I0902413

more ~~boring~~ ar

y more ~~boring~~ art.

y more ~~boring~~ art.

ny more ~~boring~~ art.

ny more ~~boring~~ art.

y more ~~boring~~ art.

y more ~~boring~~ art.

more ~~boring~~ art.

y more ~~boring~~ art.

more ~~boring~~ art.

y more ~~boring~~ art.

y more ~~boring~~ art.

any more ~~boring~~ art.

any more ~~boring~~ art.

Traffic: Conceptual Art in Canada 1965–1980

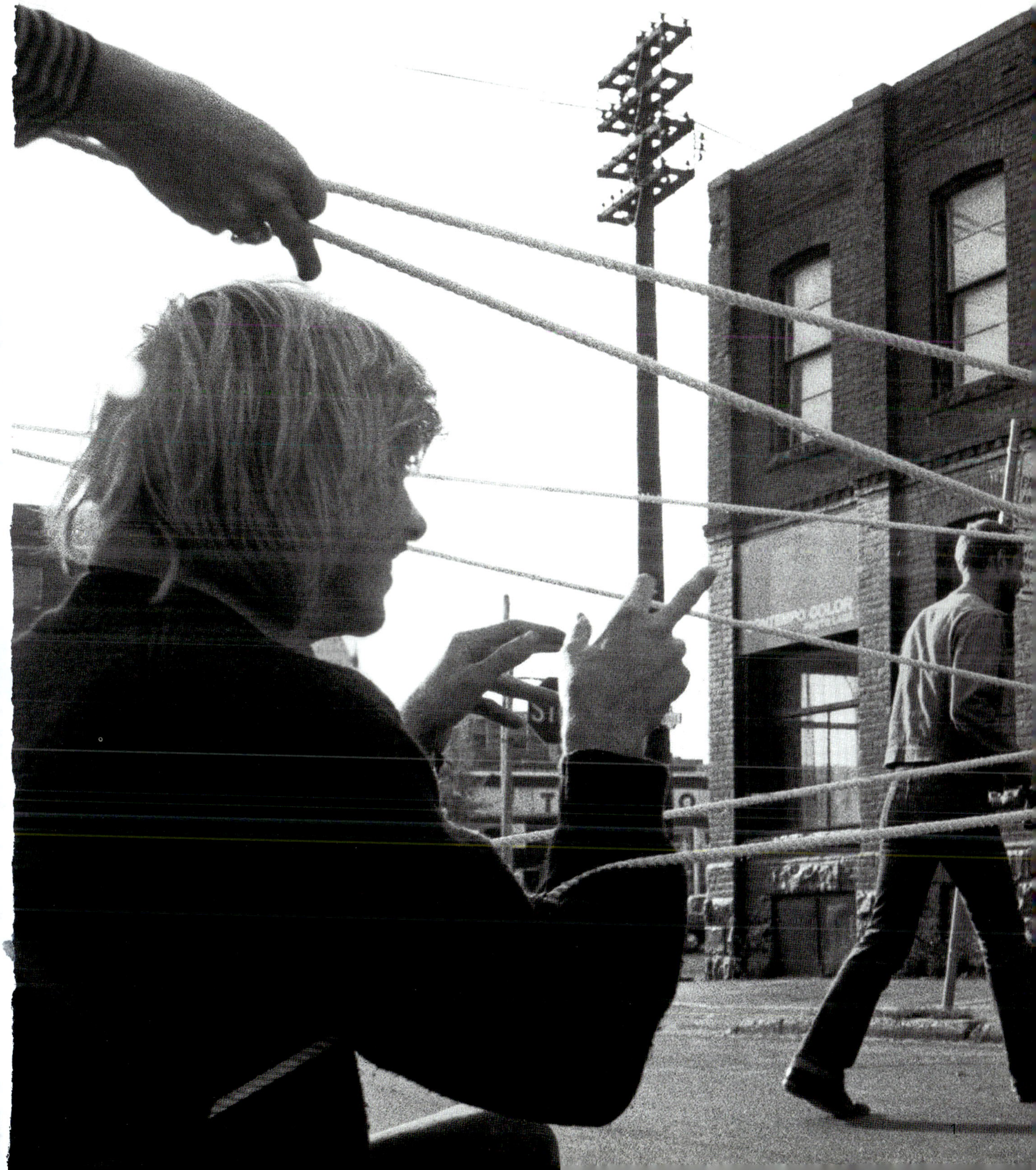

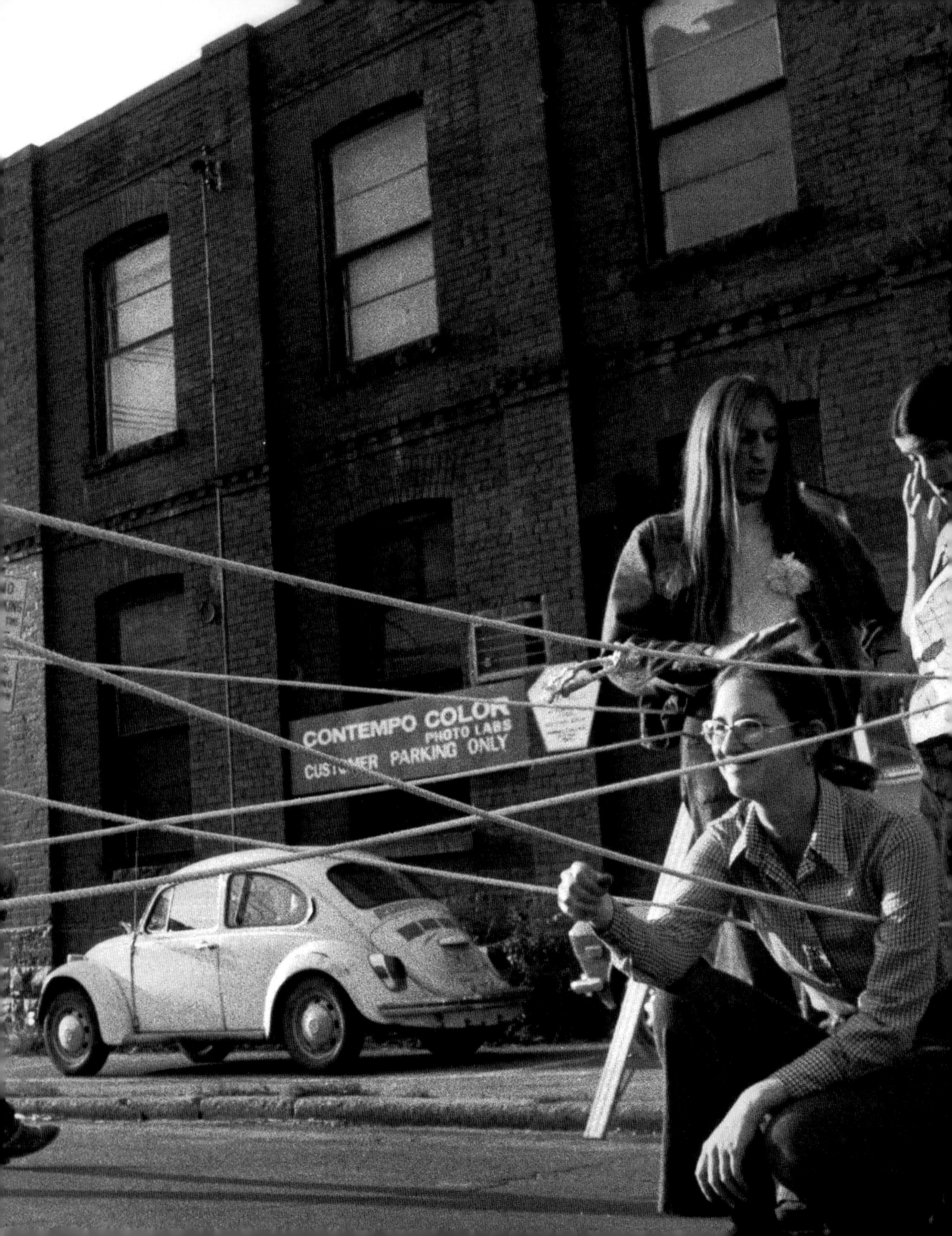
CONTEMPO COLOR
PHOTO LABS
CUSTOMER PARKING ONLY

Traffic: Conceptual Art in Canada 1965–1980

Grant Arnold and Karen Henry, Editors

Published by:
Art Gallery of Alberta
Halifax INK
Justina M. Barnicke Gallery (Hart House, University of Toronto)
Leonard & Bina Ellen Art Gallery (Concordia University)
Vancouver Art Gallery

Vera Frenkel, street rehearsal for *String Games: Improvisations for Inter-City Video*, 1974, detail

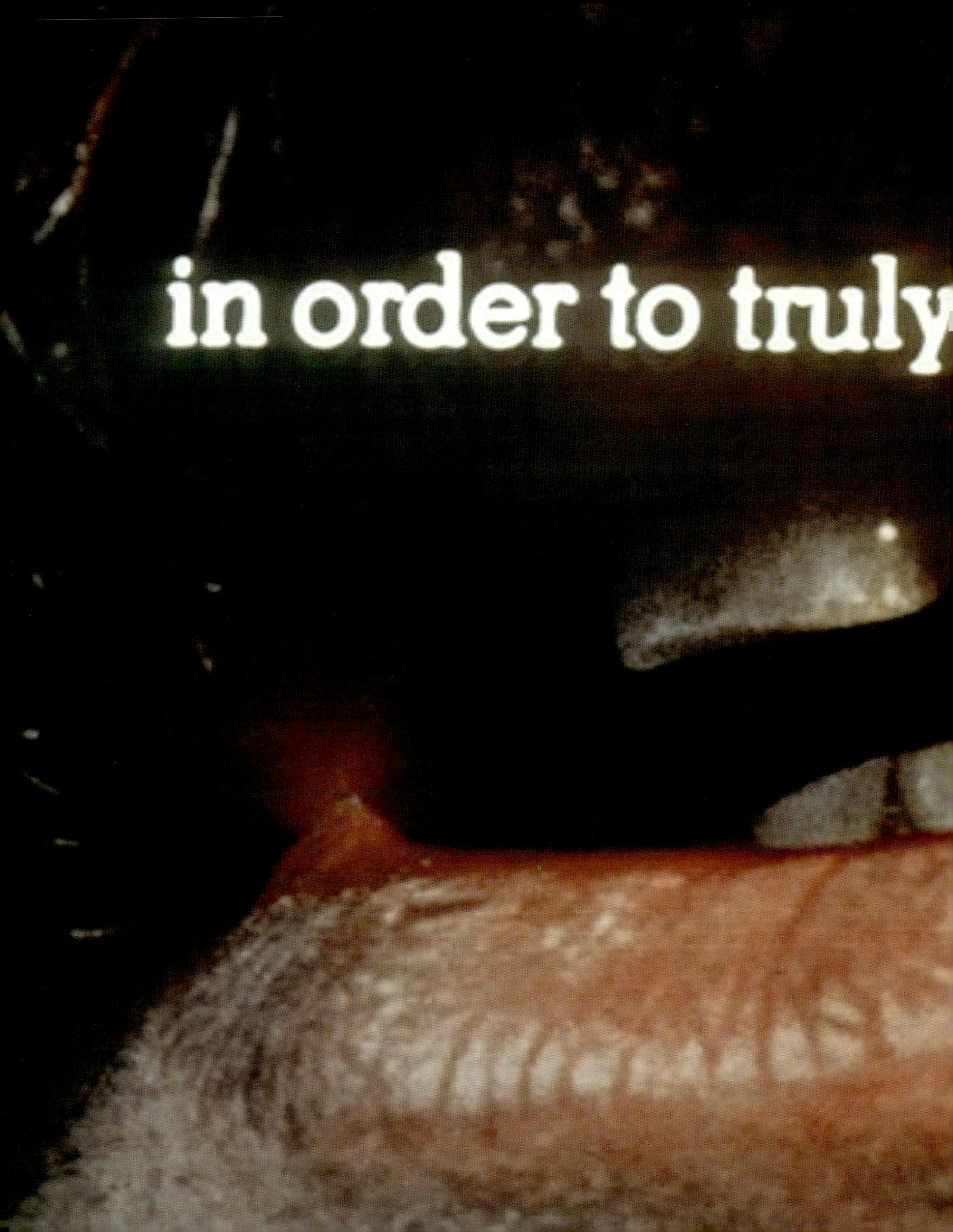
in order to truly

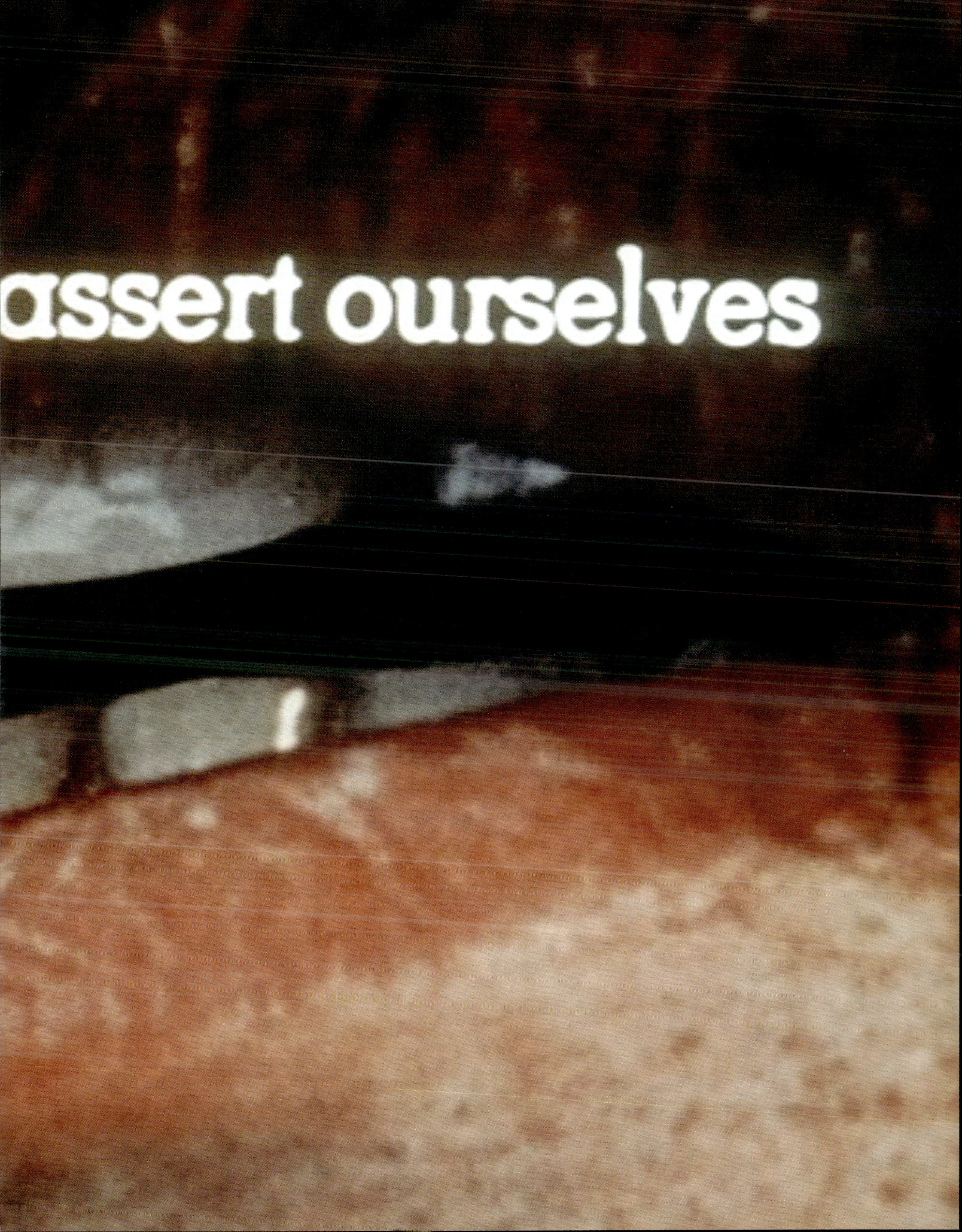
assert ourselves

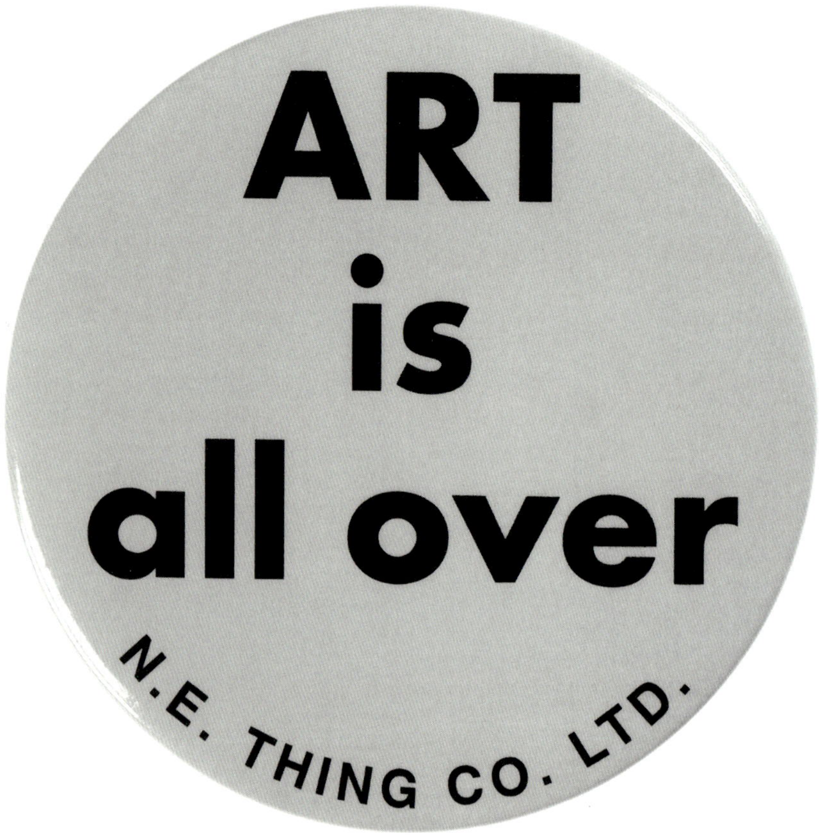

Previous page
Joyce Wieland, still from
Pierre Vallières, 1972

Above
N.E Thing Co., *ART is all over*, 1972

Contents

John Baldessari
2405 Third Street
Santa Monica, Calif. 90405
U.S.A.

Feb. 1, 1971

Charlotte Townsend
Anna Leonowens Gallery
Nova Scotia College of Art and Design
Halifax, Nova Scotia

Dear Charlotte--

Life is hard, life is earnest. Also I always seem to be occupied so with thinking about art or reading about it that I procrastinate a lot. Which is not good since I like everything all of you are doing up there.

I have no idea what your gallery looks like and I know you do not have much money for shows so that conditions my ideas. It was tough making a decision about what I wanted to do because I suppose there is never enough opportunity to do all those pieces one wants to do. Some good ideas are always waiting impatiently in the wings.

I've got a Punishment Piece for you. It will require a surrogate(s) since I can't be there to take my self-imposed punishment but that's o.k. since the theory is that punishment should be instructive to others. And there's precedent for it--Christ being punished for our sins, and think of all the others. So some students as scapegoats are necessary. If you can't induce anyone to be sacrificial and take my sins upon there shoulders, then use whatever funds there are ($50.?) to pay someone as a mercenary.

The piece is this: from ceiling to floor should be written by one or more people, one sentence under another the following statement-- " I will not make any more boring art." At least one column of sentences should be done floor to ceiling before the exhibit opens and the writing of the sentences should continue every day if possible for the length of the exhibit. I would appreciate it if you could tell me how many times the sentence has beem written by the end of the show. The sentences should be hand-written, clearly written with correct spelling. I'd like some photos of my stand-ins. This self-flagellation of mine should not be meted out by you as punishment to students that have done there art badly but only to holy innocents who will willingly take on my sins and suffer the punishment or who will do it for pay but it should be money that would normally go to me. I prefer the former--that you will find students that will freely take on my punishment.

Also would like photos of installation and close-up shots. On the mailed announcement I would like a column of sentences as in the exhibit. I include a row of my own to use.

Warm regards

John

John Baldessari

Directors' Foreword

Kathleen S. Bartels / Catherine Crowston / Peter Dykhuis / Barbara Fischer / Michèle Thériault

It is something of an understatement to say that conceptual art has had far-reaching implications for visual art since the mid-1960s. Conceptual art's challenges to the autonomy of the art object and its attention to the economies in which art circulates have radically transformed our understanding of art making and the encounter between the artwork and viewer. Over approximately the last fifteen years, the widespread and profound effects of conceptual art have been the focus of exhibitions, conferences and anthologies that have examined its specific iterations in Africa, Asia, Eastern Europe and Latin America, as well as the more widely known versions that appeared in Western Europe and North America. During this time, conceptual art has been clearly situated as a genuinely global phenomenon, one that has played a vital role in reconfiguring the conventional hierarchies of centre and margin and, at least to some extent, destabilizing the psychic geography through which the art world has traditionally been mapped. Within this context, we take great pleasure in presenting *Traffic: Conceptual Art in Canada 1965–1980*, the first exhibition and publication to survey activity related to conceptual art in Canada.

Originally conceived by Catherine Crowston and Barbara Fischer, this exhibition and publication are the outcome of an extended collaboration between the Art Gallery of Alberta, Justina M. Barnicke Gallery (Hart House, University of Toronto) and the Vancouver Art Gallery, in partnership with the Leonard & Bina Ellen Art Gallery (Concordia University) and Halifax INK (Anna Leonowens Gallery, Dalhousie Art Gallery, Mount Saint Vincent University Art Gallery, Saint Mary's University Art Gallery), and with the support of the University of Toronto Art Centre, Blackwood Gallery (University of Toronto, Mississauga) and Doris McCarthy Gallery (University of Toronto, Scarborough). We extend our gratitude to the trustees and staff of these institutions; their extraordinary support has been crucial in the realization of this project. Special thanks go to Christopher Régimbal and Meghan Bissonnette for their efforts in assembling the works that comprise the exhibition. We offer our appreciation to Karen Henry for coordinating the production of the publication and to Kelsey Blackwell for her excellent design. Thanks are due to Michèle Thériault and the Leonard & Bina Ellen Art Gallery for coordinating the French version of the publication and to Colette Tougas for her very capable work on the translation. We gratefully acknowledge the financial support for *Traffic* provided by the Museums Assistance Program of the Department of Canadian Heritage and the Canada Council for the Arts.

The project would not have been realized without the tireless efforts of curators Grant Arnold, Vincent Bonin, Catherine Crowston, Barbara Fischer, Michèle Thériault and Jayne Wark, who researched and selected their respective sections of the exhibition; thanks also to William Wood and the round-table participants for their thoughtful contributions. Most importantly we are profoundly grateful to all of the artists represented in *Traffic*. Their work continues to inspire, inform, fascinate and provoke, while expanding our understanding of the world and our place in it.

John Baldessari, letter to Charlotte Townsend, 1 February 1971

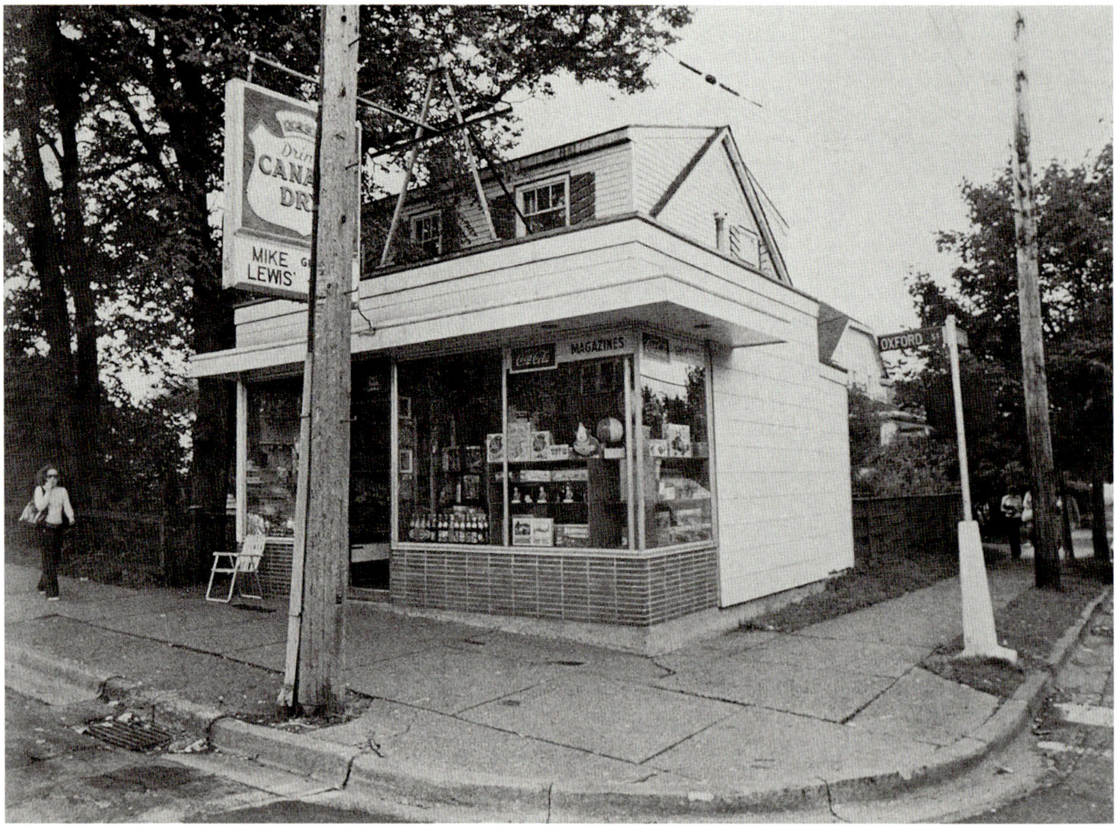

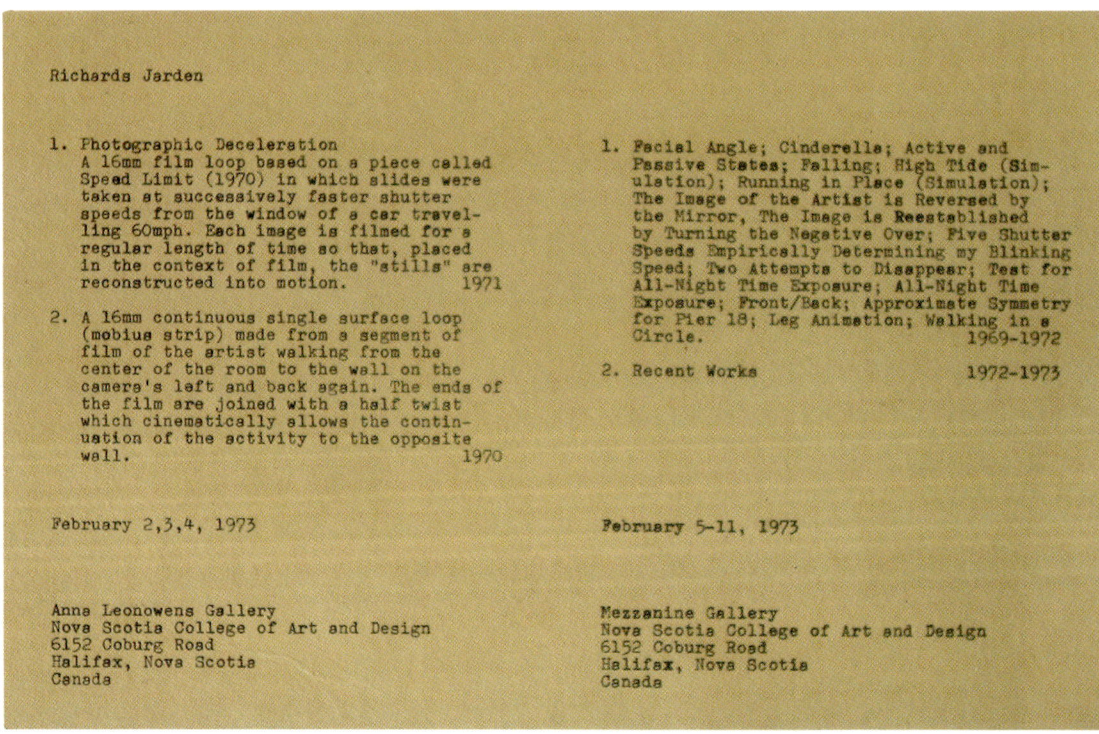

Richards Jarden

1. Photographic Deceleration
A 16mm film loop based on a piece called Speed Limit (1970) in which slides were taken at successively faster shutter speeds from the window of a car travelling 60mph. Each image is filmed for a regular length of time so that, placed in the context of film, the "stills" are reconstructed into motion. 1971

2. A 16mm continuous single surface loop (mobius strip) made from a segment of film of the artist walking from the center of the room to the wall on the camera's left and back again. The ends of the film are joined with a half twist which cinematically allows the continuation of the activity to the opposite wall. 1970

February 2,3,4, 1973

Anna Leonowens Gallery
Nova Scotia College of Art and Design
6152 Coburg Road
Halifax, Nova Scotia
Canada

1. Facial Angle; Cinderella; Active and Passive States; Falling; High Tide (Simulation); Running in Place (Simulation); The Image of the Artist is Reversed by the Mirror, The Image is Reestablished by Turning the Negative Over; Five Shutter Speeds Empirically Determining my Blinking Speed; Two Attempts to Disappear; Test for All-Night Time Exposure; All-Night Time Exposure; Front/Back; Approximate Symmetry for Pier 18; Leg Animation; Walking in a Circle. 1969-1972

2. Recent Works 1972-1973

February 5-11, 1973

Mezzanine Gallery
Nova Scotia College of Art and Design
6152 Coburg Road
Halifax, Nova Scotia
Canada

Above, top
Allan Harding MacKay with Lionel Simmons, *36 Halifax Corner Grocery Stores*, 1972, detail

Above, bottom
Invitation for *Richards Jarden*, Anna Leonowens Gallery, 2–11 February 1973

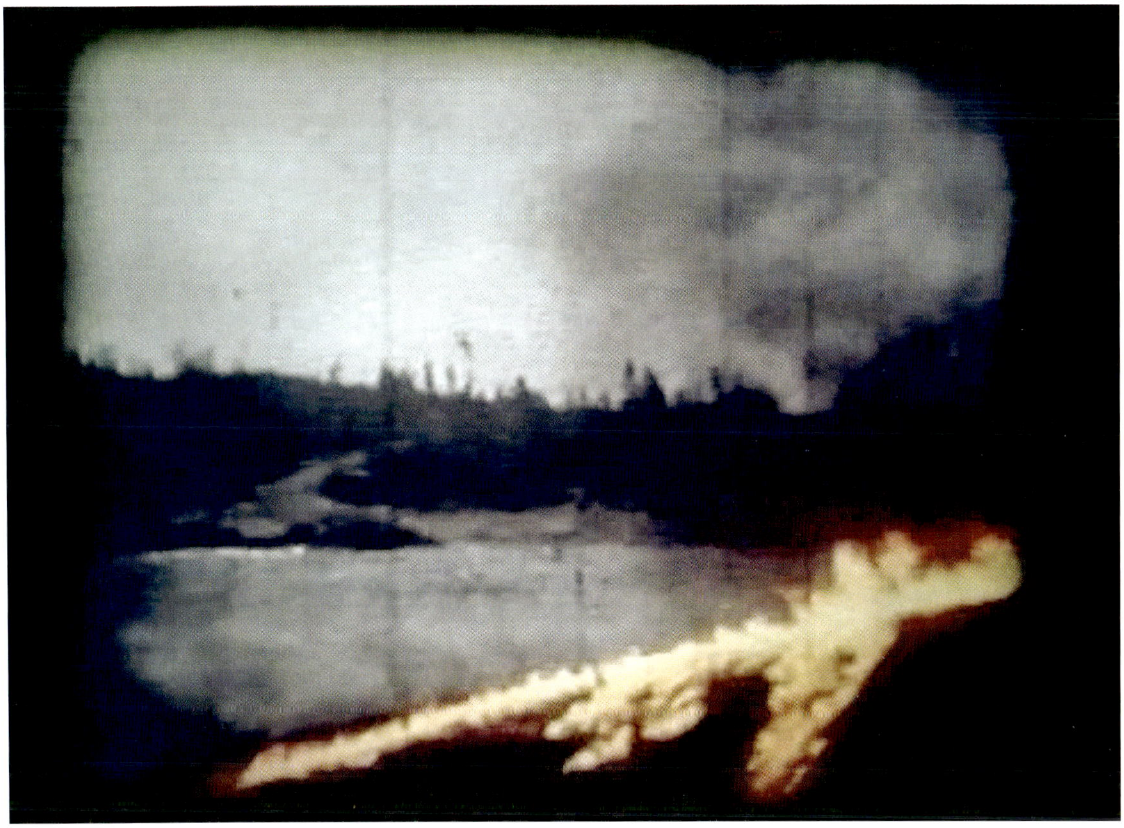

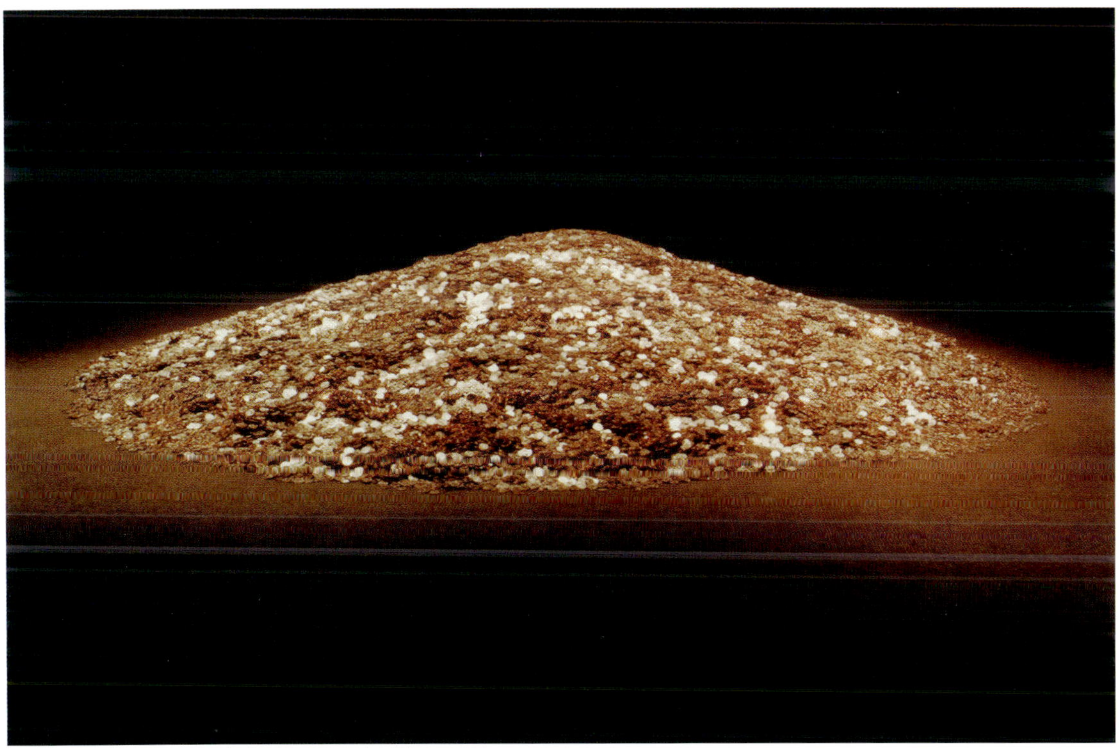

Above, top
David Askevold, still from *Nova Scotia Fires*, 1969

Above, bottom
Gerald Ferguson, *1,000,000 Pennies*, 1980

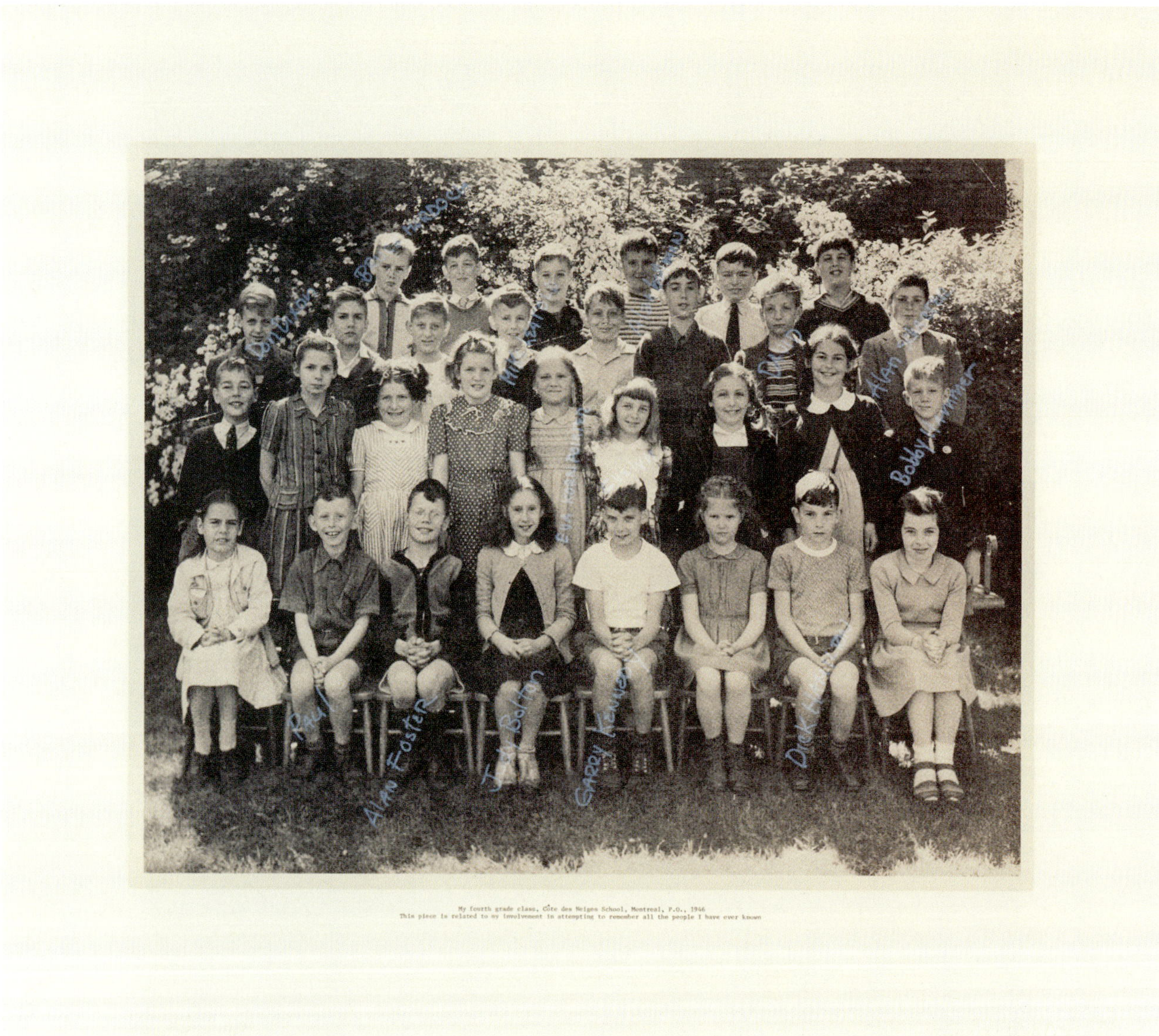

Garry Neill Kennedy, *My Fourth Grade Class*, 1972

Introduction

Grant Arnold / Vincent Bonin / Catherine Crowston / Barbara Fischer / Michèle Thériault / Jayne Wark

Conceptual art has come to be widely regarded as the most transformative art movement of the twentieth century. Responding to and partaking in the broader social upheavals that emerged in the 1960s—the rise of anti-war activism, feminism, civil rights movements and gay liberation, as well as the emergence of new information technologies including television, telecopier machines and computers—conceptual art called into question the philosophical bases and institutional frameworks within which art had come to operate during the Modernist era. Disrupting the conventional categorization of art by media, conceptual art sought to displace the traditional understanding of the artwork as an autonomous entity or discrete object. Conceptual artists downplayed the visual presence of the art object in order to question the perceptual codes through which art is experienced, the systems of representation that frame its meaning and the linguistic structures at work in the broader culture. Attempting to destabilize the understanding of art as an idiom for individual expression conveyed through specialized skills and technical acumen, conceptual art called into question the validity of an activity directed toward the production of commodities for a world already pervaded with ideologically loaded images and objects. Conceptual art thus linked the making and reception of art to a wider set of discursive fields within culture at large, radically reconfiguring the relationship between the artist, the modes through which art is circulated and the publics it engages.

Over the past fifteen years or so, conceptual art has been the subject of historical studies and exhibitions that have situated it as a global phenomenon that runs counter to the traditional mapping of the art world, in terms of centre and periphery, by focusing on its specific modes of development in Africa, Asia, Eastern Europe and Latin America, as well as its more thoroughly documented elaborations in Western Europe and the United States.[1] Although Canadian artists (including David Askevold, Gerald Ferguson, General Idea, Garry Neill Kennedy, N.E. Thing Co., Michael Snow and Joyce Wieland, among others) and institutions (most notably the Nova Scotia College of Art and Design [NSCAD]) participated in the development and dissemination of conceptual art on an international level, recent accounts have recognized artists and activities associated with Canada in relatively marginal ways. Within Canada there are regional histories of conceptual art, including Bruce Barber's *Conceptual Art: The NSCAD Connection 1967–1973* and *You Are Now In the Middle of a N.E. Thing Co. Landscape* by Nancy Shaw and William Wood,

[1] Publications that address conceptual art or Conceptualism as a global phenomenon include David Ross, *Between Spring & Summer: Soviet Conceptual Art in the Era of Late Communism* (exhibition catalogue) (Tacoma: Tacoma Art Museum, 1990); Jane Farver (Ed.), *Global Conceptualism: Points of Origin, 1950s–1980s* (exhibition catalogue) (Queens: Queens Museum of Art, 1999); Salah Hassan and Olu Oguibe (Eds.), *Authentic/Ex-centric: Conceptualism in Contemporary African Art* (exhibition catalogue) (Ithaca: Program for African Arts, Inc., 2001); Peter Osborne, *Conceptual Art* (London: Phaidon Press, 2002); Laura Hoptman and Tomas Pospiszyl (Eds.), *Primary Documents: A Source Book for Eastern and Central European Art since the 1950s* (Cambridge, MA: MIT Press, 2002); Michael Corris (Ed.), *Conceptual Art: Theory, Myth, and Practice* (Cambridge: Cambridge University Press, 2003); Luis Camnitzer, *Conceptualism in Latin America: Didactics of Liberation* (Austin: University of Texas Press, 2007); and Boris Groys, Max Hollein, and Manuel Fontán del Junco (Eds.), *Die Totale Aufklarung Moskauer Konzeptkunst 1960–1990/Total Enlightenment Conceptual Art in Moscow 1960–1990* (Ostfildern: Hatje Cantz Verlag, 2008).

and some media-specific histories that include *Videotexts* by Peggy Gale and *Performance in Canada* by Clive Robertson and Alain-Martin Richard. However, there is no overarching history of conceptual art in Canada, no comprehensive map of the contributions from the various regions of Canada and no extended consideration of the interaction between Canadian artists and practitioners from outside the country. Accounts of these developments have lingered primarily as a kind of whispered history circulated among artists and writers in "alternative" publications and artist-run centres, or within studies of particular institutions and artists, but no major exhibitions or publications have considered conceptual art's pan-Canadian effects.

This book and the exhibition it documents represent an initial attempt to address this gap by tracking the influence and diversity of conceptual art in works produced across the country and acknowledging the significance of the profoundly artist-driven nature of these iterations within a larger global phenomenon. As demonstrated by the activities represented in this publication, conceptual art was taken up across Canada in complex, rigorous and varied manifestations, with its premises enacted, hybridized and inflected by particular local and geographic needs and interests of individual artists, collectives and art communities. The activities represented here acknowledge the crucial role played by the network of artist-run centres, a unique aspect of the Canadian art world, that stretched across the country and facilitated discussions, debates and exhibitions vital to the development of conceptual art in Canada from the late 1960s on.

Both the book and exhibition that comprise *Traffic: Conceptual Art in Canada 1965–1980* are organized according to urban and regional locales. While such a geographically based structure runs the risk of obscuring differences in aesthetic positions and/or political stances and sensibilities within a given locale, the project developed around the specific circumstances that frame the locations in which artists gathered and worked—circumstances that include the success of NSCAD and the absence of an art museum in Halifax, the pervasive questions of language and identity that mark daily life in Montréal, the constellation of counterculture initiatives in Toronto, the cosmopolitan regionalism of London, the isolation of the central Canadian Prairies and the remoteness and proximity to nature of the West Coast. It became clear that these had such an impact on the art produced in Canada during this era that the viability of a regionally based structure for the project outweighed the attendant risks. Our methodology was, therefore, to work together as a group of individual curators, each with extensive knowledge about a specific geographical region, in order to achieve more depth in each area. This facilitated access to artists and local archives and interviews with other local interlocutors. Each curator problematized his or her section differently and the exhibition is, therefore, a series of curated propositions that each in themselves complicate the attempt to present a single unified picture. At the same time, we hope that the extensive interaction within the networks that linked these centres, and the dialogues between artists working in Canada and abroad, remain clearly evident within this structure. The questions concerning language, body, identity, location and geography that underscore the works presented here were constitutive elements and primary interests within communities both across the country and abroad. It is our hope that *Traffic* evokes both the manifestations in which conceptual art appeared within these particular places and histories and the effervescent, sometimes contentious, lines of traffic that connected centres across the country and facilitated the participation of artists based in Canada in the debates and developments that shaped conceptual art on an international level.

"E" Comprehension. (15 mins)

C. ...take or, and, or but out of the language... and you'll see, the whole of our epistemological tradition will become redundant.
E. what?
C. ...that's what I mean. Comprehension can't survive in the absence of criticism.
E. well, for me, I would say, the prime distinction is predicated from an absolute, a governing principle.
C. nonsense... any fool knows that every reading of a text takes place within a tradition, a living current of thought, these in turn display presuppositions and exigencies. This regardless of the quid..."that in view of which" the text was written.
E. Ricouer? An idea of culture as an assemblage of texts?
C. Yes...which are in turn assemblages.
I. No! You're both wrong. It's ensembles. And though it's reading....comprehension... it's also interpretation, understanding. And its R.i.c.o.e.u.r. - Ricoeur....not Ric-ow-er!
C. You are right...of course. Criticism is the key. It's about exposing, recovering meaning that has been submerged or collecting together that which has been dispersed.
E. Periscoping....peri-scoping is the metaphor which is, you would agree....far different....from....
C. ....telescoping or microscoping?
I. Absolutely! Saying something of something.
C. But that gets into the bind of saying something of something which has been said of something else....
E. No....only when the somethings are equivalents.
C. O.K. how about an example....?
I. O.K.

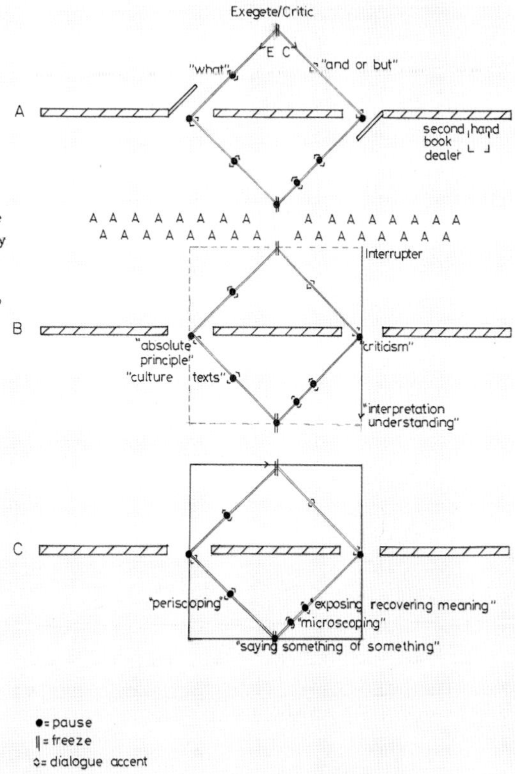

Bruce Barber, drawing with performance text for *E*, 1978

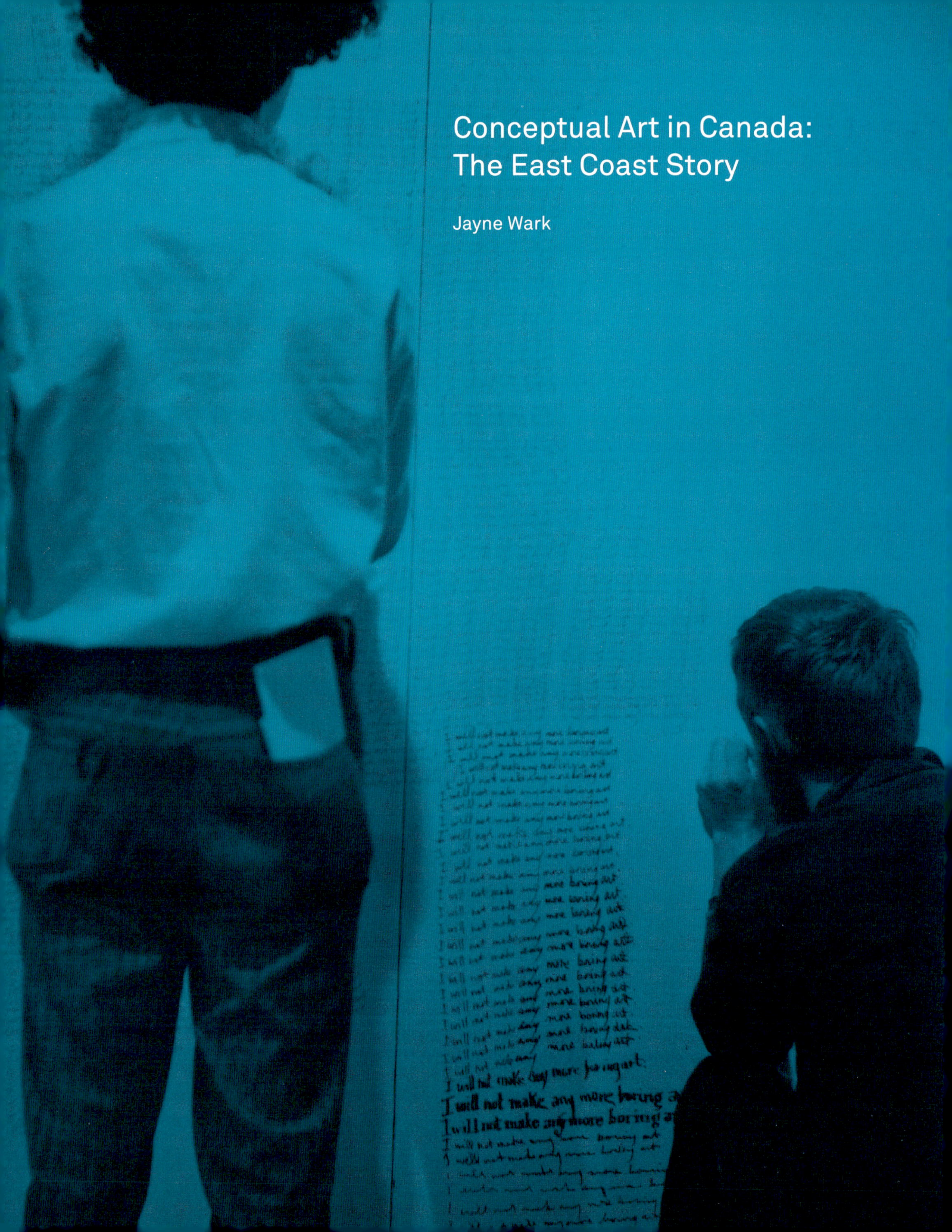

Conceptual Art in Canada: The East Coast Story

Jayne Wark

Conceptual art emerged around 1967 as an art form in which the concept or idea was primary and the execution was secondary. Although it has been associated mostly with the activities of artists in the art world's established centres, it is now acknowledged that conceptual art was a global phenomenon.[1] Conceptual art also had an unlikely but major manifestation on Canada's East Coast. The odds of such a development were hardly propitious in a place where notions of art at the time were still rooted in the beaux-arts conventions of the nineteenth century and there was no support for contemporary art of any kind, let alone something as foreign and perplexing as conceptual art.

As Vincent Bonin insightfully demonstrated in his essay "Documentary Protocols," the indifference to contemporary art in this period even in Canada's large urban centres led artists to establish their own communities and institutions.[2] The situation on the East Coast was distinctly different. It was not a matter of redressing exclusion or finding alternatives to existing institutions and markets, but rather one of establishing something in the midst of a complete void. What was needed was the creation of an entirely new community and an institutional infrastructure to support it.

In Halifax, the opportunity for such creation arose unexpectedly in 1967 with the decision of the Nova Scotia College of Art to hire Garry Neill Kennedy as president. The college had been founded in 1887 as the Victoria School of Art and Design by a group of citizens led by Anna Leonowens (later made famous by the Rodgers and Hammerstein musical *The King and I*). It survived through periods of growth and stagnation, but in 1967 it essentially remained a backwater.[3] When Kennedy was interviewed, he had just completed his MFA at Ohio University and was in his second year as head of the art department at Northland College in Ashland, Wisconsin. Upon accepting the position, he immediately set out to modernize and professionalize the school.[4] This entailed upgrading the facilities and expanding the cramped building. Kennedy also took the crucial step of establishing an art gallery, named after Anna Leonowens, to provide a venue for exhibitions by students and faculty as well as by national and international contemporary artists.

In addition to changing the name to the Nova Scotia College of Art and Design (NSCAD), Kennedy revamped the curriculum, implemented the first MFA program in Canada and hired a new roster of *au courant* faculty, including Gerald Ferguson and David Askevold, both of whom he knew from his time in the United States. These changes were avidly reported in the local

[1] See Philomena Mariani (Ed.), *Global Conceptualism: Points of Origins, 1950s–1980s* (New York: Queen's Museum of Art, 1999).

[2] Vincent Bonin, "Documentary protocols (1967–1975)." In Vincent Bonin and Michèle Thériault (Eds.), *Documentary Protocols/ Protocoles documentaries (1967–1975)* (Montréal: Leonard & Bina Ellen Art Gallery, Concordia University, 2010), 18.

This publication is the third part of the *Documentary Protocols* project conceived by Bonin, preceded by two exhibitions at the gallery in 2007 and 2008.

[3] David Soucy and Harold Pearse, *The First Hundred Years: A History of the Nova Scotia College of Art and Design* (Fredericton: University of New Brunswick and Halifax: Nova Scotia College of Art and Design, 1993), 2–8, 135–146.

[4] See Garry Neill Kennedy, "NSCAD and the sixties," in Bruce Barber (Ed.), *Conceptual Art: The NSCAD Connection, 1967–1973* (Halifax: The Anna Leonowens Gallery of the Nova Scotia College of Art and Design, 2001), 20.

Opposite
Students executing *I Will Not Make Any More Boring Art*, John Baldessari, 1971, Courtesy of NSCAD University, Gallery Archives.

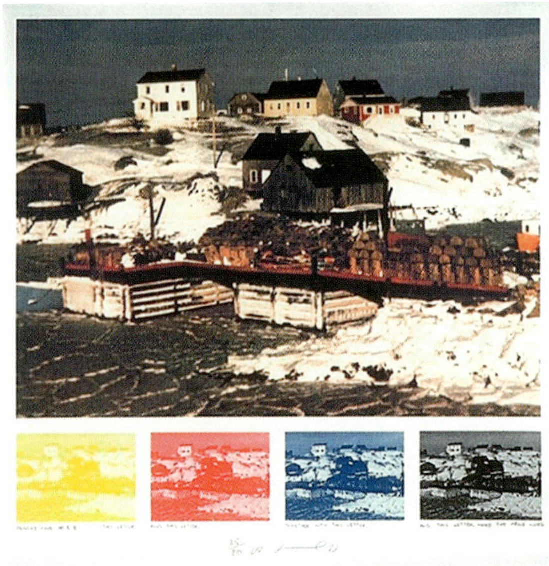

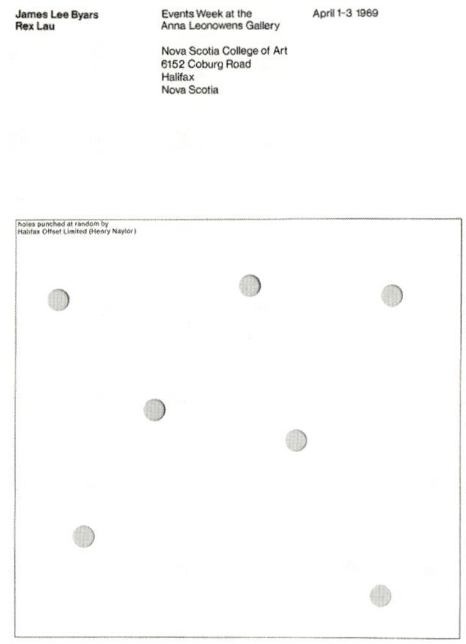
James Lee Byars
Rex Lau

Events Week at the
Anna Leonowens Gallery

April 1-3 1969

Nova Scotia College of Art
6152 Coburg Road
Halifax
Nova Scotia

holes punched at random by
Halifax Offset Limited (Henry Naylor)

press, especially his hiring of so many non-Canadians.[5] The two prominent Canadians Kennedy did attempt to recruit, Greg Curnoe and Iain Baxter, were unable or unwilling to move to Halifax.[6] By contrast, it was easy to attract Americans, many of whom saw Canada as a liberal refuge from the escalating social turmoil then afflicting the United States, especially over racial conflict and the Vietnam War.[7]

The effects of Kennedy's overhaul were sudden and sharp. Askevold, who was teaching the new Foundation course and wanted to provide opportunities for students to engage directly with contemporary art, brought about the college's first encounter with conceptual art by inviting three New York artists to conduct projects in Halifax in April 1969. The first two visitors, Rex Lau and James Lee Byars, executed installations and performance events at the Anna Leonowens Gallery. Lau poured 200 pounds of liquid urethane onto the gallery floor, while Byars orchestrated performances using various red acetate garments worn simultaneously by several people.[8] While some local reporters like Gretchen Pierce wrote enthusiastically about these strange new goings-on at NSCAD, others responded with bafflement and outright hostility. Reporter Jack Hambleton was particularly incensed at the publicity mailer Lau and Byars sent out, which consisted of a sheet of paper with the gallery information at the top and a blank box below with a header stating "holes punched at random by Halifax Offset Limited (Henry Naylor)," He decried conceptual art as a "snow job" and demanded to be taken off NSCAD's mailing list.[9]

[5] Soucy and Pearse, *The First Hundred Years*, 149. See also the press clippings in the NSCAD Archives at the Public Archives of Nova Scotia (PANS), Box 23, Scrapbook 5. For Kennedy's defence of his hiring decisions, see his letter to Dr. G. Holbrook, chairman of the board, Nova Scotia College of Art, 6 September 1968, NSCAD Archives, PANS, Box 3, File 19.

[6] Garry Neill Kennedy, letter to author, 30 November 2003.

[7] Gerald Ferguson, interview with author, 18 October 2003. Ferguson added that Prime Minister Trudeau's 1970 endorsement of the War Measures Act was profoundly disillusioning in this regard.

[8] See unattributed article, "Foam experiment produces blob," *Chronicle Herald*, 3 April 1969, 10. NSCAD Archives, PANS, Box 23, Scrapbook 5.

[9] See Gretchen Pierce, "A message from other end of garment," *Halifax Mail-Star*, 3 April 1969, and Jack Hambleton, "All about art," *Chronicle-Herald*, 11 April 1969, NSCAD Archives, PANS, Box 23, Scrapbook 5.

[10] According to Gerald Ferguson, who was very close with Weiner, the turning point was the April 1968 exhibition at Wyndham College in Vermont called *Carl Andre, Robert Barry, Lawrence Weiner.* When the outdoor installation of his piece was vandalized, Weiner concluded that it did not matter since the work could exist just as adequately in the form of its title as verbal description: *A Series of Stakes Set in the Ground at Regular Intervals to Form a Rectangle—Twine Strung from Stake to Stake to Demark a Grid—A Rectangle Removed from This Rectangle.* See Gerald Ferguson, "On NSCAD and conceptual art,"

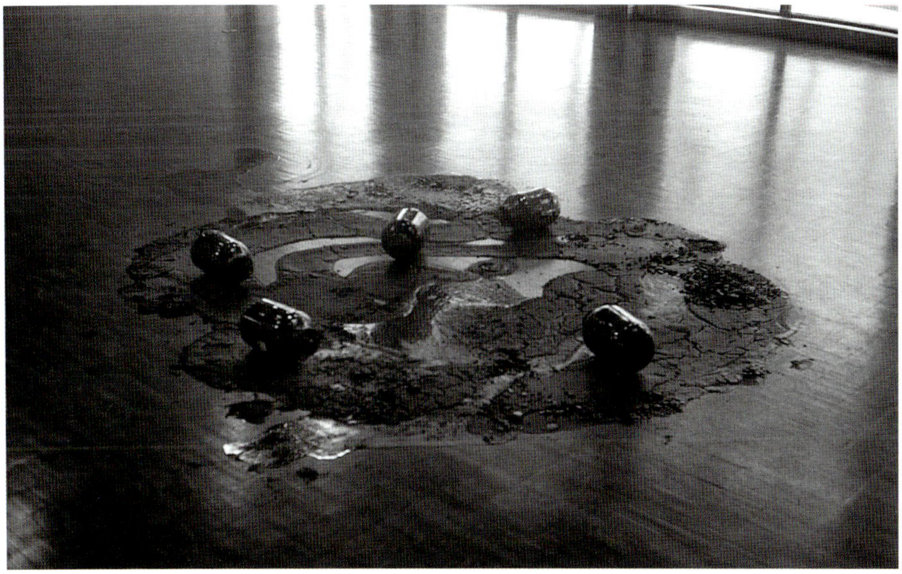

Undeterred by such local hostility, the college confirmed its commitment to conceptual art with an exhibition five days later (April 7–27) by Lawrence Weiner. By this time, Weiner had shifted from his previous minimalist orientation to adopt a format whereby the work of art would be constituted by a descriptive title that served simultaneously as the proposition for its execution.[10] For Weiner's NSCAD show, simply called 5 Works, these titles/propositions were listed on the mailer, which also reproduced, for only the second time, Weiner's now-famous "Statement of Intent":

> 1. The artist may construct the piece
> 2. The piece may be fabricated
> 3. The piece need not be built
>
> Each being equal and consistent with the intent of the artist the decision as to condition rests with the receiver upon the occasion of receivership.[11]

Some of the works in Weiner's NSCAD show were actually executed, such as FIVE GALLONS WATER BASE TEMPERA PAINT POURED DIRECTLY UPON THE FLOOR AND ALLOWED TO REMAIN FOR THE DURATION OF THE EXHIBITION. Yet Weiner's "Statement of Intent," which theorizes and explicates the premise of his works, makes their execution secondary or irrelevant. The statement also invokes several key

in Barber (Ed.), *Conceptual Art: The NSCAD Connection*, 33.

[11] This statement first appeared in *January 5–31, 1969* (New York: Seth Siegelaub, 1969), unpaginated. This was the second of three groundbreaking exhibition catalogues published by New York dealer and impresario of conceptual art Seth Siegelaub, in which the exhibition and its presentation in catalogue form were one and the same. Weiner was also included in Siegelaub's two other similar publications, *Carl Andre, Robert Barry, Douglas Huebler, Joseph Kosuth, Sol LeWitt, Robert Morris, Lawrence Weiner* (New York: Seth Siegelaub and Jack Wendler, December 1968) and *March 1969* (New York: Seth Siegelaub, 1969). Weiner's NSCAD show was especially significant, however, since it was the first solo show of his mature conceptual art practice.

From top left

Les Levine, *Peggy's Cove YR BB*, 1973, © Les Levine / SODRAC (2012)

Invitation for James Lee Byars' (with Rex Lau) *Events Week at the Anna Leonowens Gallery*, 1–3 April 1969

Lawrence Weiner, *FIVE GALLONS WATER BASE TEMPERA PAINT POURED DIRECTLY UPON THE FLOOR AND ALLOWED TO REMAIN FOR THE DURATION OF THE EXHIBITION*, as installed by Garry Neill Kennedy, Anna Leonowens Gallery, 1969, Collection of NSCAD University. Photo courtesy of Moved Pictures Archive, NYC.

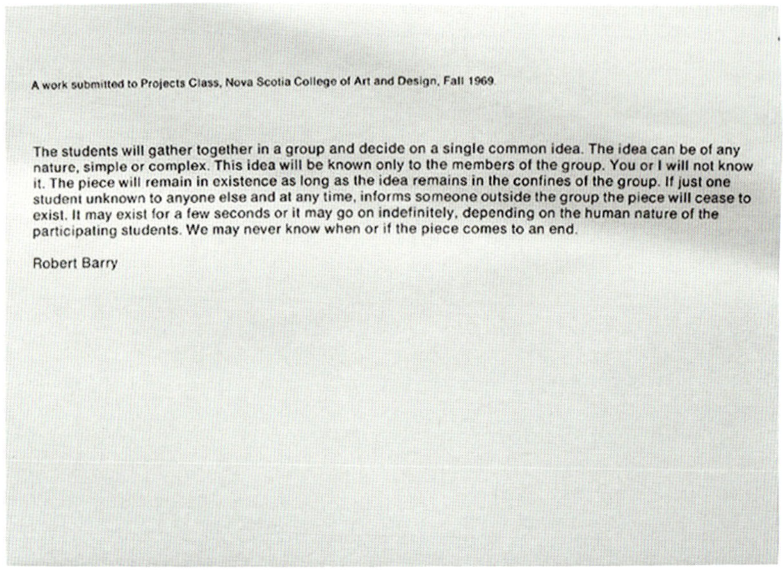

A work submitted to Projects Class, Nova Scotia College of Art and Design, Fall 1969.

The students will gather together in a group and decide on a single common idea. The idea can be of any nature, simple or complex. This idea will be known only to the members of the group. You or I will not know it. The piece will remain in existence as long as the idea remains in the confines of the group. If just one student unknown to anyone else and at any time, informs someone outside the group the piece will cease to exist. It may exist for a few seconds or it may go on indefinitely, depending on the human nature of the participating students. We may never know when or if the piece comes to an end.

Robert Barry

tenets of conceptual art, such as decentring the artist's traditional authority over the work, transforming the viewer from passive spectator to active participant, and emphasizing an egalitarian method for the production, distribution and reception of the work of art.[12]

Following the visits by Byars, Lau and Weiner, Askevold devised a new course for the 1969–70 academic year called the Projects Class. His original plan was to invite a series of artists to the college for a period of time to interact directly with students, but as this was deemed too expensive, several agreed to convey their proposals by mail or telephone to be executed by students.[13] This compromise was fortuitous, since it was both pedagogically innovative and ideally suited to overcome NSCAD's geographic isolation. Moreover, by deferring the execution of the artists' work to students, it perfectly embodied the essence of conceptual art as delineated by Sol LeWitt in his 1967 text, "Paragraphs on Conceptual Art":

> In conceptual art the idea or concept is the most important aspect of the work. When an artist uses a conceptual form in art, it means that all of the planning and decisions are made beforehand and the execution is a perfunctory affair. The idea becomes a machine that makes the art.[14]

The first Projects Class had twelve international participants: Jan Dibbets (Dutch), N.E. Thing Co. (Canadian, with co-presidents Iain and Ingrid Baxter), and Robert Barry, Mel Bochner, James Lee Byars, Dan Graham, Douglas Huebler, Joseph Kosuth, Sol LeWitt, Lucy Lippard, Robert Smithson and Lawrence Weiner (all American). Askevold subsequently published all

---

[12] For a more detailed discussion of these aspects of Weiner's work, see Alexander Alberro, *Conceptual Art and the Politics of Publicity* (Cambridge, MA: MIT Press, 2003), 92–100.

[13] See David Askevold, "The projects class," in Barber (Ed.), *Conceptual Art: The NSCAD Connection*, 38.

[14] Sol LeWitt, "Paragraphs on conceptual art," *Artforum* 5, no. 10 (Summer 1967): 80.

[15] A set of the cards as well as the original proposal letters sent to Askevold by six of the artists (Bochner, Dibbets, Huebler, LeWitt, Lippard and Weiner) are located in the National Gallery of Canada Library and Archives, Art Metropole Collection, Accession no. 9503.

[16] Most of the transmissions came from Vancouver, but some were sent from Inuvik during a brief junket (25–27 September) the Baxters made there with Lawrence Weiner, Lucy Lippard and Edmonton artist Harry Savage as part of the *Place & Process* exhibition organized by Edmonton

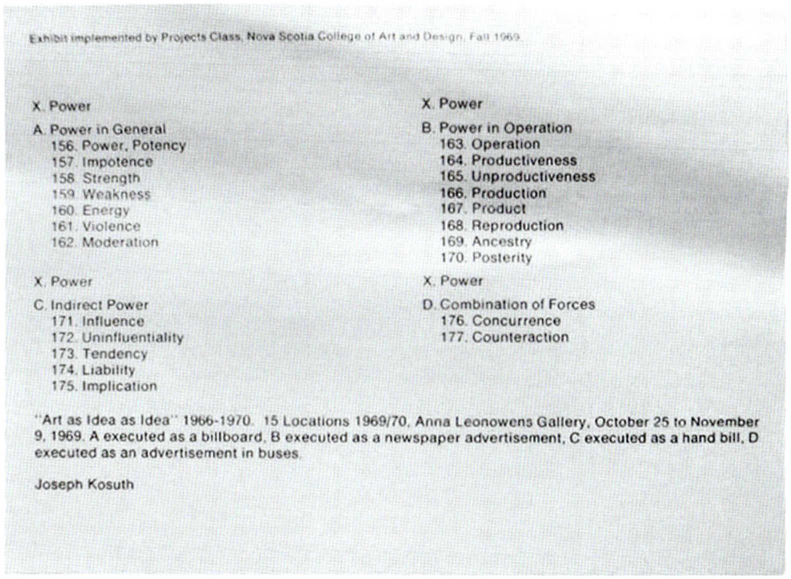

Exhibit implemented by Projects Class, Nova Scotia College of Art and Design, Fall 1969.

X. Power

A. Power in General
156. Power, Potency
157. Impotence
158. Strength
159. Weakness
160. Energy
161. Violence
162. Moderation

X. Power

B. Power in Operation
163. Operation
164. Productiveness
165. Unproductiveness
166. Production
167. Product
168. Reproduction
169. Ancestry
170. Posterity

X. Power

C. Indirect Power
171. Influence
172. Uninfluentiality
173. Tendency
174. Liability
175. Implication

X. Power

D. Combination of Forces
176. Concurrence
177. Counteraction

"Art as Idea as Idea" 1966-1970. 15 Locations 1969/70, Anna Leonowens Gallery, October 25 to November 9, 1969. A executed as a billboard, B executed as a newspaper advertisement, C executed as a hand bill, D executed as an advertisement in buses.

Joseph Kosuth

Cards describing artworks by Robert Barry and Joseph Kosuth to be executed by students during the Projects Class, NSCAD, 1969. Joseph Kosuth © SODRAC (2012)

twelve proposals as a set of individual cards.[15] Some projects required the students to enact or document an activity or event such as the recording of tree shadows (Dibbets), the fabrication and materialization of a myth (Huebler) or the dumping of 1,000 tons of mud over a cliff (Smithson). Others had little or no material manifestation. Barry instructed the students to choose a single common idea, stipulating that the piece would cease to exist if it was revealed to anyone outside the group. Bochner had them "measure/consider" the classroom objectively and subjectively in every way they could think of, but didn't care about the specifics of their findings or how they were presented. Byars' proposal merely stated: "Mr. Byars is the Artist in the Pentagon."

The projects proposed by N.E. Thing Co. (NETCO) and Joseph Kosuth included elements exhibited in the Anna Leonowens Gallery. The former called for the installation of "Teletype and Telcopier [*sic*]" machines from 15 September to 5 October, through which NETCO sent instructions to be carried out by students.[16] The printouts from the machines were posted on the gallery walls and subsequently compiled into a book called *Trans VSI Connection NSCAD–NETCO: Sept. 15–Oct. 5, 1969*.[17] This project built upon the experiments NETCO had conducted at the National Gallery in Ottawa in June–July 1969 and would serve as the format for several in the future.[18]

Kosuth's project, *Art as Idea as Idea*, was part of a larger series of word-based pieces demonstrating his fundamental premise that "the 'purest' definition of conceptual art would be that it is an inquiry into the foundations of the concept 'art'."[19] *Art as Idea as Idea* consisted

Art Gallery director Bill Kirby. For more on this expedition, see Charity Mewburn, "Sixteen hundred miles north of Denver," in Scott Watson (Ed.), *Sixteen Hundred Miles North of Denver* (Vancouver: Morris and Helen Belkin Art Gallery, 1999), 3–29. See also Lucy R. Lippard, "Art within the Arctic Circle," *The Hudson Review* 22, no. 4 (Winter 1969–1970): 665–674.

[17] Iain Baxter and David Askevold, *Trans VSI Connection NSCAD–NETCO: Sept. 15–Oct. 5, 1969* (Halifax: Nova Scotia College of Art and Design, 1970).

[18] These included, for example, NETCO's participation in the *Information* show held at the Museum of Modern Art 2 July–20 September 1970, and its *Network 70* project (7–24 October 1970), for which NETCO sent transmissions from the UBC Fine Arts Gallery in Vancouver to numerous points across North America, including NSCAD.

[19] Joseph Kosuth, "Art after philosophy II: Recent art and conceptual art," *Studio International* 178, no. 916 (November 1969): 161.

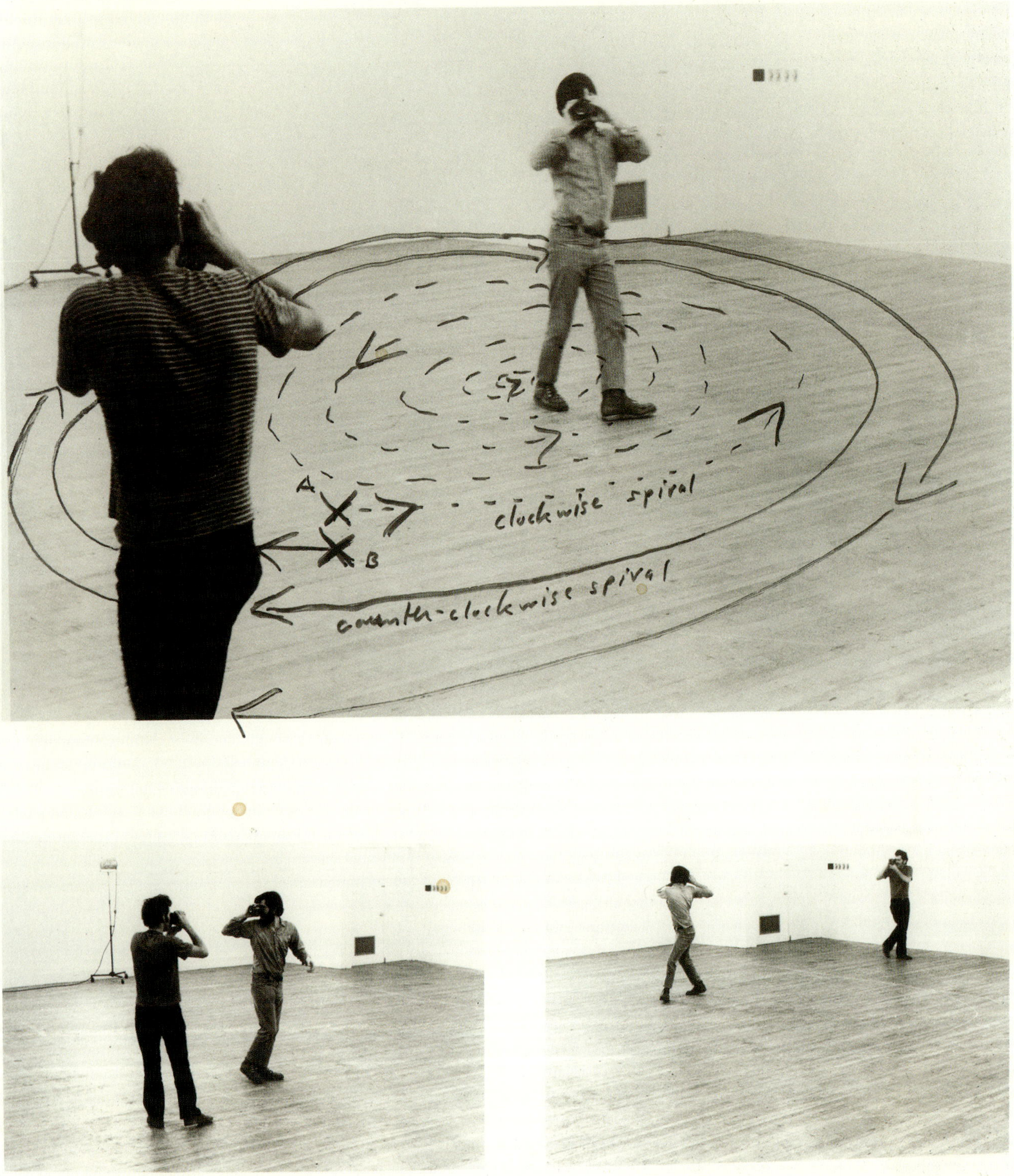

Dan Graham, rehearsal of *Two Correlated Rotations* (with Tim Zuck), 1969

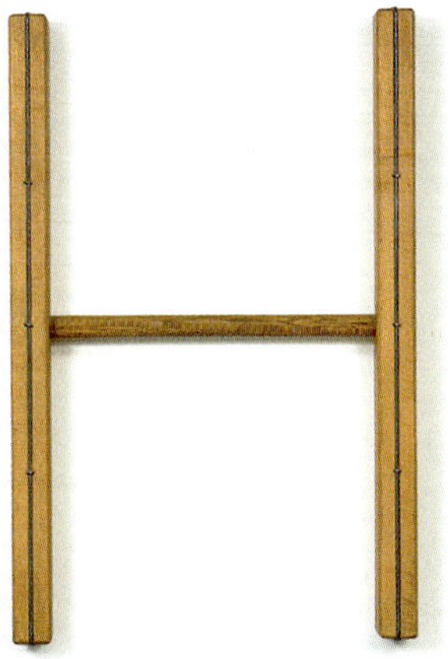

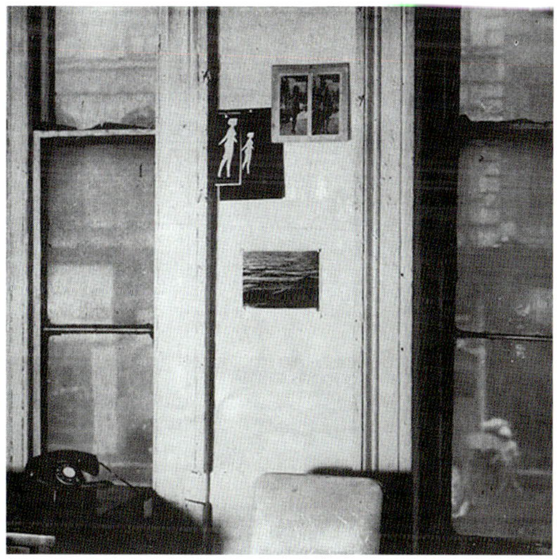

of abstract concepts such as "Intellect," "Sensation" and "Abstract Relations," each with subcategories. These concepts were exhibited in fifteen international locations in various forms of printed matter in public places. The concept for the Halifax version was "Abstract Relations: Power," and the texts for its subcategories were executed by students as a billboard, a newspaper advertisement, a handbill and a bus advertisement, with the resulting ephemera displayed in the gallery from 25 October to 9 November.

Kosuth was also one of the three Projects Class participants, along with Graham and Lippard, who visited the college in 1969–70.[20] These visits were of great value to the NSCAD community, but were equally important for many of the artists. This was particularly true for Graham. Graham initially came in September to execute his Projects Class piece, *From Sunset to Sunrise*, a series of 160 photographs of the sky from a fixed point at set intervals. Taking advantage of equipment he had access to at NSCAD but not in New York, he also made a film version of this work, his first work in this medium. Over the course of this and subsequent visits to NSCAD, Graham executed many firsts: the performance *Lax/Relax* (September 1969); rehearsal for the dual Super 8 films *Two Correlated Rotations* (October 1969); rehearsal for the performance *Like* (1971); and premieres of his video performances *TV Camera/Monitor Performance* (October 1970), *Two Consciousness Projections* (1972) and *Nude Two Consciousness Projection(s)* (1975).[21] Graham also had his first solo show at NSCAD, mounted in two parts (8–15 October 1970, and 10–22 March 1971). As Rhea Anastas notes in the exhibition catalogue, *Dan Graham: Beyond*, these experiences were so important for Graham that, even

[20] During these visits, the artists typically gave public presentations. The transcripts of many of these talks were published in Peggy Gale (Ed.), *Artists Talk: 1969–1977* (Halifax: The Press of the Nova Scotia College of Art and Design, 2004). Lippard's talk, given in November 1969, is a notable omission from this publication. Called "Toward a Dematerialized or Non Object Art," it essentially outlined the thesis of what would become her touchstone publication on conceptual art, *Six Years: The Dematerialization of the Object from 1966 to 1972* (New York: Praeger, 1973).

[21] For further discussion of these works, see Chrissie Iles, "You are the information: Dan Graham and performance," in Bennett Simpson and Chrissie Iles (Eds.), *Dan Graham: Beyond* (Los Angeles: The Museum of Contemporary Art and Cambridge, MA: MIT Press, 2009), 55–70.

Above, from left

John Greer, *Ladder of Commitment*, 1976

Invitation for Michael Snow's *Works and Films*, Anna Leonowens Gallery, 17–30 January 1972

though he had been director of the John Daniels Gallery in New York since 1964, it was only *after* doing this work and having his first solo show at NSCAD that he felt confident to request a show of his own work at Daniels' gallery.[22]

As important as the Projects Class was, it was not the only means by which NSCAD circumvented its geographic isolation and established itself as a key locus for the international production and dissemination of conceptual art. Artists were also given opportunities to exhibit at the Anna Leonowens and Mezzanine galleries, produce prints with the Lithography Workshop and publish books with The Press. As Gerald Ferguson noted, these opportunities established a quid pro quo that was of benefit both to the college and the visiting artists.[23]

The establishment of the Mezzanine in 1970 was one of the most significant of these initiatives. The Mezzanine was a small space adjoining the Anna Leonowens Gallery that was used occasionally since 1969 for projects. It became formally constituted as the Mezzanine in September 1970 with the appointment of Charlotte Townsend as director. As Townsend recalls, it was conceived as a facility rather than a gallery, with the objective of disseminating the kind of ephemeral, transient and conceptual artwork then being produced internationally.[24]

The Mezzanine ran on a shoestring budget and relied largely on shows or projects amenable to the postal and telecommunication systems. One such notable example was the 1971 exhibition by the Californian conceptual artist John Baldessari. He wrote to Townsend saying he had a "Punishment Piece" for her. But since he couldn't be there, student "scapegoats" would be needed to take the punishment for his sins by covering the gallery walls top to bottom with the handwritten phrase "I will not make any more boring art."[25]

Eleanor Antin was another Californian artist who showed work at the Mezzanine based upon instructions sent by mail. Antin's *Library Science* catalogued responses by twenty-six women to her request to provide "a piece of information" (object or document) that described themselves. Antin then catalogued each response as if it was a book, in accordance with the Library of Congress subject classification system, and exhibited the resulting cards along with the "pieces of information" at the Mezzanine.[26]

Despite their different methods and subject matter, these two exhibitions demonstrate the essential principle of conceptual art as an "idea machine" that generates the work. Both Antin and Baldessari adopted the objective logic of a system as their generative model, thus obviating what Sol LeWitt referred to as the viewer's "expectation of an emotional kick".[27] Yet their works also had a subjective and irrational aspect, and though this may seem incongruous with conceptual art, LeWitt acknowledged it as one of the art form's central characteristics

---

[22] Rhea Anastas, "Minimal difference: The John Daniels Gallery and the first works of Dan Graham." In Simpson and Iles (Eds.), *Dan Graham: Beyond*, 124.

[23] Ferguson, "On NSCAD and conceptual art," 32.

[24] See Charlotte Townsend-Gault, "Conceptual daze at NSCAD—The Mezzanine," in Barber (Ed.), *Conceptual Art: The NSCAD Connection,* 42–44. The Mezzanine Fonds are located at NSCAD in the Gallery Archives. The key document, "Mezzanine Gallery—Chronological History and Inventory of Announcement Cards," lists a total of 107 group and solo projects or exhibitions, starting in October 1970 with Bruce McLean's *King for a Day and 999 Other Pieces/Works/Stuff, etc.* and ending in July 1973 with the closing of Ian Murray's *Keeping on Top of the Top Song*. There is some crossover in this document between the Anna Leonowens and Mezzanine galleries, however, and Murray's show was probably at the former.

[25] Baldessari's letter and sample text are located at NSCAD University, Gallery Archives, Mezzanine Fonds, Halifax, Baldessari Artist's File no. 1-1.8.

[26] The documents are located at NSCAD University, Gallery Archives, Mezzanine Fonds, Halifax, Antin Artist's File no. 1-1.3. The exhibition of *Library Science* at the Mezzanine was particularly significant since it was the first time it was shown both in its entirety and in an art context (its previous and partial exhibition was at the San Diego State College Library in April–May 1971; see Lippard, *Six Years*, 231).

[27] LeWitt, "Paragraphs on conceptual art," 80.

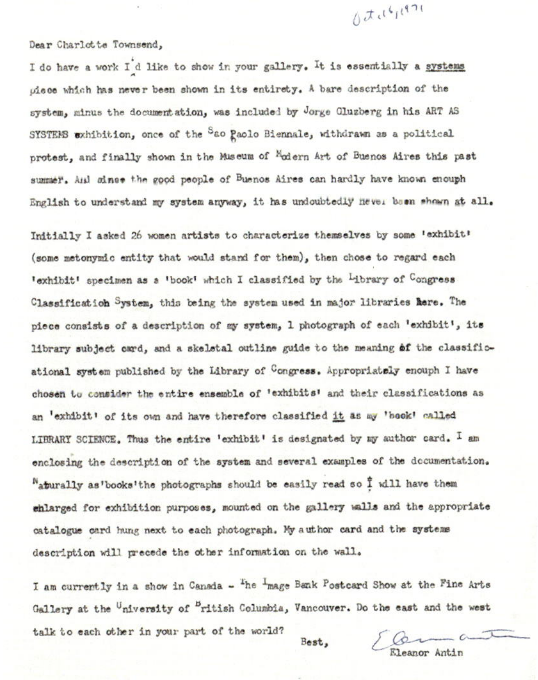

Oct. 16, 1971

Dear Charlotte Townsend,

I do have a work I'd like to show in your gallery. It is essentially a <u>systems</u> piece which has never been shown in its entirety. A bare description of the system, minus the documentation, was included by Jorge Gluzberg in his ART AS SYSTEMS exhibition, once of the Sao Paolo Biennale, withdrawn as a political protest, and finally shown in the Museum of Modern Art of Buenos Aires this past summer. And since the good people of Buenos Aires can hardly have known enouph English to understand my system anyway, it has undoubtedly never been shown at all.

Initially I asked 26 women artists to characterize themselves by some 'exhibit' (some metonymic entity that would stand for them), then chose to regard each 'exhibit' specimen as a 'book' which I classified by the Library of Congress Classification System, this being the system used in major libraries here. The piece consists of a description of my system, 1 photograph of each 'exhibit', its library subject card, and a skeletal outline guide to the meaning of the classificational system published by the Library of Congress. Appropriately enouph I have chosen to consider the entire ensemble of 'exhibits' and their classifications as an 'exhibit' of its own and have therefore classified <u>it</u> as my 'book' called LIBRARY SCIENCE. Thus the entire 'exhibit' is designated by my author card. I am enclosing the description of the system and several examples of the documentation. Naturally as'books'the photographs should be easily read so I will have them enlarged for exhibition purposes, mounted on the gallery walls and the appropriate catalogue card hung next to each photograph. My author card and the systems description will precede the other information on the wall.

I am currently in a show in Canada - The Image Bank Postcard Show at the Fine Arts Gallery at the University of British Columbia, Vancouver. Do the east and the west talk to each other in your part of the world?

Best,

Eleanor Antin

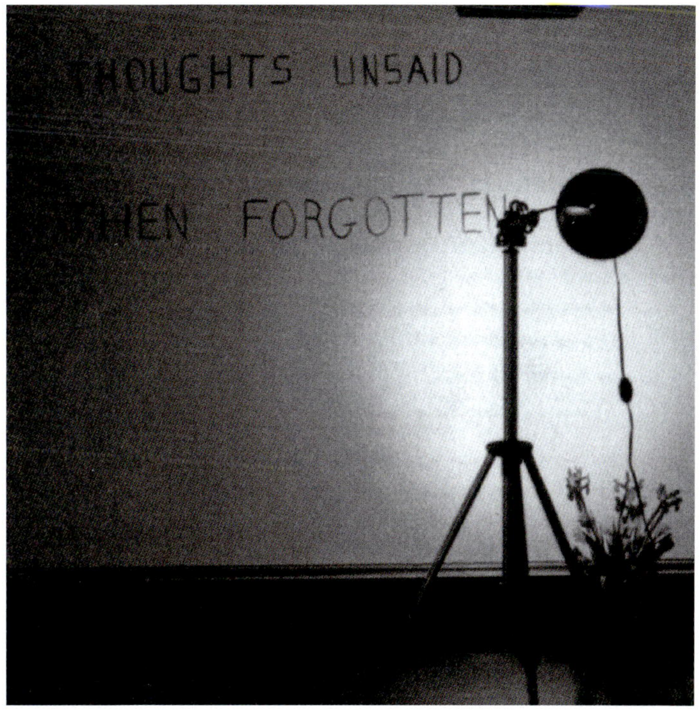

when he stated, "Conceptual artists are mystics rather than rationalists. They leap to conclusions that logic cannot reach."[28]

Two other shows held at the Mezzanine exemplify this subjective irrationalism that was inherent to much conceptual art. One was by Bas Jan Ader, the Dutch artist who went missing in 1975 while attempting to complete his triptych, *In Search of the Miraculous* (1973–75), with a solo voyage across the Atlantic in a tiny sailing boat. Ader's Mezzanine exhibition in April 1973 was an installation work called *Thoughts Unsaid, Then Forgotten*, the instructions for which were sent as a letter and sketch to Townsend.[29] They called for this phrase to be hand-painted on the wall and a vase of flowers to be placed on the floor to the right. A clip light with a reflector was to be attached to a stand set in front for illumination. After several days, the wall text was to be painted over, leaving the flowers and light undisturbed. The recent discovery of these documents at NSCAD has clarified misperceptions of this work, which was previously

[28] Sol LeWitt, "Sentences on conceptual art," *0-9*, no. 5 (January 1969): 3. Johanna Burton has examined this incongruity in "Mystics rather than rationalists," in Donna de Salvo (Ed.), *Open Systems: Rethinking Art c. 1970* (London: Tate Publishing, 2005), 65–81.

[29] The documents are located at NSCAD University, Gallery Archives, Mezzanine Fonds, Halifax, Correspondence 1970–73, File no. 1-3.1.

Above, from left

Eleanor Antin, correspondence relating to *Library Science*, Mezzanine, 1–9 February 1972

Installation view of Bas Jan Ader, *Thoughts Unsaid, Then Forgotten*, Mezzanine, 1–7 April 1973

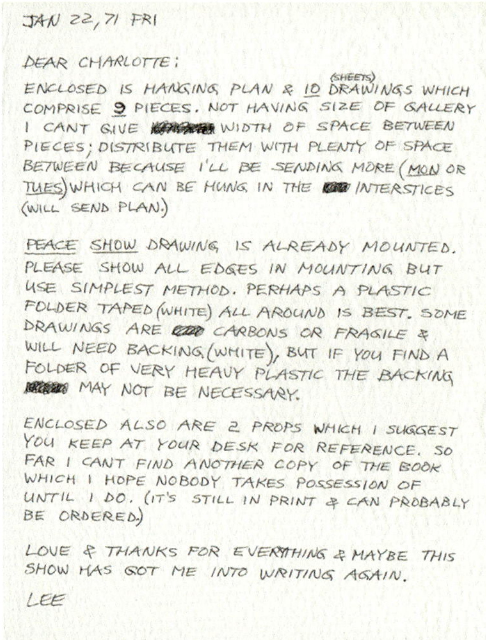
JAN 22, 71 FRI

DEAR CHARLOTTE:

ENCLOSED IS HANGING PLAN & 10 (SHEETS) DRAWINGS WHICH COMPRISE 9 PIECES. NOT HAVING SIZE OF GALLERY I CANT GIVE WIDTH OF SPACE BETWEEN PIECES; DISTRIBUTE THEM WITH PLENTY OF SPACE BETWEEN BECAUSE I'LL BE SENDING MORE (MON OR TUES) WHICH CAN BE HUNG IN THE INTERSTICES (WILL SEND PLAN.)

PEACE SHOW DRAWING IS ALREADY MOUNTED. PLEASE SHOW ALL EDGES IN MOUNTING BUT USE SIMPLEST METHOD. PERHAPS A PLASTIC FOLDER TAPED (WHITE) ALL AROUND IS BEST. SOME DRAWINGS ARE CARBONS OR FRAGILE & WILL NEED BACKING (WHITE), BUT IF YOU FIND A FOLDER OF VERY HEAVY PLASTIC THE BACKING MAY NOT BE NECESSARY.

ENCLOSED ALSO ARE 2 PROPS WHICH I SUGGEST YOU KEEP AT YOUR DESK FOR REFERENCE. SO FAR I CANT FIND ANOTHER COPY OF THE BOOK WHICH I HOPE NOBODY TAKES POSSESSION OF UNTIL I DO. (IT'S STILL IN PRINT & CAN PROBABLY BE ORDERED.)

LOVE & THANKS FOR EVERYTHING & MAYBE THIS SHOW HAS GOT ME INTO WRITING AGAIN.

LEE

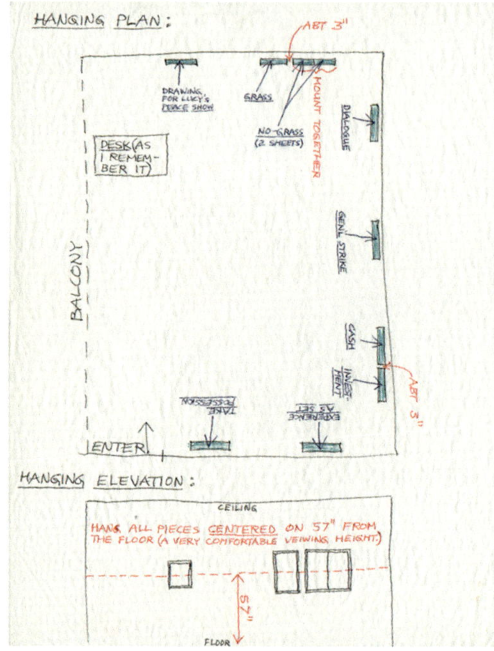

known only through a Polaroid photograph of the installation that Townsend sent to Ader. As Wade Saunders has argued, these documents reveal the extent to which the juxtaposition in this work between the chronological dimension of human consciousness (thoughts unsaid, then forgotten) and biological decay (the dying flowers) reinforces the centrality of pathos and melancholia in Ader's work.[30]

An even more pronounced irrationalism was evident in Lee Lozano's (1939–99) *Infofiction* exhibition at the Mezzanine in January 1971. Lozano was a successful New York artist in the 1960s, but by 1969 she had begun to reject the art world. Just before dropping out altogether, however, she agreed to a mini-retrospective in Halifax of her *Language Pieces*. These were derived from her journal recordings and called for the completion of self-prescribed tasks or activities within a set duration.[31] Lozano's Mezzanine show was the only individual presentation of *Language Pieces* during her lifetime.[32] These pieces attest to the highly idiosyncratic nature of Lozano's work, ranging from a scornful disdain of the art world (*Printed Matter Pile*, *General Strike*), a desire for art to foster both verbal and non-verbal communication (*Dialogue*, *Experience as Set*) and the self-examination of extremely

Above, from left

Lee Lozano, correspondence relating to *Infofiction*, Mezzanine, 27 January–13 February 1971

Lee Lozano, installation plan for *Infofiction*, Mezzanine, 27 January–13 February 1971

[30] Wade Saunders, "In dreams begin responsibilities," *Art in America* 92, no. 2 (February 2004): 61–62.

[31] See Helen Molesworth, "Tune in, turn on, drop out: The rejection of Lee Lozano," in Adam Szymczyk (Ed.), *Lee Lozano: Win First Dont Last/Win Last Dont Care* (Basel: Kunsthalle Basel, 2006), 133–135.

[32] The documents are located at the Anna Leonowens Gallery Archive, MG Fonds, Lozano Artist's File no. 1-1.37. Included in the show were *Printed Matter Pile*, *Grass* and *No-grass*, *Dialogue*, *General Strike*, *Cash*, *Investment*, *Experience as Set*, *Masturbation Investigation* and *Take Possession*, all from 1969–70. For a brief synopsis of the significance of Lozano's *Infofiction* show at the Mezzanine as well as reproductions of the individual pieces, see Adam Szymczyk, "Infofiction, January

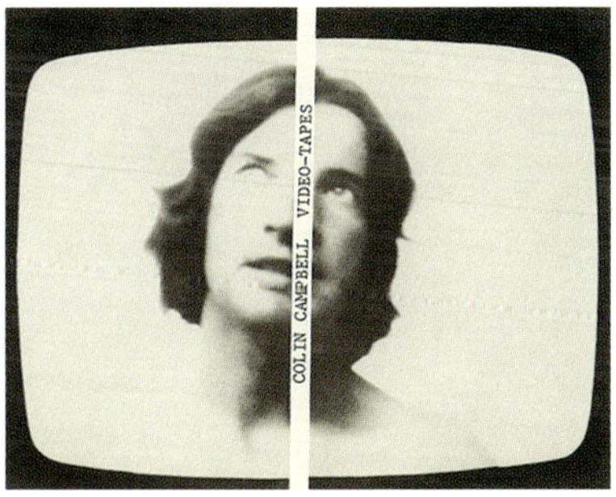

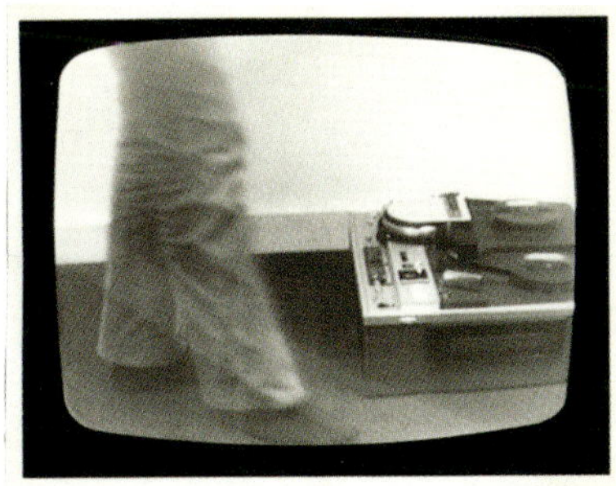

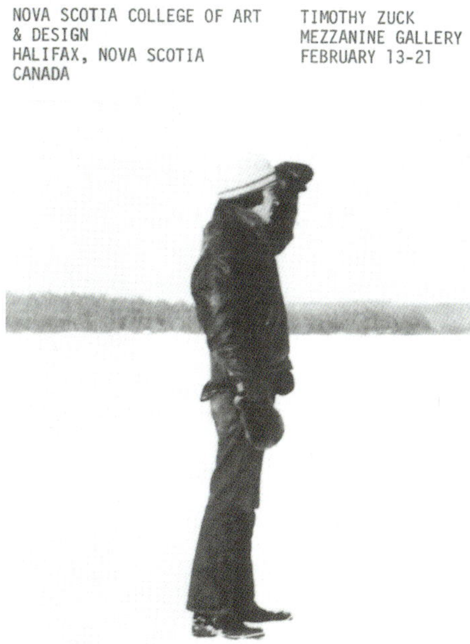

Top, left
Invitation for Colin Campbell's *Video Tapes*, Mezzanine, 1–10 December 1972

Bottom, left
Douglas Waterman, still from *Shuffle*, 1971

Right
Invitation for Tim Zuck's *Untitled*, Mezzanine, 13–21 February 1971

private experiences (*Grass* and *No-Grass*, *Masturbation Investigation*). While the linguistic and documentary aspects of Lozano's *Infofiction* pieces conform broadly to the tenets of conceptual art, the works also demonstrate how those tenets could be radically stretched to accommodate her uniquely irrational predilections.[33]

While the exhibitions outlined here demonstrate how the Mezzanine's innovative programming structure facilitated projects by international artists, the gallery also sponsored many shows by Canadian artists as well as by NSCAD faculty and students. Notable examples of the former include shows by N.E. Thing Co. (1971); Karl Beveridge, Colin Campbell, Ian Carr-Harris and Bill Vazan (1972); and Christos Dikeakos (1973). Some of the faculty and students who showed at the Mezzanine were David Askevold (1970); Richards Jarden, Pat Kelly, Douglas Waterman and Tim Zuck (1971); and Wallace Brannen and Sharon Kulik (1972).

Whereas the Mezzanine operated only from 1970 to 1973, the Anna Leonowens Gallery also played a vital role in fostering the dissemination of conceptual art at NSCAD during the entire period covered by the *Traffic* exhibition.[34] In addition to the previously cited exhibitions by Lau,

---

27–February 13, 1971," in *Lee Lozano: Win First Dont Last/Win Last Dont Care*, 144–160.

[33] These predilections were further evident in Lozano's participation in David Askevold's Projects Class on 16 July 1971. For this she realized her *3-State Experiment*, which entailed giving a "lecture" to students in three states: sober, stoned on marijuana and stoned on LSD. Three days later, Lozano reflected on her Halifax experience in an entry containing phrases that seem to constitute the key aperçu to her work: "Information is content. Content is fiction. Content is messy . . . Form is reduplicable, content is not reduplicable. Fiction has meaning, but only in a given instant of time." For further documentation of Lozano's activities in Halifax, see Adam Szymczyk and Charles Esche, "Lee Lozano's lecture at NSCAD, Halifax, July 16, 1971" and "Halifax *3-State Experiment*," and David Askevold, "David Askevold on Lee Lozano," in *Lee Lozano: Win First Dont Last/Win Last Dont Care*, 161–178.

[34] The gallery's exhibition records are located at NSCAD University, Gallery Archives, Anna Leonowens Gallery Exhibitions Fonds, Halifax

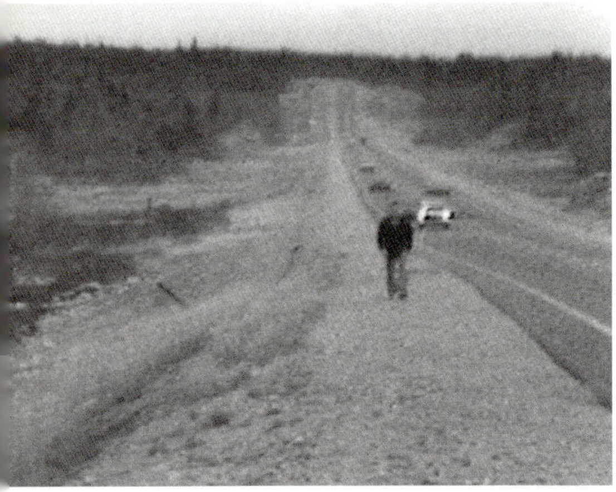

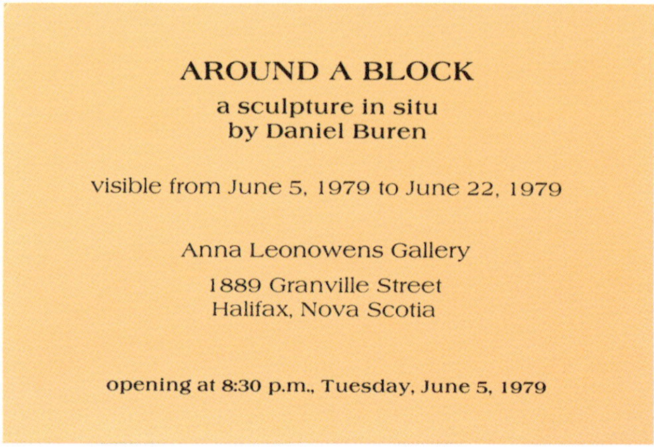

AROUND A BLOCK
a sculpture in situ
by Daniel Buren

visible from June 5, 1979 to June 22, 1979

Anna Leonowens Gallery

1889 Granville Street
Halifax, Nova Scotia

opening at 8:30 p.m., Tuesday, June 5, 1979

Nova Scotia College of Art and Design
6152 Coburg Road
Halifax Nova Scotia
Canada

Sharon Kulik

March 13-17 1972

(Trying to become another person)

Copying another person for a week in an attempt to become him. Others,simultaneously and unconciously,copy my copy(of a copy) destroying the original by breaking the mirror,concluding in diminishment of my dissappearance.

Winter 1972

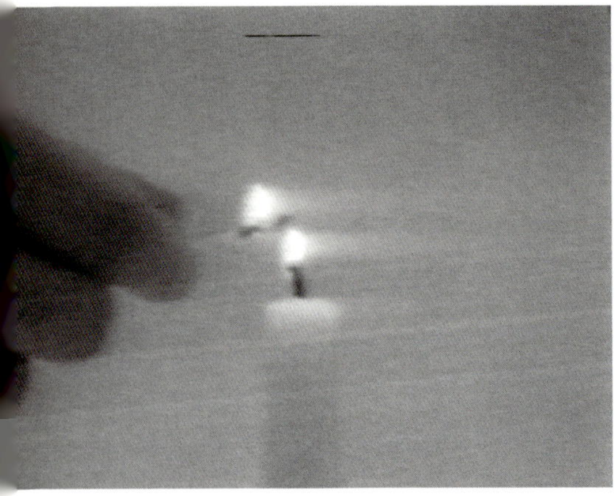

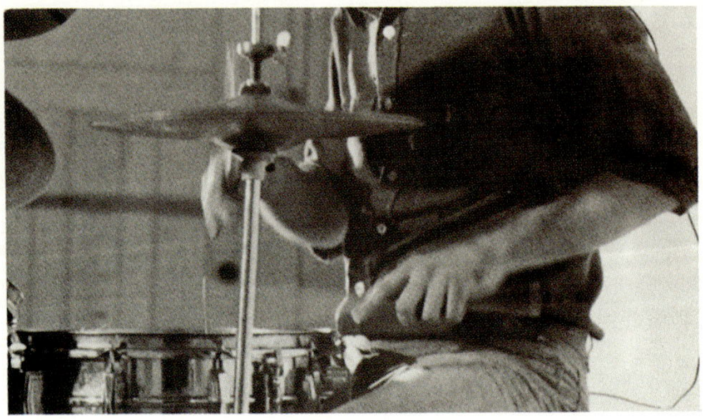

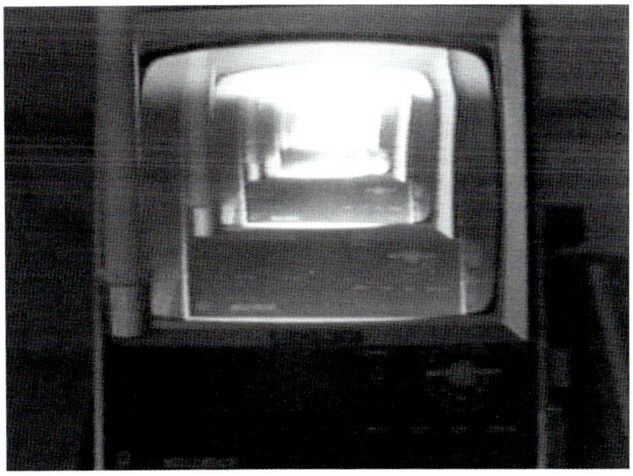

Brian MacNevin, still from *Audio Visual Feedback (completing two cycles) (The Vancouver Tapes No. 1)*, c. 1970

Byars, Weiner, NETCO and Kosuth, other notable artists who showed there include Gerald Ferguson, John Greer and Michael Snow (1972); Les Levine and Ian Murray (1973); Michael Asher, David Askevold and Carole Condé (1974); Daniel Buren (1979); Dara Birnbaum, Jenny Holzer, Martha Rosler and Allan Sekula (1980); and Mary Kelly (1981).

Yet no matter how significant these exhibitions were both for the artists and for the history of conceptual art in Canada, the main function of the Anna Leonowens and Mezzanine galleries was to serve students. This meant providing them with opportunities to see work by professional artists in a city where they could not otherwise have done so. Equally important, it meant providing students with a gallery where they could exhibit their own work alongside professional artists, and be treated as professionals themselves. The Anna Leonowens Gallery still operates this way and its integration of student and professional exhibitions remains unique in Canada.

Along with the Projects Class and the galleries' exhibition programs, the founding of the Lithography Workshop and The Press were key gambits in NSCAD's overall strategy for creating innovative connections with the larger contemporary art world. When the Lithography Workshop started up in January 1969 it emulated the Tamarind Lithography Workshop, founded by June Wayne in Los Angeles in 1960 "to rescue . . . the art of the lithograph" by having artists work directly in the shop with the master printer.[35] The main objectives of the NSCAD Lithography Workshop were to attract prominent artists to the school through the incentive of producing a limited edition print (normally a run of 50, split between the artist

[35] June Wayne, "Preface." In Garo Z. Antreasian and Clinton Adams, *The Tamarind Book of Lithography: Art and Techniques* (Los Angeles: Tamarind Lithography Workshop, 1971), 7.

Opposite, clockwise from top left
Wallace Brannen, still from *Mile Walk (The Vancouver Tapes No. 3)*, c. 1971

Invitation for Daniel Buren's *Around a Block: A Sculpture in Situ by Daniel Buren*, Anna Leonowens Gallery 5–22 June 1979

Invitation for *Sharon Kulik*, Anna Leonowens Gallery, 13–17 March 1972

Invitation for Ian Murray's *Keeping on Top of the Top Song*, Anna Leonowens Gallery, 25 June–2 July 1973

Barry MacPherson, still from *Untitled (The Vancouver Tapes No. 1)*, c. 1970

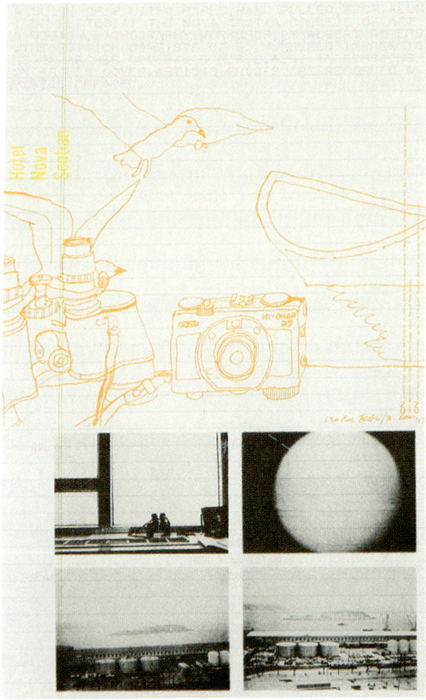

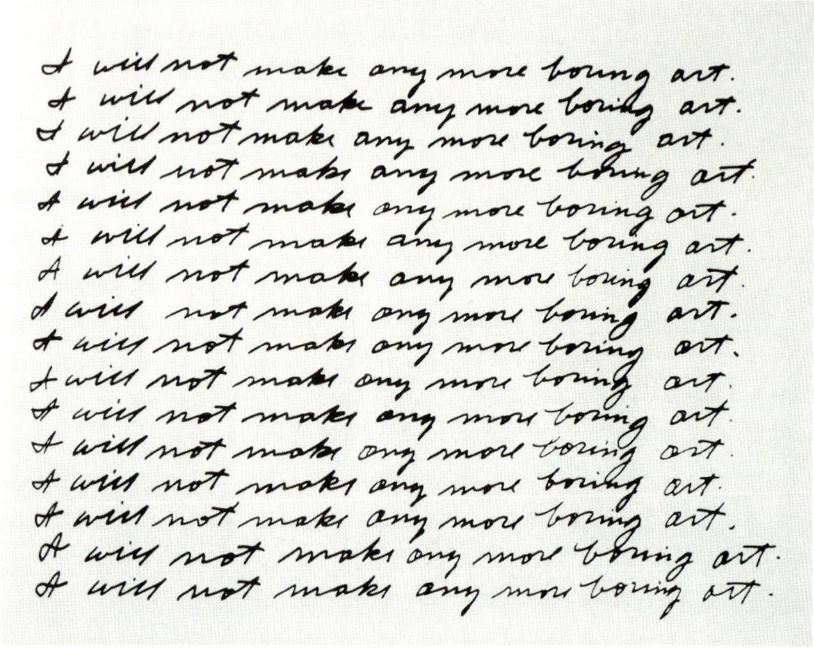

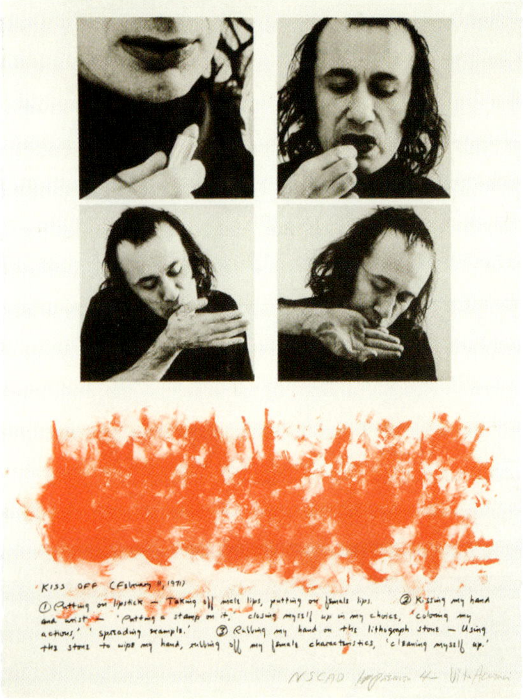

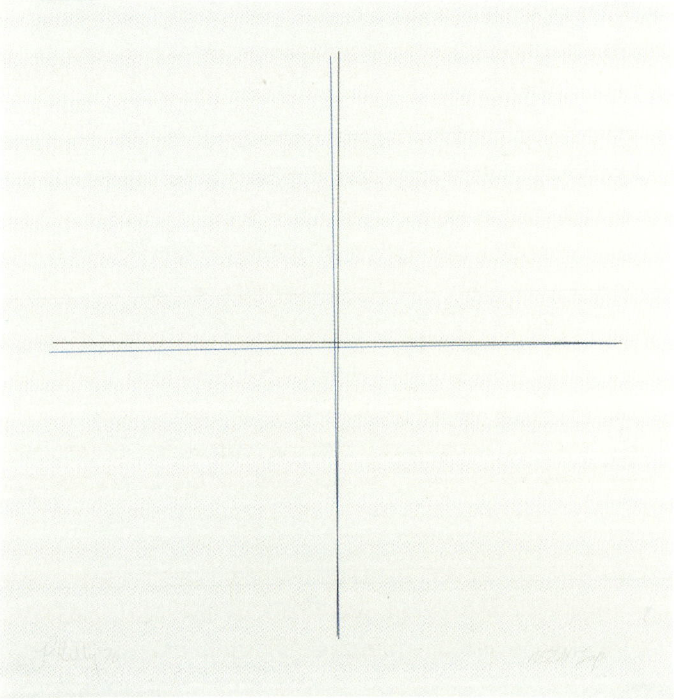

Top, left
Greg Curnoe, *Homage to Sam Langford*, 1970, detail © Estate of Greg Curnoe / SODRAC

Bottom, left
Vito Acconci, *Kiss Off*, 1971

Top, right
John Baldessari, *I Will Not Make Any More Boring Art*, 1971

Bottom, right
Pat Kelly, *A Shot in the Dark*, 1971

and the college); provide students with opportunities to interact with artists during their residencies; and generate revenue through sales of prints.[36]

During its first eighteen months, under the directorship of Jack Lemon, the Lithography Workshop produced a series of technically spectacular works, including *Homage to Sam Langford*, a suite of 10 prints by Greg Curnoe that simulate a writing pad with accounts of his visit to Halifax to work on the prints in February–March 1970. When Lemon left in mid-1970 and Gerald Ferguson took over as director, however, the Lithography Workshop took a very different direction. As Eric Cameron has said, it often went so far against the Tamarind ideals as to travesty them.[37] Ferguson's goal was to increase the Workshop's marketability by producing prints with artists who were then establishing international reputations as innovators of conceptual art. This objective accorded with Ferguson's lack of commitment to the aesthetics of lithography per se, which he considered "no more or less valuable than any other medium for the demonstration of an idea by an artist."[38]

This new orientation showed the unexpected ways in which such a traditional medium as printmaking could be reinvented under the principles of conceptual art. In some cases, such as John Baldessari's *I Will Not Make Any More Boring Art* (based on his 1971 Mezzanine show) and Sol LeWitt's 1971 suite of 10 prints, the execution was deferred to students and/or the master printer, thus exemplifying LeWitt's definition of conceptual art as a practice where "the execution is a perfunctory affair."[39] In other cases, the basis of the prints was a self-reflexive reference to the process of printmaking. Pat Kelly's *A Shot in the Dark* (1971), for example, entailed registering two black lines intersecting at the centre of the paper and then having the artist attempt to match these by repositioning each paper manually on the printing bed, the results of which were superimposed in blue ink.

Other Lithography Workshop prints incorporated conceptual art principles through methods that indexed systems, locations or memories. Gerald Ferguson's *Length 4* (1970) was an excerpt from his systematic cataloguing of dictionary words in his book *The Standard Corpus of Present Day English Language Usage arranged by word length and alphabetized within word length*. For his *Location Piece #25* (1973), Douglas Huebler reproduced his own composite photograph of a postcard of the Trevi Fountain in Rome. Below this image, the print gave instructions for the purchaser to contact the artist, who would have a postcard of the fountain sent from Rome to the purchaser, who was then to affix it to the print in order to complete the work. Garry Neill Kennedy's print, *My Fourth Grade Class* (1972), was an index of

[36] For a more detailed discussion of the Lithography Workshop history, see my article "Conceptual lithography at the Nova Scotia College of Art and Design," *Journal of Canadian Art History* 30 (Fall 2009): 60–88.

[37] Eric Cameron, "The Lithography Workshop." In Garry Neill Kennedy (Ed.), *NSCAD: The Nova Scotia College of Art & Design* (Halifax: The Press of the Nova Scotia College of Art and Design, 1982), 9.

[38] Gerald Ferguson, "Lithography Workshop." In Michael Knigin and Murray Zimiles (Eds.), *The Contemporary Lithographic Workshop Around the World* (New York: Van Nostrand Reinhold Co., 1974), 117.

[39] LeWitt, "Paragraphs on conceptual art," 80.

~~EVNA~~ ALSO AWAY BEDE BOAR BULB CATS COED CURD DENT DOUG EDGY FAIM FLAW FUND GNAW GYMS HENA HOYT IRAN JOWL KNEE LAYS LITZ ~~MAEQ~~ MEET MOOD NEX
~~EV-T~~ ALTO AWED BEDS BOAT BULK CATT COGS CURE DENY DOUR EDIT FAIN FLAX FUNK GOAD GYRO HEAD HUAI IRAQ JOYS KNEW LAZE LIVE MACK MEIR MOON NIC
~~AVO~~ ALUM AWRY BEEF BOAZ BULL CAVE COHN CURL DEOR DOVE EDNA FAIR FLEA FURS GOAL HABE HOSE HUBS IRMA JUAN KNIT LAZY LOAD MADE MELD MOOS NIC
~~AXLG~~ ALVA AXES BEEN BOOK BUMP ~~CCI~~ COIL CURT DEPT DOWN EGGS FAKE FLED FURY GOAT HACK HERO HUCK IRON JUDE KNOB LBJ. LOAF MAGI MELT MOOT NIC
~~AY-S~~ AMEN AXIS BEEP BODY BUMS ~~CCI~~ COIN CURY DERE DRAB EGON FALL FLEE FUSE GODS HADD HERR HUES ISIS JUDY KNOE LEAD LOAN MAHT MEME MOPS NIG
~~-10~~ AMID AXLE BEER BOGY BUNK CEIL COKE CUSA DESK DRAG EIES FAME FLEM FUSS GOES HAEC HERS HUEY ISLE JUET KNOT LEAF LOHE MAID MEMO MORE NIL
ABBE AMIS AYES BEES BOHN BUNS CELL COLD CUSP DEUS DRAM EINE FANS FLEW FUZZ GOGH HAIL HESS HUFF IT'D JUJU KNOW LEAK LOBO MAIL MEND MORT NIN
ABED AMMO AYUB BEGS BOIL BUNT CENT COLE CUTE DEUX DRAW EIRE FARE FLEX GAGE GOGO HAIR HICK HUGE IT'S JUKE KNOX LEAN LOCK MAIN MENU MOSE NIN
ABEL AMOS BABE BEIN BOIS BURI CEPT COLO CUTS DIAL DRED EKED FARM FLIP GAGS GOIN HALE HIDE HUGH ITCH JULY KOAN LEAP LOEB MAIS MERC MOSK NIP
ABER AMRA BABY BELA BOLD BURL CERV COLT CZAR DIAM DREW ELAN FARO FLNG GAIN GOLD HALF HIGH HUGO ITEM JUMP KOCH LEAR LOEN MAKE MERE MOSS NIS
ABLE ANDY BACH BELL BOLO BURN CHAP COMB ~~DILL~~ DICE DRIP ELBA FARR FLOC GAIT GOLF HALL HIKE HULK IVAN JUNE KOHI LEES LOFT MAKU MERZ MOST ~~NO~~
ABLY ANEW BACI BELT BOLT BURR CHAR COME ~~DIUN~~ DICK DROP ELEC FAST FLOE ~~GAL~~ GONE HALO HILL HULL ~~JIAI~~ JUNK KOLA LEET LOGS MALE MESA MOTH NOA
ABRA ANNA BACK BEND BOMB BURT CHAT CONE DADE DIDI DRUG ELKS FATE FLOG GALA GOOD HALS HILO HUME JABS JURE KOLB LEFT LOIN MALI MESH MOVE NOD
ACES ANNE BADE BENT BONA BURY CHAW CONG DAER DION DRUM ELLA FATS FLOP GALE GORD HALT HILT HUMP JACK JURY KONG LEGS LOIS MALL MESS MSEC NOE
ACEY ANTA BADS BERN BOND BUSH CHEF CONN DAIS DIED DUAL ELLO FAWN FLOR GALL GORE HAMM HIND HUNG JADE JUST KOOP LENA LOLA MALT METS MUCH NOE
ACHE ANTE BAER BERT BONE BUSS CHEN CONS DALE DIEM DUCK ELMS FAZE FLOW GALS GOSH HAMS HINO HUNK JAHR KAHN KRIM LEND LOND MAMA MICA MUCK NOI
ACID ANTI BAGH BESS BONG BUST CHES COOK DALI DIES DUCT ELOI FEAR FLUX GALT GOTT HAND HINT HUNT JAIL KALE KUHN LENI LONE MAME MICE MUFF NOL
ACRE ANTS BAGS BEST BONN BUSY CHEW COOL DALY DIET DUDS ELSE FEAT FOAL GAME GOUT HANG HIPS HURL JAKE KALI KURD LENS LONG MANA MICH MUGS NOL
ACTS ANYE BAHI BETA BONY BUTT CHIC COOP DAME DIEU DUEL EMIL FEDS FOAM GANG GOWN HANK HIRE HURT JAMS KANS KURT LENT LOOK MANN MICK MUIR NOL
ADAM APEX BAIL BETE BOOK BUYS CHIN COPE DAMN DIGS DUET EMIT FEED FOCI GAPS GPD, HANS HISS HUSH JANA KANT KWHR LEON LOOM MANO MIDI MULE NON
ADDS ARAB BAIT BETH BOOM BUZZ CHIP COPP DAMP DILL DUKE EMMA FEEL FOES GAPT GRAB HARD HITS HUTS JANE KARE KYNE LESS LOON MANS MIEN MUSE NOO
AEON ARAK BAKE BETS BOON BYRD CHMN COPS DAMS DIME DULL ENDS FEES FOGG GARB GRAD HARE HIVE HYDE JAPS KARL LACE LEST LOOP MANU MIGS MUST NOP
AFAR ARCH BAKU BEVO BOOS ~~CAPO~~ CHOP COPY DANA DINE DULY ENGH FEET FOGY GARY GRAM HARK HMPF HYMN JARS KATE LACK LETS LOOT MANY MIKE MUTE NOR
AGED ARCO BALD BEVY BOOT ~~CLUN~~ CHOU CORD DANE DINH DUMB ENNY FEIS FOIL GASH GRAN HARM HOAG HYTT JAVA KAVA LACY LEVY LOPE MAPS MILD MUZO NOR
AGEE ARCS BALE BHOY BORE CABS CHOW CORE DANG DION DUMP ENOS FELL FOLD GASP GRAS HARP HOAK ~~I-TH~~ JAWS KAYO LADS LEWD LORD MARC MILE MYNE NOS
AGES AREA BALI BIAS BORN CADY CHUM CORK DANK DIOR DUNE ENVY FELT FOLK GATE GRAY HART HOBO ~~ILLE~~ JAZZ KEEL LADY ~~LILL~~ LORE MARE MILK MYRA NOT
AGIN ARES BALL BIBB BOSS CAFE CIAO CORN DANS DIPS DUNG ENZO FENS FOND GAUL GREG HASH HOES ~~HIVE~~ JEAN KEEN LAFE LIAR LOSE MARK MILL MYTH NOT
AGUE ARID BAND BICH BOTH CAGE CINQ CORP DARE DIRE DUNK EPIC FERN FOOD GAVE GRET HAST HOGS ICED JEEP KEEP LAGS LICE LOSS MARR MILT ~~NAIO~~ NOU
AHAH ARIZ BANG BIDE BOUN CAIN CITE COST DARK DIRT DUNN EONS FESS FOOL GAZE GREV HATE HOLD IDAL JEFF KEGS LAHK LICK LOST MARS MIMI ~~N-NB~~ NOV
AHEM ARMS BANI BIDS BOUT CAKE CITO COSY DARN DISC DUSK ERAS FETE FOOT GEAR GREW HATH HOLE IDEA JENA KEHL LAID LIDS LOTS MART ~~MIN.~~ ~~NATH~~ NOV
AIDA ARMY BANK BIEN BOWL CALF CITY COTT DASH DISH DUST ERDE FEUD FORD GEMS GREY HATS HOLY IDJE JENS KELP LAIN LIED LOUD MARV ~~MIN.~~ NAIL NUC
AIDE ARTE BANS BILE BOWS CALL CLAD COUD DATA DISK DUTY ERIC FIAT FORE GENE GRIM HAUL HOME IDLE JERK KEMM LAKE LIEN LOVE MARX MIND NAME NUF
AIDS ARTS BARD BILL BOXY CALM CLAM COUP DATE DIST DWOR ERIE FIDE FORK GERM GRIN HAVE HOMO IDLY JESS KENG LAMB LIES LOWE MARY MINE NAPS NUF
AIMS ARTY BARE BIND BOYD CAME CLAN COVE DAVE DIVA DYED ERIK FIFE FORM GETS GRIP HAWK HONE IDOL JEST KENO LAME LIEU LOWN MASH MINH NARA NUI
AINU ARYL BARI BING BOYS CAMI CLAP COWS DAVY DIVE DYER EROS FIGS FORT GETZ GRIS HAYS HONG IFNI JETS KENT LAMP LIFE LOWS MASK MINK NARY NUL
AIRS ASCH BARK BINI BRAD CAMP CLAW COZY DAWN DOAN DYKE ERRS FIKE FOSS GIBE GRIT HAZE HOOD IGBO JEWS KEPT LANA LIFT LUCK MASS MINN NATE NUM
AIRY ASIA BARN BINS BRAE CAMS CLAY CRAP DAYS DOCK ~~EARO~~ ESSE FILE FOUL GIDE GROK HAZY HOOF IGOR JINX KERN LAND LIKE LUCY MAST MINT NAVY NUN
AJAR ASKS BARK ~~BIO~~ BRAG CANE CLIP CREW DEAD DOOD EACH ~~EIIS~~ FILL FOUR GIFT GROW ~~HEIB~~ HOOK IKLE JIST KERR LANE LILA LUIS MASU MIRA NAWT NUT
AKIN ASSN BARS BIRD BRAN CANS CLOD CRIB DEAF DOES EARL ETES FILY FOWL GILD GRUB ~~JEIS~~ HOOP ILKA JOAN KEYS LANG LILI LUKE MATE MIRO NAZI ~~OIL~~
~~ALAS~~ ~~ATHL~~ BASE BITE BRED CANT CLOG CRIP DEAL DOGS EARN EVEN FIND FOXX GILL GUAM HEAD HOOT ILLE ~~JOB~~ KHAN LAOS LILT LULL MATH MISO NEAL OAF
ALAI ATUM BASS BITS BREW CAPE CLOT CRIS DEAN DOIN EARP EVER FINE ~~FOG~~ GILT GUAR HEAL HOPE ILLS JOBS KICK LAPS LILY LULU MATS MISS NEAR OAK
ALAN ATOP BAST BIWA BRIG CAPO CLOV CROP DEAR DOLE EARS EVIL FING FRAN GINO GULF HEAP HOPS INCA JOCK KIDS LARD LIMB LUMP MATT MIST NEAT OAT
ALAS ATTA BATH BLDG BRIM CAPS CLUB CROW DEBS DOLL EASE EWEN FINK FRAU GINS GULL HEAR HORD INCH JODY KIKA LARK LIME LUND MAWR MITE NECK OAT
ALBA ATTU BATS BLED BROD CAPT CLUE CRUS DEBT DOME EAST EXEC FINN FRAY GIRD GULP HEAT HORN INGO JOEL KILL LARS LIMP LUNG MAYE MMES NEED OBE
ALDO ATTY BAUM BLEW BROK CARD CMDR CRUX DECK DOMI EASY EXIT FINS FRED GIRL GUMS HECK HORS INKS JOEY KIND LASH LINE LURA MAYO ~~MMMM~~ NEHF ODD
ALEC AUBR BAWH BLOB BROS CARE COAL CRUZ DEED DONE EATS EYED FIRE FREE GIST GUNK HEED HOSE INNA JOGS KING LASS LINK LURE MAYS MOAN NEIL ODE
ALEX AUNT BAYS BLOC BROW CARL COAT CUBA DEEM DOOM EAVE EYES FIRM FRET GIVE GUNS HEEL HOSS INNS JOHN KIRA LAST LINT LURK MAZE MOBS NELL ODD
ALFA AURA BEAD BLOT BRYN CARR COAX CUBE DEEP DOOR EBBS EYKE FISH FROG GLAD GURU HEIR HOST INTO JOIE KIRK LATE LINZ LUSH ~~MGAH~~ MOCK NEO- ODO
ALIA AUTO BEAM BLOW BUCK CARS COBB CUBS DEER DOPE EBEN EZRA FISK FROM GLEE GUSH HELD HOOK IONE JOIN KISS LATH LION LUST ~~MEAR~~ MODE NEON OHI
ALIX AVEC BEAN BLUE BUCS CART COCK CUES DEFT DORA EBER FACE FIST FUCK GLEN GUST HELL HOUR IONS JOKE KITE LATS LIPS LUTE MEAD MOLD NERO OIL
ALLA AVID BEAR BLUM BUDD CASE COCO CUFF DEFY DORR ECHO FACT FITS FUDO GLIB GUTE HELM HOVE IOTA JOLT KITS LAUE LISA LYIN MEAL MOLE NEST OIL
ALLY AVIS BEAT BLUR BUDS CASH COCU CULT DEJA DOSE EDDY FADE FIVE FUEL GLOW GUTS HELP HOWE IOWA JOSE KIVU LAVA LISE LYLE MEAN MOLL NETS OKA
ALMA AVIV BEAU BLVD BUFF CASK CODE CUPS DELL DOST EDEN FADS FLAG FUJI GLUE GUYS HENH HOWL IPSO JOSS KLAN LAWN LISS LYNN MEAT MONK NEWS OKL
ALPS AVON BECK BOAL BUGS CAST CODY CURB DENS DOTS EDGE FAIL FLAT FULL GLUM GWEN HENS HOXA IRAJ JOUR KLUX LAWS LIST LYON MEEK MONT NEWT OLA

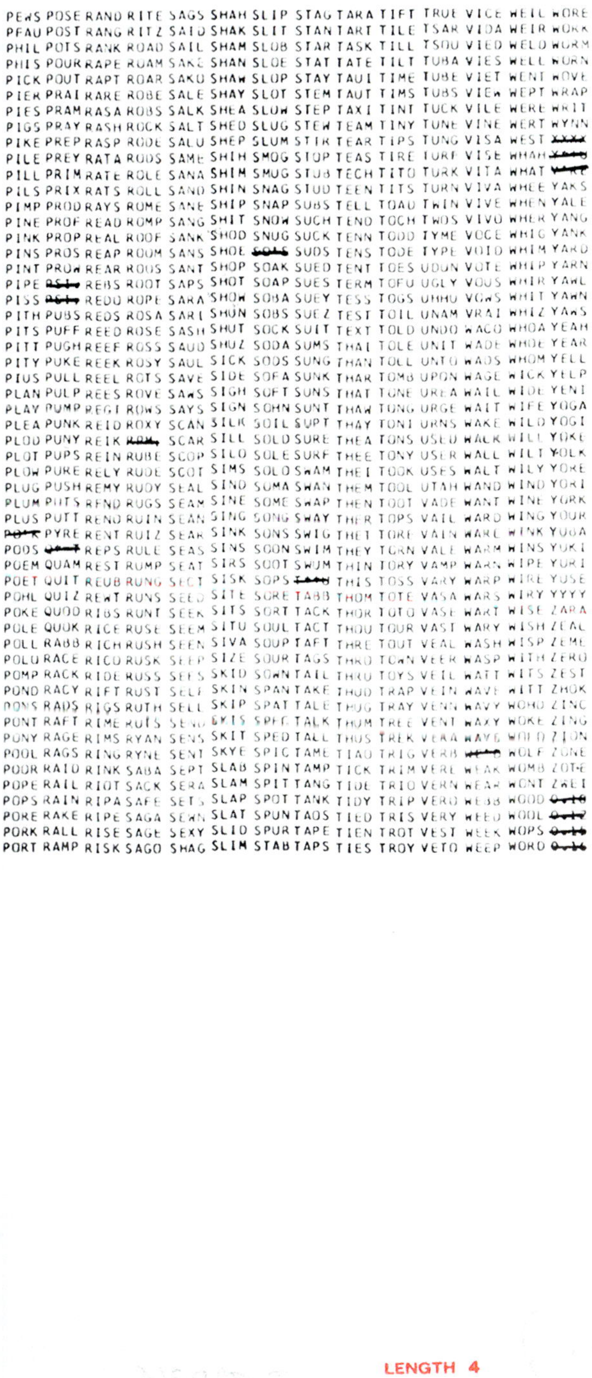

Gerald Ferguson, *Length 4*, 1970

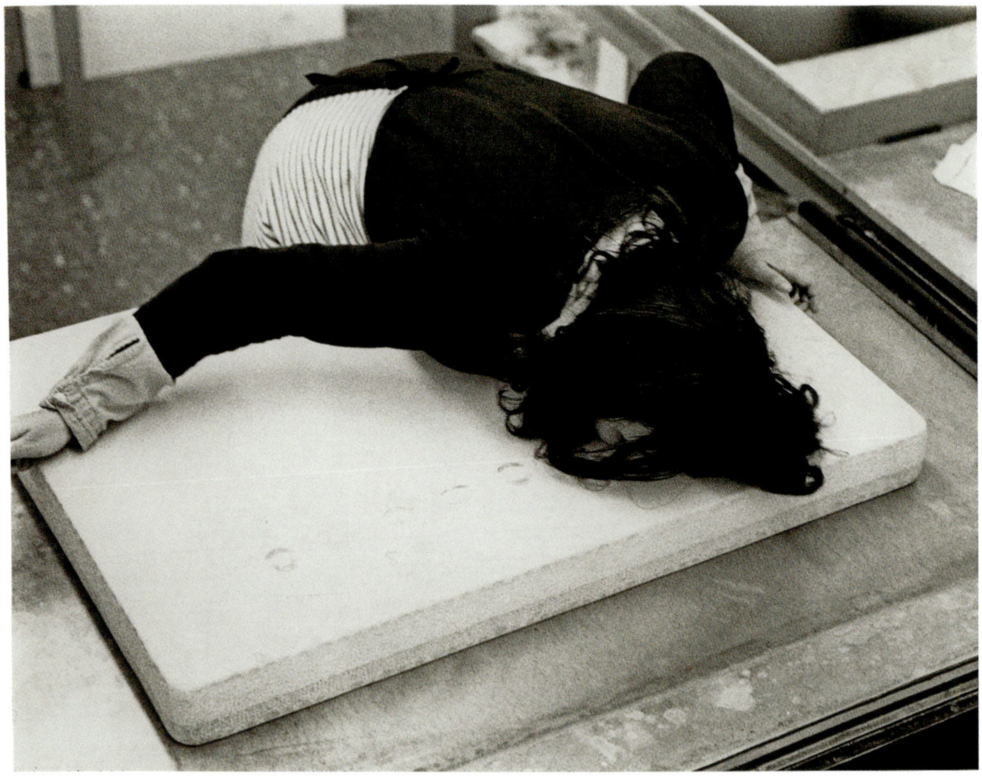

memory consisting of his class photograph with the names written in for all the children he could remember.

Still other prints employed this indexing principle by referring to the artists' own embodied subjectivities. For her iconic _O Canada_ (1970), Joyce Wieland applied lipstick and then mouthed the words of the national anthem on the litho stone. Shortly afterward, in February 1971, Vito Acconci produced _Kiss Off_ and _Trademarks_. _Trademarks_ documented a previous performance by Acconci where he attempted to bite as much of his body as he could reach, but _Kiss Off_ was a unique production for the Lithography Workshop. By covering his mouth with lipstick and then wiping it off on the stone in a process described on the print as "rubbing off my female characteristics, 'cleaning myself up,'" Acconci clearly seems to have responded directly to the gendered implications of Wieland's _O Canada_.

The Lithography Workshop was very successful both in demonstrating how printmaking could become a vehicle for conceptual art and in attracting artists to the college. But by 1976 it was deemed financially unsustainable and was closed. This decision was eased, however, by the founding of The Press in 1972. The suggestion for initiating a press came from Dan Graham, who also suggested the appointment of German curator and book dealer Kasper Koenig as editor.[40] On the advice of NSCAD art historian Dennis Young, The Press adopted the mandate

Above
Joyce Wieland executing *O Canada*, 1970.
Photo: Robert Rogers

[40] Kennedy, "NSCAD and the sixties," 26. For a detailed overview of the history of The Press, see Benjamin H.D. Buchloh, "The Press of NSCAD: A brief incomplete history and its future books," in Kennedy (Ed.), *NSCAD: The Nova Scotia College of Art & Design*, 64–75.

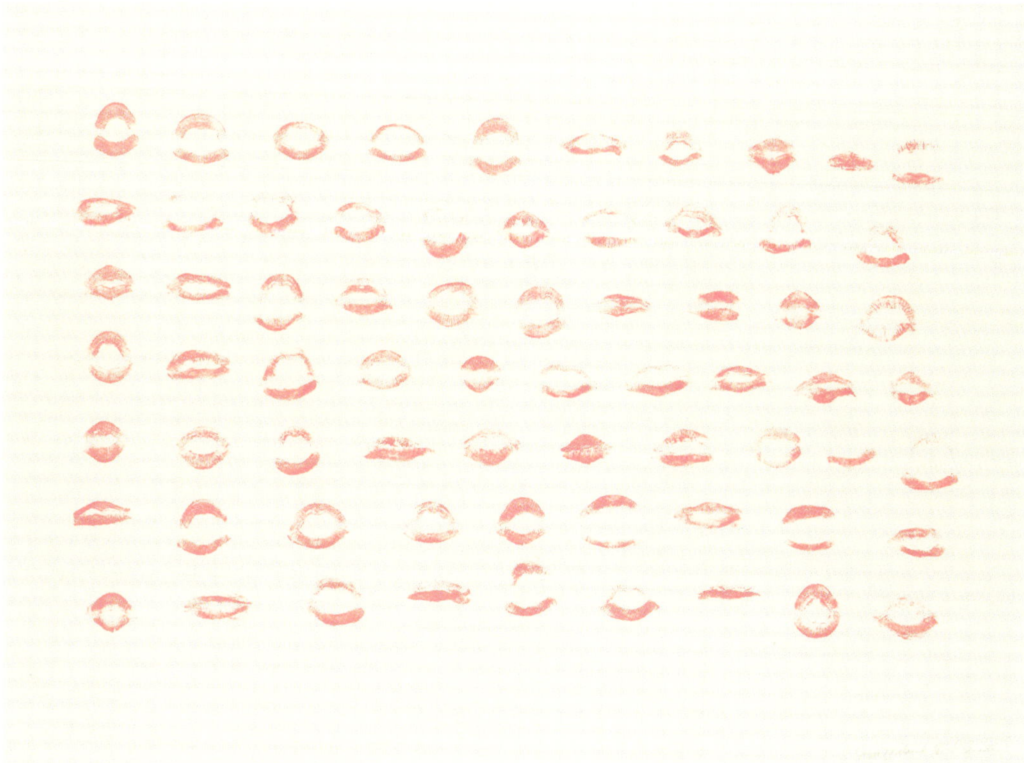

of publishing "Source Materials of the Contemporary Arts." This mandate suited the college's commitment to advancing research and knowledge in the contemporary visual arts and, like the Lithography Workshop, it provided a means to bring contemporary artists to NSCAD to work with the editor and interact with students.

The Press published nine books with Koenig, including three by leading dancers and musicians of the New York performance scene (Yvonne Rainer, Simone Forti and Steve Reich) and five by visual artists (Claes Oldenburg, Hans Haacke, Michael Snow and two by Donald Judd). After a two-year hiatus, The Press resumed activity in 1978 under the editorship of Benjamin H.D. Buchloh, previously the editor of the German journal *Interfunktionen*. Buchloh published seven books with The Press, including several by international conceptual artists such as Michael Asher, Dan Graham and Daniel Buren. He also started a second series called the Nova Scotia Pamphlets, which published books by Martha Rosler, Allan Sekula, Jenny Holzer, Dara Birnbaum, Gerhard Richter and Lawrence Weiner. The Press closed again in 1983 after Buchloh took a teaching position in New York. It was relaunched in 2002.

This overview of the history of conceptual art on Canada's East Coast has necessarily focused on NSCAD. To be sure, there were other instances of conceptual art in the region, such as the book *Exzéo* (1975) that Sylvain Cousineau and Francis Coutellier produced as a document of

Above
Joyce Wieland, *O Canada*, 1970

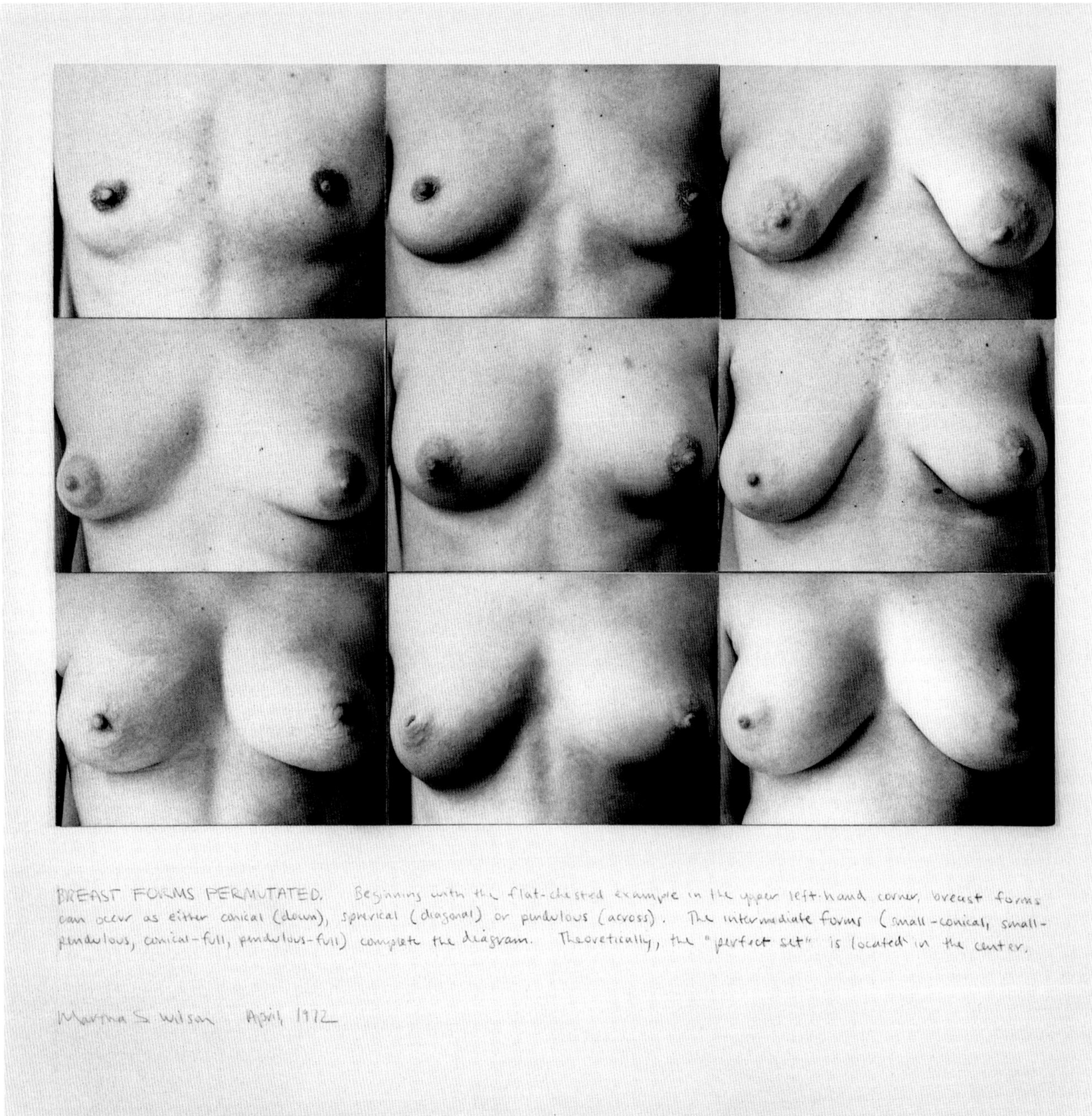
BREAST FORMS PERMUTATED. Beginning with the flat-chested example in the upper left-hand corner, breast forms can occur as either conical (down), spherical (diagonal) or pendulous (across). The intermediate forms (small-conical, small-pendulous, conical-full, pendulous-full) complete the diagram. Theoretically, the "perfect set" is located in the center.
Martha S. Wilson April, 1972

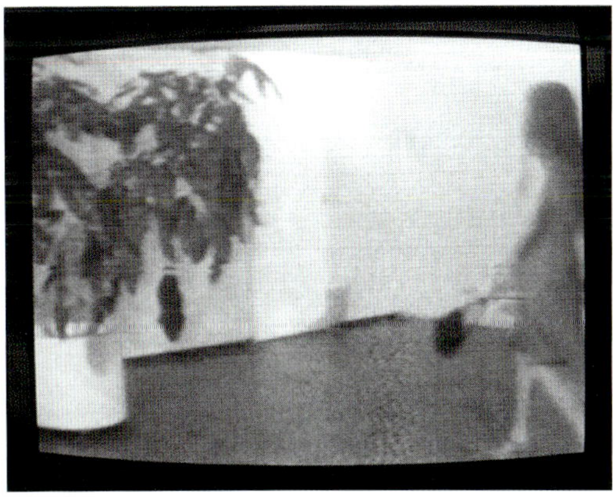 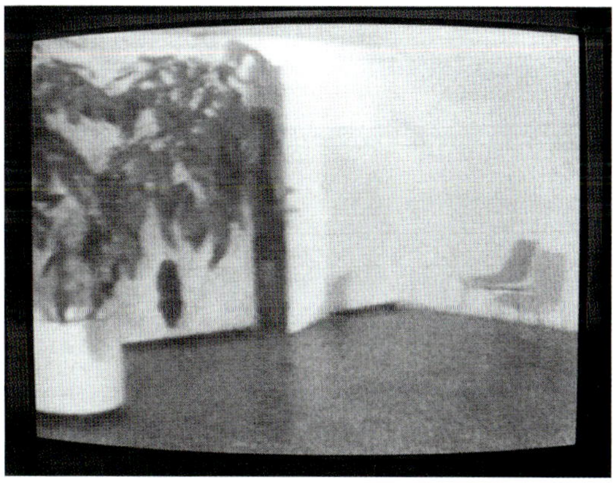

their road trip along New Brunswick's Acadian Peninsula, and the 1974 exhibition that Chris Youngs organized at the Owens Art Gallery in Sackville called *Investigations: Ian Carr-Harris, John Greer, N.E. Thing Co. Ltd*.[41] Eye Level, the artist-run centre founded in Halifax in 1974, also held exhibitions of conceptual art, such as Michael Fernandes' *AD.AP.TA.TIONS.* (1975) and John Murchie's *Opening.Open.Closed*. (1980). On the whole, however, the concentration of conceptual art was at NSCAD.

For all the reasons cited at the beginning of this essay, it was implausible and yet possible that such a flourishing of conceptual art could take place in such a remote and provincial outpost as Halifax was at the time. It never would have happened without the institutional context of an art school with a critical mass of students and an administration and faculty dedicated to fostering rigorous thinking about what art is or might be. At NSCAD, this dedication extended not only to supplying professional-quality facilities and initiating a range of innovative courses and programs, but also to creating an intellectually challenging environment that has attracted scores of artists and students over the years. It seems fitting to close by quoting the late Gerald Ferguson, who summed up what he regarded as the pivotal importance of the Visitors Program in words that succinctly captured NSCAD's tough yet supportive ethos: "An aggressive visitor program will be controversial, make some angry and threaten others. No one in their right mind votes for that. Only the President can endorse such a program, and that was done here beginning in 1968."[42]

[41] Sylvain Cousineau and Francis Coutellier, *Exzéo* (Moncton: Editions d'Acadie, 1975). Youngs had previously founded the Nightingale Gallery in Toronto and served as director of the Owens Art Gallery from 1970 to 1976.

[42] Ferguson, "On NSCAD and conceptual art," 33.

Opposite
Martha Wilson, *Breast Forms Permutated*, 1972

Above
Eric Cameron, stills from *Keeping Marlene Out of the Picture*, 1973–76

Language Is Not Transparent : Translating Conceptual Art in Montréal

Vincent Bonin

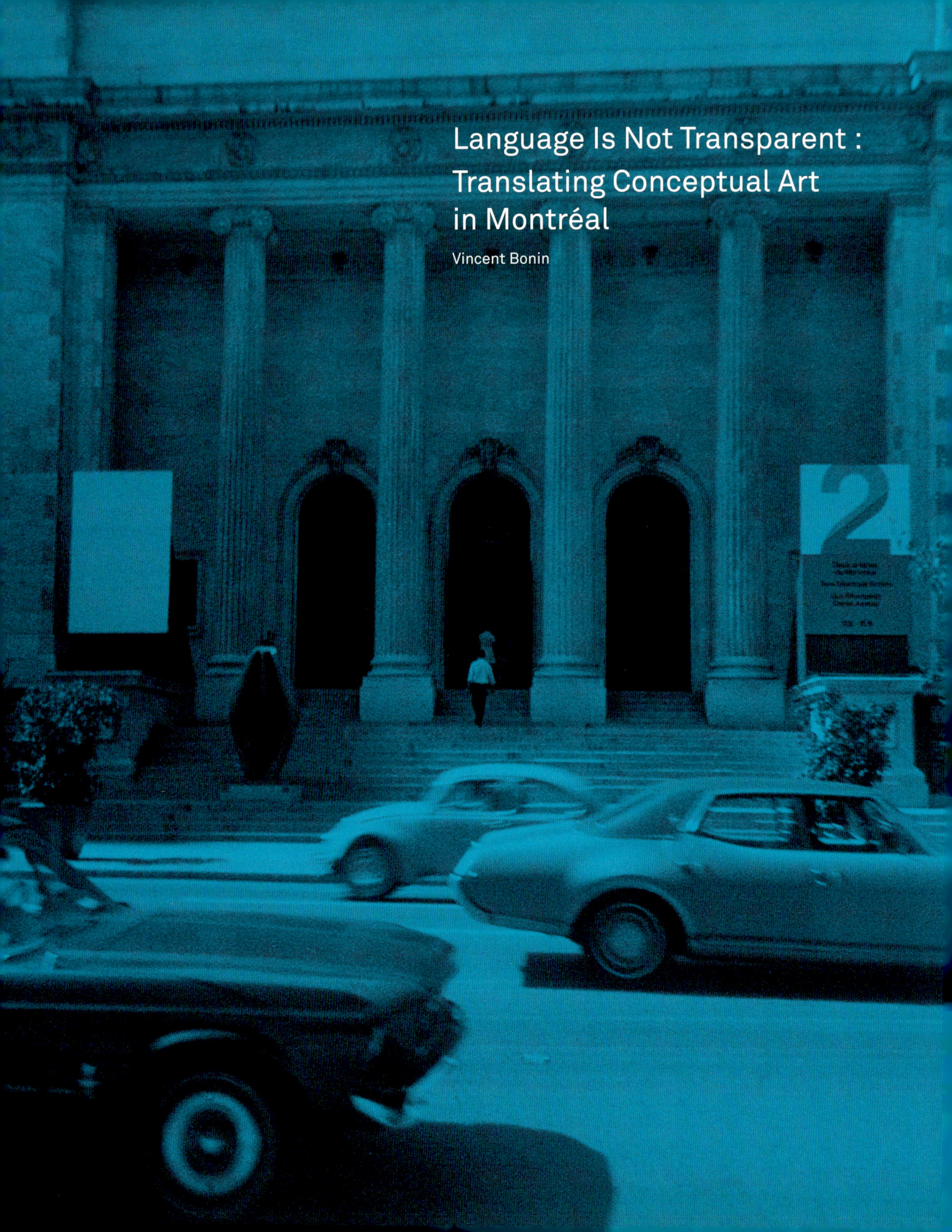

Though in 1990 the Musée d'art contemporain (MACM) in Montréal hosted *L'art conceptuel: une perspective*, the first institutional re-evaluation of the conceptual art movement since its temporary eclipse in the 1980s,[1] there has been no previous attempt to consider the local and national manifestations of these practices in Montréal or Canada.

The Montréal section in the exhibition *Traffic* is the outcome of a process in which the emergence of conceptual art in Canada was mapped across major urban centres, namely Halifax, Montréal, Toronto, Edmonton/Winnipeg and Vancouver. This curatorial approach was adopted to avoid the risk of overshadowing a number of contextual factors linked to the production of the works through a critical apparatus that would reproduce, on a smaller scale, the tension between the centre and the periphery.

Much like their peers in Vancouver, Toronto and Halifax, certain (mostly Anglophone) members of Montréal's artistic community absorbed the American and European canons of conceptual art. However, a set of historical circumstances in Québec rendered its reception somewhat more problematic for a larger group of Francophone protagonists. Although the present analysis addresses the effects of this linguistic divide, it also takes into account attempts made by certain cultural players (artists, critics, curators) to bridge this rift, if only in part, and to facilitate the work of cultural transfer.[2]

At the beginning of the 1960s, a heightened sense of public debate and the founding of new institutions led to the secularization of Québec society, which was previously dominated by the clergy during the 1945–59 period called *la grande noirceur* (great darkness). Founded in 1968, the Parti Québécois provided the people with the political tools that would give impetus to the project of sovereignty, which had been nascent in the social imagination since the 1950s. Artistic undertakings of all kinds, along with the modernization of the state apparatus, helped consolidate this nationalism.

In 1965, the Fusion des arts group, led by art historian Yves Robillard and printmaker Richard Lacroix, published a manifesto redefining the role of the artist as a key agent in the radical restructuring affecting other spheres of Québec society.[3] The following year, students from Montréal's École des beaux-arts went on strike and demanded that the institution re-evaluate its outdated teaching methods. In the face of their professors' indifference, the students requested that the *ministère des Affaires culturelles* create an ad hoc commission to assess the situation. During a second strike in the autumn of 1968, the students called for the implementation of a self-run management model (autogestion), fearing that the promised reforms would replace academicism with even more rigid forms of institutionalization.

In 1968, the sociologist Marcel Rioux endorsed both Fusion des arts' theoretical agenda as well as the students' demands in a report in which he advocated this paradigm of self-determination.

---

[1] *L'art conceptuel: une perspective* (Paris: Musée d'Art Moderne de la Ville de Paris, 1990).

[2] Few art historians have addressed the difficulty involved in transmitting the canon of conceptual art in Québec. For a study that analyzes materials stemming from the critical reception of conceptual art exhibitions, see Julie Turcotte, *L'art conceptuel au Québec entre 1969 et 1975* (master's thesis, Université du Québec à Montréal, 2003).

[3] For an account of the Fusion des arts group, whose activities spanned this transitional moment in the history of art in Québec, see Yves Robillard (Ed.), *Québec Underground 1962–1972*, Vol. 1 (Montréal: Les éditions Médiart, 1973). Also see Francine Couture (Ed.), *Les arts visuels au Québec dans les années soixante: la reconnaissance de la modernité* (Montréal: VLB éditeur, 1993).

Françoise Sullivan, *La promenade entre le Musée d'art contemporain et le Musée des beaux-arts de Montréal*, 1970, detail.

Rioux announced the coming of a "post-industrial" age in which artworks would foster a range of collective experiences at the margins of the capitalist system's mode of rationality (which Rioux linked to the pervasiveness of American culture).[4] According to Rioux, the 1967 World's Fair was to be regarded as the paragon of the total work of art, for it emblematized both the sociality of the media sensorium and Québec's opening up to the world. Rioux's conclusions were similar to observations made by Marshall McLuhan in *Understanding Media* (1964), which was translated into French that same year.[5]

Artists across Canada adapted McLuhan's theses as they created "environments" that sought to combine the emancipatory utopias of countercultural movements with the technological innovations now available to them. The Festival of Contemporary Arts in Vancouver, particularly the fifth one, entitled "The Medium Is the Message" (1965), held on the campus of the University of British Columbia, had Montréal counterparts in the activities of the Fusion des arts group, the installations of Maurice Demers and the happenings of Serge Lemoyne. In keeping with McLuhan, who envisioned a new dialectics between territory and telecommunications systems, several Canadian conceptual artists used maps as a form of agency to counter the state of isolation in which they found themselves at the end of the 1960s.

In August 1969, Bill Vazan and Ian Wallace traced diagonal lines on the beaches of Paul's Bluff (Vazan) and Vancouver (Wallace) to create parentheses of sorts between the country's two extremities. The resulting work, *Canada in Parentheses,* is composed of a series of photographs taken at each of the two sites. To produce *Canada Line* (1969–70), Vazan asked several Canadian institutions (museums, universities) to place a strip of adhesive tape on the ground according to predetermined angles obtained by means of geodesic calculations, thus tracing a line connecting each site. *World Line*, the project's second phase, included, in a similar fashion, sites around the globe.[6] Vazan coordinated these interventions from his family residence at 5171 Orleans Avenue in Montréal, which functioned both as an office and as a studio. He then published documents taken from his correspondence with institutions or individuals.[7]

As Vazan skillfully avoided the limitations inherent to borders, he also relayed the conceptual idiom to the periphery that was then Montréal. In 1971, he organized *45°30' N—73°36' W* with art critic Arthur Bardo and artist Gary Coward.[8] The exhibition was held simultaneously at the Saidye Bronfman Centre and the Sir George Williams University Art Galleries, two institutions with strong ties to Montréal's English-speaking cultural community.[9] In the spirit of Lucy Lippard's exhibitions from the 1960s and '70s, whose titles cited the number of inhabitants of each of the cities in which a given show was held,[10] *45°30' N—73°36' W* referred to Montréal's geodesic coordinates. Using yet another aspect of Lippard's curatorial strategy, the organizers asked participants to send written instructions or schematic drawings that would serve as the basis for site-specific works. Such a decision, which was above all of a pragmatic nature, inflected the design of the ensuing publication, conceived by Gary Coward and Arthur Bardo, in which some of these proposals were assembled on index cards.[11] The publication also

---

[4] Marcel Rioux, "La société, la culture et l'éducation. Rapport Rioux (1968)." In *École et Société au Québec. Éléments d'une sociologie de l'éducation* (Montréal: Éditions Hurtubise HMH, 1975).

[5] Marshall McLuhan, *Pour comprendre les medias*, translated by Jean Paré (Montréal: Éditions Hurtubise HMH, 1968)/Marshall McLuhan, *Understanding Media: The Extensions of Man* (New York: McGraw Hill, 1964).

[6] For an overview of the work Bill Vazan produced from 1969 to 1971, see Marie-Josée Jean (Ed.), *Bill Vazan: Walking into the Vanishing Point: Art conceptuel/Conceptual Art* (Montréal: VOX, centre de l'image contemporaine, 2009).

[7] Bill Vazan, *World Line* (artist's book, 1971).

[8] The *45°30' N—73°36' W* exhibition contained works by David Askevold, Robert Barry, Greg Curnoe, Tom Dean, Jean-Marie Delavalle, François Déry, Mervyn Dewes, Christos Dikeakos, Gerald Ferguson, Douglas Huebler, Sol LeWitt, N.E. Thing Co., Harold Pearse, Michael Snow, Françoise Sullivan, Ian Wallace and Lawrence Weiner.
[9] Bardo, who was born in the United States, was friends with Lucy Lippard and other representatives of the neo-avant-garde

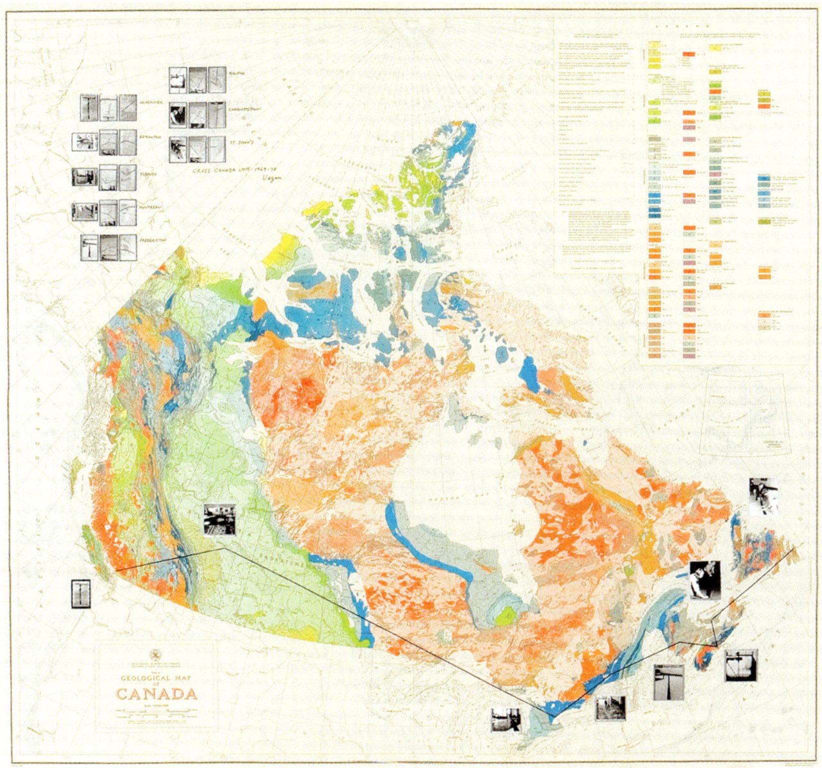

Bill Vazan, *Canada Line*, 1969–70

reproduced quotes from American artists (many of whom did not take part in the exhibition), as well as excerpts from texts by influential theorists (Jack Burnham, Buckminster Fuller, Herbert Marcuse, Marshall McLuhan, Alfred North Whitehead, Charles Sanders Peirce, etc.). This segment can be regarded as a cross-section of the intellectual family to which Bardo, Coward and Vazan aspired to belong.

The abstract nature of the project and its accompanying publication gave it the appearance of a manifesto, but one that, oddly enough, avoided the political.[12] In fact, one of the catalogue's first index cards contains a statement written by the curators that precludes, if only provisionally, a certain brand of provincialism by equating the works' context of production with their simplest common denominator: "They [the coordinates] locate us by a coding system that is outside the usual ones, with their references to the histories of culture, race or politics. They relate to the history of technology, and are purely informational."[13] During this important transitional period (1969–72), Halifax, Vancouver and Toronto became the juncture points of a pan-Canadian and international network of emergent conceptual art practices. Although Montréal hosted Expo '67—an event that was symptomatic of globalization in its

when he lived in New York in the 1960s. Along with Normand Thériault he was one of the key mediators of American conceptual art in Montréal.

[10] See *557,087: An Exhibition* (Seattle: The Council, 1969); *955,000: An Exhibition* (Vancouver: Vancouver Art Gallery, 1970), unpaginated.

[11] Arthur Bardo and Gary Coward (Eds.), *45°30' N—73°36' W + Inventory* (Montréal: Sir George Williams University, 1971), 162 card files.

[12] Irwin and Myra Gopnik recount that a symposium entitled "Art and Its Social Responsibilities" was organized jointly by Concordia University's Art Education Department and the Saidye Bronfman Centre. See Irwin and Myra Gopnik, "The semantics of concept art," *artscanada* XXVIII, no. 2, issue 154/155 (April/May 1971): 81–83.

[13] Coward and Bardo (Eds.), *45°30' N—73° 36' W + Inventory*. This statement is printed along with a quote from Sun Ra that emphasizes the authors' apolitical stance: "One Nation, One Planet."

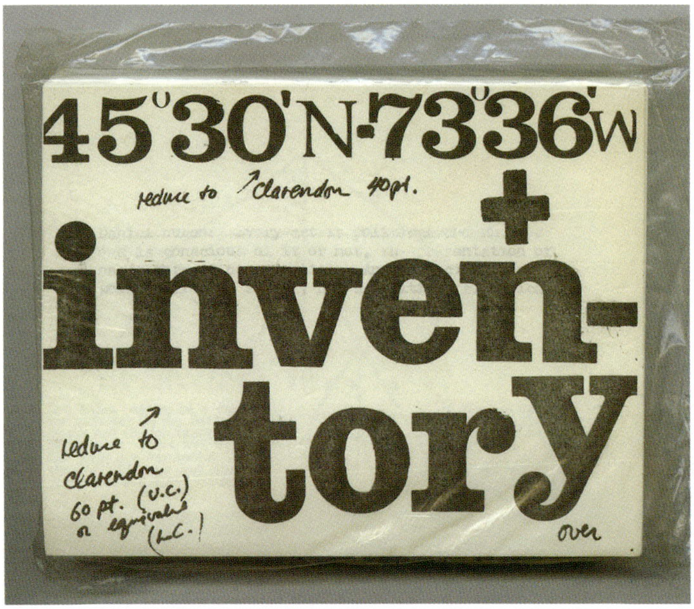

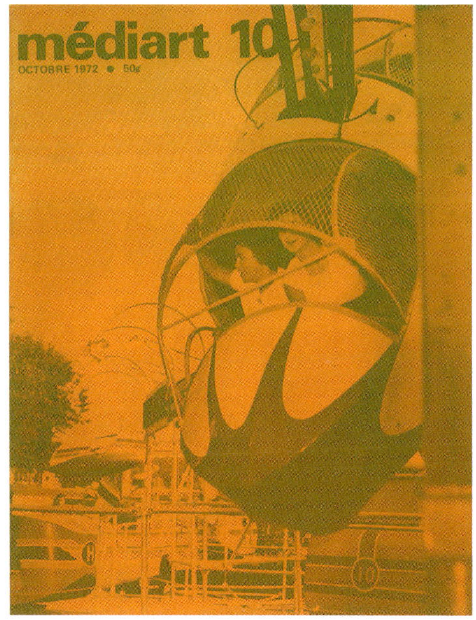

embryonic stage—the city was to remain an opaque zone within this configuration of sites and discourses. Despite Fusion des arts' disciplinary program of interdisciplinarity, which the Rioux report openly advocated, the influence of painter Paul-Émile Borduas and his associates, called the mouvement automatiste, remained an important reference point around which Québec's project of emancipation evolved during what was called the Quiet Revolution. In this context, painting in the late 1960s and throughout the 1970s did not represent the object of cultural inertia that had to be challenged, but was an indisputable marker of identity. As a result, the debate that polarized artistic circles was generally framed around an opposition between passing down such a painterly heritage or updating it by way of a formalist agenda advocated by the *néo-plasticiens* painters (Guido Molinari, Claude Tousignant).

Throughout this period certain representatives of the conceptual art movement regarded language as a heuristic tool capable of calling into question the very foundations of the ideology of medium-specificity, as well as an apparently inalienable definition of artistic subjectivity. In Québec, however, this overall pragmatic approach was bound up with the terms of a complex equation involving painting as a marker of cultural identity and a "linguistic over-consciousness" (*surconscience linguistique*) that pervaded the literary field.

Lise Gauvin coined the concept of linguistic over-consciousness to describe a set of strategies deployed by certain Francophone authors writing outside of France who attempt to disrupt their relationship to a hegemonic language:

> To write in Québec is truly to perform a speech act. More than just the mere process of integrating the oral within the written, or of representing social languages in a more or less mimetic way, [to write in Québec] is to unveil the very status of a

Above, from left

Catalogue for Gary Coward and Arthur Bardo, *45°30' N—73°36' W + Inventory*, 1971

Médiart, Vol. 1, No. 6, October 1972

Catalogue for *Québec '75*

Beaux-Arts, Spring/Summer 1972

[14] Lise Gauvin, "D'une langue à l'autre: la surconscience linguistique de l'écrivain francophone." In *L'écrivain francophone à la croisée des langues* (Paris: Karthala, 2006), 7. Quote translated by Eduardo Ralickas.

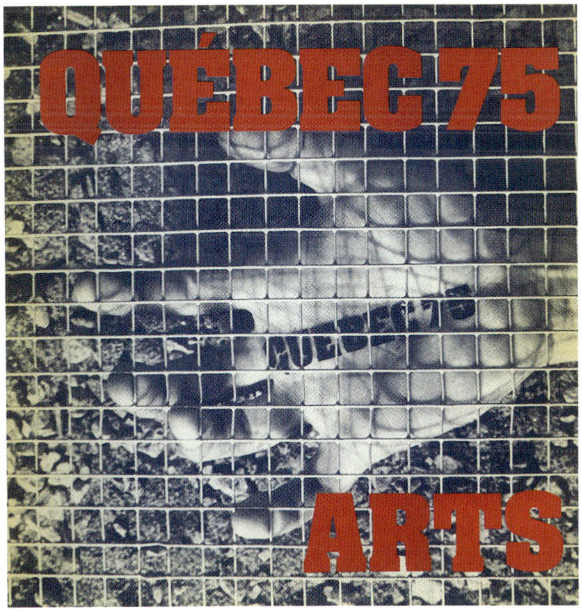

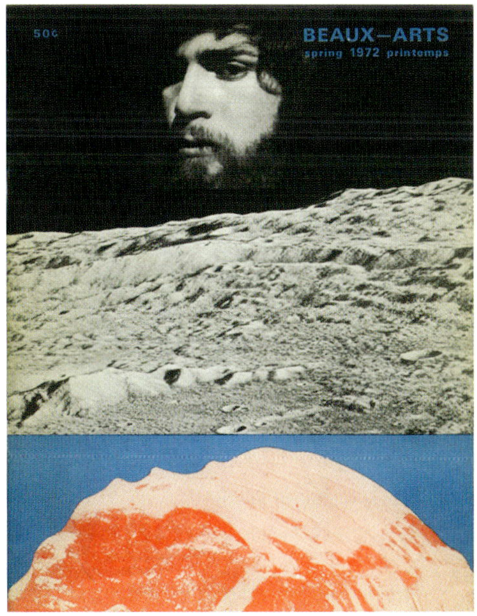

literature, its integration/definition of codes, and a whole set of reflections on the nature and workings of the literary.[14]

These strategies append a surplus reflexivity to the act of writing, which is never reducible to the modalities of communicational transparency. Johanne Lamoureux contends that it is possible to apply some of Gauvin's observations to the visual arts in Québec.[15] Lamoureux analyzes a group of works produced in the 1980s that address issues of language or speech by means of metaphors and other stylistic devices that create semiotic interferences. However, her analysis sidesteps an important period (spanning the end of the 1960s to the mid-1970s) in which the gap between English- and French-speaking communities became an open, rather than a latent, matter.

In general, conceptual artists who produced language-based works saw them as carriers of "pure" information, but English was nevertheless the code they all shared. Most of the propositions compiled in the *45°30' N—73°36' W* catalogue were published in English, including a text by Serge Lemoyne. However, contributions by Jean-Marie Delavalle and art critic Normand Thériault were exceptions, as they appeared in their authors' mother tongue. Much like his colleague Arthur Bardo from the *Montreal Star*, Thériault was one of the first to promote conceptual art to a wider audience in his capacity as art critic writing reviews for the newspaper *La Presse*. Excerpted from one of his articles, Thériault's contribution to *Inventory* takes note of a certain status quo: "In Québec, irrespective of a glorious past, when it comes to action we have returned, in art, to year zero. Let us hope that year one will one day begin."[16] For Thériault, this point of origin does not denote a tabula rasa of sorts; rather, it heralds the coming interdisciplinarity in artistic practices by taking into account recent developments in the history of Québec. A few years later, Thériault organized *Québec 75* at the Musée d'art

[15] Johanne Lamoureux, "Le bout de la langue: les arts visuels et la langue au Québec." In *Le bout de la langue: Les arts visuels et la langue au Québec = Seeing in Tongues: A Narrative of Visual Art and Language in Quebec* (Vancouver: Morris and Helen Belkin Art Gallery, University of British Columbia, 1995).

[16] Coward and Bardo (Eds.), *45°30' N—73°36' W + Inventory*. Quote translated by Eduardo Ralickas.

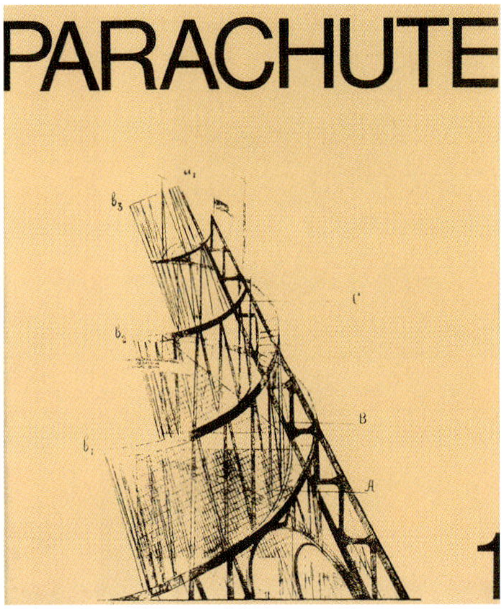

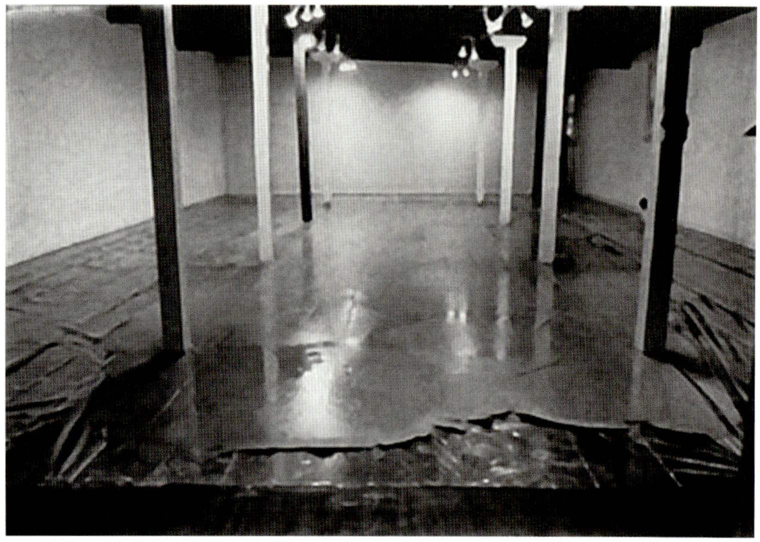

contemporain, which aimed to take stock of art produced in Montréal five years after the October Crisis. His project stood out among exhibitions with similar designs in its attempt to rise above the limitations of provincialism and provide equal visibility to Anglophone and Francophone artists.[17]

Alongside his work as an art critic and curator, Thériault assumed a more educational role in 1971 when he became director of the Groupe de recherche en administration de l'art, which was founded by Rose-Marie Arbour at UQÀM. Composed of students who were to become key art world protagonists in the following decade (France Morin, Chantal Pontbriand, Claude Gosselin, René Blouin), the group launched *Médiart*, a magazine that eschewed disciplinary boundaries as it reviewed current trends in Canadian and international art, and took stock of the rise of countercultural movements. Contrary to *FILE Megazine*, *Médiart*'s readership was limited by its exclusively French content. In 1972, Tom Dean founded *Beaux-Arts* as a local, English-language complement to *FILE* (Toronto) and *Avalanche* (New York). It was only with the appearance of *Parachute*, a bilingual magazine co-founded in 1975 by Chantal Pontbriand and France Morin, that a Montréal-based publication would be able to reach readers beyond the borders of Québec. *Parachute* soon became an indispensable platform for critical discourse on international contemporary art.

At the time of the *45°30' N—73°36' W* exhibition, certain artists began planning for the creation of the cooperative Véhicule Art (Montréal), which was incorporated in 1972. In keeping with the title of the 1971 exhibition, the organization's name was meant above all to define the space as a "neutral" dissemination tool circumscribed by its users. The members of Véhicule Art distanced themselves from the orthodoxy of conceptual art as they embraced the more inclusive programs of post-Minimalism and process art.[18] For many, the concept of

Above, from left
Parachute, No. 1, October–December 1975

Installation view of Gunter Nolte, *Intervention*, A Space, 1972

[17] Normand Thériault (Ed.), *Québec 75* (Montréal: Institut d'art contemporain, 1975). Also see Véronique Rodriguez, "Québec 75/Arts, Cinéma, Vidéo: pour une nouvelle vision de l'art contemporain au Québec," in Francine Couture (Ed.), *Exposer l'art contemporain du Québec: discours d'intention et d'accompagnement* (Montréal: Centre de diffusion 3D, 2003), 17–71.

[18] In 1974, the *Périphéries* exhibition held at the Musée d'art contemporain paid heed to this state of affairs as it included most of the artists who were members of Véhicule

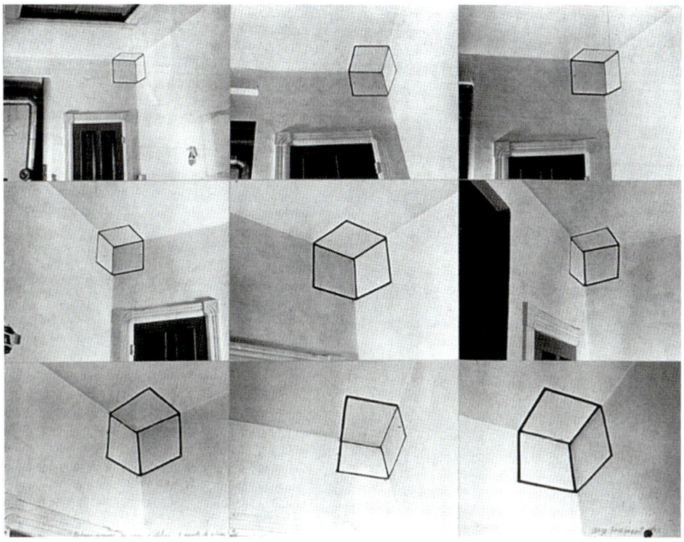

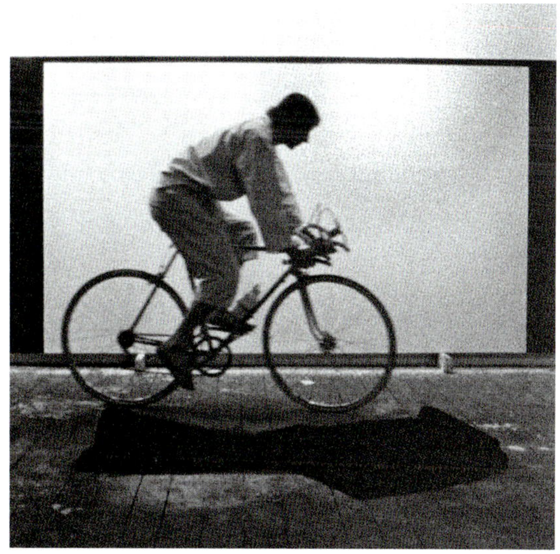

dematerialization no longer represented the key reference for avant-gardism; rather, it was regarded as one aesthetic strategy among others that could be recycled depending on the nature of the project at hand.

The creation of systems and the representation of their contingent nature characterized the work of many artists, including Gunter Nolte, whose practice from the early 1970s evoked the early propositions produced by Hans Haacke during the previous decade. In 1972, Nolte created Intervention, which involved placing 100 gallons of glaze on polystyrene sheets that covered the floor of A Space gallery in Toronto. As the glaze dried and cracked, it disclosed the usually invisible effects that environmental factors such as humidity and ambient temperature have on a perennial, architectural situation.[19] In his series entitled Coins d'ateliers (1971–72), Serge Tousignant placed adhesive tape on the walls of his studio, which he then photographed to counter the illusion of perspective and emphasize the surface of the image itself.

Although the works made by artists such as Françoise Sullivan and Suzy Lake partook of the same formalist approach as their male colleagues, they tacitly addressed issues related to the formation of identity and feminism. Sullivan's contribution to the history of art in Québec stems from her work as a painter, choreographer and member of the Automatistes group. However, during the first part of the 1970s she momentarily set this past aside for aesthetic and political reasons. The parameters of her conceptual works involved circumscribing a site or location to accommodate the singularity of her own body, which would then override the pragmatic framework of the strategies deployed. For the *45°30' N—73°36' W* exhibition, Sullivan indicated the height of her children by marking the pillars of the Saidye Bronfman Centre. In the catalogue, she also generated a self-portrait of sorts in the guise of an identification sheet composed of collated personal biological data. In similar fashion, Lake's

Art. See *Périphéries: Exposition organisée en collaboration avec les artistes membres de Véhicule Art (Montréal)* (Montréal: Musée d'art contemporain, 1974).

[19] This work was shown the following year at Véhicule Art during the *Set of 3* exhibition, which also included works by John Heward and Bill Vazan.

Above, from left
Serge Tousignant, *Ruban gommé sur coin d'atelier—Neuf points de vision*, 1973

Charles Gagnon, still from *Le son d'un éspace/The Sound of Space*, 1968

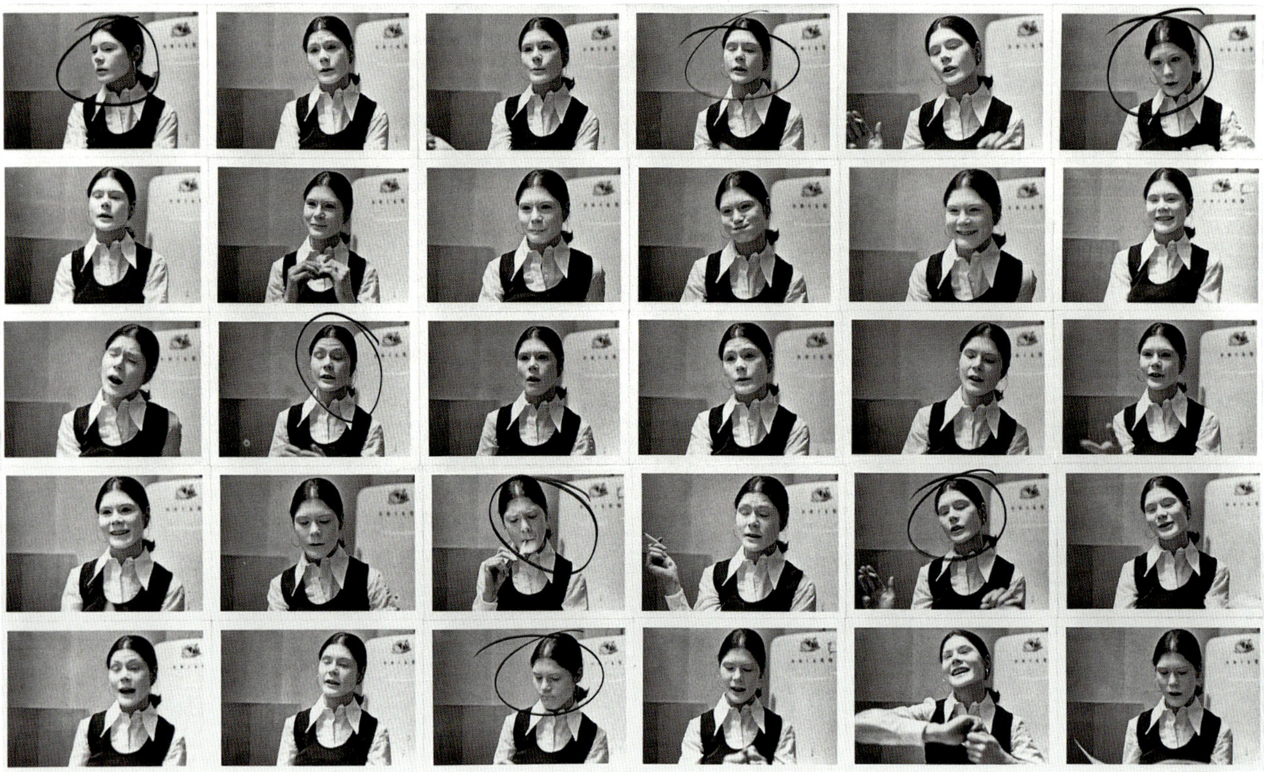

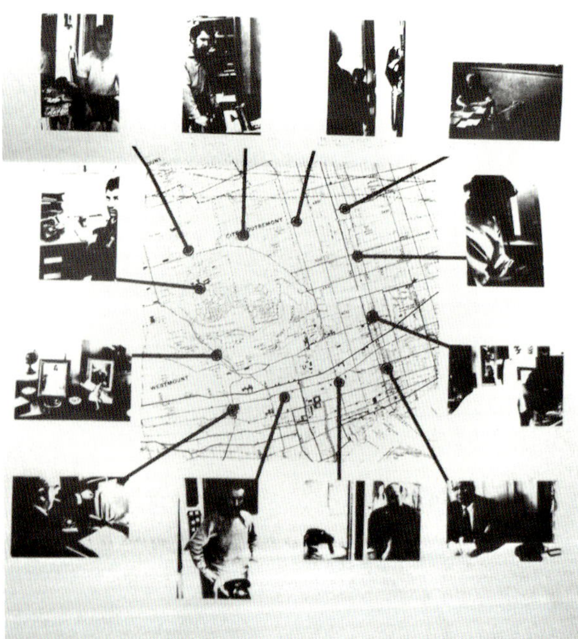

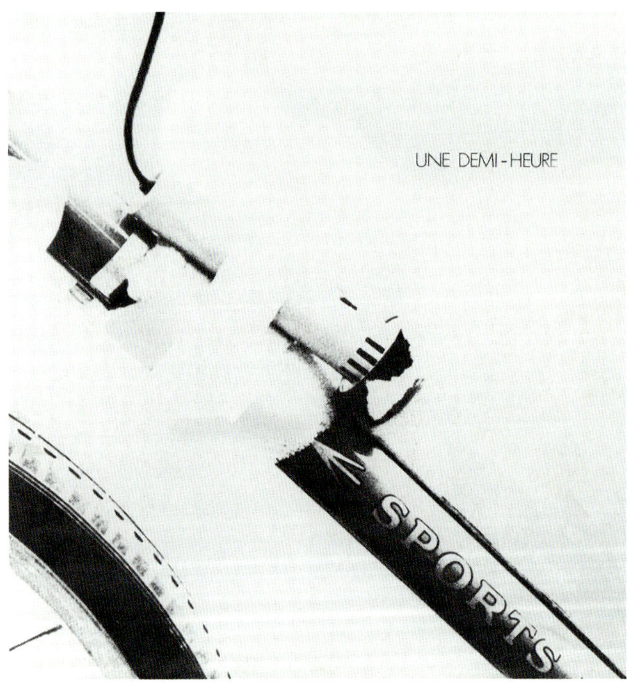

Clockwise from top left

Suzy Lake, *A One Hour (Zero) Conversation with Allan B.*, 1973. Photo: Ernest Mayer, Winnipeg Art Gallery

Jean-Marie Delavalle, *Une demi-heure*, 1973

Tom Dean, *Telephone Square,* 1970

use of protocols stemming from Minimalism (modular repetition, grids) subtly alluded to autobiographical referents. Thus, the question of intersubjectivity progressively came to the fore in her practice. The work *A One Hour (Zero) Conversation with Allan B.* (1973) is made up of several snapshots of Lake's face covered in white makeup taken while the artist was speaking to a person beyond the camera's frame. In the *Suzy Lake as . . .* series (1974–75), the artist transposed her colleagues' facial features (Bill Vazan, Gary Smith, Andrea Stannard, Gilles Gheerbrant) onto photographic images of herself, thereby creating composites that recall the extent to which her peers were present in both her personal and professional lives.

While producing projects such as *World Line*, which established an imaginary network between geographically disparate points, Bill Vazan also undertook walks in Montréal in view of circumscribing his immediate surroundings. In *Sainte-Catherine Street Walk* (1969), the artist photographed each intersection he encountered on the commercial thoroughfare. In *Tour d'autobus* (1970), Vazan took photographs from inside a bus every time the vehicle would stop to allow passengers to enter or exit.[20] In 1970, Françoise Sullivan photographed landmarks that lay on her trajectory between the Montreal Museum of Fine Arts and the Musée d'art contemporain. Sullivan explains retrospectively that she decided to undertake this photographic walk to explore a residual experiential field during a period in which artists abandoned the museum.[21] The walk's two sites also function as markers of identity: whereas the Museum of Fine Arts is tied to Montréal's English-speaking elite, the Musée d'art contemporain denotes the 1960s Québécois utopia of French-language cultural democratization. In the installation *Vue d'une portion du trajet* (1973), Jean-Marie Delavalle juxtaposed a vinyl sound recording (produced as a multiple) with a series of photographs to represent a bicycle ride in the countryside. Similarly, the works produced by Pierre Boogaerts at the end of the 1970s also make use of sequential imagery to represent the artist's architecturally over-determined walks (*Série Écran Promenade*, 1979).

In 1972, the artist and architect Melvin Charney was invited to organize the *Montréal, Plus or Minus?* exhibition at the Montreal Museum of Fine Arts.[22] His project attempted to assess daily life in a "metropolis" that had lost much of its appeal since Expo '67. His proposal did not seek to equate the city with its abstract, geodesic coordinates, such as Vazan, Bardo and Coward had done. Instead, the exhibition foregrounded the effects the new political and economic context had on the urban fabric; consequently, the documentary approach to photography was pervasive (Groupe d'action photographique, Westmount Action Committee). However, the works produced for the exhibition by such artists as Tom Dean, Robert Walker and Bill Vazan were still conceptual in nature. For the piece *Telephone Square* (1970), Dean photographed several individuals engaged in simultaneous telephone conversations on 11 November 1970; the photographs were then placed on a map, thereby showing the locations in which each image was taken. For *Hochelaga* (1972), in a gesture that differed from the work of his peers, who regarded cartographic devices as quasi-neutral instruments for circumscribing space, Robert Walker used a map to delineate the site once occupied by the native village of Hochelaga, to which he juxtaposed a print representing the meeting of Jacques Cartier and the village's inhabitants. In another project entitled *Le sacré et le profane* (1972), Walker drew up an inventory of all the churches and bars he encountered during a walk in the eastern districts of Montréal.

[20] For an analysis of these projects by Vazan, see Johanne Sloan, "Bill Vazan: Coordonnées urbaines/Urban Coordinates," in Jean (Ed.), *Bill Vazan: Walking into the Vanishing Point*, 85–89.

[21] Françoise Sullivan, telephone conversation with author, 23 March 2010.

[22] Melvin Charney, *Montréal, plus ou moins?/Montréal, Plus or Minus?* (Montréal: Montreal Museum of Fine Arts, 1972).

Enclosed Slide & Photographic Material ①

① . A New Theory of Light and Colours, Isaac Newton, 1672
Discovery of Radio-activity, H. Bequerel, 1896, 1975, Seven volume book, $8\frac{1}{2}$" x 11"

1-2 . Example of Title Pages

3 . Violet

4 Indigo

5 Blue

6 Green

7 Yellow

8 Orange

9 Red

10 Installation shot — The First photograph to be Interpreted as a Positive Electron (Published 1933) - Approx 23' each panel $6\frac{1}{4}$"x$38\frac{1}{2}$" Pencil - Coloured Pencils + Hand Written book, 1976

11 Installation shot — The Positive Electron, 1933. 4 panels 14"x28" - Pencil + 4 Volume Hand Written Book 1976

12 Detail 7"x14"

13 Detail 14"x28"

14 Detail "

15 Detail "

16 Detail "

17 An Unusual Event Recorded in Il Nuovo Cimento Vol I No3. March 1955 and Volume III No 2 Februarg 1956. 14"x21" — Pencil + 2 Xeroxed Books, 1976

18 Detail 14"x21"

19 Detail

20 Opticks, Isaac Newton, 1704, 1st English Edition with Newton's Notes, (Newton's copy) Xeroxed book, 1976

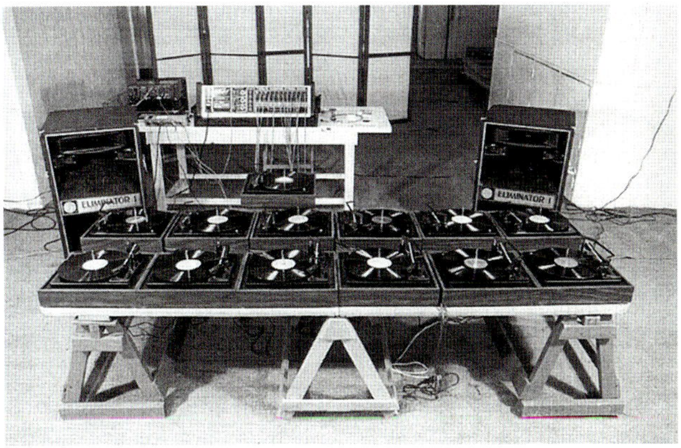

Opposite
David Tomas, detail of draft slide list of works from 1972–79 relating to *Works on the History of Physics*, 1975–76

Left
Raymond Gervais, *12+1=*, 1976.
Photo: Roland Poulin

Raymond Gervais, Rober Racine, David Tomas and Tim Clark gravitated toward the margins of the circle of artists who founded Véhicule Art. Their respective practices sought to give tangible form to various overlapping historical or theoretical references. Tomas' first works, produced from 1974 to 1975 while the artist was still a student, addressed the way in which meaning is either lost or supplemented as one shifts from one specialized discursive field (the scientific paper) to another, namely the enunciative space underpinning the field of art.[23]

Gervais took part in the founding of *Parachute* in 1975 and was a regular contributor to the magazine with texts of a hybrid nature that crossed the history of the avant-garde in music with that of the visual arts.[24] Presented at the galerie Média in 1976, the work *12+1=* comprised thirteen turntables that simultaneously played different sound samples. The resulting configurations each represented an improbable encounter between geographically disparate recording contexts and regional locales. In a written statement handed to visitors, Gervais drew a list of possible juxtapositions:

> a) Thirteen authentic works of popular music from thirteen different countries. The encounter of music from around the world in a precise, defined location.
> b) Thirteen solo instruments from thirteen different countries. An international ensemble whose counterpoint and harmony are completely improvised. [They play] simultaneously. Etc.[25]

Far from being an ideological program that levelled cultural difference, Gervais' intervention emphasized the sonic tensions produced by these juxtapositions as well as the narrative possibilities they triggered. In 1978, Rober Racine performed Erik Satie's *Vexations* at Véhicule Art, a score in which the performer must play a very short musical passage 840 times without interruption. Much like the works Gervais produced during the same period, Racine's practice explored interconnected references to the histories of musical, literary and artistic avant-gardes. With the *Le Terrain du dictionnaire* cycle begun in 1979, the artist physically separated words from their definitions in the French dictionary *Le Robert*, thereby forming a new "text" articulated according to spatial parameters. Thus, the artist's identity as reader became inscribed within the vacant, interstitial spaces he created throughout the French language's lexicon.

[23] *1000 Seconds: five permutations on the theme of the last 200 seconds before 7:30 am, July 1916, The First Battle of the Somme* (1974); *Works on the History of Physics* (1975–76).

[24] Among others, Gervais was instrumental in having the Philip Glass Ensemble and Steve Reich perform in Montréal in 1973.

[25] See Raymond Gervais, *12+1 = pour treize tourne-disques automatiques et les musiques du monde* (artist's statement given to exhibition visitors, 1976).

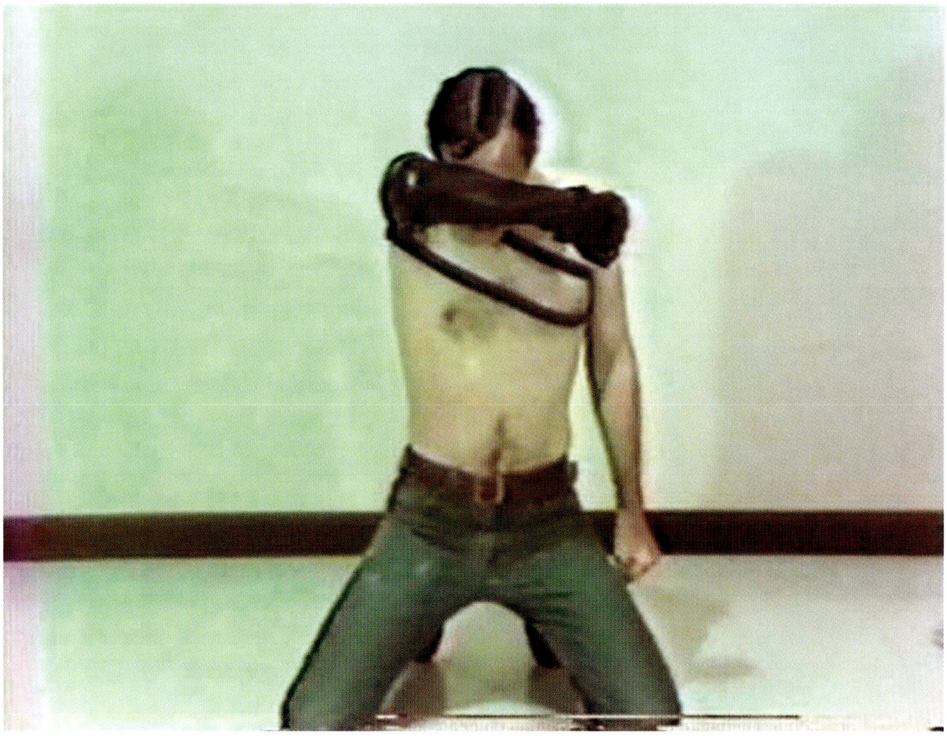

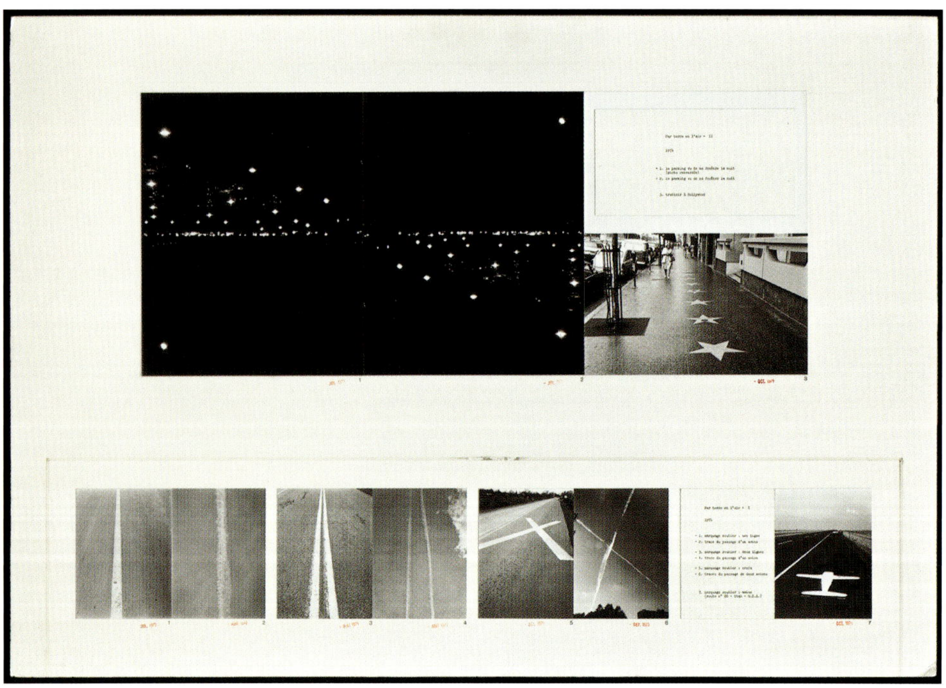

Top
Tim Clark, still from *A Reading of "On Obedience and Discipline" from* The Imitation of Christ *by Thomas à Kempis*, 1979

Bottom
Pierre Boogaerts, *Par terre en l'air I—Par terre en l'air II (Version b)*, 1974

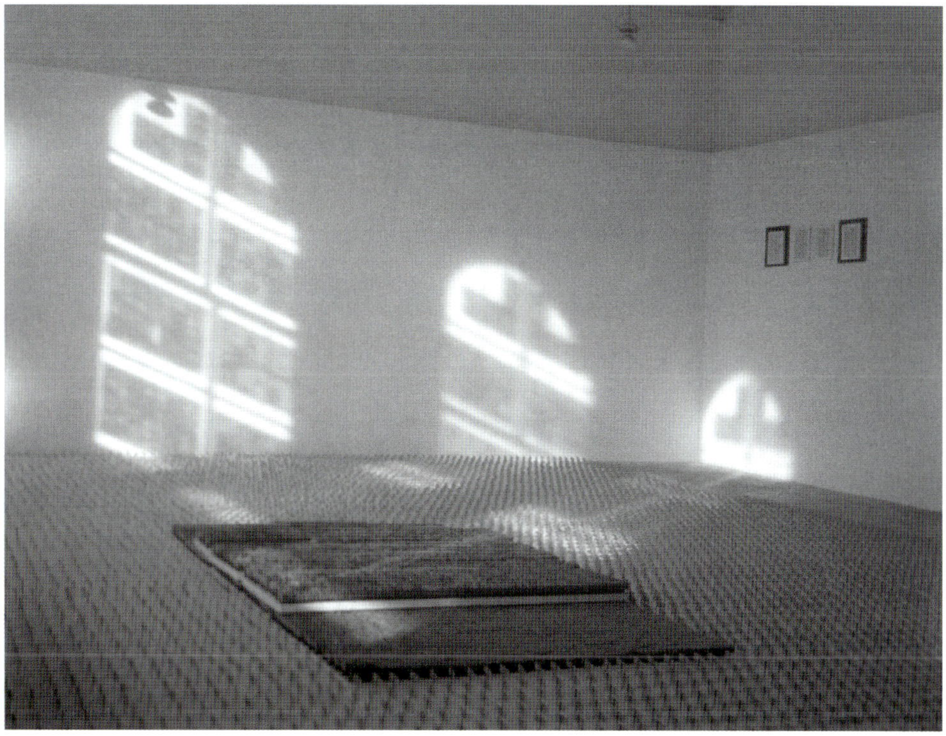

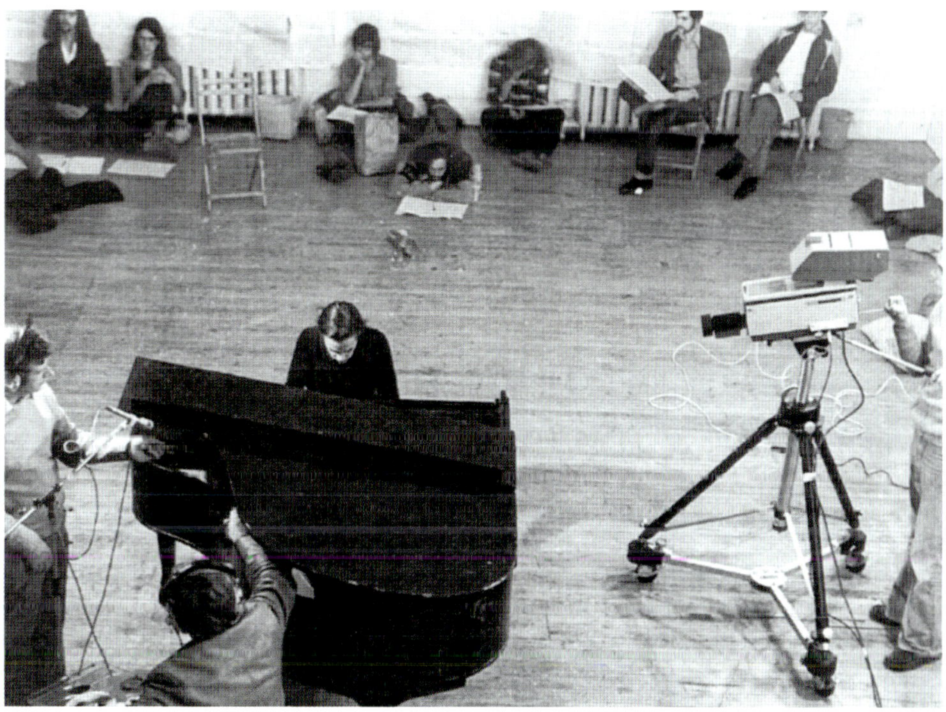

Top
Installation view of Rober Racine, *Le Terrain du dictionnaire A/Z*, 1980–81, PSI, New York, 1981. Photo: Rober Racine

Bottom
Rober Racine performing Erik Satie's *Vexations* at Véhicule Art, 1978. Photo: Bernard Lamy

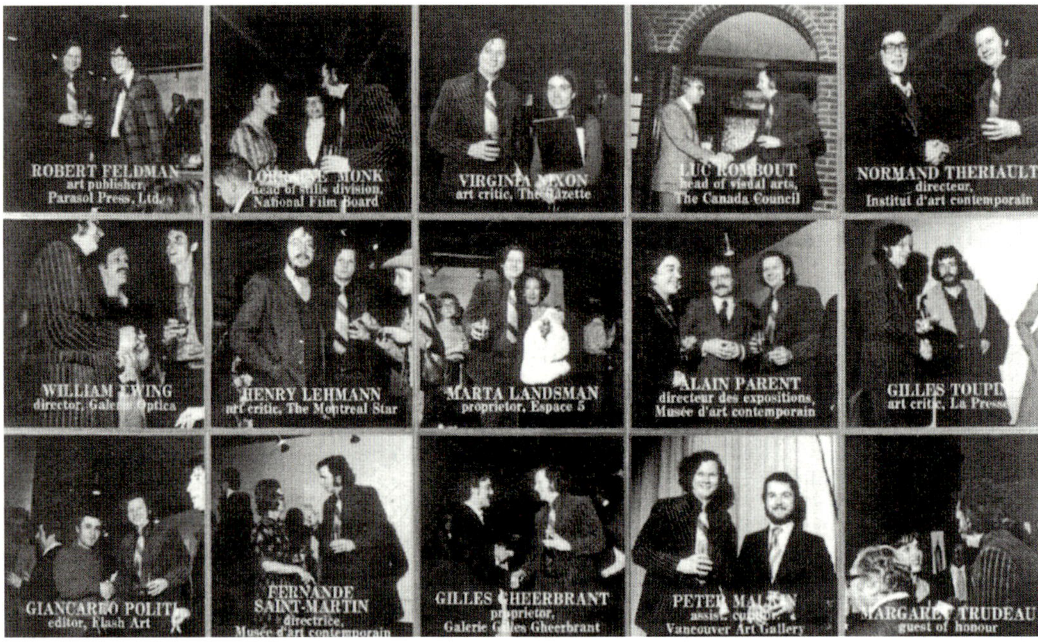

Authors who have recently examined the rise of Conceptualism within peripheral sites have emphasized artists' political commitments as opposed to the practice of merely mimicking strategies stemming from the New York or European canons of conceptual art.[26] Few similar cases exist in Montréal, although the period was characterized by a shift toward the left on the part of intellectuals. The English-language collective Insurrection Art Company is an exception. Founded in 1970 by Robert Walker, Michael Haslam and anthropologist Paul Heyer, it sought to counter the apathy that pervaded the world of "bourgeois art" in Montréal in the wake of the October Crisis.[27] The group's performances existed in the grey zone between the activism of the previous decade's countercultural movements and an embryonic form of institutional critique. Insurrection Art Company quickly disbanded, though, and its members pursued individual careers that sustained the collective's political leanings.

Walker's work Is Politics Art? shown in Québec 75, revisits many of the issues raised by the projects he produced in collaboration with Haslam and Heyer. A series of photographs hung in a grid depict the artist shaking hands with museum directors, curators and other key individuals he encountered at exhibition openings. While producing a synoptic tableau of the Montréal art world at a given moment of its existence, Is Politics Art? reveals the degree to which Walker was complicit in the system he denounced in order to safeguard his economic survival.

The previous year, William A. Ewing, director of Galerie Optica, asked Walker to organize Camerart, which attempted to provide an overview of the diversity of photographic practice in Montréal.[28] Walker's strategy was similar to Normand Thériault's in Québec 75, insofar as it involved the decompartmentalization of aesthetics and the will to overcome the linguistic divide. Beyond the fact that the selected artists shared photography as a common denominator,

Above
Robert Walker, *Is Politics Art?*, 1975

[26] See *Global Conceptualism: Points of Origin, 1950s–1980s* (New York: Queens Museum of Art, New York, 1999).

[27] See Paul Heyer, "Insurrection Art: Conscience et responsabilité," *Médiart*, no. 3 (February 1972): C2–C3. Also of interest is an interview Claude Gosselin conducted

Walker's curatorial choices exceptionally brought together three important currents in art at the time: a post-minimalist vein of Conceptualism, a documentary approach and formalism. The exhibition did not attempt to highlight or resolve ideological differences between these approaches. However, the authors invited to contribute to the catalogue did underscore such gaps. Les Levine conceived the camera as an apparatus that elided subjectivity; he thus summoned artists to acknowledge this form of alienation when they made use of the technology. Chantal Pontbriand analyzed the common threads found in the work made by the group who gravitated to Véhicule Art. For his part, ex-FLQ member Pierre Vallières addressed a topic that at first glance appeared unrelated to his usual preoccupations, namely the aesthetic polarities of the exhibition's content as such. Avoiding the commonplace, he reproached Francophone photographers working in the documentary tradition (Groupe d'action photographique) as well as Anglophone "conceptualists" who "imitate a bit too closely [work] that had already been made with more vigour in the United States."[29] By equating conceptual art with a "post-artistic" and "ideologically impoverished" situation, Vallières' position about the exhibition was fundamentally ambivalent: these two bodies of work were artificially brought together under the rubric of an expanded definition of photography, but their political efficacy was rendered indeterminate.

Vallières' 1974 contribution to the catalogue for _Camerart_ was not his only foray into the field of contemporary art. Two years prior he became the subject of a structural film made by Ontario-based artist Joyce Wieland, which, at a formal level, seems to cancel the polarizations underpinning his _Camerart_ text by enacting an impure synthesis. At the time the film was produced Vallières was living in Mont-Laurier and had distanced himself from the position he held in the 1970s, namely that one had to take up arms in order to achieve the independence of Québec. Wieland's work is composed of three reels of film spliced together to reproduce the duration of Vallières' reading of a three-part manifesto in which the independence movement is associated with the project of feminist emancipation and the fight for native rights. Wieland's camera focuses on a close-up of the militant's mouth as a point of origin that exacerbates Vallières' will to speak. The artist thereby juxtaposes formal minimalist elements with the irreducible nature of the political content she hopes to convey. Subtitles emphasize the gap between the reading of the original text and its later reception by an English-speaking public. However, the recording of Vallières' performance no longer corresponds to the functional equivalence of languages under the diktat of bilingualism. Rather, the film inscribes the viewer within the site of two subjectivities—Wieland's and Vallières'—thereby negotiating the measure of the visible and the intelligible. Bound to one linguistic group (or listening to the voice and simultaneously reading the subtitles), the viewer must integrate the effects of translation protocols in his or her experience of the work.

Pierre Vallières (1972) functions as a strategic anomaly within the discursive configuration that gives shape to this part of *Traffic*. It foregrounds the impossibility of constituting a coherent set of artistic propositions around a single aesthetic category (conceptual art) and one geographical marker (Montréal) without addressing the effects of cultural transfer. Much like the film's close-up shot, the attempt to foreground, in retrospect, the stakes that shaped this important period of transition turns out to be a kind of amplification process whose product—a cross-sectional view—calls for other forms of analysis.

---

with Robert Walker, "Insurrection Art Company : une conscience sociale," *Le Devoir* (1 November 1975).

[28] *Camerart : 24 artistes du Québec* (Montréal: Galerie Optica, 1974).

[29] Pierre Vallières, "L'absurde fonctionnel," in *Camerart*, 43.

Dated Conceptualism: Toronto, London, Guelph

William Wood

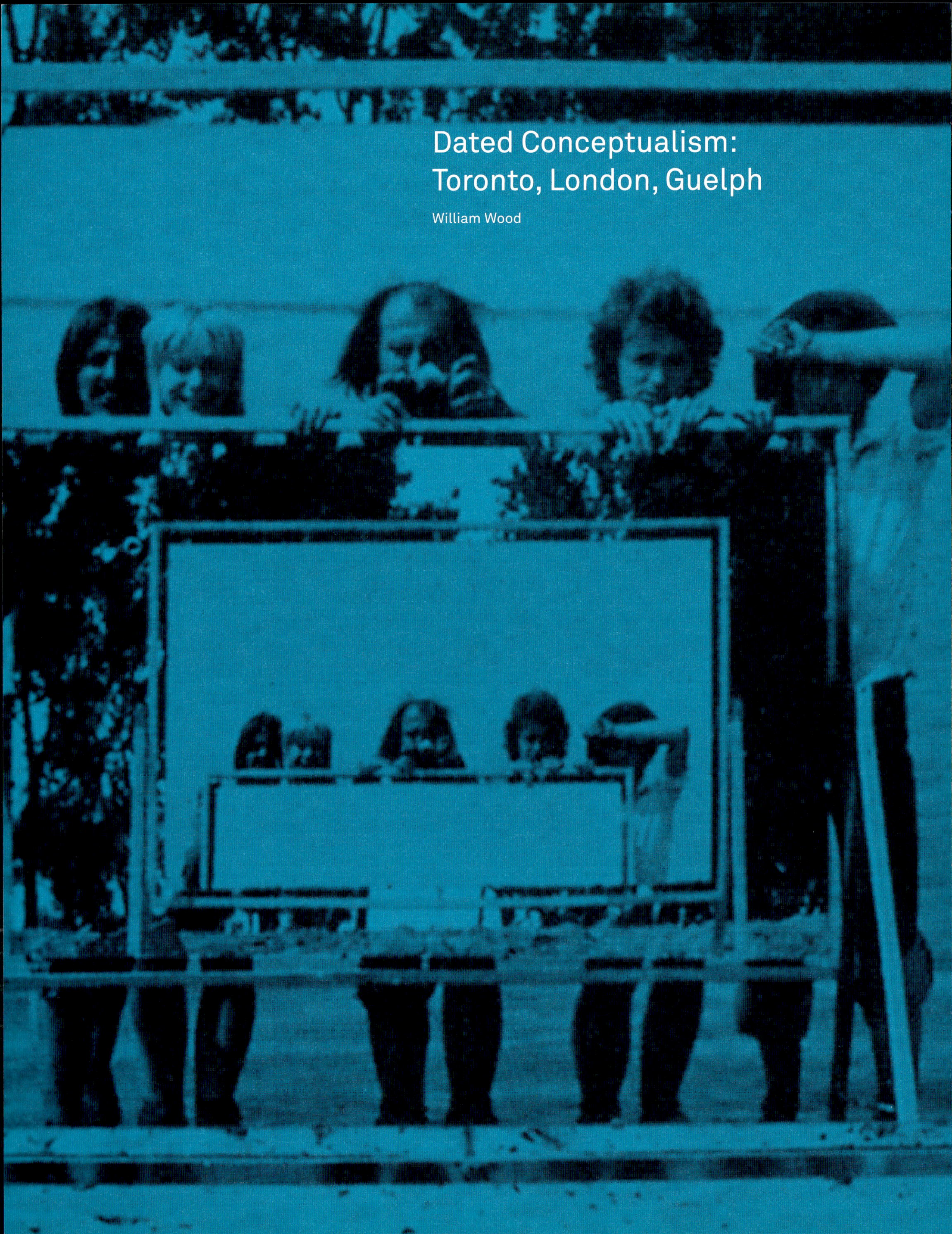

The history I want to discuss, which may be the history of art in Canada, is a history of subjects and objects, where the objects have been replaced by subjects.[1]

In 1983, freelance critic and curator Philip Monk published three related essays focusing on works displayed and mostly produced in Toronto from the 1960s and '70s. Without doubt one of the most perceptive writers on the period, he offered an account of a structural shift from self-reference to social reference in "Colony, Commodity and Copyright," a thick description of a 1973 Ian Carr-Harris exhibition in "Staging Language, Presenting Events, Representing History," and a polemic concerning General Idea and their systematic inhabitation of capitalist values and forms in "Editorials."[2] The Toronto portion of *Traffic*, curated by Barbara Fischer, includes works by artists discussed by Philip Monk in the first essay, such as Robin Collyer, Andy Patton, Tom Sherman and Michael Snow, as well as several of Carr-Harris' from 1973 and issues of General Idea's *FILE Megazine* (which form the basis for the argument of "Editorials"). Yet, re-reading Monk's astute take on the work, I never met the term conceptual art—and discovered only one occurrence of its near-cognate, Conceptualism. Recounting Carr-Harris' work of 1973, Monk writes: "Looking now, we might too readily read the image-text conjunction alone and forget the presentation. Thus we might reject the work as a dated conceptualism or simplistic semiotics."[3]

Although he went on to urge readers to realize that both the sculptural and linguistic aspects of the art were fresh when first encountered—and remained ripe for his explication—the notion that by 1983 an alert and supportive critic would wearily refer to "dated conceptualism" should remind us that as its influence waned, conceptual art was something many wanted to put behind them. As Victor Burgin opened his defence of conceptual art in 1984, there is an "almost universal tendency . . . to 'lose' an entire decade—the 1970s—as a period when 'nothing happened.'"[4] Instead of losing the decade, Monk was on a recovery mission, so he worked to separate the work he was discussing from the stale-dating that Conceptualism connoted in 1983.

I raise this anomaly to recall not only that Monk was rejecting the term but that conceptual art was not then nor is it now a current or often-used term to describe art from Ontario, historical or contemporary. This might be because of the way the "image-text conjunction" Monk named had become a fairly standard marker of artistic sophistication after conceptual art's deployment of the form, but also because, unlike in places such as the Nova Scotia College of Art and Design (Garry Neill Kennedy et al.) or the Vancouver School of Art (Ian Wallace) or Simon Fraser University (Iain Baxter, Jeff Wall), conceptual or former conceptual artists had not taught nor were they teaching full time in Ontario colleges or universities during the 1960s

1 Philip Monk, "Colony, commodity and copyright: Reference and self-reference in Canadian art," *Vanguard* 12, no. 5/6 (June 1983): 14.

2 Philip Monk, "Colony, commodity and copyright," 14–17; "Staging language, presenting events, representing history: Ian Carr-Harris, September 1973," *Vanguard* 12, no. 9 (September 1983): 18–21, "Editorials. General Idea and the myth of inhabitation," *Parachute* 33 (Winter 1983): 12–23. All reprinted in Philip Monk, *Struggles with the Image: Essays in Art Criticism* (Toronto: YYZ Books, 1988).

3 Monk, *Struggles*, 113.

4 Victor Burgin, "The absence of presence: Conceptualisms and postmodernisms." In Hilary Gresty (Ed.), *1965 to 1972: When Attitudes Became Form* (Cambridge: Kettle's Yard Gallery, 1984). Reprinted in Victor Burgin, *The End of Art Theory: Criticism and Postmodernity* (London: Macmillan, 1986), 29.

General Idea, still from *Double Mirror Video*, 1971, detail

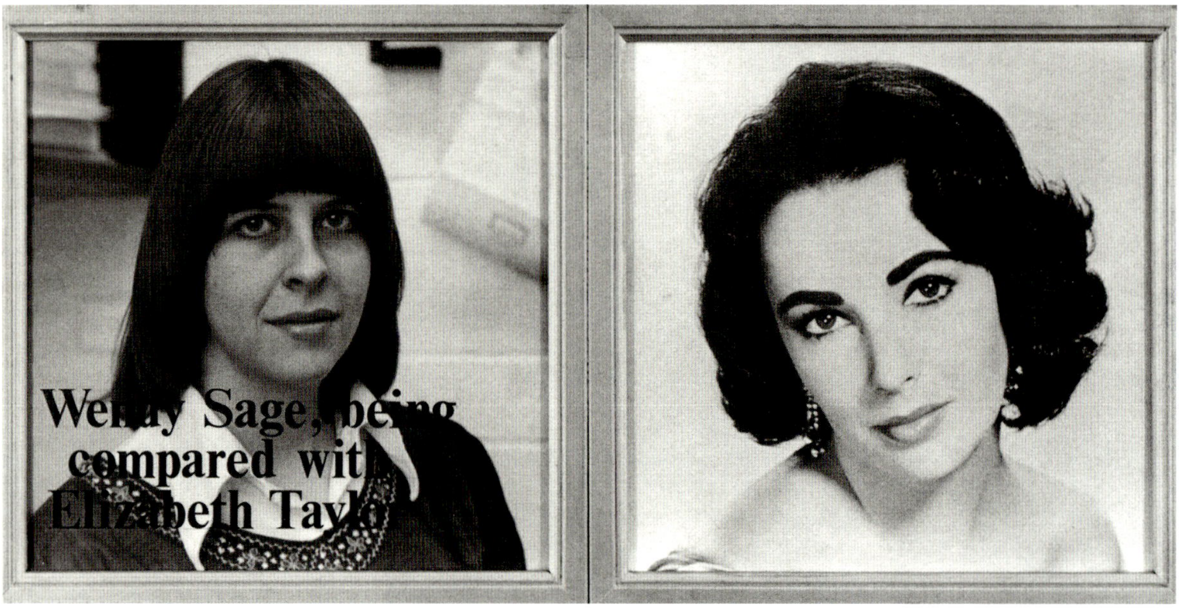

and '70s—with the important exception of Eric Cameron at the University of Guelph from 1969 to 1976.[5] It could be argued that the perseverance of conceptual art as a paradigm for art making was kept going after the mid-1970s only in the academies and colleges where erstwhile conceptual artists held positions. In addition, it could be that conceptual art never took hold in Toronto, even though many types of art and formulations of artistic projects took the form of conceptualist or conceptual-like endeavours and are treated under different rubrics such as image-text, video art, performance art, installation art, artist-run centre . . . Also, there is the persistent question of historical memory and historical research, what Monk again, almost thirty years ago, cryptically lamented by stating, "The history of art in Canada is short. That is to say there is no history. Or there are many. This is one of them."[6]

One response to this condition ("This is not a postmodern condition: it is our condition"),[7] was General Idea's fictionalization of a purportedly self-generated and self-serving history. With the Miss General Idea pageants and the plans for the Miss General Idea Pavilion, and with *FILE*, they concocted a story that was also a strategy and a system of mythographic, nested self-reference. Part of this strategy was also embedded in the celebration of the new organizations that had fostered the type of self-generated and self-regulating autonomy that General Idea both took advantage of and travestied—especially the artist-run centre and its affiliates. In his essay "The Humiliation of the Bureaucrat," also published in 1983, AA Bronson offered the image of "a dream community connected by and reflected in the media" as the idealist projection of the artist-run centre. By seeking to be "authenticated by its own reflection in

Above
Ian Carr-Harris, *Wendy Sage Being Compared*, 1973

[5] Ian Carr-Harris was head librarian at the Ontario College of Art after 1970 but taught only one studio seminar after 1976. He began teaching studio and criticism full time in 1988.

[6] Monk, *Struggles*, 91.

[7] Philip Monk, "Axes of difference," *Vanguard* 13, no. 4 (May 1984). Reprinted in Monk, *Struggles*, 189.

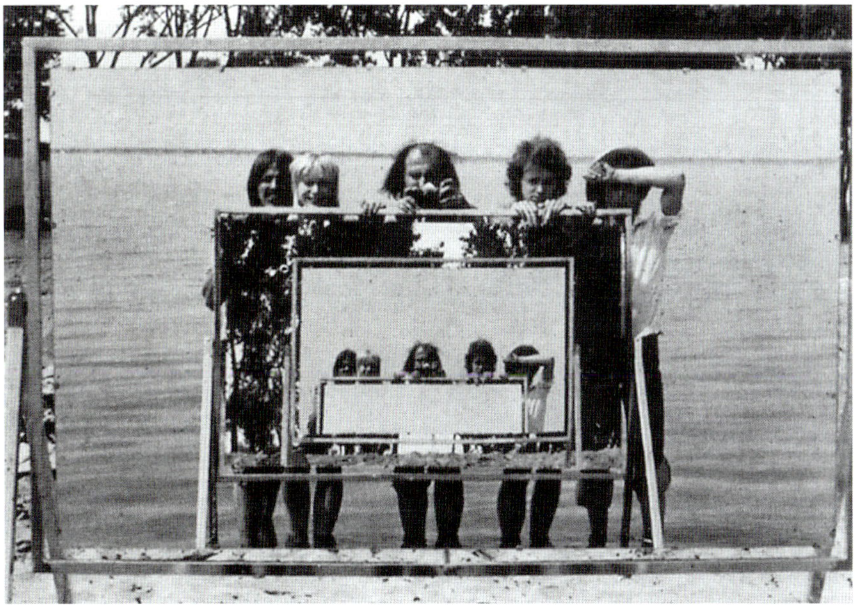

the media," the Canadian artist was, he wrote:

> desiring to see not necessarily himself but the picture of his art scene pictured on TV; and knowing the impossibility of an art scene without *real* museums (the Art Gallery of Ontario was not a *real* museum for us), without *real* art magazines (artscanada was not a *real* magazine for us), without *real* artists (no, Harold Town was not a *real* artist for us), we forgot that we ourselves were real artists, because we had not seen ourselves in the media . . . as such an artist desiring such a picture of such a scene, such a reality from sea-to-shining-sea, then, it was natural to call upon our national attributes—the bureaucratic tendency and the protestant work ethic—and working together, and working sometimes not together, we laboured to structure, or rather to untangle from the messy post-sixties spaghetti of our minds, artist-run galleries, artists' video and artist-run magazines. And that allowed us to see ourselves as an art scene. And we did.[8]

Bronson presents at once the worthy aim of "working together" and the less than worthy aim to create not great art or national identity but, through institutional pastiche, the conditions for generating visibility through an art scene. The desire to see "the picture of his art scene pictured on TV" sounds trifling when it is based on "the bureaucratic tendency and the protestant work ethic," and such incongruity is surely the point. What Bronson offers is a recipe for a "real" art scene, not for real art, and the forms his putative institutions take—FILE Megazine replacing Life magazine on the coffee table, video by artists replacing

[8] AA Bronson, "The humiliation of the bureaucrat." In AA Bronson and Peggy Gale (Eds.), *Museums by Artists* (Toronto: Art Metropole, 1983), 30.

Above
General Idea, still from *Double Mirror Video*, 1971

THE 1984 MISS GENERAL IDEA PAGEANT PAVILLION

DEPARTMENT 1. THE SEARCH FOR THE SPIRIT OF MISS GENERAL IDEA

PAGE | PAGE

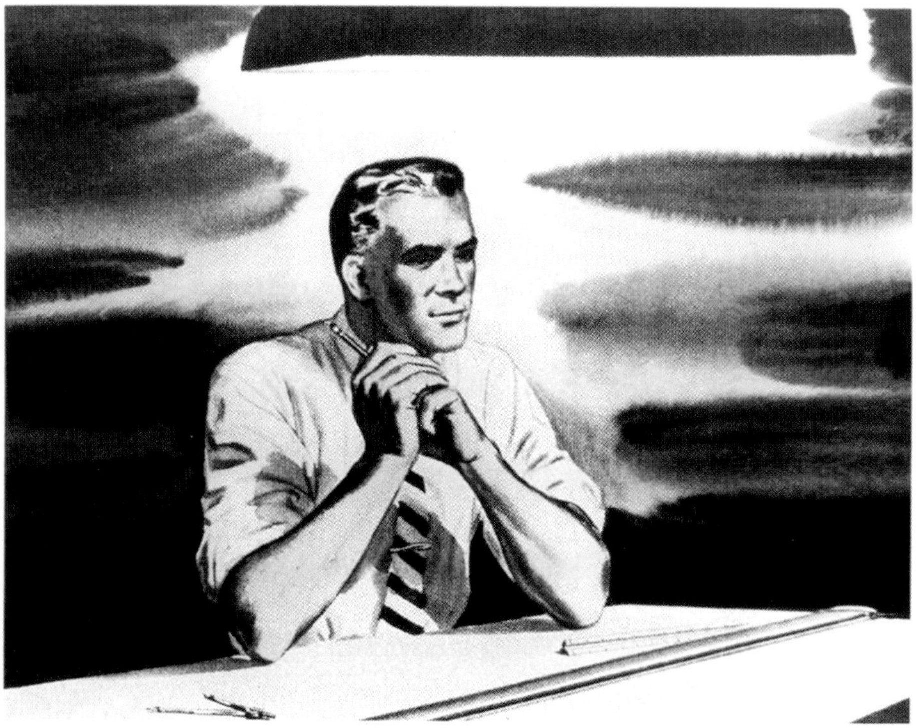

'GENERAL IDEA'

General Idea is basically this: a framing device within which we inhabit the role of the artist as we see the living legend. We can be expected to do what is expected within these bounds. We are aware of the limitations of this and refer to it as our Frame of Reference and act accordingly behind the lines. Projecting our roles gives us some perspective to start with so we can see clear to project our frames frame by frame.

ADDENDA

PHOTO: General Idea from Fortune Magazine

COPY NUMBER 1/2 1-001

LAYOUT DATE OCT 18 1975

SIGNATURE GENERAL IDEA

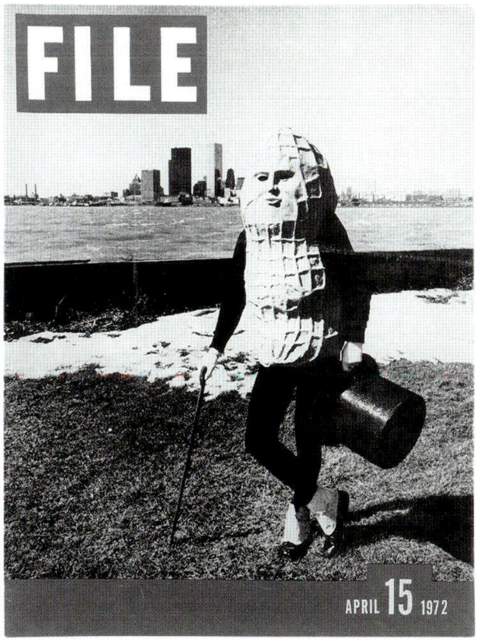

Opposite
General Idea, *Showcard 1-001 "General Idea"*, 1975

Left
General Idea (with Image Bank), *FILE Megazine,* Mr. Peanut Issue, Vol. 1, No. 1, April 1972

broadcast television in the living room, artist-run centres replacing the art museum as the public sphere, with the Canada Council handing out grants just like the Academy of Motion Picture Arts and Sciences hands out the Oscars—all are parasitic on the existence of the "real" thing. Indeed, this was fitting, since General Idea had based their output on filling the empty shells of advertising and fashion with camp, kitsch and a quasi-Warholian gang of Canadian and international superstars, the followers of the "scene" they had generated and would document. As in their claim to be "mirrors mirroring mirrors," the leaders and followers circled each other, or, more likely, they mimed ballroom dancing together for the cameras, and the aura of self- and mutual admiration sustained the project so that, as Monk intimated, "objects have been replaced by subjects."

Another response, in some ways as intricately self-referential, was the parochial sort of regionalism propounded by Greg Curnoe in London. He, too, promoted artist-run organizations such as the magazine *20 Cents* and the magazine and gallery *Region*, as well as collaborated on opening the still extant Forest City Gallery and forming the Nihilist Spasm Band. As art, Curnoe's most persuasive works argue for the integrity of immediate experiences of family, community and place—even as his callow anarchistic and nihilistic politics conceal the fundamental hayseed conservatism of this stance. Diaristic and list-like records using stamp pads—of his boyhood friends, of his daily activities on an artist's visit to NSCAD in Halifax, of his timed-out visit to see the ailing Jack Chambers in hospital—suggest that this is a charmed life and it needs nothing but noting to convey the richness of the everyday and the essential rightness of recording the most arbitrary but revealing events as constituting a kind of art. There is a brilliance in this, related both to a history of artists in Southern Ontario recording specific places (Homer Watson and Carl Schaefer come to mind) and to the simple equation of Curnoe's immediate surroundings and his deadpan documentation of them as nothing more than facts—beautifully spare, plain, uninterpreted and unalloyed occurrences and

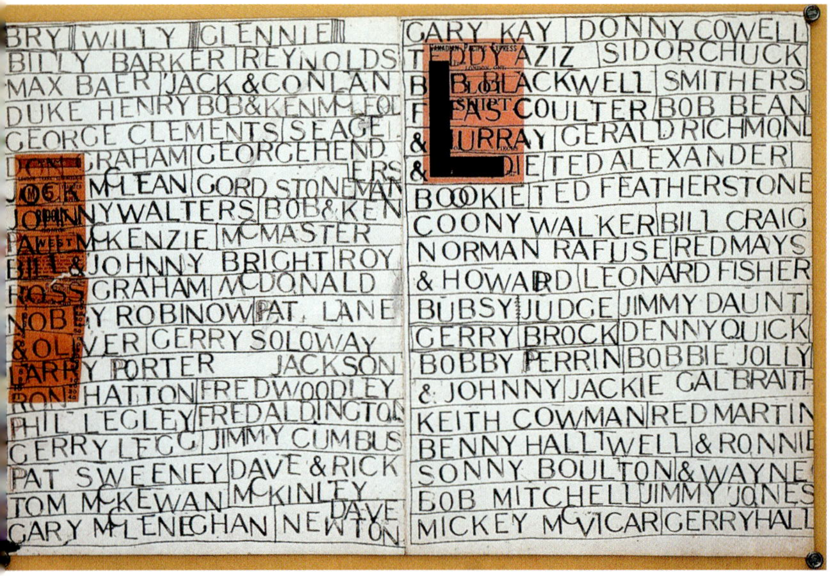

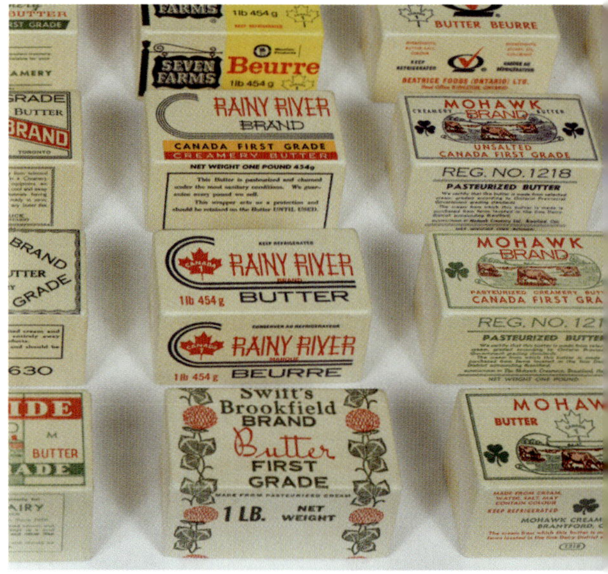

memories. In what was perhaps a more properly anthropological and non-autobiographical mode, Londoner Robert Fones collected matchbooks featuring foliage for his *Leaf Collection* (1968) and the paper coverings used by creameries to advertise their pounds of butter in *Butter Models* (1979)—preserving evidence of a once flourishing variety of conflicting identities for the region based in images of pastoral plenty and indigenous peoples.

Between the cosmopolitan cleverness of General Idea and the pastoralism of Curnoe and Fones there is a particularly opaque use of combined language and image in work from Toronto. Deployed in video, seen in photographs, placed and printed on walls and on what counts as sculpture (but is probably best seen as tableaux), there is an overwhelming presence of written and spoken language. You could also draw an analogy, loose but workable, between the mostly uninflected character of the prose and the plain procedures and actions recorded on videotape or presented as photography. Michael Snow's *Authorization* (1969) and *Venetian Blind* (1970) are exemplary here, for each follows a specific protocol, much as in Sol LeWitt's statement: "When an artist uses a conceptual form of art, it means that all of the planning and decisions are made beforehand and the execution is a perfunctory affair. The idea becomes a machine that makes the art."[9]

When these works were conceived, Snow was living in New York and had ties to LeWitt. *Authorization* enacts a LeWitt-like serial process while also possessing the level of tautologous self-reference characteristic of Robert Morris' *Box with the Sound of Its Own Making* and *Card File* (both 1962), using Polaroid prints and a mirror to gradually replace the image of the camera and operator in the mirror's reflection with photographic prints that depict the mirror, camera and silhouette of Snow behind the camera. Produced while Snow was representing Canada at the Biennale, *Venetian Blind* showed a grid of 24 colour photographs of the artist in Venice, "blinded" by the sun on the lagoon. As with LeWitt, an uncomplex protocol issues a machine-

Above, from left

Greg Curnoe, *List of Names of Boys I Grew Up With*, 1962. © Estate of Greg Curnoe / SODRAC (2012)

Robert Fones, *Butter Models*, 1979, detail

Michael Snow, *Authorization*, 1969

Installation view of Michael Snow, *Portrait*, 1967, Doris McCarthy Gallery, University of Toronto, 2010. Photo: Tony Hafkenscheid

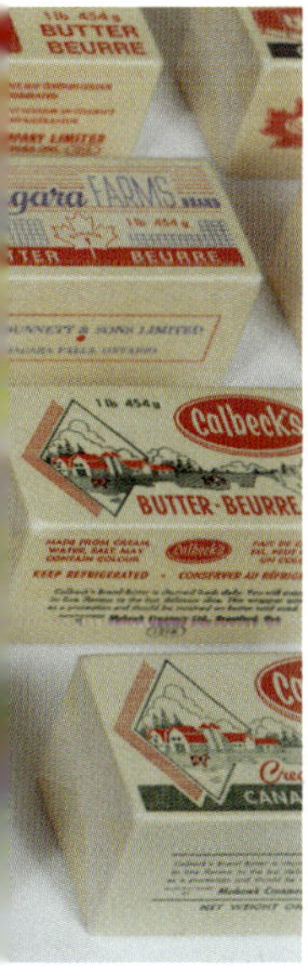

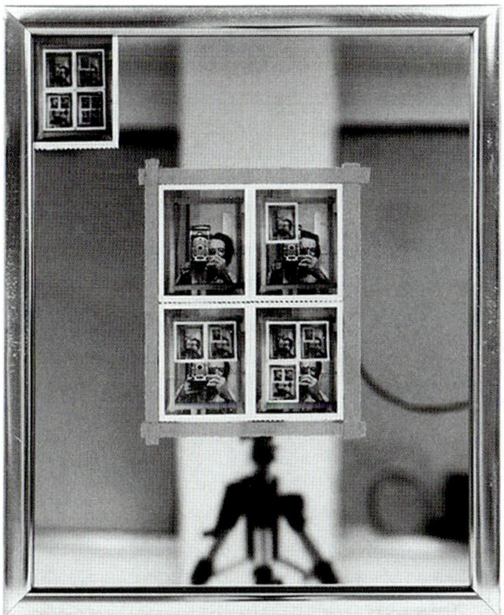

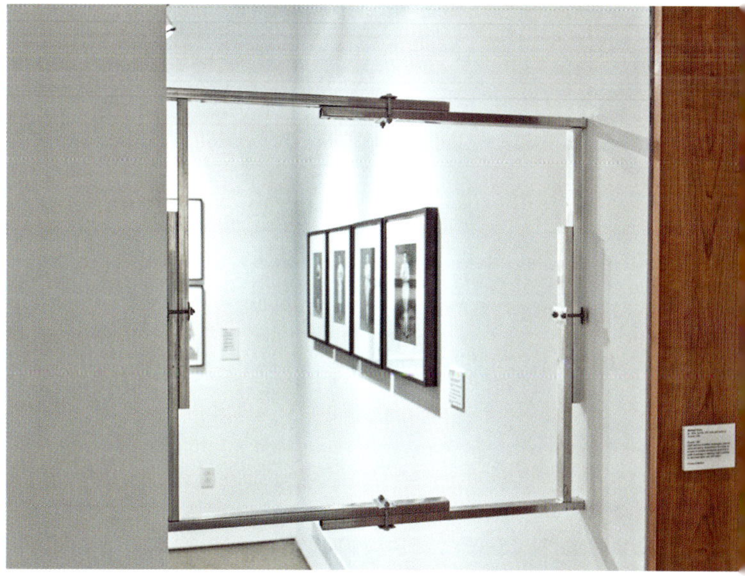

like system, but one, in Snow's case, that produces a cover-up or requires sightlessness. The enacted subtraction of vision or its enforced elimination is also present in the framing device of *Portrait* (1967), in which four aluminum bars contrive to create a sited frame that also blocks passage. If Snow's image is gradually covered in *Authorization* and he is shown visionless in *Venetian Blind*, in *Portrait* the spectator is set up, is framed, in order to become the unwitting subject of an artistic procedure. Later examples of such procedural approaches to portraiture and photography include Arnaud Maggs' documentation of German youth in *Kunstakademie* (1980) and Rebecca Singleton's four images of Margareth Kluka demonstrating such operations as *How to hold a chihuahua* or *How to wear a raincoat while wearing a slip* (both 1981).

Much as Snow's works either subtract vision or add to it—making the viewer the portrait—so the deployment of language veers away from the type of straightforward noting seen in Curnoe's stampings. In Carr-Harris' *A Man Illustrating* (1973), the two phrases "A man illustrating the muscles in his back" and "Lynn, demonstrating that her work is never done" would seem to be, as Monk notes, simply illustrative. But as captions beneath photographs—one removed from a printed book showing a man's back and buttocks with one arm raised to enhance his musculature, the other showing front torso and legs of a naked woman in a relaxed pose—they exceed the illustrative to become a nest of oppositions and "relations between bodies, classification and power."[10] Robin Collyer's *Untitled Magazine* (1979) continues such an analysis, being composed of a complete mock-up of a popular magazine forming an extensive investigation into the semiotics of the mass media as it continually overlaps and reinforces the biased links between image and text, word and picture, assertion and tendentious interpretation.

In a similar way, Lisa Steele's videotapes *Birthday Suit—with scars and defects* (1974) and *Internal Pornography* (1975) concern themselves with the descriptions of events and dreams,

[9] Sol LeWitt, "Paragraphs on conceptual art," *Artforum* 5, no. 10 (Summer 1967): 79.

[10] Monk, *Struggles*, 120.

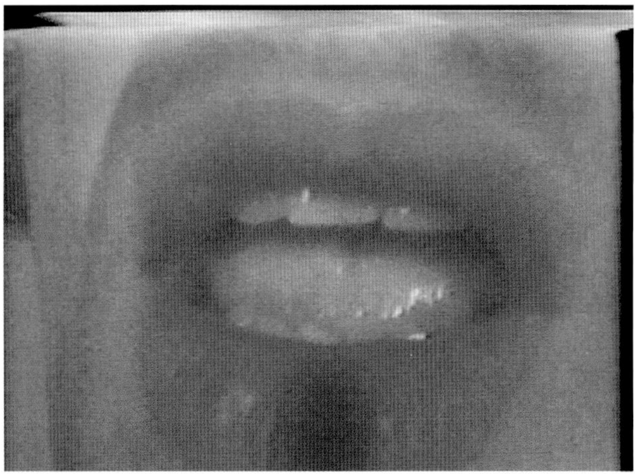

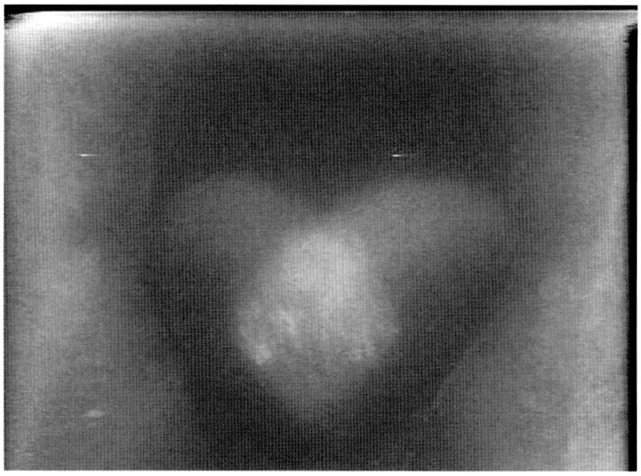

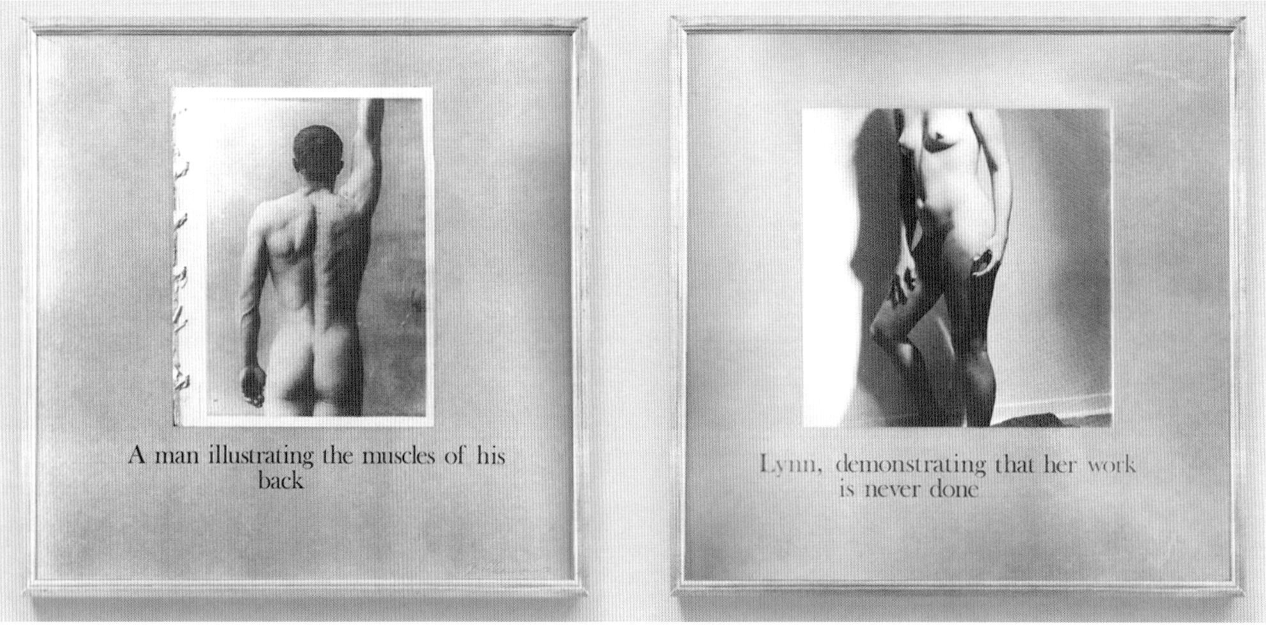
A man illustrating the muscles of his back
Lynn, demonstrating that her work is never done

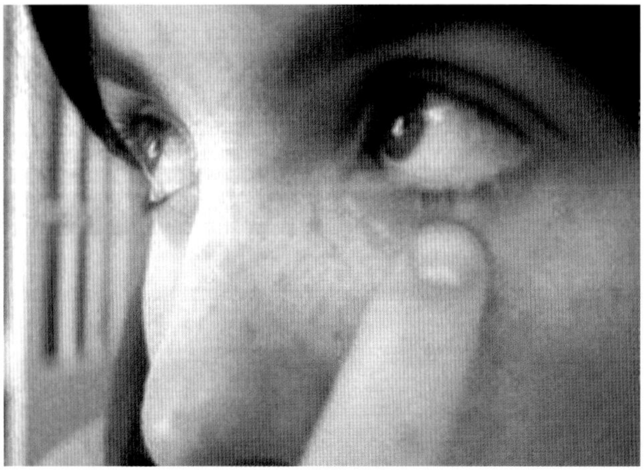

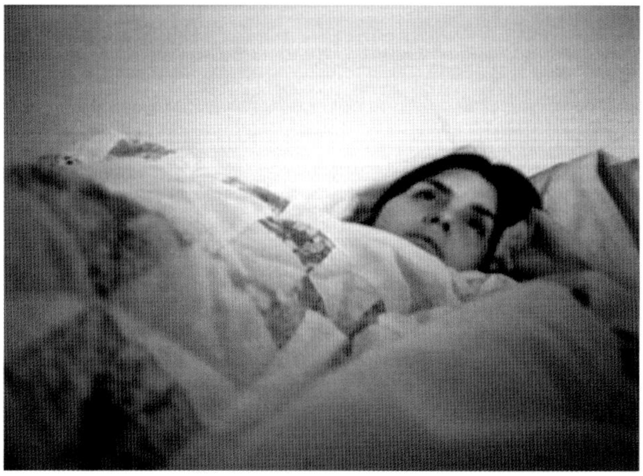

but in each case the image and the language are lightly disrupted—in the first case as Steele not only clinically recounts the date and cause of the scars she accumulated up to her twenty-seventh birthday, but also allows her fingers to linger after pointing out each scar, rubbing the differential skin, telltale of a pleasure and sense of accomplishment in recalling accidents and illness. The three monitors of *Internal Pornography* display Steele in bed reciting fragments from her dreams—short, sometimes violent, sometimes comforting phrases that convey images and sights from beyond consciousness—while her naked torso on the far monitor is slowly written over by gynecological diagrams and, in the middle, leaves are sensuously rubbed—like the scars in *Birthday Suit*. Once again, touch, talk and image do not add up, and there is a surplus in Steele's confessional gambit that is countered by the pain sustained and the distance of the dream imagery from felt reality.

A related surplus—or perhaps excess—is met with in Eric Cameron's videos. As chair of visual arts at Guelph, in 1972 Cameron took over a course in video production after a colleague who had purchased equipment, Alan Lite, left the university.[11] Heading into the teaching year he composed "Notes for Video Art" based on the question: "What can you do with a television camera?"[12] Answers included dropping the recording camera from the Empire State Building, inserting its lens into someone's mouth, or running the lens over the body of a naked model or the surface of the walls of a room. Save the Empire State drop, Cameron followed through on these possibilities, seemingly tracing a path close to structural filmmaking with its concentration on cinematic apparatus. Yet the camera rhythmically entering and exiting Cameron's mouth in *Insertion (My Mouth)* (1973) or the same instrument surveying Sue Sterling's body in *Es In Arcadia Id: (Figure)* (1972) are conspicuously erotic, as is the voyeuristic editing required to excise the traces of a female figure in the video and installation *Keeping Marlene Out of the Picture* (1973–76)

Perhaps indicating how and why the tactile and documentary properties of early video overshadow its visual interests, Steele's still camera recording parts of her body and

---

Opposite, from top, left to right
Eric Cameron, stills from *Insertion (My Mouth)*, 1973

Ian Carr-Harris, *A Man Illustrating*, 1973

Lisa Steele, still from *Birthday Suit—with scars and defects*, 1974

Lisa Steele, still from the 3-channel video *Internal Pornography*, 1975

[11] See the informative and singularly insightful essay, Diana Nemiroff, "The 'imperfect' artist: Eric Cameron's video work," in Ann Davis (Ed.), *Cover and Uncover: Eric Cameron* (Calgary: University of Calgary Press, 2011), 85–111.

[12] Eric Cameron, "Notes for video art." In *Video Circuits* (Guelph: University of Guelph, 1973). Reprinted in Peggy Gale and Lisa Steele (Eds.), *Video re/View* (Toronto: Art Metropole and Vtape, 1996), 106.

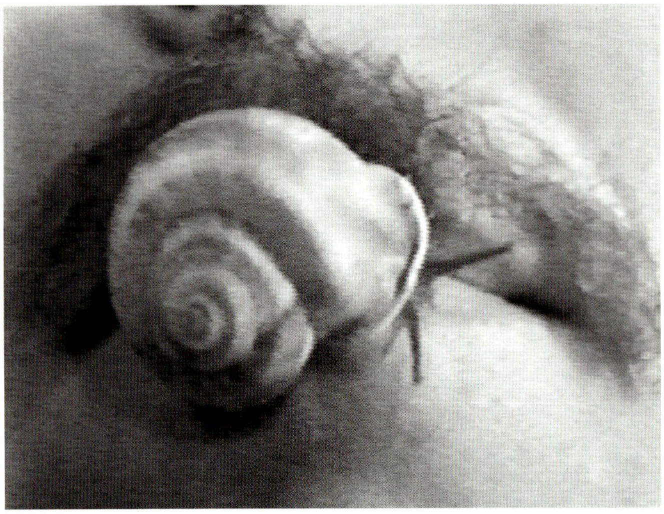

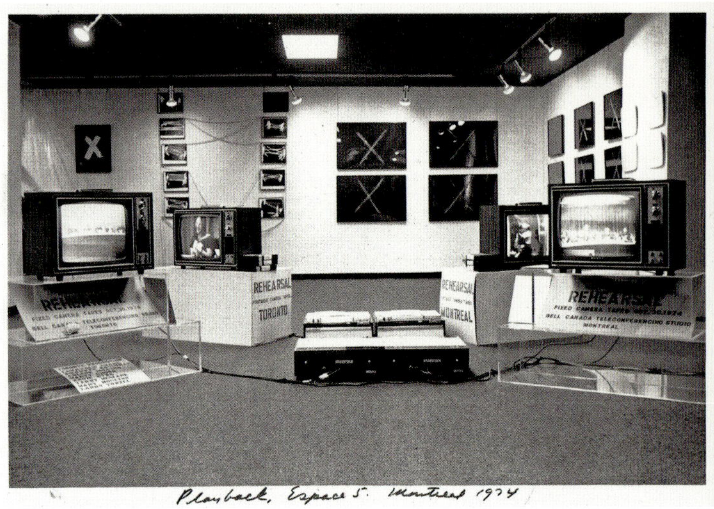

Cameron's overt attempts to touch or cut out the figure are devoted to traces, often nearly impossible to visualize, while their conceptual clarity is unquestioned. Similar conclusions could be drawn regarding the more immediately corporeal video work produced out of Toronto's premier artist-run centre, A Space, including by artists Vito Acconci and Dennis Oppenheim, who held artist's residencies at the centre in spring and summer 1971, making videotapes and performances often involving the use of the body as an instrument—as in Acconci's *Sounding Board* (1971), in which an accomplice beats on parts of the artist's naked body in an attempt to replicate the sounds of a Frank Zappa tune. The sort of body art documentation featured in Robert Bowers' *Kiss* (1971) or John McEwen's *Blood Tap (or Pressing out/Pressing Down)* (1971) extend such practices, as do sonically based works such as John Watt's threatening repetition of indistinct phrases involving homicide in *I'm a Killer* (1973) or Steele's remarkable verbal gymnastics in her homage to her grandfather, *The Ballad of Dan Peoples* (1977). These videos invoke language as a type of miscommunication or a device for dividing people. A concentration on communications leading to informational mayhem also prompted the enactment—if not the rhetoric—of Vera Frenkel's *String Games: Improvisations for Inter-City Video* (1974). Here, through then-magical teleconferencing technology, Frenkel attempted to have two groups make body-sized cat's cradles simultaneously in Montréal and Toronto, resulting in yet another proof of the persistence of at least "two solitudes" in an ever increasingly connected electronic world.

Such conceptual clarity only reinforces the opacity of communications in the document, and is suggestive of the narrative potential of language's subtle veering away from intelligibility in works by Colin Campbell and Tom Sherman. Campbell's *True/False* and *Sackville, I'm Yours* (both 1972) assume the television conventions of talking head and interview question-and-answer, but do so askance of the implausible straightforwardness of those devices. In *True/*

Top, from left
Robert Bowers, still from *Kiss*, 1971

Installation views of Vera Frenkel, *String Games: Improvisations for Inter-City Video*, 1974, Espace 5, 1975 (original installation) and Doris McCarthy Gallery, University of Toronto, 2010

Colin Campbell, still from *Sackville, I'm Yours*, 1972

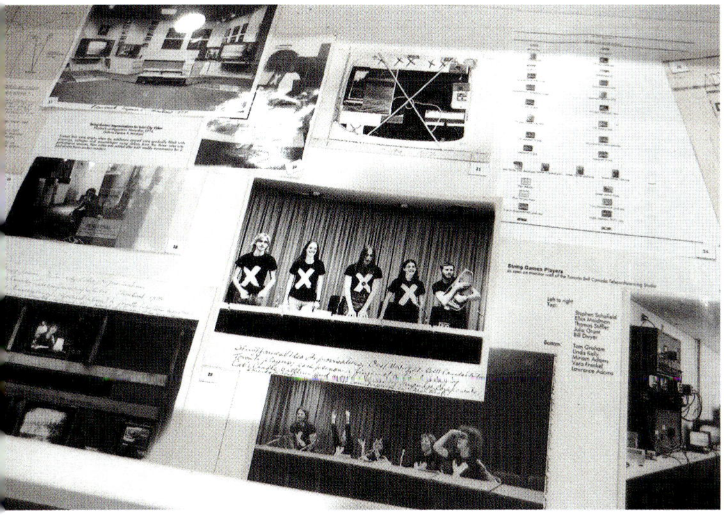

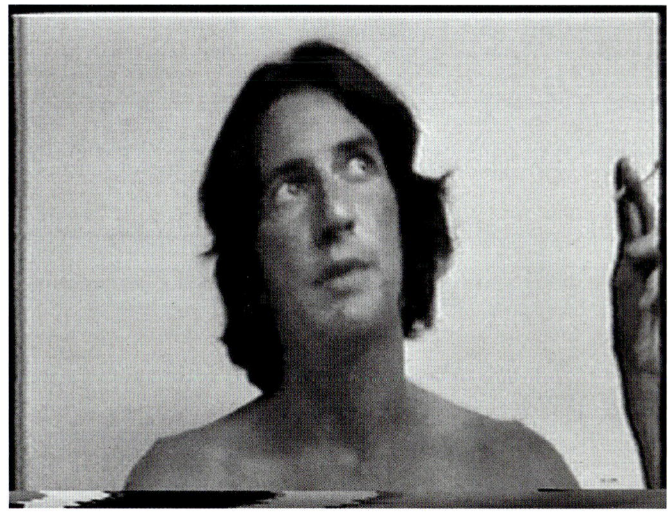

False, as the person making statements ("I am an exhibitionist," "My real name is Colin") and the respondent to those questions (all uniformly answered "True" and subsequently "False"), Campbell interrupts the circuits of transparency that televisual and videographic media would seem to require. When he adopts the pose of Art Star in *Sackville, I'm Yours*, the role of the interviewer is left out so that he is responding without standard prompting. Of course the plight of Art Star as teacher at Mount Allison in Sackville, New Brunswick, is a constant challenge of the small fish in the big pond of art stardom, while being the art star of a small town is traduced by the opposite—the knowledge that "there's a timeless quality here, the countryside, the ocean, goodness it's just so timeless. Time just goes by in Sackville."[13]

Art Star is the first of the many heroic-loser personae Campbell would adopt, developing video's narrative and serial potential. Sherman's work, including his bookwork *3 Death Stories* and his meticulous text panel *Distant Interior Sound, from a Photograph by Lynne Cohen* (both 1977), absorbs some of the thickening agents of repetition and parataxis used in the *nouveau roman*, but adds this to a demotic blend of ordinary reference and extraordinary perceptiveness and meta-commentary. In the video *Envisioner* (1978), the monitor becomes the teleprompter for a voice that keeps running on once the televised text is spelled out, although intermittently a close-mouthed, silent, mustachioed head appears as a cipher for the voice-over. Sandwiched between the type of statement made ("THERE IS INSTABILITY IN MY SELF-IMAGE, JERKY TRANSITIONS IN MY MECHANICAL METHOD OF SURVIVAL," "WHAT PISSES ME OFF IS THE WAY PEOPLE GENERALIZE WHEN THEY DON'T KNOW WHAT THEY ARE TALKING ABOUT, THE ONLY WAY TO CUT THROUGH THEIR GENERAL BABBLE IS TO ASK SPECIFIC QUESTIONS OF DETAIL") and the running text is a commentary on what we now call multi-tasking or information overload. The narrator spies people in their homes reading while watching television or talking while listening to musical recordings, while he admits to

[13] Colin Campbell in *Sackville, I'm Yours*, single-channel video, 1972.

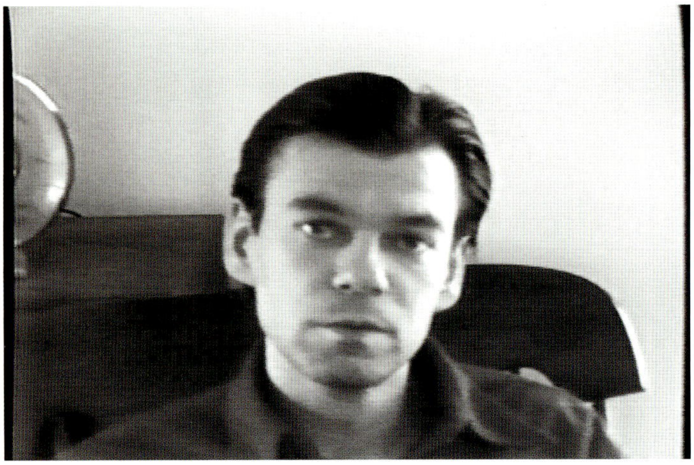

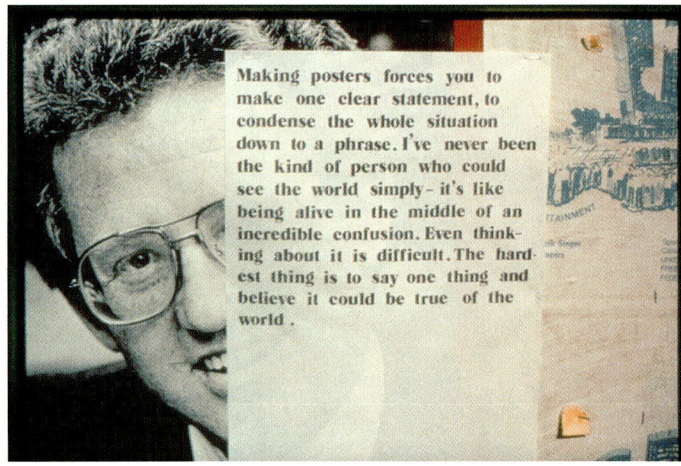

tailoring his discourse to modes of greatest rhetorical effectiveness and presents an analysis reminiscent of Roland Barthes and his discussion of the "reality effect" in narrative fiction.[14] The effect is to produce a real that is replete with oversight and understatement, a world of watchers and liars, lazybones and scrupulous, active discernment—a vanity fair that also sounds familiarly suburban and homely, as in Sigmund Freud's discussion of the uncanny, or *unheimlich*.

Even more immediately uncanny is Sherman's *TVideo* (1980), in which the narrator is literally at home in his kitchen and living room discussing his habits, ailments and approach to making coffee, travelling and so on—or not so on, since the entire exercise is prefaced by the statement that by the time the video is shown the speaker present on screen will be dead. The statement, grounded in the distinct temporal shift between the contraction "TV" and the short term "video"—between the immediacy of television broadcast and the past tense of videotape playback—means that viewers are split before the sight of a dead man talking and the knowledge, hard to bear, that we interpret his entire talk as symptomatic: is his back pain the trouble, or his insomnia, too much coffee . . . ? *TVideo* is 28 minutes long and was made for broadcast as part of a series of artists' video commissioned by TVOntario, the provincial educational network, so its temporal slippage was complemented by its mirroring of the viewer's domestic setting in the speaker's homely context—only underlining the uncanny aspect. In contrast, General Idea's *Pilot* (1977), also produced for broadcast on TVOntario, fits quite comfortably in the mediatized context of advertising commodities that constitute the base of broadcast television. The show—it is entertainment, after all—is yet another version of the story of General Idea, a series of voiceovers and trio presentation where the *FILE* "editorials" and the *Showcards* (1975) come to life as an infomercial. *Pilot*'s imitation of television—its "inhabitation" of the media environment, as Monk would have it—may be as parasitic

Top, from left
Tom Sherman, still from *TVideo*, 1980

Andy Patton, *Municipal Election Poster*, 1978

Carole Condé and Karl Beveridge, *Cultural Signs: Lower East Side, New York*, 1975

Carole Condé and Karl Beveridge, *Cultural Signs: Carmen Lamanna Gallery, Toronto* (with Carmen Lamanna), 1975

[14] Roland Barthes, "The reality effect," *Communications* 11 (1968). Reprinted in Roland Barthes, *The Rustle of Language*, translated by Richard Howard (Berkeley: University of California Press, 1989), 141–168.

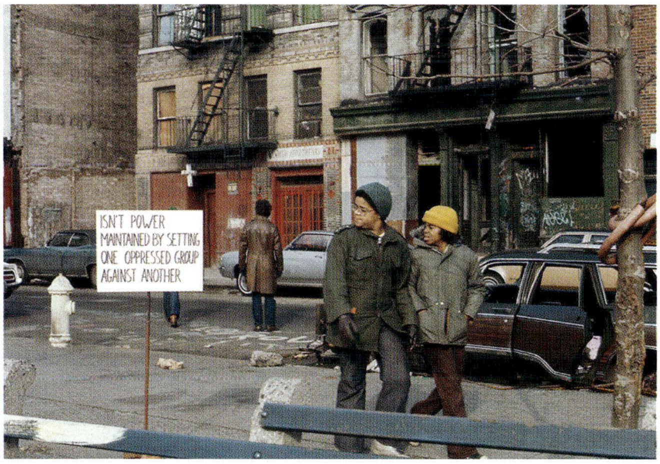

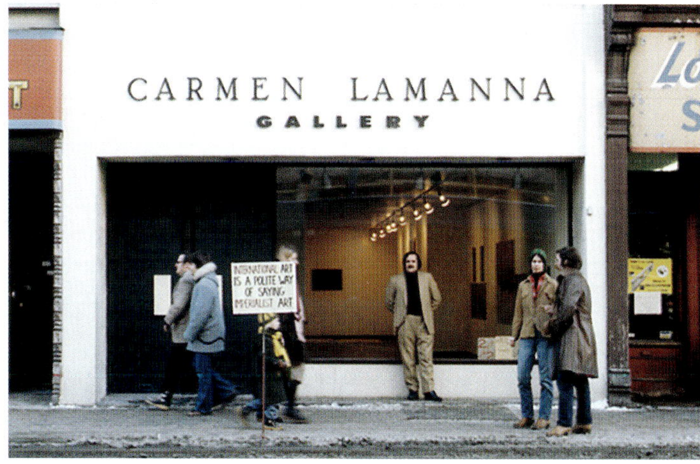

as General Idea's other manifestations, yet it may also be symptomatic of the peculiar preoccupation of Toronto art with the language and rhetoric of bureaucracy and marketing. Although Conceptualism's incorporation of the "aesthetics of administration" and its "politics of publicity" have been highlighted,[15] and the local legacy of Harold Innis and Marshall McLuhan referred to,[16] Toronto's longstanding role as the national centre for English-language communications, marketing and financial and corporate administration has not been much explored in relation to artistic practice. However, with the art community moving south toward Queen Street West in the 1970s, the close proximity of the towers of Bay Street and University Avenue—or the shadow of the CN Tower—would have been constant reminders of the source and persistence of dominance.

As the example of General Idea reminds us, such a position in the field of cultural production, what Pierre Bourdieu referred to as the position of the "dominated dominant,"[17] is often emulative rather than critical. Indeed, when in public, as in Carole Condé and Karl Beveridge's *Cultural Signs* (1975) or Andy Patton's *Municipal Election Poster* (1978), statements such as "International Art is A Polite Way of Saying Imperialist Art" photographed posted in front of the Carmen Lamanna Gallery (the proprietor is pictured on the sidewalk), or the admission that "The hard thing is to say one thing and believe it could be true of the whole world" partly covering the face of civic political candidate (and future Toronto mayor) Art Eggleton, appear more drenched in pathos than effectively oppositional. *. . . It's Still Privileged Art* (1976) was the title of the Art Gallery of Ontario exhibition marking the return of Condé and Beveridge to Canada after a period working with Art & Language New York. Although fueled by the fervent left politics of the residual counter culture, the slogans in the accompanying catalogue were ironic against the comic book images of the artist's life struggle with conventional career concerns and leftist guilt over the privileges still due to art and artists.

[15] See Benjamin H.D. Buchloh, "Conceptual art 1962–1969: From the aesthetic of administration to the critique of institutions," *October* 55 (Winter 1990): 105–143, and Alexander Alberro, *Conceptual Art and the Politics of Publicity* (Cambridge, MA: MIT Press, 2004).

[16] For example, the previously cited anthology *Video re/View*, edited by Gale and Steele, opens with the essay "The Bias of Communication" by Innis and "Media Hot and Cold," an extract from McLuhan's *Understanding Media*.

[17] Pierre Bourdieu, "The field of cultural production, or: The economic field reversed." In Randal Johnson (Ed.), *The Field of Cultural Production* (New York: Columbia University Press, 1993), 35.

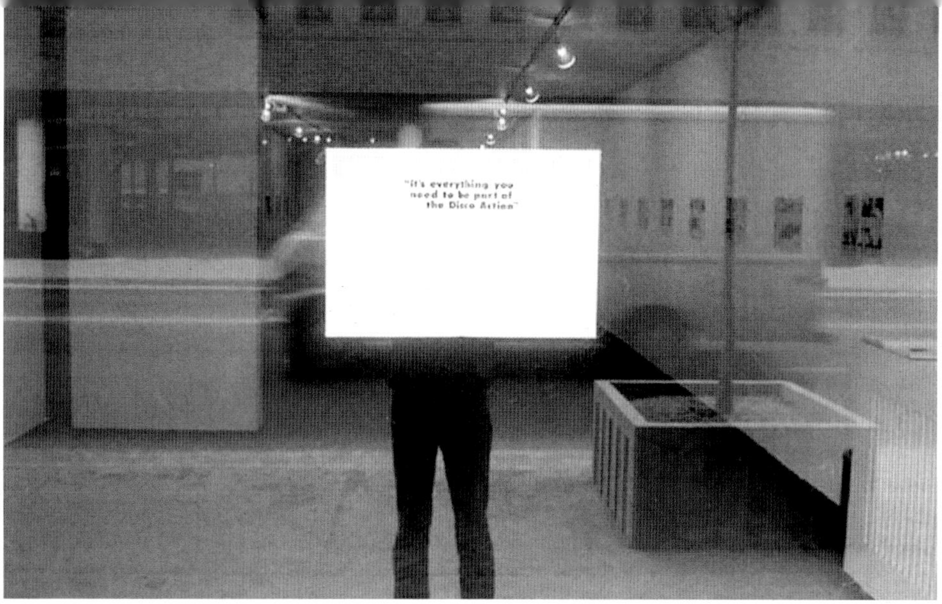
"It's everything you
need to be part of
the Disco Action"

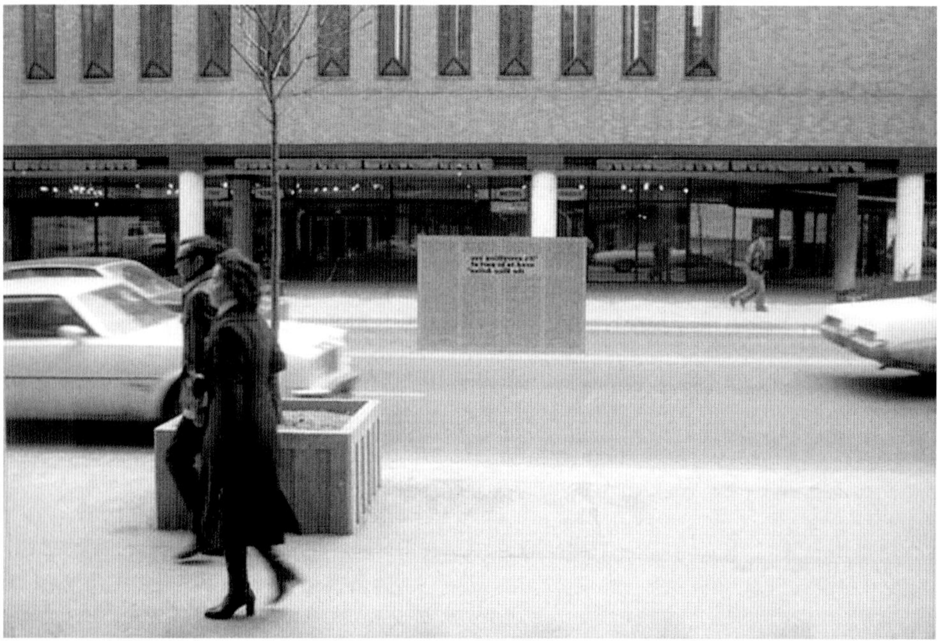

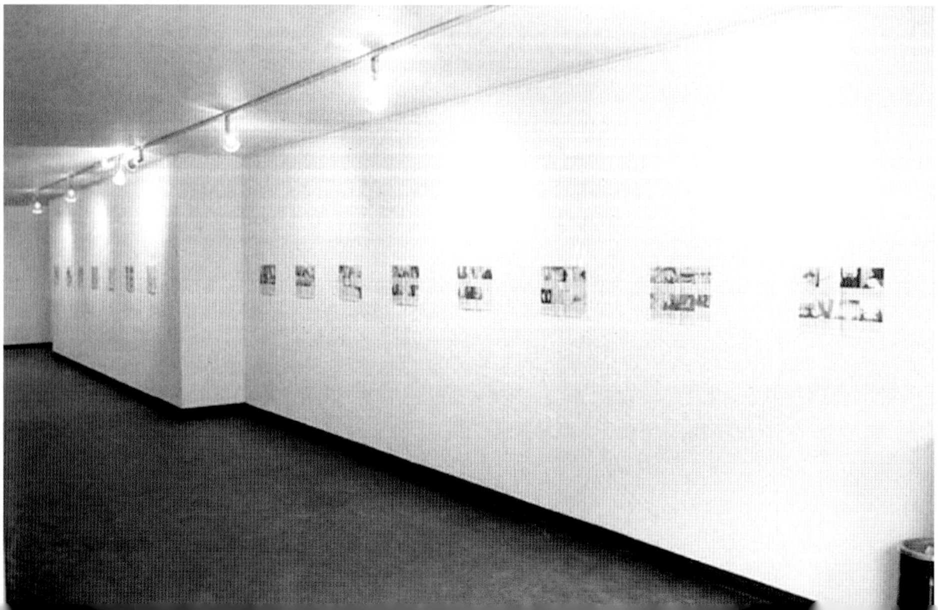

Condé and Beveridge's ties to Art & Language were perhaps the closest Ontario artists came to the international movement of conceptual art, outside of exhibitions by Joseph Kosuth (at the Carmen Lamanna Gallery) and N.E. Thing Co. (at both the Art Gallery of Ontario and the National Gallery of Canada) and the Kensington Arts Association's presentation of the touring group exhibition *Language & Structure in North America* in 1975. Although NETCO's corporate impersonation and their takeover of the National Gallery's first floor for their corporate headquarters had indubitable influence on the Miss General Idea Pavilion, and Kosuth's definitional and "purely" conceptual art would find resonance in the deconstructive text works of Gordon Lebredt, the late 1970s in Ontario saw a move toward a cultural politics focused on nationalism and radicalism that seemed to echo the Art & Language journal *The Fox* and the invidious collapse of the organization in 1976. With the changing of the name of the Kensington Arts Association to the Centre for Experimental Art and Communication (CEAC), the connection to New York was highlighted, as well as through the appearance of Kosuth and Sarah Charlesworth at the Contextual Art Symposium at CEAC in November 1976. There, CEAC members deliberately fomented debate between the conceptual art of New York and the European notion of "contextual art" espoused by Jan Świdziński and Hervé Fischer,[18] with the aim to confront American artists with resistance to imperialist aesthetics via alignment with the European revolutionary left. Eighteen months later, the identification of CEAC ideologue Amerigo Marras with the terrorist aims of the Brigate Rosse led the Canada Council for the Arts and the Ontario Arts Council to revoke funding to the organization after CEAC published images of the Italian bodyguards slain by the Brigate Rosse during their kidnapping of former prime minister Aldo Moro (whom the group subsequently shot).

In order to provide distance from the ideological idiocy displayed by CEAC, attention was increasingly focused on insular regard for such local struggles as Ontario government attempts to censor videos or Toronto police invading gay bathhouses and universal struggles against racism and sexism. The international aspect of conceptual art, whether associated with US imperialism or with the arcana of analytic philosophy, or the Conceptualism of the non–North American leftist artists, was subdued or disavowed in Ontario, ironically making a "dated conceptualism" a legacy to recover rather than revise.

[18] On CEAC, see Dot Tuer, "The CEAC was banned in Canada," *C Magazine* 13 (1986): 24–37.

Opposite
Details and installation view of Robin Collyer, *Untitled Magazine*, Carmen Lamanna Gallery, 1979

Episodes in Conceptual Art on the Prairies

Catherine Crowston with Grant Arnold

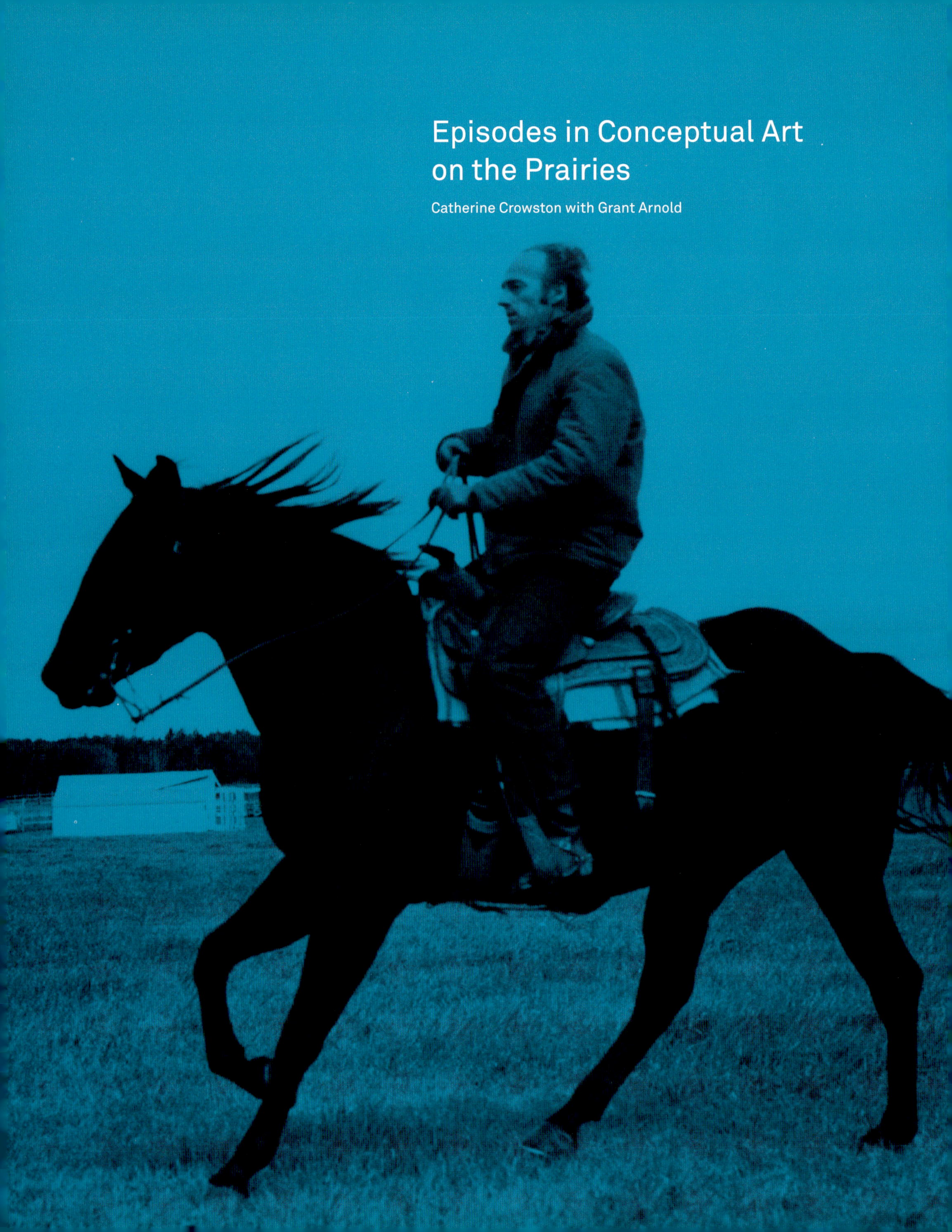

The development of conceptual art in the prairie provinces was episodic in character. It flourished in specific places, at specific moments, around particular groups of artists and artist-run centres, and sometimes in singular events. In this part of the country, the lines of continuity running from 1965 to 1980 are more difficult to trace than in locations such as Halifax or Vancouver. Institutions such as the Edmonton Art Gallery (EAG), the Alberta College of Art, the Winnipeg Art Gallery (WAG) and the University of Manitoba's Gallery One One One at times provided crucial support; however, this often was contingent on specific individuals and dissipated as they moved on and were replaced by directors, curators and faculty with different interests. Artist-run centres, including Winnipeg's Plug In, founded in 1972, and Calgary's Clouds 'n' Water Gallery (later Off Centre Centre and then The New Gallery) and Parachute Center for Cultural Affairs (later known as Arton's), both founded in 1975, provided the most sustained support for conceptually based work. These organizations offered a vital platform for connecting artists working in relative isolation with the most current developments in the wider world of contemporary art. In keeping with the intermittent character of conceptual art in central Canada, this essay looks at the conditions and individuals who shaped the emergence and dissemination of conceptually based art in Edmonton, Calgary and Winnipeg.

Edmonton (and the Arctic)

In the mid-1960s, visual art in Alberta was characterized by a well-established tradition of landscape painting and by experimentations in abstraction and Expressionism undertaken by artists such as Marion Nicoll and Maxwell Bates. While Nicoll, Dates and a number of their colleagues produced accomplished and powerful paintings, they drew upon an idiom of art making grounded in traditions specific to the region. This approach informed much of the programming of the province's few art institutions, including Calgary's Alberta College of Art (founded in 1926), the University of Alberta in Edmonton (where the art and design department was established in 1945) and the province's primary art museum, the EAG (founded in 1924). On September 24, 1969, however, the EAG opened *Place & Process*, an exhibition featuring six outdoor projects executed in downtown Edmonton that radically departed from the traditional aesthetic positions inhabited by Alberta-based artists. Organized by American artist and curator Willoughby Sharp, *Place & Process* was part of a program initiated by EAG director Bill Kirby to engage local audiences with new non-material, process-based art in a format that purposefully occupied highly visible public spaces.

The works created for *Place & Process* were unlike anything previously seen in the province. Robert Morris' *Pace and Process* (the artist riding twelve horses consecutively back and forth over a white chalk line until either he or the horses tired) and Dennis Oppenheim's *Condensed 220 Yard Dash* (a run across Sir Winston Churchill Square, with the artist's footprints later cast in plaster) were similar in their emphasis on measured distance, duration and physical endurance. John Van Saun's *Flour Drop* (in which the artist dropped 500-pound bags of flour and hit them with a 2 x 4 inch piece of lumber) and Les Levine's *Cornflakes* (250 jumbo boxes of cornflakes thrown into the air) emphasized action, chance and the use of everyday materials. Hans Haacke's untitled work consisted of plastic bottles released to float down the North Saskatchewan River, each containing a message and a request that the finder record the time

Robert Morris, *Pace and Process*, 1969, detail. © Robert Morris / SODRAC (2012)

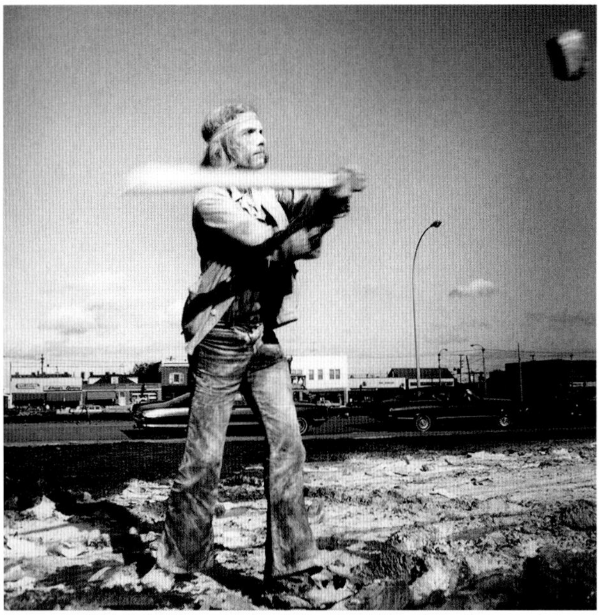

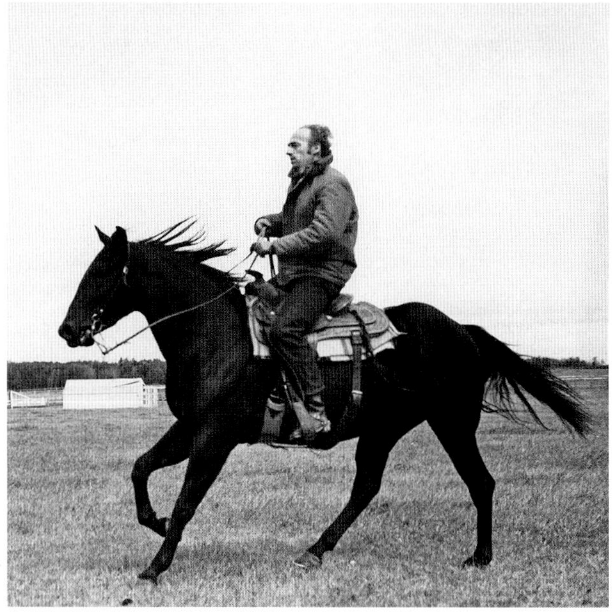

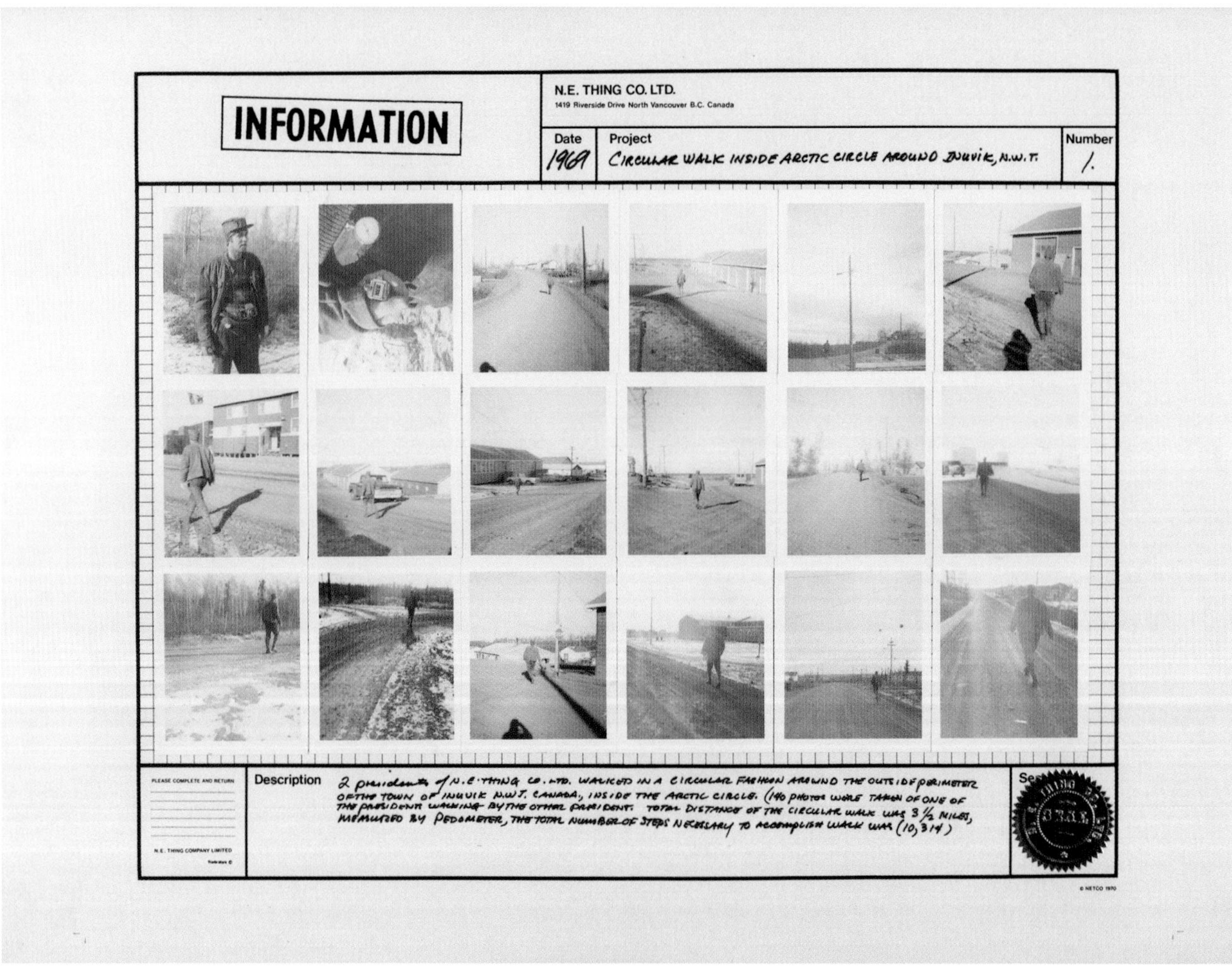

INFORMATION

N.E. THING CO. LTD.
1419 Riverside Drive North Vancouver B.C. Canada

Date	Project	Number
1969	CIRCULAR WALK INSIDE ARCTIC CIRCLE AROUND INUVIK, N.W.T.	1.

PLEASE COMPLETE AND RETURN

N.E. THING COMPANY LIMITED
Trade-mark ©

Description: 2 presidents of N.E. THING CO. LTD. WALKED IN A CIRCULAR FASHION AROUND THE OUTSIDE PERIMETER OF THE TOWN OF INUVIK N.W.T. CANADA, INSIDE THE ARCTIC CIRCLE. (140 PHOTOS WERE TAKEN OF ONE OF THE PRESIDENTS WALKING BY THE OTHER PRESIDENT. TOTAL DISTANCE OF THE CIRCULAR WALK WAS 3 1/2 MILES, MEASURED BY PEDOMETER, THE TOTAL NUMBER OF STEPS NECESSARY TO ACCOMPLISH WALK WAS (10,314)

Seal

© NETCO 1970

and place of discovery and report the information back to the EAG. When their original plan to exhibit a herd of sheep went awry, Vancouver's N.E. Thing Co. (Iain and Ingrid Baxter) produced alternative works such as the *Nothing Project (Nothing is impossible. Nothing is Something)*, which included a tree spray-painted green and a performance in the EAG theatre by Ingrid Baxter wearing an inflated dress. A unique exhibition of international conceptual art, *Place & Process* was the first project of its kind to be presented in a Canadian museum.[1]

Immediately following the opening of *Place & Process*, American artist Lawrence Weiner, art critic Lucy Lippard, Edmonton artist Harry Savage, arts writer Virgil Hammock, the Baxters and Kirby flew from Edmonton to the northern settlement of Inuvik. This Arctic trip was made under the auspices of the EAG as a complement to the *Place & Process* project. Over the following three days, the artists created works that engaged with the specific environs of the Arctic.

Weiner had conceived of his work, *AN ABRIDGEMENT OF AN ABUTMENT TO ON NEAR OR ABOUT THE ARCTIC CIRCLE*, prior to travelling to Inuvik. He executed an iteration of the work by taking an object immediately at hand, a cigarette package, and leaning it against a pile of dirt. The work was then donated to the EAG. Weiner created a second work, titled *A natural water course diverted reduced or displaced,* by creating two channels (one curved and one straight) to divert the course of a river. He also produced a work specifically for Lippard, *The Arctic Circle Shattered*, by marking a rock with shots from a .22-calibre rifle.

On arriving in Inuvik, N.E. Thing Co. began a walk piece that would encircle the town. Wearing a pedometer, the artists counted 314 miles or 10,314 steps. On discovering in a Rand McNally star chart that the constellation Sculptor had a similar structure to the map of Inuvik's few miles of road, the Baxters marked a section of road with round mirrors to approximate the position of the constellation's stars. Expanding this attempt to delineate the sky, N.E. Thing Co., in collaboration with artists in Halifax and Vancouver, drew invisible but convergent lines in the sky in the shape of a triangle formed from the projected viewpoints of the three participants all looking north. The Baxters also executed *This statement will be is being has been sent from inside to outside the Arctic Circle*, in which a message was transmitted by ham radio from the Arctic Circle to the Antarctic. For a third work, they placed a large black and white sign reading "You Are Now in the Middle of an N.E. Thing Co. Landscape" in the midst of the tundra, continuing their practice of "aesthetic claiming" as seen in their earlier *ACT (Aesthetically Claimed Thing)* works.

Savage, known for his pop-inspired and politically satirical print works, filled a 20-foot length

[1] Coincident with *Place & Process* was the exhibition *AIR ART* (4–8 September 1969) inside the EAG. *AIR ART* featured inflatable, intangible works by the Architectural Association Group, Hans Haacke, Akira Kanayama, Les Levine, Preston McClanahan, David Medalla, Robert Morris, Marcello Salvadori, Graham Stevens, John Van Saun and Andy Warhol. Organized by Willoughby Sharp, *AIR ART* travelled to venues across the United States, with the EAG its only Canadian venue.

Opposite, clockwise from top left
John Van Saun, *Flour Drop*, 1969

Robert Morris, *Pace and Process*, 1969
© Robert Morris / SODRAC (2012)

N.E. Thing Co., *Circular Walk Inside Arctic Circle Around Inuvik, N.W.T.*, 1969. Photo: Howard Ursuliak, Belkin Art Gallery

of clear plastic hot-dog casings with water and set them outside to freeze. The remaining sausage casings were later given to a group of local children, who inflated and flew them in the wind. Savage would produce two other works on the trip: *Exposed Light Silhouette,* in which the artist lay on a sheet of light-sensitive paper to create a temporary silhouette, and an installation of fifty bright red flares that were lit, dispersed over a large area and left to illuminate the night until they burned out.

Response to *Place & Process* was enthusiastic, at least in some quarters. In an article published in the *Edmonton Journal*, Hammock wrote, "This exhibition is not only a first for Edmonton but a first for Canada. Because of our gallery's daring, Edmonton is becoming known throughout Canada as a centre for Avant Garde art exhibitions."[2] This perception was bolstered by the inclusion of Sharp's article on the exhibition in the November 1969 issue of *Artforum*.[3]

Following on *Place & Process,* the EAG hosted Bill Vazan's *Tape Across Canada* in January 1970 and the solo exhibition *Les Levine Graphics: Conceptual/Decorative* in February 1972.[4] Despite these early and historically important institutional engagements with American and Canadian conceptual art, Edmonton never generated its own practitioners and the *Place & Process* exhibition had little, if any, lasting impact on the local community. Following the departure of Bill Kirby in July 1971, the EAG realigned its exhibition mandate to champion abstract painting and sculpture produced by American and western Canadian artists working within the tenets of Greenbergian Modernism—a direction reinforced by new faculty hires at the University of Alberta in 1971 and 1972.

Calgary

At this same time, Calgary participated in the emergence of the new radical, anti-establishment mentality shared by a generation of young people across North America. In 1971, the University of Calgary and the Alberta College of Art initiated a series of faculty hires that were instrumental in bringing young American and British artists to the city, artists who embraced the idea of the counterculture and the notion of the alternative or off-centre. These artists included Paul Woodrow (who had worked with N.E. Thing Co. in Vancouver), Jeff Funnell (who would later move to Winnipeg) and Don Mabie (who shifted his correspondence/mail art practice from Toronto to Calgary in 1972). Of equal significance was the arrival of Clive Robertson to the city in late 1971.

The work produced by these artists during the 1970s may not be seen to be conceptual art in its strictest sense; their activities were a confluence of Fluxus-influenced happenings and

Opposite, from top
Brian Dyson, *I will not make any more art (after John Baldessari, 1971)*, 1977

Jeff Funnell, *Sistine Tons*, 1980

[2] Virgil G. Hammock, "One needs a full stomach to be honest about art," *Edmonton Journal*, 5 September 1969.

[3] Willoughby Sharp, "Place & Process," *Artforum* VIII, no. 3 (November 1969): 46–49.

[4] A solo exhibition of N.E. Thing Co. was also held at the University of Alberta Fine Arts Building Gallery in Edmonton, 15 January–10 February 1971.

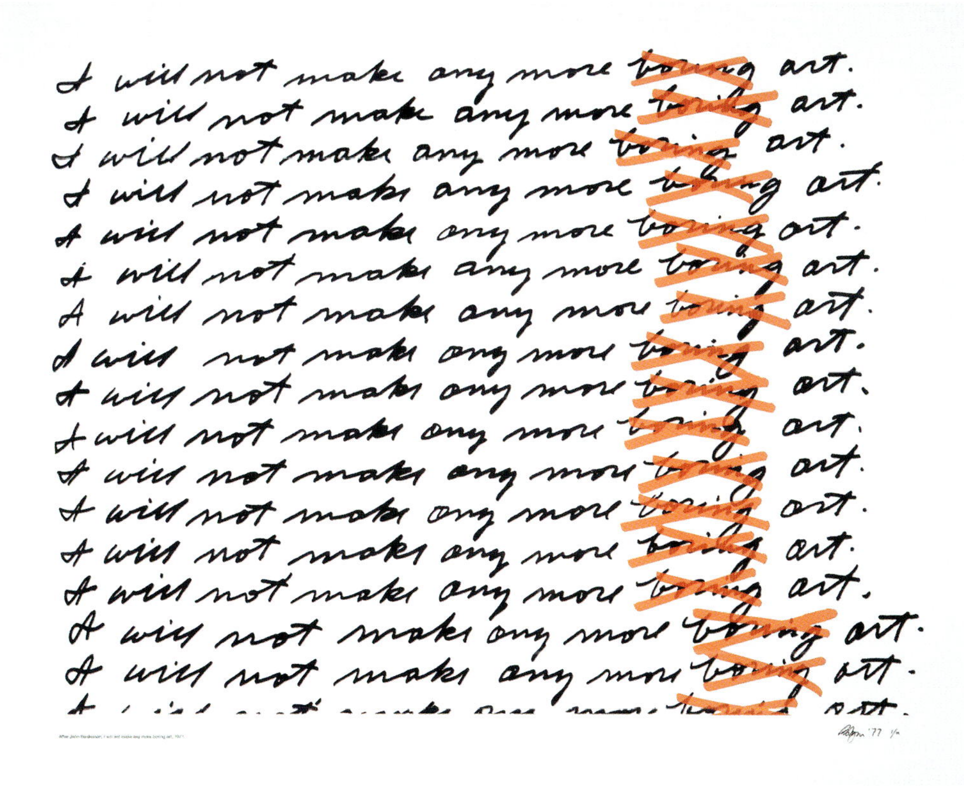
I will not make any more boring art.
I will not make any more boring art.
I will not make any more boring art.
I will not make any more boring art.
I will not make any more boring art.
I will not make any more boring art.
I will not make any more boring art.
I will not make any more boring art.
I will not make any more boring art.
I will not make any more boring art.
I will not make any more boring art.
I will not make any more boring art.
I will not make any more boring art.
I will not make any more boring art.
I will not make any more boring art.
I will not make any more boring art.

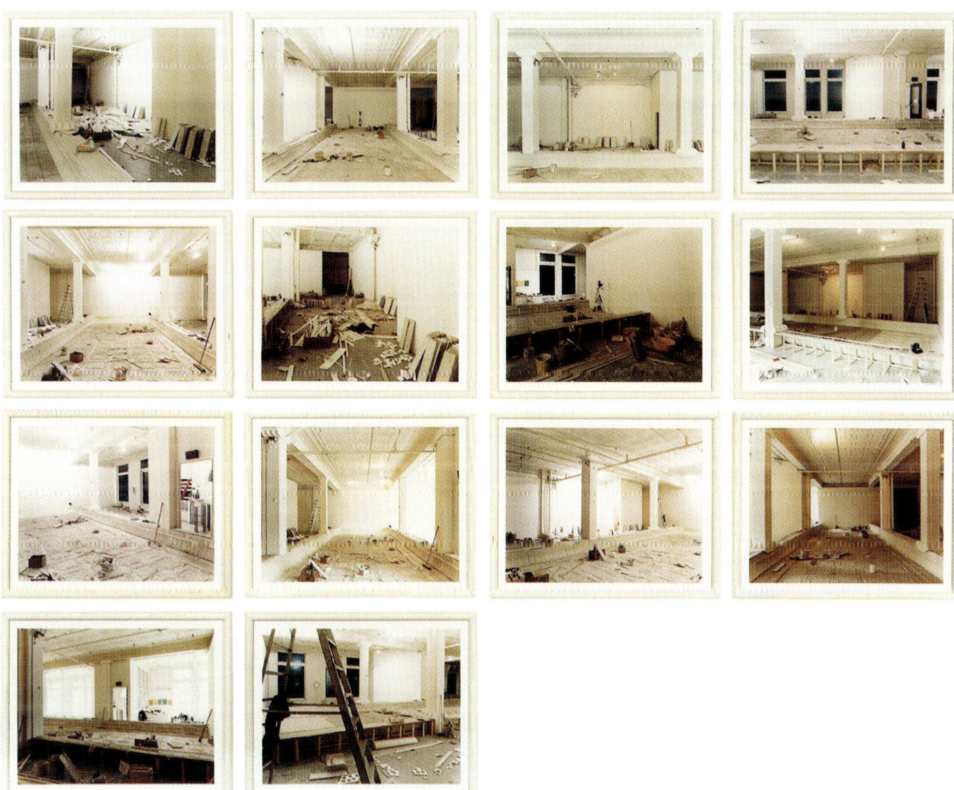

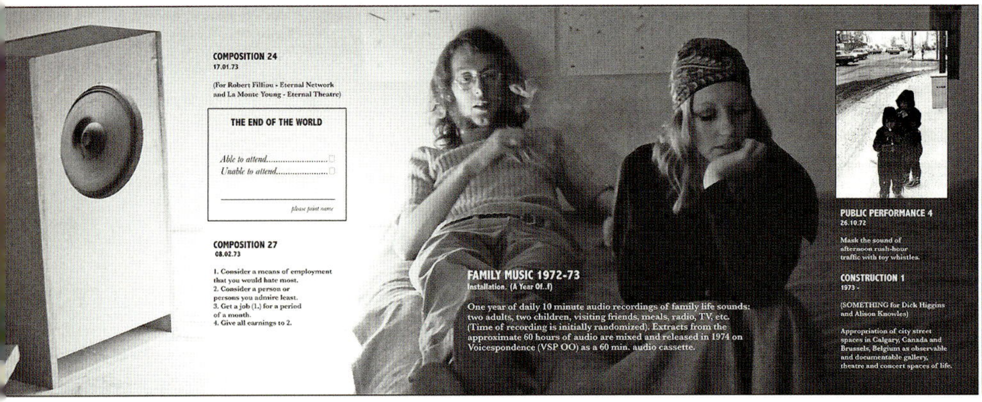

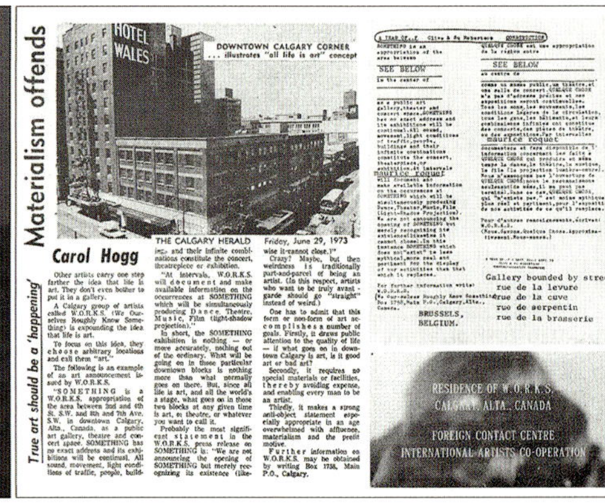

experiments in new media and interdisciplinarity that, in a conceptualist vein, emphasized process over product and examined the interstitial space between art and daily life. In June 1972 and again in December 1973, Robertson and Woodrow organized the *World Festival of W.O.R.K.S.* (an acronym for "we ourselves roughly know something"). Initiated through an open invitation for projects that was distributed worldwide, and including projects performed in Calgary by the *W.O.R.K.S.* artists and other willing participants, the *World Festival of W.O.R.K.S.* presented early experiments with non-object, instruction-based performance actions.

The *w.o.r.k.s.c.o.r.e.p.o.r.t.*, which documented many of the *W.O.R.K.S.* activities, was part of a series of books edited by David Mayor and Felipe Ehrenberg and published by Beau Geste Press (Cullompton, England) from 1971 to 1974. The series focused on an international selection of artists and artists' groups who circulated process artworks grounded in the idea of exchange, and included separate volumes on individual and/or group activities from Iceland, France, Germany, Czechoslovakia, Japan and Canada.

Throughout the 1970s, networking and distribution were an imperative for artists working in Calgary. These strategies articulated the desire to overcome a sense of geographic and cultural isolation by engaging with artists in other parts of the world through exchanges, residencies and collaborative and/or coincident projects. The *W.O.R.K.S.* 1973 project, *A Conceptographic Reading of Our World Thermometer,* for instance, was an international artist-produced television series composed of six one-hour videotapes derived from internationally circulated calls to participate. Artists submitted instructions for episodes that were performed in Calgary by the *W.O.R.K.S.* group. Conceived and coordinated by Robertson for broadcast as *W.O.R.K.S.* Cable TV, the programs appeared on Community Antenna TV in Calgary, providing an opportunity for artists to both produce and disseminate content within a mass media format.

Calgary artists were focused on embodying and manipulating mass communication systems, using television, radio and magazine platforms to reach a wider audience. In 1972 came the founding of Radio Cora, an independent, artist-fueled radio program operated through cable

Top, from left
Clive Robertson, *Family Music*, 1972–73

Clive Robertson, *Identity Transfer*, 1972–78

[5] Ron Moppett took on the persona of Vincent van Gogh in a series of works produced in the mid-1970s.

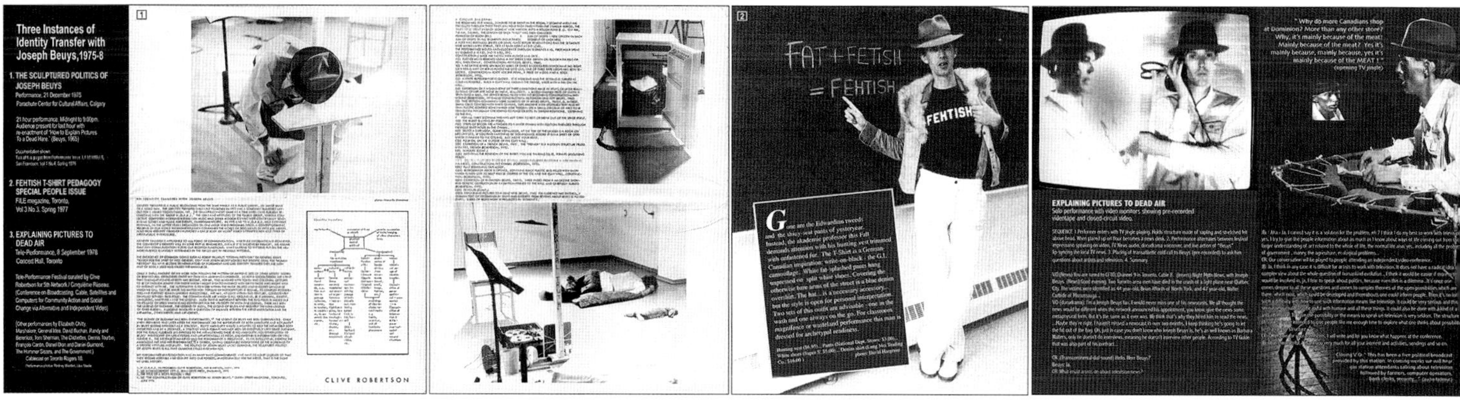

and broadcast radio and featuring live performances, interviews with artists, alternative music and an artists' open forum. In 1974, Clive Robertson founded *Voicepondence*, an audio magazine distributed on cassette tape. The first issue featured his work *Family Music*, which compressed 365 days of the daily sound of Robertson's domestic environment, which included a partner and two young children, into a sixty-minute cassette. *Family Music* was one result of Robertson's year-long project, *A Year of..f*, which focused on an extended series of events and collaborations as a way to connect with artists working in other parts of the world. A major component of Robertson's work at this time was his concept of "identity transfer"—inhabiting other people's daily lives and work—which was manifest in performances in Calgary, Montréal, Hastings (England) and Amsterdam. These performances culminated in 1975 in a composite remake of Joseph Beuys' actions and sculptures, entitled *The Sculptured Politics of Joseph Beuys*.

The concept of inhabiting the work of others or adopting another artistic persona was perhaps most apparent in the work produced by Brian Dyson in the late 1970s. After working briefly with N.E. Thing Co. in Vancouver, Dyson arrived in Calgary in 1974 to take a position as assistant curator at the Alberta College of Art Gallery, where fellow artist Ron Moppett was curator.[5] Throughout the 1970s, Dyson's work was focused on the idea of the "remade ready-made," in which he extended Marcel Duchamp's conception of the ready-made by reproducing and manipulating an existing artwork. For example, Dyson's *I will not make any more art (after John Baldessari, 1971)* (1977) was a remake of Baldessari's famous print, *I Will Not Make Any More Boring Art*, originally produced in the Nova Scotia College of Art and Design (NSCAD) Lithography Workshop in 1971.[6]

Many of the W.O.R.K.S. activities were produced by Robertson in collaboration with Woodrow, who came to Calgary to teach at the University of Calgary in 1972. Woodrow, a fellow British artist, had recently completed studies at Sir George Williams University in Montréal and worked as information officer for N.E. Thing Co. in the early 1970s.[7] In addition to his collaborative work, Woodrow produced independent works in a variety of media. From February 3 to 16, 1977, Woodrow set up the office of the *Bureau of Imaginary Exchange* in the Alberta College of Art Gallery. As described in the exhibition catalogue, the project was "a para-bureaucratic

[6] The Baldessari print was made as a response to an invitation to create an exhibition at NSCAD's Mezzanine. Baldessari requested that students be invited to write the words "I will not make any more boring art" repeatedly on the gallery wall. The handwritten example for the text that Baldessari mailed to the gallery was used as the image for the lithograph.

[7] In 1971, working in Montréal, Woodrow produced a number of single-channel video works such as *Triple Roll Out*, *Cover-Up* and *Character Generator*, at times in collaboration with Harold Pearse.

- 2 -

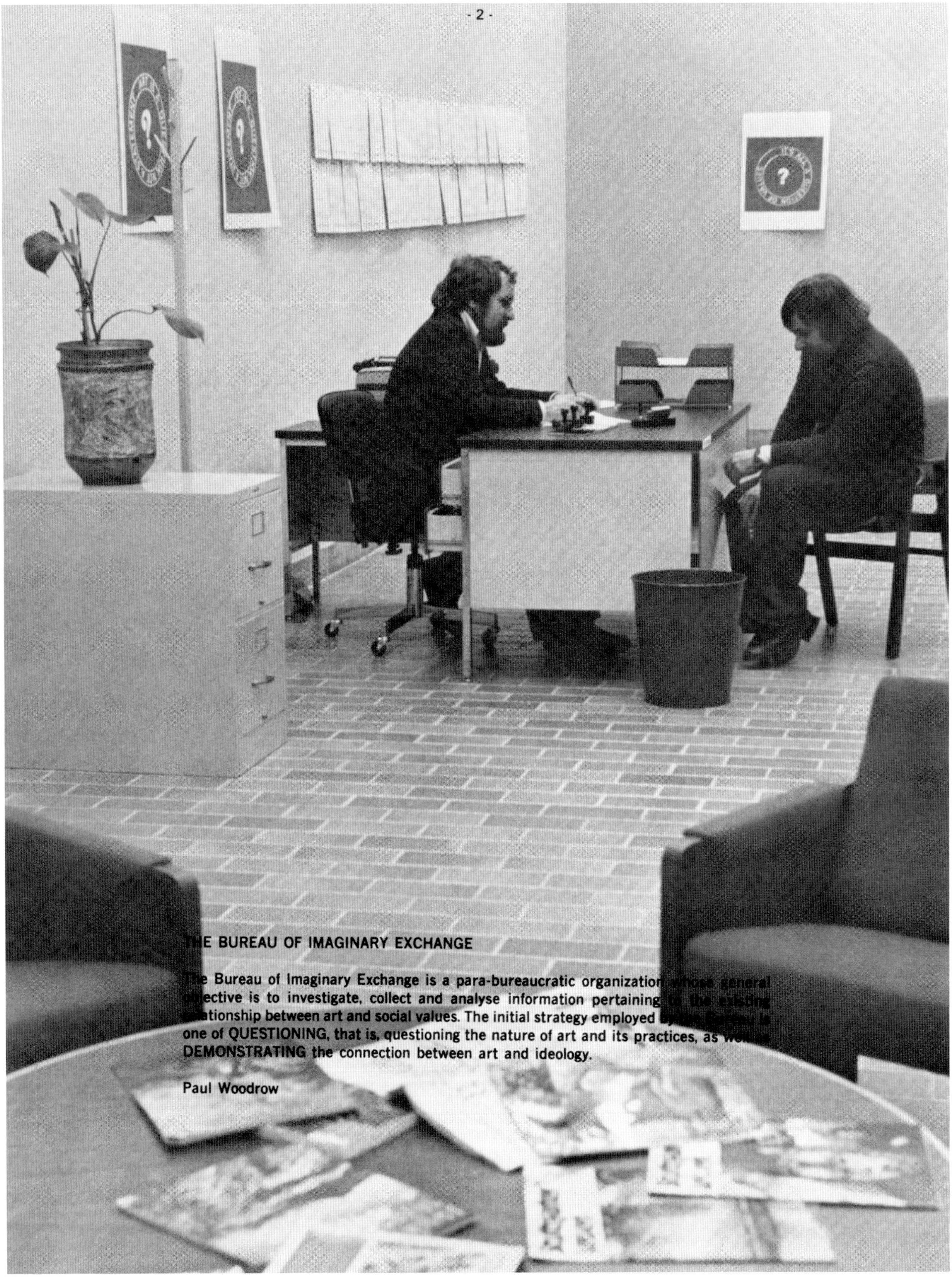

THE BUREAU OF IMAGINARY EXCHANGE

The Bureau of Imaginary Exchange is a para-bureaucratic organization whose general objective is to investigate, collect and analyse information pertaining to the existing relationship between art and social values. The initial strategy employed by the Bureau is one of QUESTIONING, that is, questioning the nature of art and its practices, as well as DEMONSTRATING the connection between art and ideology.

Paul Woodrow

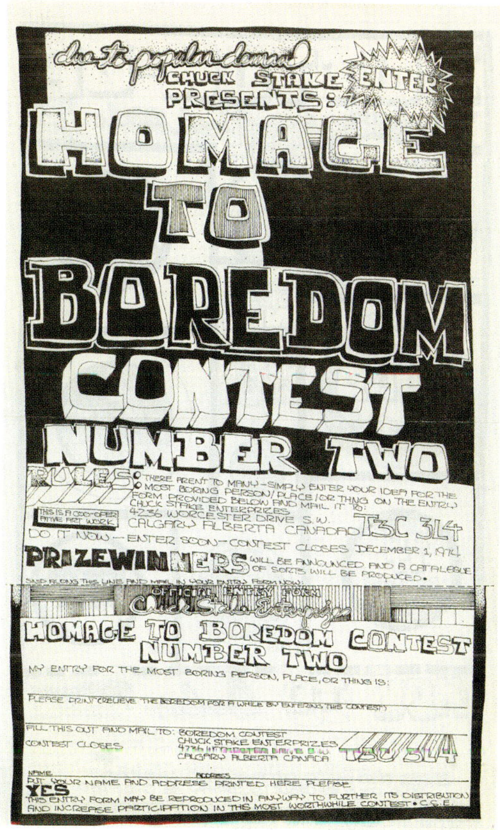

Don Mabie, Chuck Stake Enterprizes mailer for *Homage to Boredom Contest Number Two*, 1974

organization whose general objective is to investigate, collect and analyse information pertaining to the existing relationship between art and social values." Participants filled out questionnaires about the idea of value in relation to colour, art and social services. Another work, *Imaginair Travel*, was based on the concept of a fictive travel agency in which customers would create their own dream travel adventure as an act of imagination.

Calgary artist Don Mabie produced performance art and photocopy works, but was primarily known for his correspondence/mail art during this time. Mabie lived in Toronto from 1970 to 1974, where he organized the *First Annual Correspondence and Junk Mail Exhibition* and founded Chuck Stake Enterprizes. He returned to Calgary in 1972, where he co-founded the Clouds 'n' Water Gallery. Mabie's practice emphasizes both the use of language and text as its primary visual structure and the mass dissemination of ideas through the postal network, demonstrating the connection between correspondence art and conceptual art. The works included in *Traffic* consist of original drawings (created with pen and ink, pencil and collage) that were then, most pertinently, offset printed and mailed internationally.

The common characteristic linking Robertson's, Woodrow's and Mabie's practices was the

Opposite
Paul Woodrow, *Bureau of Imaginary Exchange*, 1976

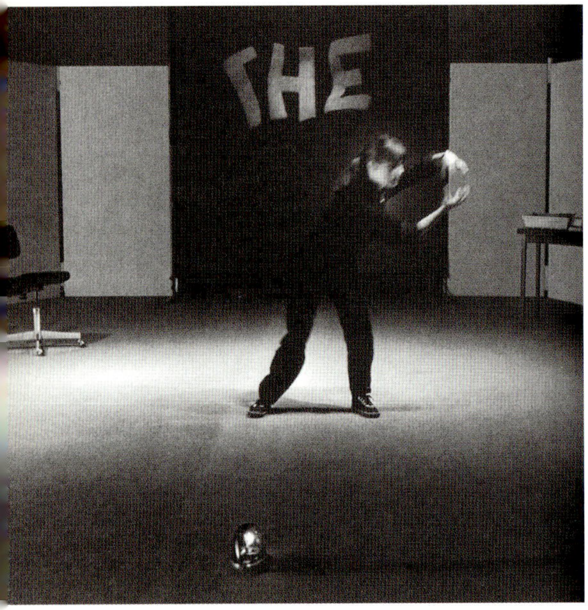

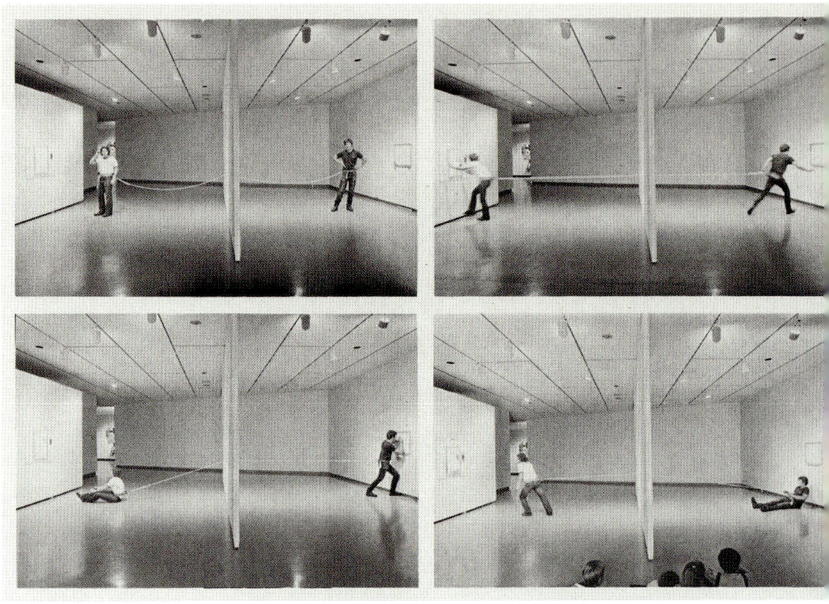

engagement with national and international artists' exchange networks to connect the relatively isolated Calgary art community to the larger world. Their use and manipulation of existing communication systems—radio, community television and the postal service—was complemented by the development of a series of visiting artist projects initiated through Calgary art institutions in the mid to late 1970s.

Marcella Bienvenue was another important Calgary-based artist during the 1970s. She worked primarily as a performance artist, and although her works went largely undocumented, some, such as *I Believe in Myself* from 1978 and later works from the 1980s, were recorded on video.

In 1975, Robertson, Woodrow, Mabie and Bienvenue founded the Parachute Center for Cultural Affairs as an intermedia facility that administered an artist-in-residence program, a national video festival and the publication of *Centerfold,* a magazine edited by Robertson and Bienvenue that was published from 1976 to 1979.

In 1977, the Parachute Center was renamed Arton's. As with General Idea's play on the title of *LIFE* magazine in their journal *FILE,* Arton's referenced the giant of Canadian corporate identities, Eaton's. Similar parodic enactments of corporate culture can be seen in Dyson's SPacific company and Mabie's pseudonym, Chuck Stake Enterprizes. With a new space for performances, exhibitions and events, Arton's expanded its artist-in-residence program, bringing artists such as General Idea, Margaret Dragu and Anna Banana to Calgary.[8] Moppett and Dyson, working at the Alberta College of Art Gallery (later the Illingworth Kerr

Above, from left
Marcella Bienvenue, *I Believe in Myself*, 1979

Max Dean, *Drawing Event*, Winnipeg Art Gallery, 1977

[8] As in other parts of the country, this move toward artist-run culture was also apparent in Edmonton. In 1973, artists Harry Savage (who was part of the *Place & Process* Arctic trip) and Sylvain Voyer established Latitude 53 out of concern that the EAG offered little support for local artists. Painting and sculpture remained the primary focus of Latitude's visual arts programming in the 1970s. In 1981, however, Don Mabie/Chuck Stake Enterprizes organized Edmonton's first correspondence art exhibition.

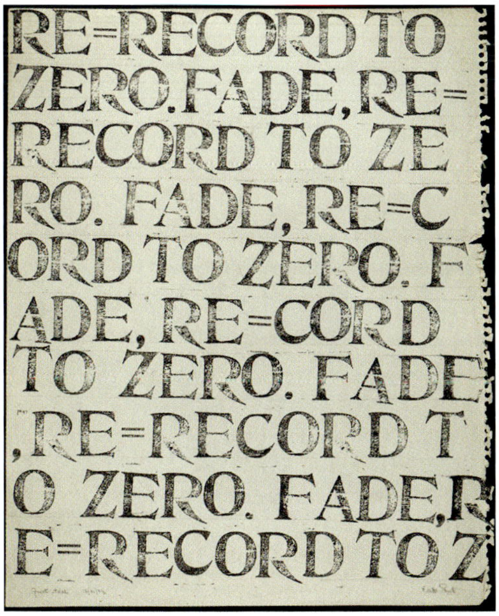

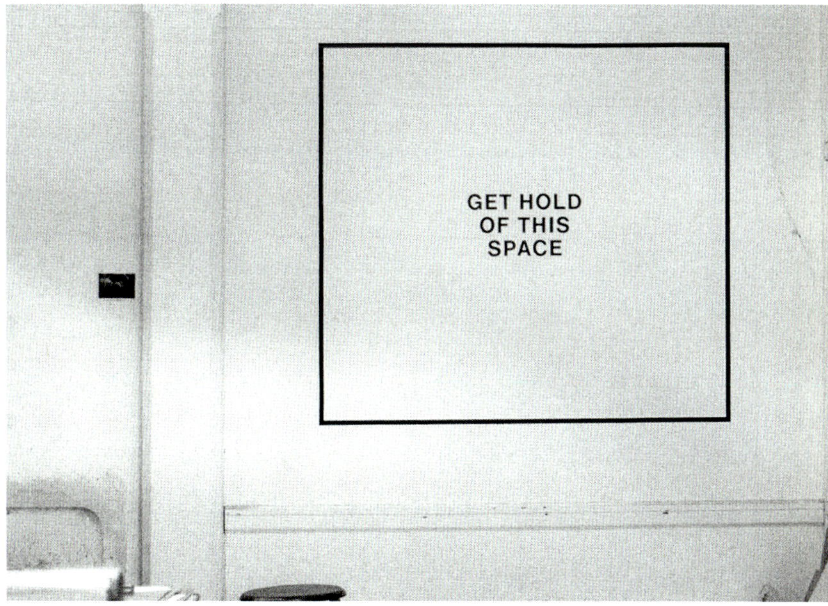

Gallery), also made significant contributions to building an international network for the city by featuring visiting artists such as Chris Burden and Robert Filliou. Burden's performance *Do You Believe in Television*, produced at the Alberta College of Art on 18 February 1976, became an iconic moment for Calgary's art community, reinforcing the idea that the city could both host and present the work of senior international artists. The gallery's visiting artists program was augmented in 1978 by the arrival of Jeffrey Spalding and Peter White at the Glenbow Museum, where they organized the series *Issues in Contemporary Art* and *Presentations in the Arts* from 1978 to 1981. Like Robertson and Woodrow, Spalding understood the importance of inviting international artists, performers, musicians, art historians, critics and curators to Calgary. Participants in these programs included Laurie Anderson, Benjamin Buchloh, Philip Glass, Meredith Monk, Linda Nochlin, Robert Pincus-Witten, Yvonne Rainer, Robert Rosenblum, Leo Steinberg, Marcia Tucker and William Wegman.

Winnipeg

In Winnipeg, conceptual art grew from a distinctive mix of local art histories and the influence of international art movements such as Minimalism, Situationism and Fluxus. Given Winnipeg's geographical isolation within Canada and the absence of an overriding regional economic or ideological imperative, a heterogeneous and dynamic community constituted the art scene. New groups and organizations formed around interests in emerging media, experimentation and exchange. Winnipeg could be seen as a crossroads that allowed artists investigating the possibilities of Conceptualism (including Max Dean, Aganetha Dyck, Jeff Funnell, Milly

Above, from left

Kenneth Coutts-Smith, *Artext (RE=RECORD TO . . .)*, 1974. Photo: Michael Barrick, Belkin Art Gallery

Gordon Lebredt, *Get Hold of This Space*, 1974

Giesbrecht, Gordon Lebredt and Alex Poruchnyk) to take risks with supportive institutions and audiences.

Under the directorship of Suzanne Gillies and Doug Sigurdson, Plug In supported experimental and process-based approaches to art and art making. Curiously, many of the "conceptual" works at Plug In employed decidedly elemental building materials: concrete, lumber, drywall, glass, rebar and plaster. For his 1977 exhibition *Loci*, Lebredt erected two opposing 12- × 1-foot mirror templates and a metal mesh screen, creating a *mise en abyme* reflective of the gallery's architecture. Poruchnyk had himself enclosed in a large concrete block for his 1978 *Work in Process (The Cube)*, and then spent twelve hours smashing it to bits in order to escape. Funnell covered the floor of the gallery in plaster panels cast from the tin ceiling tiles for *Sistine Tons* (1980) and Rita McKeough (then living in Winnipeg) filled the gallery with a "town" of shingled houses and almost 1,000 square feet of concrete sidewalks for her exhibition *Sidestreet* in 1980. Plug In was also the site of numerous sound, video and performance pieces, including Linda Tooley and Reid Dickie's *Mechanical Bliss* (1980) and Jon Tupper's *Fall* (1980).

Painter, writer, curator and thinker Kenneth Coutts-Smith, who had moved to Canada in 1970 to teach art history at the University of Calgary and was a contributor to *Centerfold* in its early years, relocated to Winnipeg in 1974 to become director of the University of Manitoba's Gallery One One One (founded in 1965), a position he held for much of the late 1970s. In addition to his important critical texts and writings, Coutts-Smith produced film and video works, mail art and text-based paintings, notably the *Artexts* series shown at the Anna Leonowens Gallery at NSCAD in Halifax in 1980. His work as director at Gallery One One One and the programming of the WAG (which had moved into an expansive new building in 1971) played key roles in expanding the aesthetic, social and political discourses of conceptual art through exhibitions featuring artists' books and multiples, image/text works, installations and performances by local, national and international artists.

The arrival of new WAG curators Millie McKibbon and Bill Kirby in the 1970s was critical to the growth of conceptual art in the city. Kirby's receptivity to works by Dean, Lebredt and other conceptual artists (including Americans Dan Graham and Sol LeWitt) and McKibbon's inclusion of both Dean and Lebredt in the exhibition *Form & Performance* sent clear signals that conceptual art was no longer to be confined to alternative spaces or relegated to the borders of curatorial practice. Also of note is the University of Manitoba's visiting artist program from 1977 to 1980, in which Funnell brought to Winnipeg artists such as Lynda Benglis, Robert Irwin, Joseph Kosuth and Robert Morris, as well as art critic Lucy Lippard.

Key WAG exhibitions and publications such as *Artists' Prints and Multiples* (1977) and *Form & Performance* (1978) took up issues of authorial and institutional critique, presenting works that balanced aesthetics of negation with language play and performativity. In 1977, Dean performed *Drawing Event*, in which he and Dennis Evans, bound by a length of rope, dragged each other back and forth as they each tried to execute a wall drawing. Dean also created a number of important works, including performance pieces, for the exhibition *Sculpture on the*

---

[9] Additional links between NSCAD and Alberta occurred in the southern city of Lethbridge when Allan Harding MacKay (former director of the Anna Leonowens Gallery) was appointed as the first director of the newly founded Southern Alberta Art Gallery in 1975. At the same time, artist and faculty member Billy McCarroll, in the position of director/curator of the University of Lethbridge Art Gallery, brought the work of NSCAD artists Garry Neill Kennedy and Gerald Ferguson, as well as N.E. Thing Co., to the city.

Prairies (1977), curated by Bill Kirby. The following year, Lebredt installed Fence, a 14- × 70-foot chain-link barrier that ran through the main exhibition space for *The Winnipeg Perspective*.

Afterword

By the late 1970s in Calgary, graduates of NSCAD, including Jeff Spalding and later Mary Scott and Rita McKeough, took up curatorial and teaching positions, bringing with them conceptually driven strategies and defining the Calgary art community in opposition to the scene in Edmonton, where high Modernism had become the dominant idiom. [9] In 1978, Arton's moved from Calgary to Toronto. A number of prominent figures in Winnipeg's conceptual art scene also relocated to other centres. Max Dean left for Ottawa in 1979 and Gordon Lebredt moved to Toronto in the early '80s; also in 1979, Bill Kirby left to become the Canada Council's visual arts officer in Ottawa and Kenneth Coutts-Smith departed for Halifax and Toronto. Nonetheless, the approaches to art making associated with the emergence of conceptual art in central Canada—with their emphasis on process over the object and the interest in connecting with the broader world of contemporary art—continued to shape and inform artwork seen and produced in the region up to the present day.

Reference/Cross Reference: Conceptual Art on the West Coast

Grant Arnold

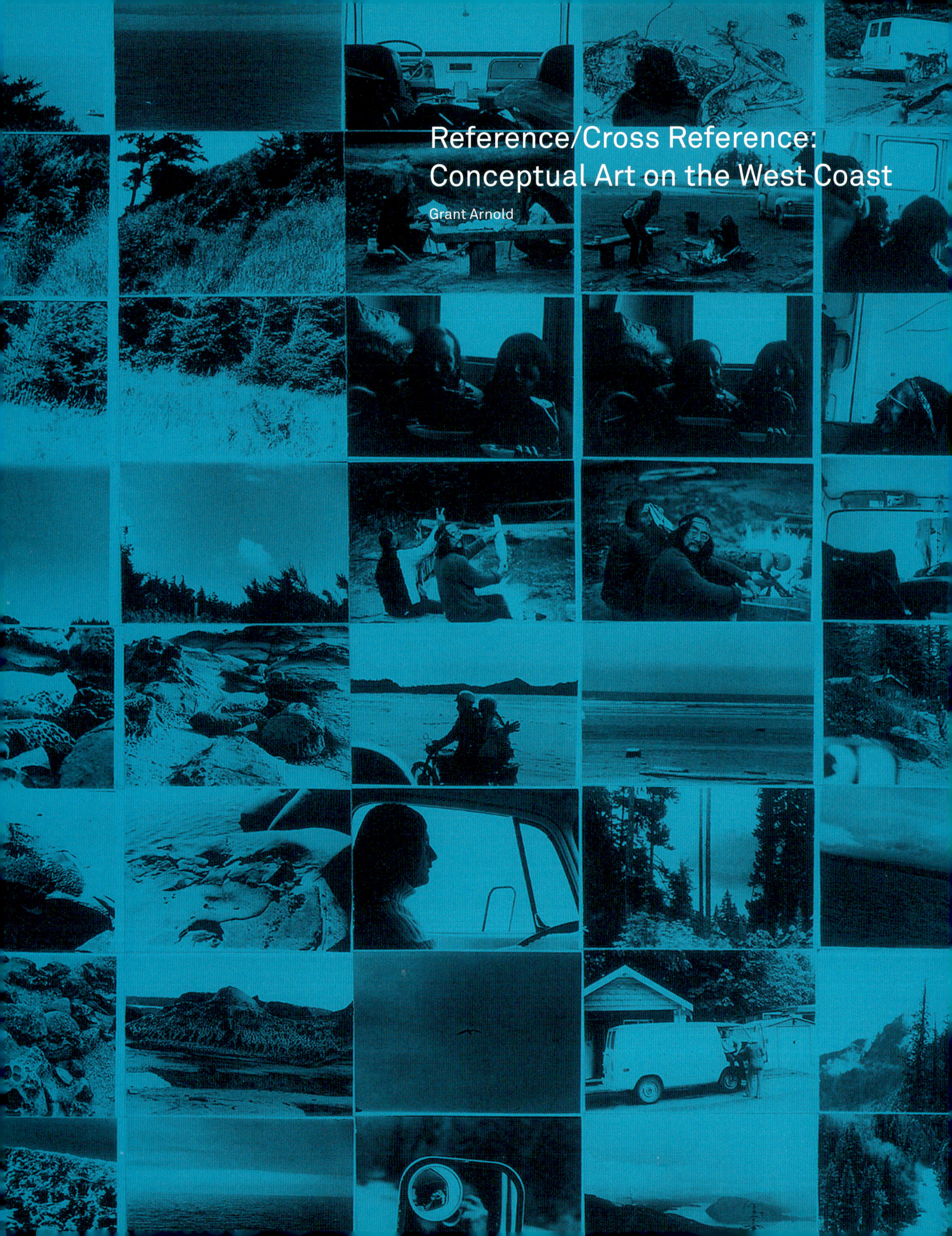

Ideas that are rapidly transmissible and photographic cross-references and information about objects or sites are more stimulating to the isolated artist than the reproductions of objects that are fundamentally un-reproducible, objects intended primarily as physical presences.[1]

In the spring of 1967 Philip Leider, then editor of *Artforum*, travelled to the Canadian west coast to examine the state of Vancouver's art scene. The trip was in response to an invitation extended by Alvin Balkind, curator/director of the University of British Columbia's Fine Arts Gallery, who was interested in developing dialogues with critics, curators and artists from outside the country. Leider was one of several prominent Americans who travelled to Vancouver in 1967; his time in the city was bracketed by visits from John Coplans, Walter Hopps, Kurt von Meier, and Maurice Tuchman. Leider's report, which appeared in the June 1967 issue of *artscanada*, presented a paradoxical situation. Although he identified a number of Vancouver-based artists who were "talented" and "energetic," his impression was that Vancouver had "virtually no [art] scene at all."[2] Most of the components associated with a vital artistic milieu—serious collectors, commercial galleries that presented advanced contemporary art and critics who could extend the level of dialogue—were conspicuously absent from the city. Rather than a full-fledged art scene, the Vancouver situation consisted of a small set of "forward-looking individuals"[3]—artists and curators who acted as conduits between Vancouver and the outside world. While Leider asserted that the prevailing attitudes among artists in Vancouver—their openness and interest in dialogue with contemporary work from the United States and Europe—were strikingly similar to those of many Los Angeles–based artists, he argued that the circumstances that confronted Vancouver-based artists were considerably more difficult than those in the larger American city.

Much of Leider's report consisted of an analysis of what it meant to make art outside of the major cultural capitals of the world (for Leider, any North American city other than New York). According to Leider, artists working in such a situation had three positions to choose from. The first was to pursue an idiosyncratic mode of art making that abandoned any relationship with the advanced work of the time, an approach that, in Leider's judgment, is usually "disastrous." The second was to develop a deliberately regional idiom, a mode of working that "consciously seeks to draw its strength from the surroundings, arts and traditions" of a specific geographic area. Such movements, Leider held, relate only obliquely to the main thrust of modern art, but often result "in works of considerable strength and beauty."[4] He cited Jack Shadbolt and Gordon Smith as examples of Vancouver artists who had successfully taken up this position.

The third possibility, and the one clearly favoured by Leider, was to develop an art that is "international in character, which is capable of being absorbed into the mainstream of

[1] Lucy R. Lippard, "Iain Baxter: New spaces," *artscanada* XXVI, no. 3 (June 1969): 6.

[2] Philip Leider, "Vancouver: Scene with no scene," *artscanada* XXIV no. 6/7, issue 109/110 (June/July 1967): 4.

[3] Ibid.

[4] Ibid.

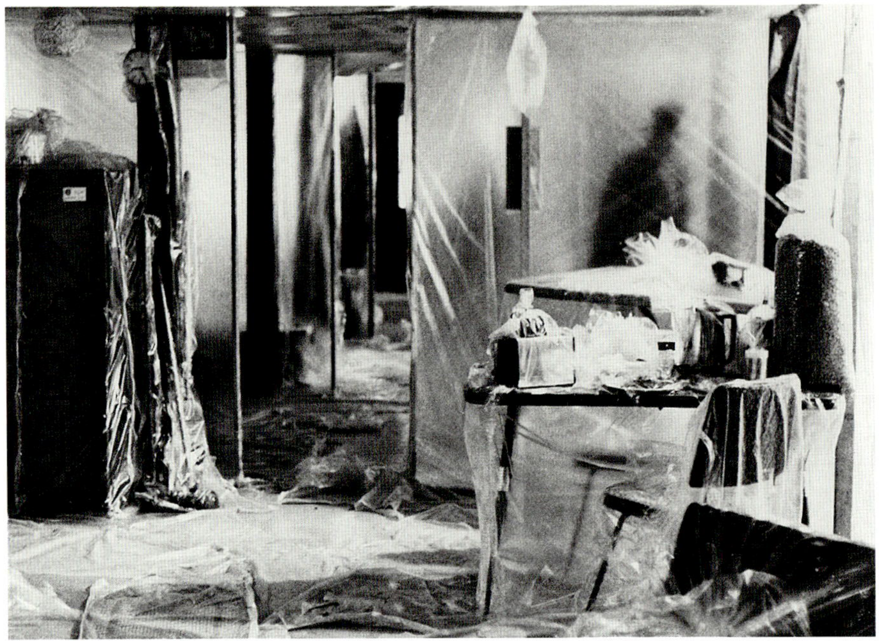

contemporary painting and sculpture."[5] Larry Bell, Robert Irwin and Ed Ruscha were among the artists cited as exemplars of this approach. For Leider, one of the basic difficulties confronted by artists who pursued this option was that "the very artifacts which make up a tradition are accessible only in the treacherously imperfect form of reproduction."[6] Rightly or wrongly, he linked what he identified as the principal deficiency in the work of ambitious Vancouver painters—their uncertainty in approach to surface—to the fact that they had experienced a great deal of modern and contemporary art only through reproductions, which cannot convey the character of an artwork's surface. Although he didn't state it explicitly, and despite his emphasis on painting and sculpture, Leider implied that the Vancouver artist who had most successfully taken up this third approach was Iain Baxter. An English-born Canadian, Baxter, together with his wife Ingrid, had arrived in Vancouver two and a half years earlier after studying Zen Buddhism in Japan and completing an MFA at Washington State University. Tellingly, Baxter had abandoned painting in the early 1960s. Driven in part by an interest in Marshall McLuhan's investigations into the way media shapes the transmission of information, he had begun to work with photography, vacuum-formed plastics and other materials and motifs associated with consumerism. Baxter's mode of working embraced reproduction as a pervasive aspect of contemporary culture, thereby sidestepping the problem of first-hand experience versus knowledge obtained through images in books and journals.

Leider was particularly enthusiastic about Bagged Place—a project that has been cited as the first major environment constructed and exhibited in Canada[7]—which Baxter had mounted a year prior to Leider's arrival in Vancouver. Bagged Place reconstituted a four-room furnished apartment within the UBC Fine Arts Gallery, in which every element—walls, furniture,

Above
Installation view of Iain Baxter, *Bagged Place*, UBC Fine Arts Gallery, 1966

[5] Leider, "Vancouver," 5.

[6] Leider, "Vancouver," 4.

[7] Marie Fleming, "Baxter and N.E. Thing Co. 1965–70." In *Baxter2: Any Choice Works* (Toronto: Art Gallery of Ontario, 1982), 24.

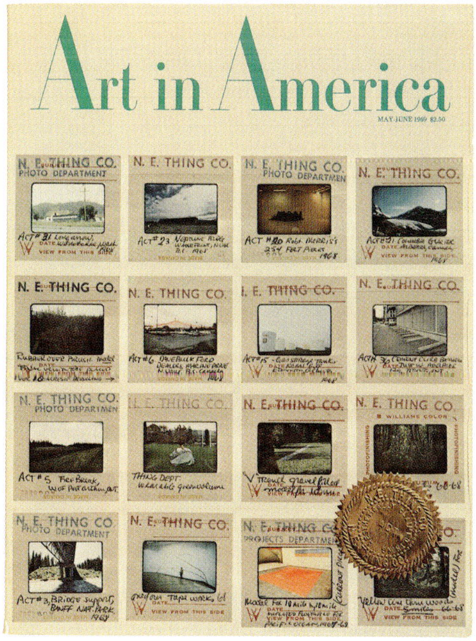

mops, clocks and pictures—was carefully bagged in clear plastic. The exhibition invitation deliberately parodied real estate advertising, informing each recipient that *Bagged Place* was for rent.[8]

It would be simplistic to draw a direct line from Leider's analysis of Vancouver's remoteness to the various forms of conceptually based work subsequently produced in the region. The development of these modes of activity on the West Coast did not have a single point of origin or follow a clearly defined path, but rather emerged from a complex and multi-faceted milieu that contained very different and sometimes antagonistic aesthetic programs. Nonetheless, Leider's text reflects an unavoidable situation to which West Coast artists had to respond if they were to elude a provincial condition and participate in the art world's most current developments and debates, a situation in which the production of traditional objects such as painting and sculpture seemed to be diminished in viability, and work that could be easily transported, transmitted and/or realized as documentation held out greater possibilities. The apparent ascendance of this approach would have been bolstered by the appearance of work by the Baxters' N.E. Thing Co. (NETCO) on the cover of the May–June 1969 issue of *Art in America*, the opening of NETCO's solo exhibition at the National Gallery of Canada that same year and the inclusion of Jeff Wall's *Landscape Manual* in *Information*, the Museum of Modern Art's 1970 exhibition of conceptual art, land art and arte povera.

Leider had arrived in Vancouver at a moment of transition in which the ground for radical transformations within the city's art community was being shaped. The annual Festival of the Contemporary Arts mounted at UBC beginning in 1961 provided a forum in which

[8] Leider also lamented the lack of attention the exhibition received due to Vancouver's geographic isolation. "What is tragic is that the exhibition of *Bagged Place* went, for all practical purposes, utterly unnoticed in the world of art . . . not a single publication reviewed it, nor has a single reproduction of it been seen, except those which accompany this article." See Leider, "Vancouver," 6.

Above
Art in America, cover of May–June 1969 issue with images by N.E. Thing Co.

interdisciplinary links between art, dance and literature were developed and McLuhanesque notions of communication were discussed.[9] The staging of the festival coincided with the emergence of 1960s counter-cultures, which resonated with particular intensity in Vancouver. The anarchic character of this environment spurred attitudes in which tradition was to be challenged and the culture of the commodity overturned. These sensibilities were widely embraced by the city's art community, which was sufficiently isolated and small enough to sustain an impulse toward total reinvention, a process in which Roy Kiyooka abandoned his career as a successful and accomplished abstract painter and turned to photography, poetry and performance as his principal areas of activity in the late 1960s; Michael Morris paralleled the move at about the same time.

This reformulation of art production materialized at a moment when new forms of institutional support were being put in place by various levels of government in the effort to modernize Canadian culture, providing a financial framework crucial to the development of new approaches to art making. On a federal level these efforts were part of a larger program aimed at inscribing a sense of national identity that could unify a country often divided along regional lines. They included a substantial increase in the budget of the Canada Council[10] and the development of mechanisms such as the Local Initiatives Program (LIP), which would provide support for businesses and cultural organizations. In Vancouver these measures coincided with the expansion of UBC, where Balkind had achieved a national profile for its Fine Arts Gallery and Ian Wallace was among Iain Baxter's students; an increasing profile of the Vancouver Art Gallery under directors Richard Simmons and then Tony Emery and curator Doris Shadbolt; and the opening of Simon Fraser University in Burnaby, where Baxter taught after leaving UBC.

The most emblematic manifestation of this scenario was the formation in 1967 of Intermedia, an artist-run umbrella organization initially funded through the Canada Council and later through LIP. Intermedia challenged the traditional categories of art, emphasized process over product and fostered collaborative approaches to art making that included sculpture, sound, video, performance, dance, poetry, film and photography. As Nancy Shaw has argued, members were engaged in "a counter-cultural rebellion against the homogenizing constraints of postwar society, as they attempted to blur the boundaries between art and life in order to expand consciousness and assert a creative, participatory and active subjectivity."[11] Although it was disbanded in 1972, Intermedia laid the ground for subsequent artist-run organizations in Vancouver, including the Satellite Video Exchange Society and the Western Front (both founded in 1973), that supported the development, production and exhibition of conceptually based work in their programs. Intermedia also provided some impetus toward the formation of feminist organizations, including Reelfeelings (founded in 1973), ISIS: Women and Film, and Women in Focus (both founded in 1974).[12]

Practices that favoured process over the completed object found support in venues such as UBC's Fine Arts Gallery and SUB Gallery, the Vancouver Art Gallery, the Burnaby Art Gallery

[9] Iain Baxter co-organized a symposium with Roy Kiyooka and Alvin Balkind, among others, on McLuhan for the fifth festival in 1965. He produced *Bagged Place* for the sixth festival the following year.

[10] When it was formed in 1957, the Canada Council's budget was $2.7 million. By 1967 it was $16.9 million. See Canada Council for the Arts, "History of the Canada Council," http://canadacouncil.ca/aboutus/Background/kd127229037949843750 (accessed March 10, 2011).

[11] Nancy Shaw, "Expanded consciousness and company types: Collaboration since Intermedia and the N.E. Thing Co." In Stan Douglas (Ed.), *The Vancouver Anthology: The Institutional Politics of Art* (Vancouver: Talonbooks, 1991), 86.

[12] Much of the feminist activity of the time focused on providing higher visibility to social issues that impacted the lives

ARTISTS IN THE EXHIBITION: VANCOUVER

Vito Hannibal Acconci	Rafael Ferrer	Bruce Nauman
Carl Andre	Dan Graham	N.E. Thing Co.
Keith Arnatt	Hans Haacke	George Nikoliadis
Richard Artschwager	Alex Hay	N.Y. Graphic Workshop
Terry Atkinson	Michael Heizer	Dennis Oppenheim
John Baldessari	Eva Hesse	John Perreault
Michael Baldwin	Douglas Huebler	Adrian Piper
Robert Barry	Robert Huot	Robert Rohm
Rick Barthelme	Stephen Kaltenbach	Alan Ruppersberg
Gene Beery	On Kawara	Robert Ryman
Mel Bochner	Edward Kienholz	Ed Ruscha
Bill Bollinger	Robert Kinmont	Fred Sandback
Jon Borofsky	Joseph Kosuth	George Sawchuk
Donald Burgy	Christine Kozlov	Richard Serra
Daniel Buren	John Latham	Randy Sims
Rosemarie Castoro	Barry Le Va	Robert Smithson
Greg Curnoe	Sol LeWitt	Keith Sonnier
Hanne Darboven	Roelof Louw	Jeff Wall
Walter de Maria	Duane Lunden	Lawrence Weiner
Jan Dibbets	Bruce McLean	Ian Wilson
Christos Dikeakos	Robert Morris	

Catalogue for *955,000*, 1970

and an emerging private gallery scene with Douglas Christmas' Ace Gallery, Willard Holmes and Kitty Byrne's Pender Street Gallery and later Claudia Beck and Andrew Gruft's Nova Gallery, which emphasized photography. During the late 1960s and through the 1970s these galleries presented exhibitions that included conceptually based work by Vancouver artists such as Tom Burrows, Rodney Graham, Carole Itter, Roy Kiyooka, Robert Kleyn, Michael Morris, NETCO, Vincent Trasov and Ian Wallace, among others, as well as by American artists such as Carl Andre, Bruce Nauman and Robert Smithson. Among the most important and influential exhibitions to be mounted in Vancouver during this era was *955,000*. Curated by Lucy Lippard for the Vancouver Art Gallery, *955,000* opened in January 1970 and was presented at venues throughout the city. It comprised work by about sixty artists from Europe and North America, including Vito Acconci, Carl Andre, Michael Asher, Hanne Darboven, Christos Dikeakos, Dan Graham, Hans Haacke, Duane Lunden, Bruce Nauman, N.E. Thing Co., Adrian Piper, Robert Smithson, Jeff Wall and Lawrence Weiner.

Much of the relevant work made in Vancouver between 1965 and 1980 resists easy classification and often straddles the boundary between conceptual art, which has come to be associated with strategies of negation, dematerialization and institutional critique, and the sensibilities of the Fluxus movement, with its emphasis on play, humour and the incorporation of art into daily life. The situation is further complicated by the work of artists like Gathie Falk, Glenn Lewis, Kiyooka and Itter who worked in different idioms simultaneously. Conceptualism as a platform

of women and drawing attention to the overlooked contributions of women to the larger culture. These projects usually took a more traditional documentary form; thus, as in other centres in Canada and abroad, conceptual art on the West Coast was largely a male domain. For an outline of feminist activity in Vancouver during this era see Carole Williams, "A working chronology of feminist cultural activities and events in Vancouver: 1970–1990," in Douglas (Ed.), *The Vancouver Anthology*, 171–205. See also Terry Atkinson's remarks on this question in Judith Mastai (Ed.), *VAG Documents 2: An Evening Forum at the Vancouver Art Gallery with Terry Atkinson, Jeff Wall, Ian Wallace and Lawrence Weiner* (Vancouver: Vancouver Art Gallery, 1992), 44.

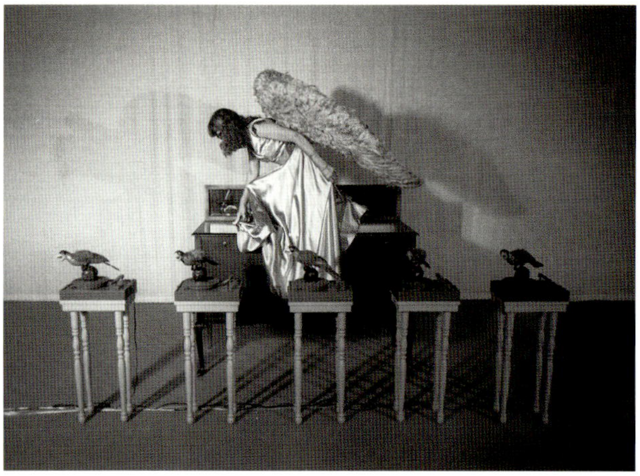

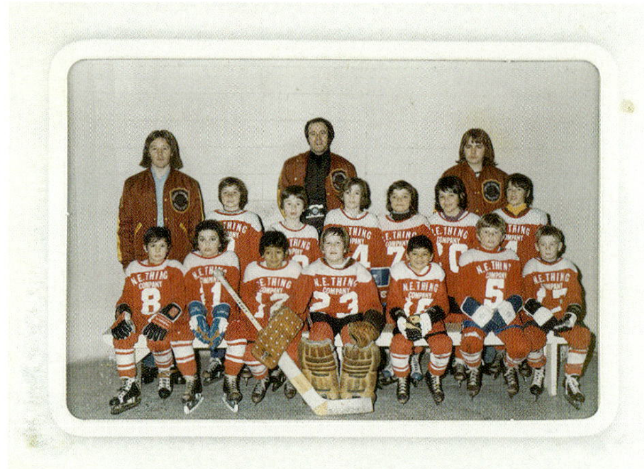

was traversed from many directions during this time. For the purposes of this text and the work that comprises the West Coast section of the related exhibition, I have chosen to focus on work that downplays the primacy of the visual over concept and process and addresses (at least obliquely) the context of its presentation and/or the role of the viewer in the production of meaning.

Beginning in the late 1960s, the widespread challenges to the traditional preciousness of the art object were taken up by West Coast artists in work that was performative in character, was dispersed in form or existed as multiples rather than singular objects. Among the performance projects of the time, the "theatre art works" of Gathie Falk had the most rigorously conceptualized structure. In *Red Angel*, first performed at the Vancouver Art Gallery in 1972, for example, Falk, dressed in a white wedding dress with large-scale wings, sat on a red sideboard behind five red record players with red plastic parrots and red ceramic apples. As the parrots rotated on the turntables they were accompanied by the round song "Row, Row, Row Your Boat," with Falk joining in as the final participant. The repetitive character of the performance, as Marina Roy has noted, situated Falk as a "broken record, driven to repeat the same lines over and over like a parrot, [reflecting] her role as a woman trapped within the vicious cycle of repeated acts, as a woman passively displaying herself as a decorative ornament, repeating what she is taught to say."[13]

While the reconfiguration of art making in the city didn't involve a wholesale rejection of the museum or gallery as a venue, artists actively pursued alternatives for the presentation and distribution of their work in order to engage audiences outside the boundaries of the art world and/or maintain some control over the context in which their work was received and interpreted. In its dissemination of "visual sensitivity information," for example, N.E. Thing Co. took out membership in the Vancouver Board of Trade, distributed information through NETCO booths at trade fairs, operated a restaurant in Vancouver's Kitsilano neighbourhood

Above, from left
Gathie Falk, still from video of *Red Angel*, 1972

N.E. Thing Co., *N.E. Thing Co. Hockey Team*, 1972

[13] Marina Roy, "Corporeal returns: Feminism and phenomenology in Vancouver video and performance 1968–1983," *Canadian Art* 18, no. 2 (Summer/June 2001): 61. I'm grateful to Karen Henry for bringing this essay to my attention.

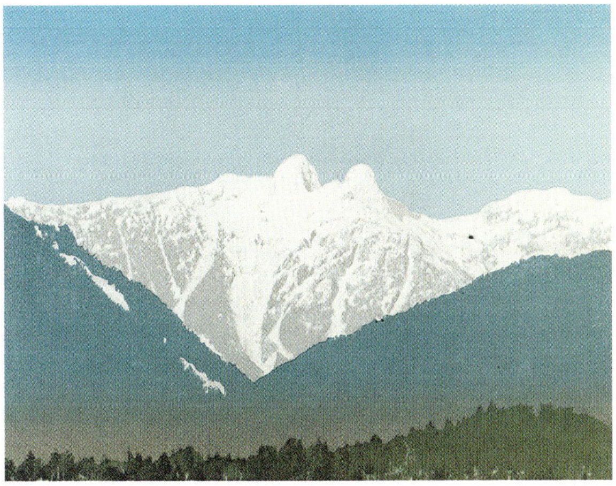 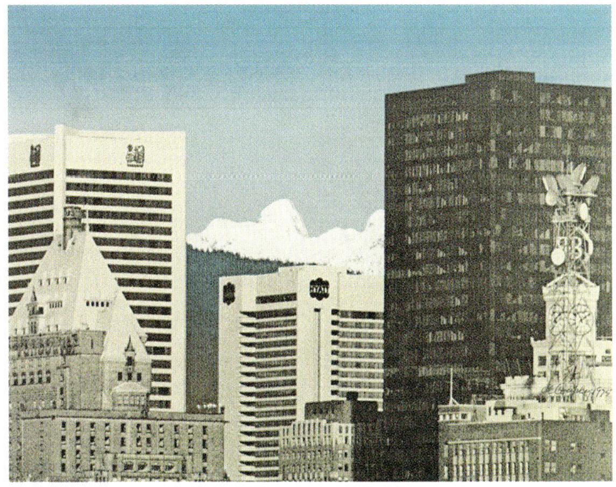

and sponsored a kids' hockey team. Michael de Courcy's A Vanishing View of the Lions (1975), a series of photographic screenprints that depict a pair of lion-shaped mountains as they disappear into a maze of telephone wires and signage, led to an expanded project titled Greetings from the Urban Wilderness (1976), which guided participants along three "nature trails" de Courcy charted through Vancouver's downtown core using maps and sign markers that appeared on sidewalks, hoardings and telephone poles. Tom Burrows situated large-scale, constructivist-inflected sculptures on the intertidal mudflats of North Vancouver, where the kind of form articulated in Kazimir Malevich's drawings could interact with the rhythms and openness of the landscape, while Christos Dikeakos and Jeff Wall, drawing upon the examples of Dan Graham's Homes for America and Robert Smithson's A Tour of the Monuments of Passaic, New Jersey, combined text and photographs in cheaply printed booklets that could be purchased for a nominal price.

The most fully realized mode of independent distribution was developed by Image Bank. Founded in 1969 by Michael Morris, Vincent Trasov and Gary Lee-Nova,[14] Image Bank was conceived as a network through which participants could communicate and exchange ideas and information, primarily through the mail. Characterized by a Fluxus-oriented sense of play and humour, the "bank" served (and continues to serve) as a repository for mail art projects by artists working throughout North America and Europe, an assemblage of "mythic materials generated from the media" in which the act "of isolating and defining artistic activities" might suggest a way to move beyond the "image bondage" of the broader culture.[15] The network was largely built through image requests that were published in vehicles such as General Idea's journal, *FILE*, and Image Bank's *International Exchange Directory*. In contrast to the populist ambitions of NETCO and de Courcy, the activities of Image Bank can be linked to an avant-garde tradition of counter-media—the limited-circulation journals and reviews associated with Dada, Surrealism and the Situationist International—that the Dutch critic Sven Lütticken has described as attempts "to forge a different publicness . . . on the grounds of a radical

[14] Although Lee-Nova was a co-founder of Image Bank, he was involved for only a short time. It's worth noting that he had begun research into colour bars prior to the formation of Image Bank.

[15] Michael Morris, "The artist as curator of the imagination," *artscanada* XXXV, no. 2 (April/May 1978): 41–42.

Above, from left
Michael de Courcy, *A Vanishing View of the Lions*, 1975, details

dissent from the dominant form of publicness, and the society it represented."[16] For Image Bank (and many of their collaborators), this alternate conception of publicness was closely intertwined with the articulation of sexual identity through the sense of irony, camp and overt homoeroticism that marked the image world they assembled.

Photography took on a particularly important role for West Coast artists during the 1970s and became central to the development of conceptual art here. Photographs appeared as project documents in the work of NETCO, representations of performances undertaken by Theodore Wan and others, a link to the everyday in the work of Kiyooka and an index of the

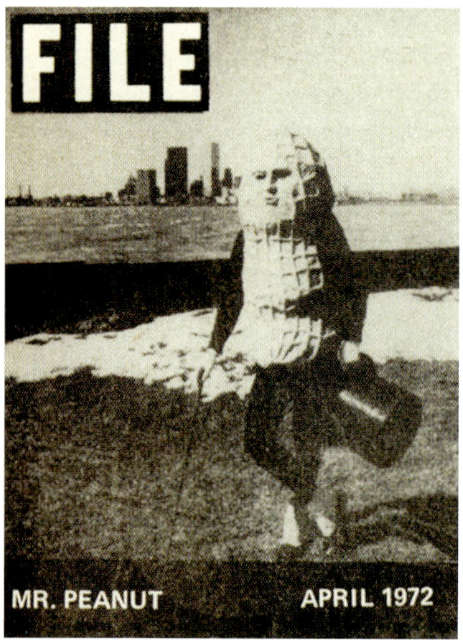

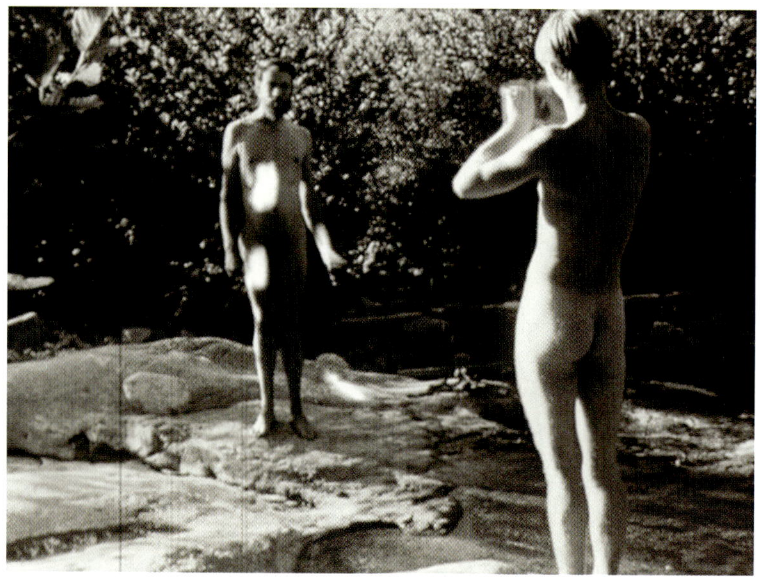

semiotics of urban space in the work of Christos Dikeakos, Jeff Wall and Ian Wallace. Extensive examinations on the nature of the photograph as a model of acculturated perception were undertaken by Bill Jones, Robert Kleyn and Dean Ellis. Beginning in the late 1960s, Jones focused on the photograph as both an object and a regime of depiction. For *Landscape #1* (1970), which was exhibited at the Vancouver Art Gallery in 1972, Jones photographed the window of a house reflecting a Vancouver landscape, then bolted a glass panel, cut precisely to the size and shape of the window's image, onto the mural-sized photographic print. Through its title and materials, the work plays off the idea of the "picture window" as the perceptual model for painting and a feature of middle-class housing, as well as the relationship between the physical presence of the glass, its reflection of the surrounding space and the photographic

Above, from left
General Idea (with Image Bank), *FILE Megazine*, Mr. Peanut Issue, Vol. 1, No. 1, April 1972

Image Bank with Gordon Kidd and Martin Bartlett, still from *Light-On*, 1970–1971

Opposite, from top
Image Bank Request List, *FILE Megazine*, May/June 1972, detail

Bill Jones, *Landscape #1*, 1970

[16] Sven Lütticken, *Secret Publicity: Essays on Contemporary Art* (Rotterdam: NAI Publishers, 2006), 30.

EXPLOSION OF A MYTH

IMAGE BANK REQUEST LIST

Pin this list on your bulletin board and plug in to the subliminal.

Church Bank	5972 Whitcomb Pl., Tsawwassen, B.C. request images of sacrilege, any religion, crumbling churches, pissing buddhas, plastic flowers in graveyards, toppled gravestones, the pope Jesus as chicken etc.
Stan Jantos	19 Rowland St., Toronto 9, Ont., requests images of paint tubes or paint containers full, empty, or partially full or empty.
Leo Labelle	555 Hamilton St., Vancouver, requests images of wheelchairs, EYES, anteaters.
Dave Gilhooley	253 Finch Ave. E., Willowdale, Ont. requests pictures of QUEEN VICTORIA, local Diefendemons, and classical erotic art.
Carman Dawson	21 Livingston St. Point Edward, Ont. requests unique one shots of a lifetime and joy filled anythings.
David Zack	Box 1, Silton, Sask. requests a supply of different issues of Canadada or new currency.
Jane Vasey	82 Sullivan St. Toronto, would like old photos, old music, and rubber legs and knock knees.
C&C Santon	PO Box 472, Canal St. Stn, NYC 10013 request more Chinese masters (unearthed)
Vicki Hurrop	3090 Saddle Dr., Port Coquitlam, B.C. requests combs or pieces.
Lana B. Anal	General Idea, 87 Yonge St. Tor., requests something by mouth images, and candid pictures of Miss Harland.

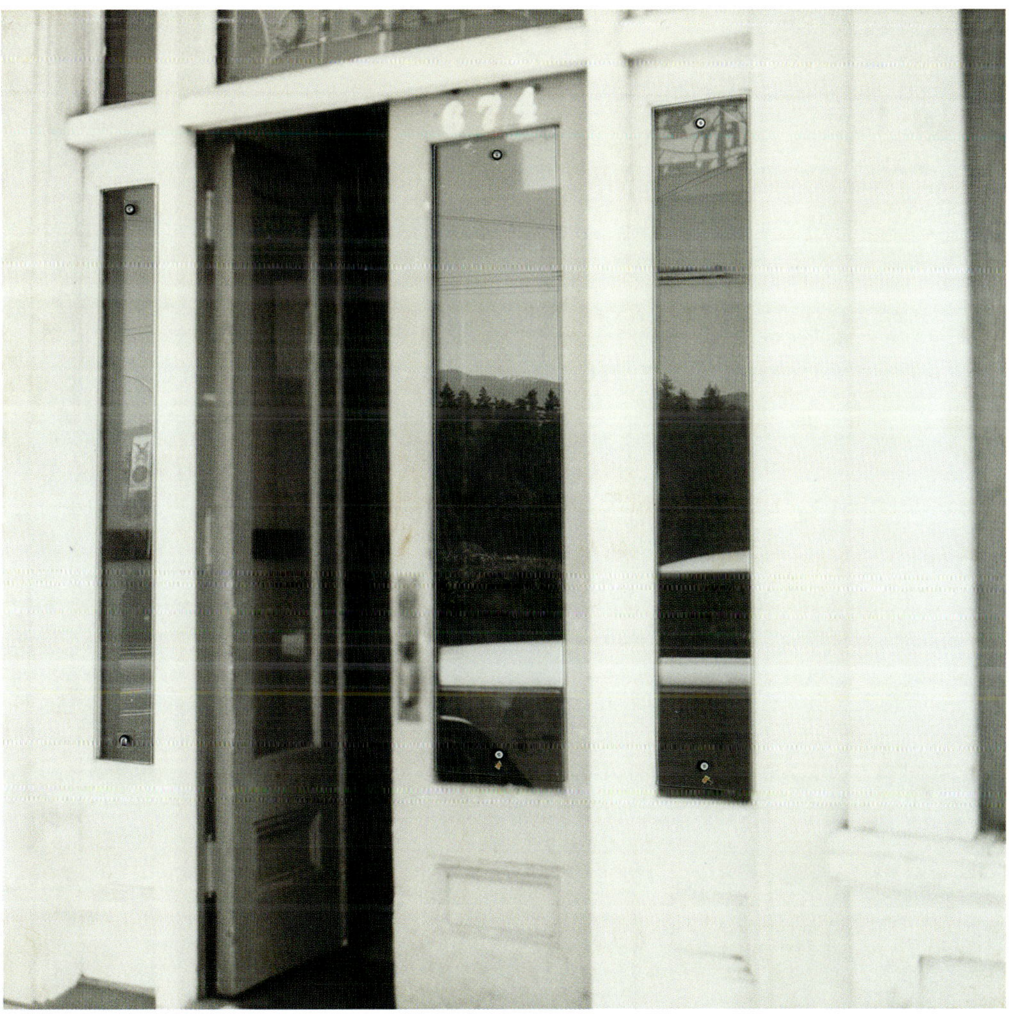

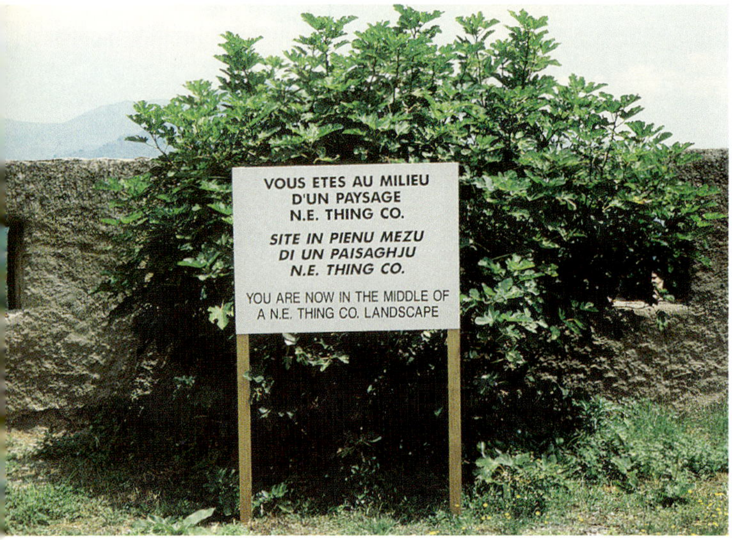

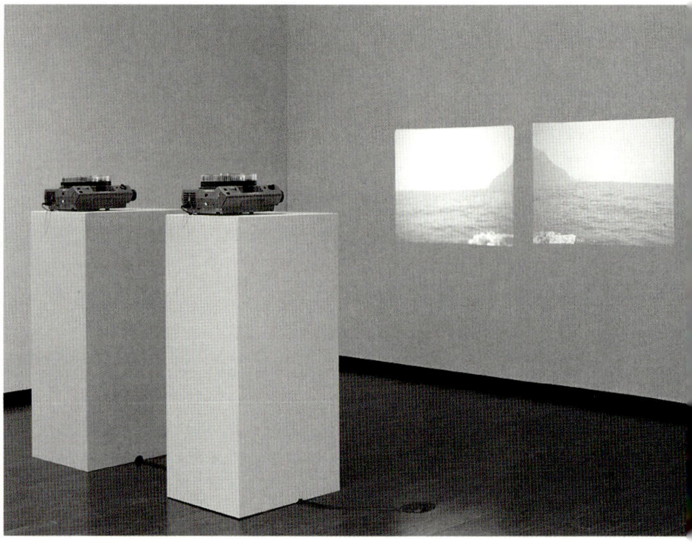

recording of the reflected landscape. The reflected landscape as a phenomenon, presumably influenced by Smithson's mirror works, also appears in work by Image Bank, Glenn Lewis and others.

At about the same time, Kleyn produced a number of proto-cinematic works that considered the mediating character of photography and language through sequences of slides or colour prints exhibited at the Pender Street Gallery, UBC's SUB Gallery and the Vancouver Art Gallery. These include *Island* (1972), which consists of two sets of projected slides that depict a journey to and from an island near Capri in the Tyrrhenian Sea. One set of 81 slides depicts the island becoming larger and larger during the inbound journey; the other set shows the island as it recedes into the distance during the trip back to the mainland. The images are projected side by side in a bifocal structure that disrupts the viewer's relationship to the illusion of space in the images and the narrative presented in each set of slides, while the mechanical noise of the projectors blends into the recorded sound of the boat's motor and the waves generated in its wake.

Ellis' *Landscape Morphology and Perceptual Tools*, exhibited at the Vancouver Art Gallery in 1972 and the Nova Scotia College of Art and Design's (NSCAD's) Mezzanine in 1973, included slide works documenting interventions in which the artist arranged found elements—rocks, boulders, logs—in semi-wilderness areas on the west coast. The particular sense of order between these elements was clearly one imposed on the scene through the specific location of Ellis' camera so that, as Dennis Wheeler noted, "the play on the illusory properties of the medium becomes the semantic basis"[17] for the work, and the intersection between the ordering impetus of human perception and its perceived object is located as the work's primary subject matter. Shot on Hornby Island, Ellis' untitled video from 1972 presents a

Above, from left
Installation view of N.E. Thing, *You Are Now in the Middle of a N.E. Thing Co. Landscape*, 1968, FRAC Corse, 1997

Installation view of Robert Kleyn, *Island*, 1972

[17] Dennis Wheeler, "Dean Ellis: Landscape morphology and perceptual tools," *artscanada* XXX, no. 1 (Feb/March 1973): 23–27.

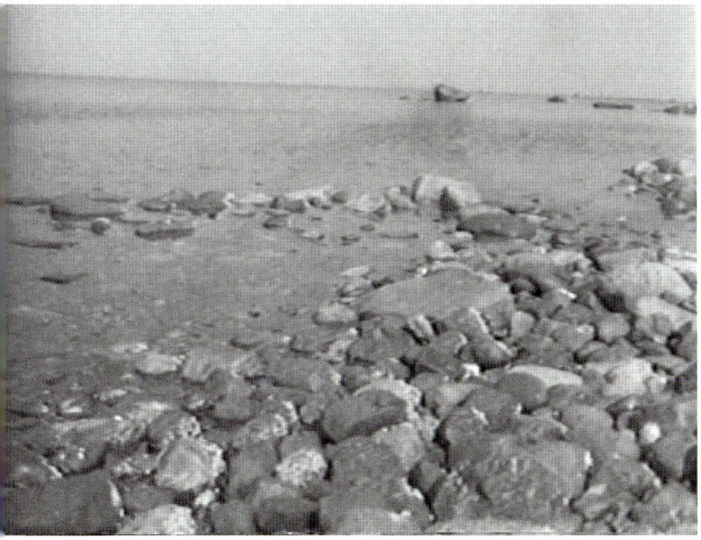 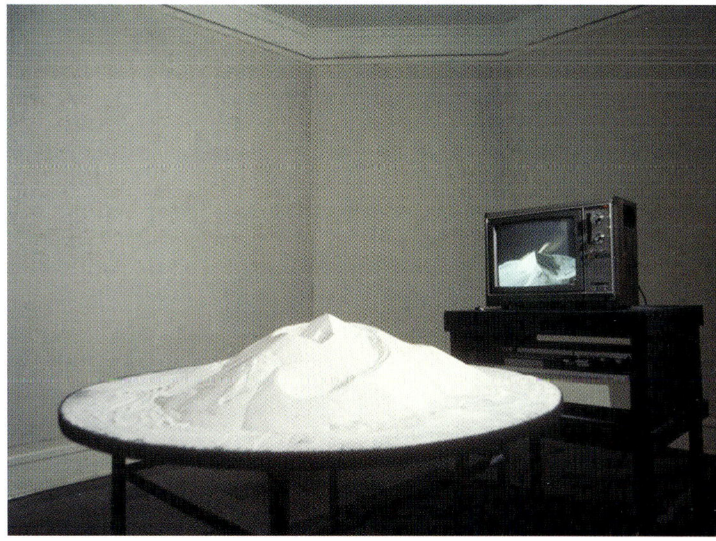

static, real-time view of the rising tide, with rocks thrown into the frame at regular intervals. The viewer is left to consider the pervasive structure of abstract time, with its division into quantifiable units, in relation to rhythmic cycles of the ocean tide.

While these works maintained a strong link to the landscape, the emergence of conceptually based practices marked a conscious break with the lyrical landscape tradition that informed much of the work of the previous generation of West Coast painters. To varying degrees, a number of Vancouver-based artists came to see the ideal of spiritual union with nature that informed that tradition as a conciliatory fantasy that masks the real relationship between the rapacious economic order of capitalism and the natural environment upon which it feeds. Nonetheless, questions regarding the intersection of the spiritual and the political remained a compelling problem for a number of artists working on the West Coast during the 1960s and '70s. By the late 1960s, Jeff Wall, for example, was interested in Zen Buddhism as a political philosophy;[18] Tom Burrows, in a 1971 interview with Gary Lee-Nova, acknowledged that he had "yet to make the separation between some sort of spiritual trip and political ideology, but that's the ultimate problem."[19] This question inflects Burrows' *Sand Pile* (1973), a kind of scaled-down earthwork that consists of a round table covered with sand and a behaviourally instructive video depicting the artist's arms and hands as he gently forms the sand into a pyramid and then obliterates the form. This decidedly non-instrumental, entropic activity, in which the viewer's participation in forming the sand holds out the possibility of joining mind and body, counters the increasingly purpose-driven character of daily life in its proposal of an activity that exists for and of itself while, within the space of the museum, implying a level of transgression in its invocation to touch.

Landscape persisted as a motif for West Coast artists, not as an inexhaustible container for

[18] Scott Watson, "Discovering the defeatured landscape." In Douglas (Ed.), *The Vancouver Anthology*, 251.

[19] Tom Burrows cited in Gary Lee-Nova, "Our beautiful west coast thing," *artscanada* XXVIII, no. 2 (June/July 1971): 37.

Above, from left
Dean Ellis, still from *Untitled*, vers 1972

Tom Burrows, *Sand Pile (Sand to Pyramid to Sand)*, 1973

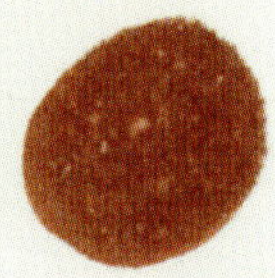

TWO DOTS

N. E. THING CO. TRANSV. S.I. INFORM

TITLE SEND A LIE RECEIVE THE TRUTH 1968-70

PRODUCER N.E.THING CO. LTD 10/16/70

TRANSMISSION	RECEIVING
PLACE N. VANC.	PLACE Henry Gallery
TIME 11 2/am PST	TIME
BY NETCO	BY
BY TELECOPIER	BY TELECOPIER

COMMENTS THE LIE IS IN VANC. AT NETCO OFFICE AND TRUTH IS IN THE HENRY GALLERY

1419 RIVERSIDE DRIVE, N. VANCOUVER, B.C.
Canada Cable: "ANYTHING" (604) 929-3662

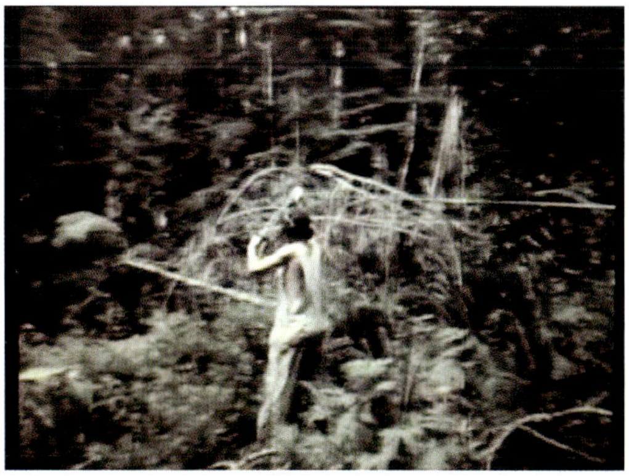 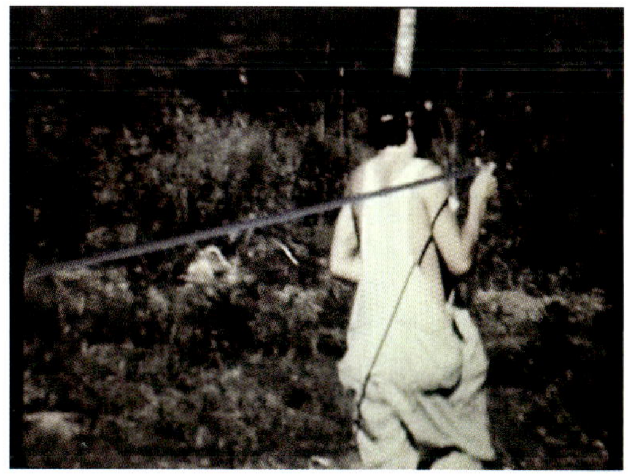

personal expression, but as something to be mapped and analyzed, or as a kind of theatre in which an alternative to the existing conditions of domination might be glimpsed. Babyland, Image Bank's bucolic retreat near Roberts Creek on the Sunshine Coast, was a kind of utopian laboratory in which much of Image Bank's research was undertaken. It appears regularly in the documentation of Image Bank projects, including *Colour Bar Research* (1972–74), in which an "endless painting" of a thousand wooden blocks painted to mimic the greyscale and colour test strips used in film and television were arranged in the landscape (often accompanied by nubile men and women), as well as the film *Light-On* (1970–71) and videos such as *My Five Years in a Nutshell* (1975), which depicts Vincent Trasov's time as Mr. Peanut. Babyland had carefully constructed edenic connotations, with the images of playfully cavorting young bodies calling up both a theatrical innocence and an aura of "nature boy" eroticism.

Given Vancouver's remoteness from the centres of power of both the art world and the state, it's not surprising that strategies associated with mapping and networking informed much of the work from this time. In the late 1960s, NETCO undertook a variety of projects using telex and telecopier machines that located their North Vancouver headquarters in relation to the Museum of Modern Art in New York and NSCAD in Halifax, as well as in relation to places as diverse as Inuvik and Chicago. Telex projects such as *Telex: Trans VSI: Send a Lie, Receive the Truth (Two Dots)* (1970), in which "truth" is realized only through the transmission of information, provides an indication of the close affinities between NETCO's activities and McLuhan's theorization of the impact of telecommunications technology on quotidian experience and the way in which space is imagined. NETCO also addressed the abstract systems through which landscape is apprehended in works that include *Black Arctic Circle* (1968), a hypothetical undertaking in which a jet plane would fly low over the Arctic Circle, physically tracing it by spraying black paint onto the polar icecap. Similarly, Glenn Lewis marked out basic units for the quantification of space in *Blue Tape Around a City Block* (1969), a filmed performance in which he used blue surveyor's tape to accentuate the rationalized grid that commonly structures urban space, and *Forest Industry* (1969), a two-hour, real-time performance in which he used the same type of surveyor's tape as he bushwhacked through the undergrowth to delineate a square kilometre of the forest near Image Bank's Babyland.

Opposite
N.E. Thing Co., *Telex: Trans VSI: Send a Lie, Receive the Truth (Two Dots)*, 1970, detail

Above
Glenn Lewis, stills from *Forest Industry*, 1969

Lewis' work can be related to a poetics of "localism"—a sensibility associated with the work of the American poet Charles Olson, whose influence was significant in Vancouver's literary scene[20]—that focused on the tension and potential transcendence of the constraints placed upon the local and immediate through ideological structures at work in the broader culture. This aesthetic can also be seen in works like Carole Itter's *Personal Baggage* (1972) and Roy Kiyooka's *Long Beach to Peggy's Cove* (1971) and *Untitled (Opposite Blue Mule Studio, Powell Street)* (1978–80). Produced for the *Halifax/Vancouver Exchange*, Itter's work responded to the geographic poles of the project by cutting a large cedar log that had washed up on the beach at Roberts Creek into luggage-sized sections. Carrying handles were attached to each section and both the log and Itter travelled by train to Nova Scotia, where the log was reassembled and positioned near the beach in the town of Lockeport. Like Lewis' *Forest Industry*, *Personal Baggage* engaged in a gently absurd application of instrumental logic to a sign of nature and homeliness in a manner that both undercuts the humanist model of a man-centred world

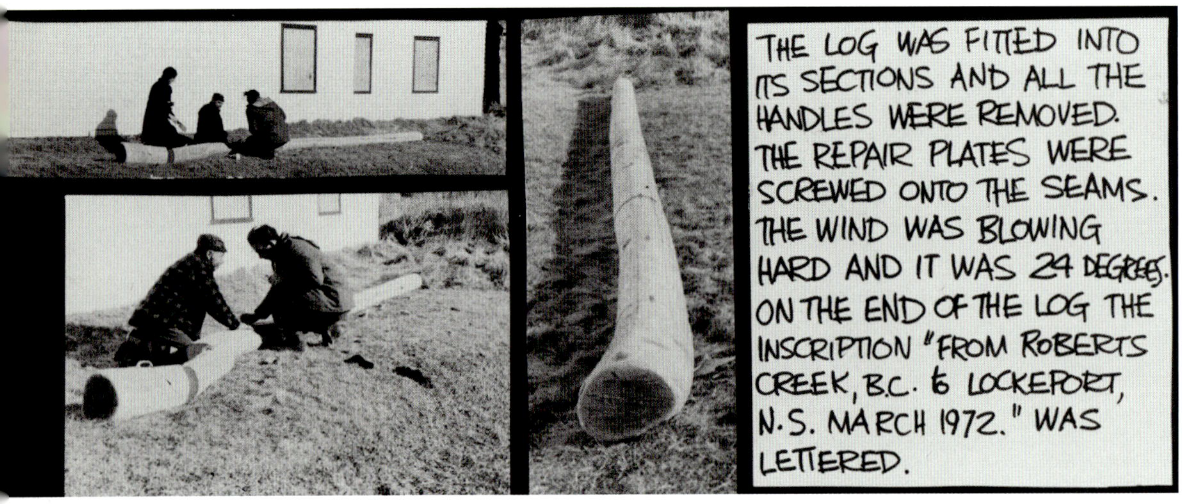

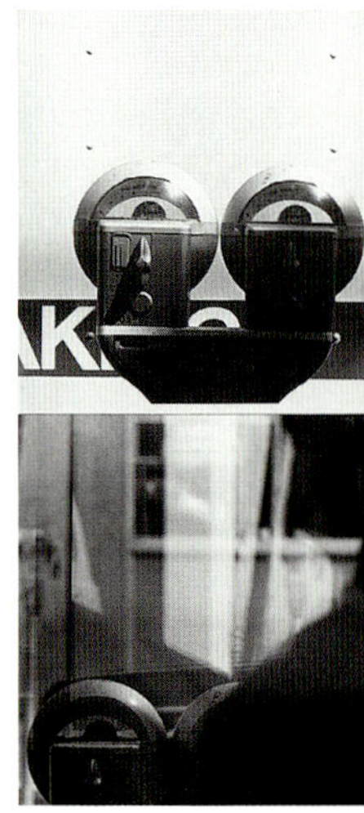

and posits the potential for lived experience to counter the fragmentation of subjectivity in contemporary culture. Similarly, Kiyooka's *Long Beach to Peggy's Cove* depicts a road trip Kiyooka took from British Columbia to Nova Scotia to take up a teaching position at NSCAD; 573 small black and white photographs, mostly banal snapshot views of tanker trucks, gas stations, roadside cafés, overpasses, bridges and friends along the way, are arranged in a grid so they can be read as a chronological sequence. Thus, the transit of the convivial private space of the automobile is contained by a systematic, anti-organic structure that echoes the system of roads on which Kiyooka travelled in pursuit of work. This ordering power of the grid is more explicitly countered in *Untitled (Opposite Blue Mule Studio, Powell Street)*, which comprises images shot through the front window of Kiyooka's street-level studio. The location of Kiyooka's studio in the centre of what was Vancouver's "Japantown" was a

Above
Carole Itter, *The Log's Log*, documentation of *Personal Baggage*, 1972–73, detail

[20] See Sharla Sava, "Roy Kiyooka: Photographing the local from the inside out," *C Magazine* no. 60 (November 1998–January 1999): 26–32.

deliberate positioning of his activity in relation to a history in which the wartime internment he experienced as a child was a defining feature. The regulating appearance of a parking meter is the only presence that persists from one frame to the next. The passage of time is clearly central to the work, but any logic that might indicate a definitive temporal succession is broken down and the viewer is left to struggle with the relation between past and present in the arrangement of images.

Continuities can be traced between works like *Long Beach to Peggy's Cove* and Duane Lunden's emphatically minimal drawings and prints, in which a grid is the principal formal element, as well as Jeff Wall's *Landscape Manual* (1969–70) and Christos Dikeakos' *Instant Photo Information* (1970), in which photographs made through an automobile window figure prominently. Lunden's *Untitled* (1967) is related to *The Locator*, an extended project based on mapping and modular structures with interchangeable units that was exhibited in different

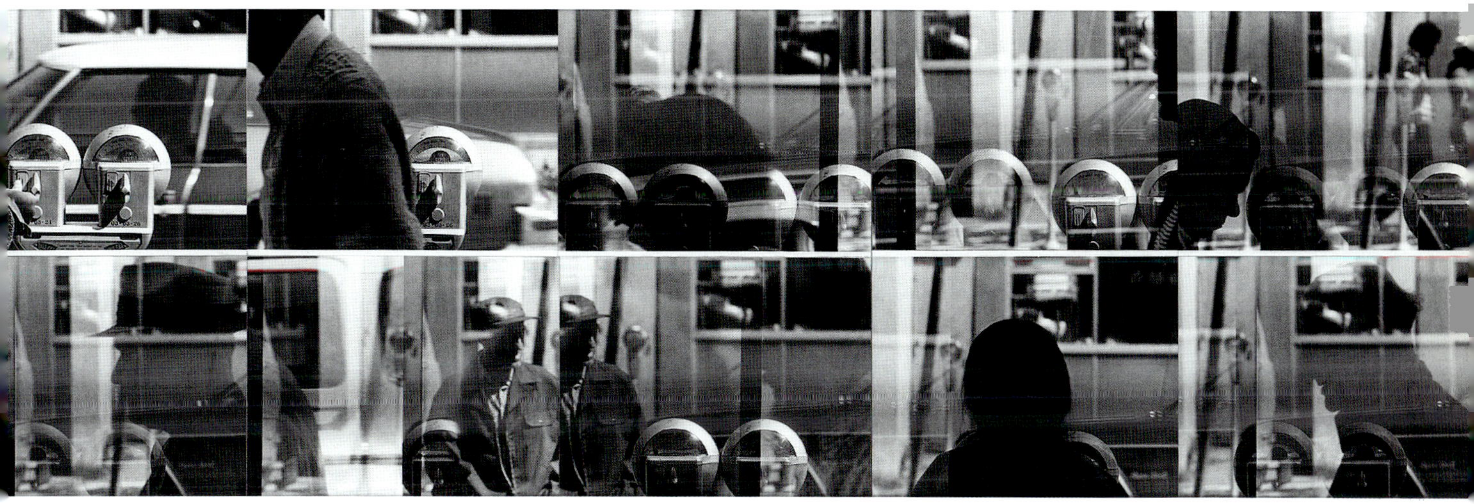

iterations at Vancouver's Bau-Xi Gallery in 1969 and the UBC Fine Arts Gallery the following year. The "composition" of *Untitled* is based on a process in which a single unit is divided into quarters, then the resulting four identical units are divided into quarters, and so on, potentially to infinity. The resulting grid operates as a kind of telescoping view that implies shifts in scale, but also content that is undifferentiated and interchangeable within its abstract framework.

Printed in the National Film Board publication *BC Almanac*, Dikeakos' *Instant Photo Information* includes a text and diagram that propose the automobile as a scanning device for photographing the urban landscape, and 72 black and white photographs made through the window of Dikeakos' car as he travelled through a light industrial zone on Vancouver's east side. Wall's *Landscape Manual* also includes black and white photographs of Vancouver shot randomly

Above
Roy Kiyooka, *Untitled (Opposite Blue Mule Studio, Powell Street)*, 1978–80, detail

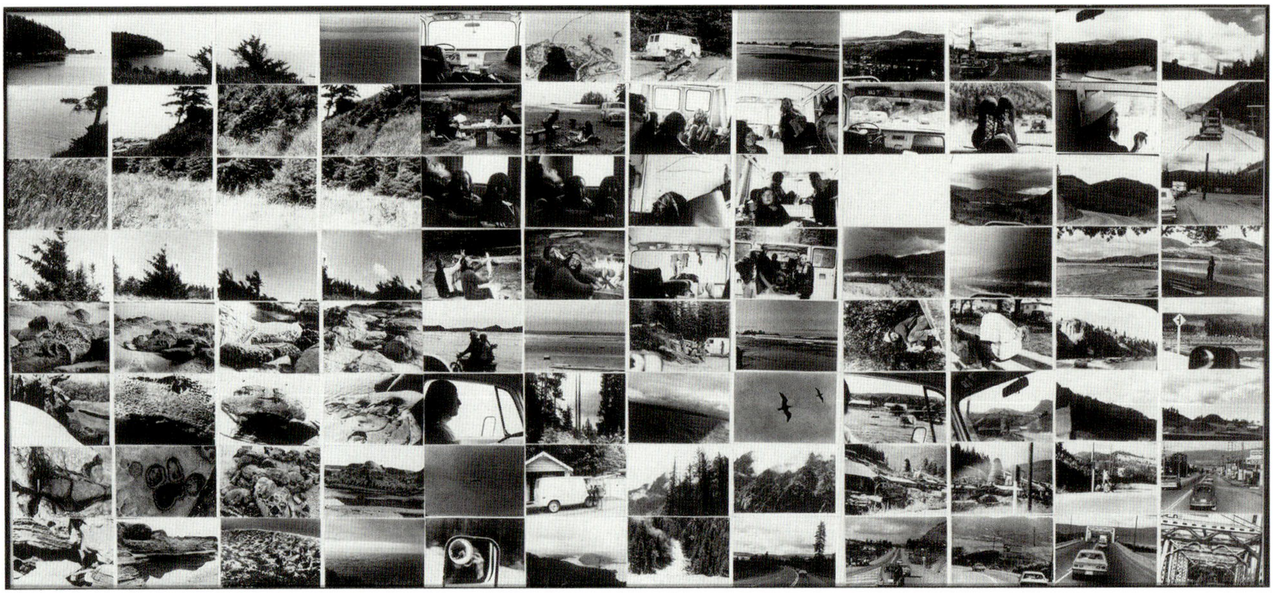

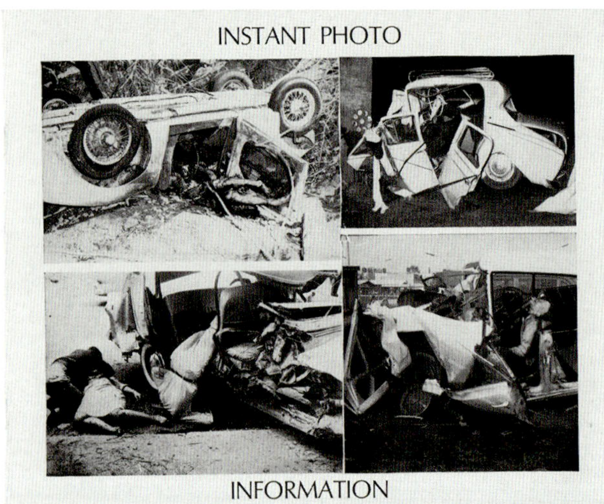

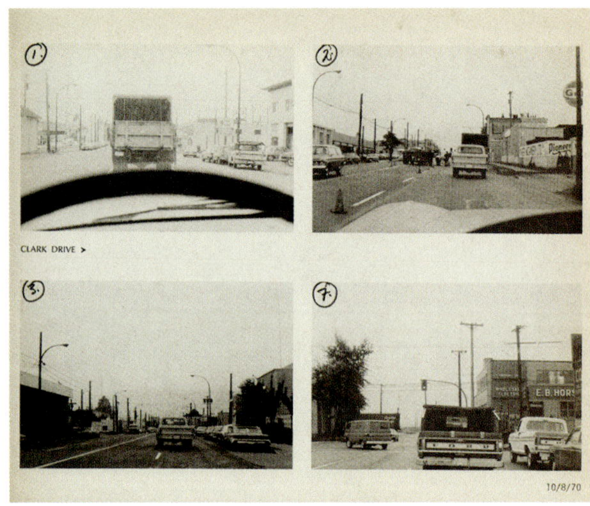

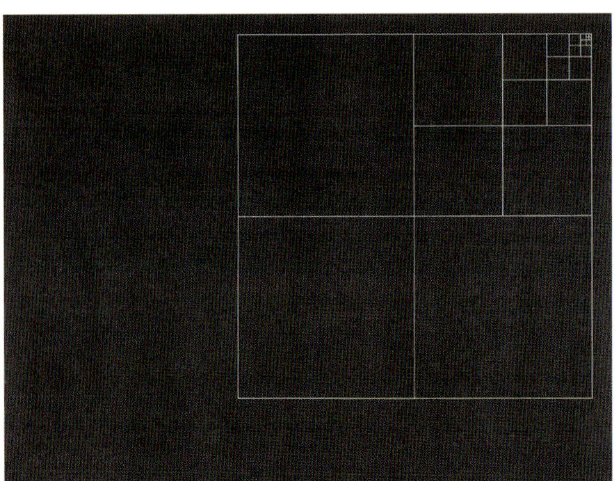

Clockwise from top left

Roy Kiyooka, *Long Beach to Peggy's Cove*, 1971, detail

Christos Dikeakos, *Instant Photo Information*, 1970, detail

Duane Lunden, *Untitled*, 1967

Christos Dikeakos, *Instant Photo Information*, 1970, detail

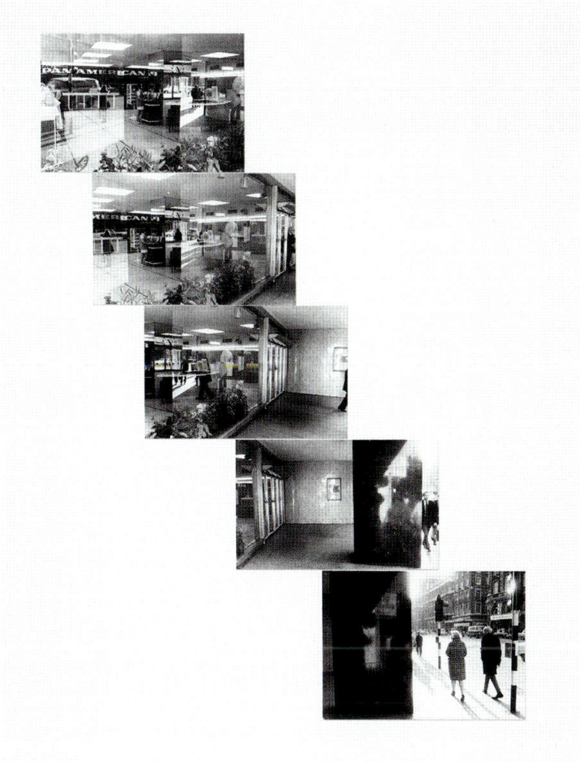

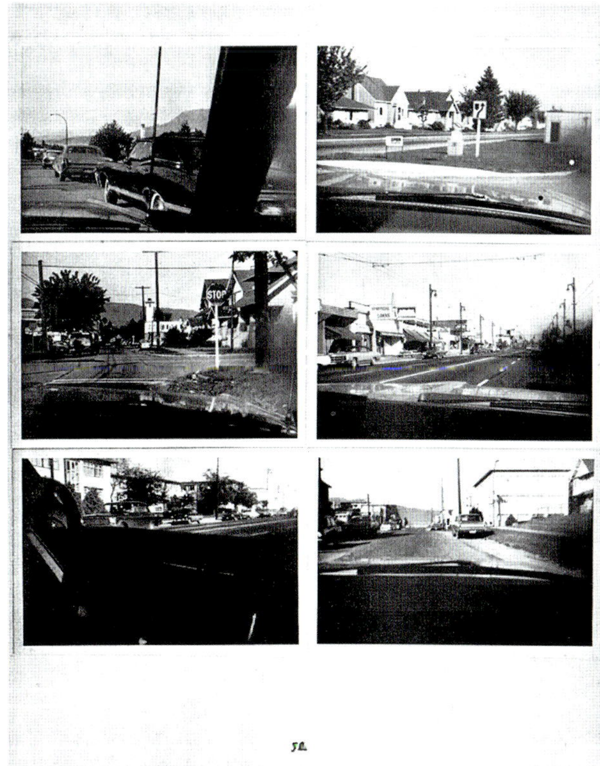

through the window of a moving car, but in Wall's work the images are combined with a lengthy text that records the intense alienation between the consciousness of the narrator and the surrounding urban environment. The scanning technique, especially that of *Instant Photo Information*, also informs Ian Wallace's *Pan-Am Scan* (1970), a sequence of photographs made in London that mechanically scans from a modernist, mirrored office lobby to pedestrians passing by on the street, the distorted reflections alluding to the complex relation between corporate architecture and urban life.

In reviewing *Photo Show*, an exhibition organized by the UBC SUB Gallery in late 1969 that included work by Dikeakos, Lunden, Wall and Wallace, Charlotte Townsend noted that through its ubiquity and ability to take in everything, photography had come to function as "the great equalizer [in] which everything is reduced to the celluloid or printed surface." The impersonal photographs of Dikeakos and Wall, she argued, engaged with this social operation through their inexpressive character, the sense they were "shots taken, not made."[21] This quality of arbitrary equalization and artlessness was crucial to the aesthetic of the defeatured landscape that came to be articulated in the work of Dikeakos, Wall and Wallace, with its focus on the city as the paradigmatic public space of modernity and the manifestations of capitalism's abstract systems within the urban environment. Their interest in effacing personal expression and what Dennis Wheeler termed "micro-identity," together with the sense that their work could just as

[21] Charlotte Townsend, "Photo Show, SUB Art Gallery, University of B.C., December 1969–January 1970," *artscanada* XXVII, no. 3, issue 144/145 (June 1970): 49.

[22] Dennis Wheeler, "The limits of the defeated landscape: A review of *Four Artists*, Fine Arts Gallery, University of B.C., February 1970," *artscanada* XXVII, no. 3 (June 1970): 51.

Above, from left
Ian Wallace, *Pan-Am Scan*, 1970

Jeff Wall, *Landscape Manual,* 1969–70, detail

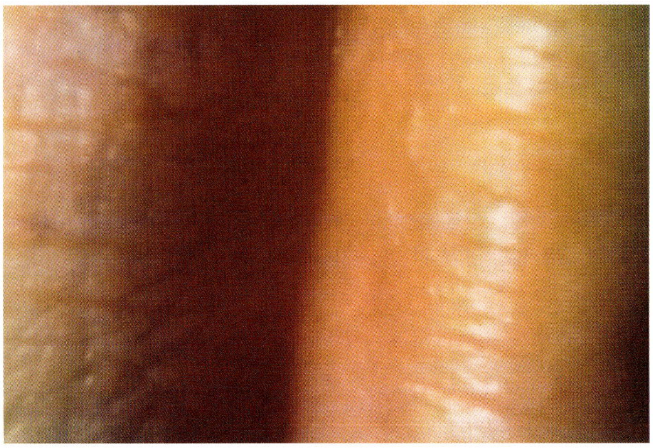

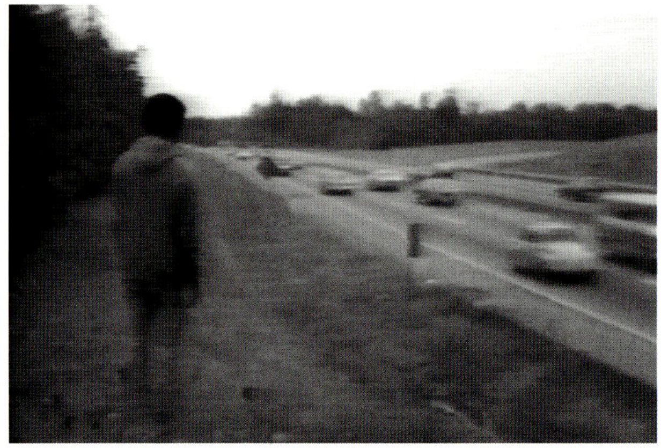

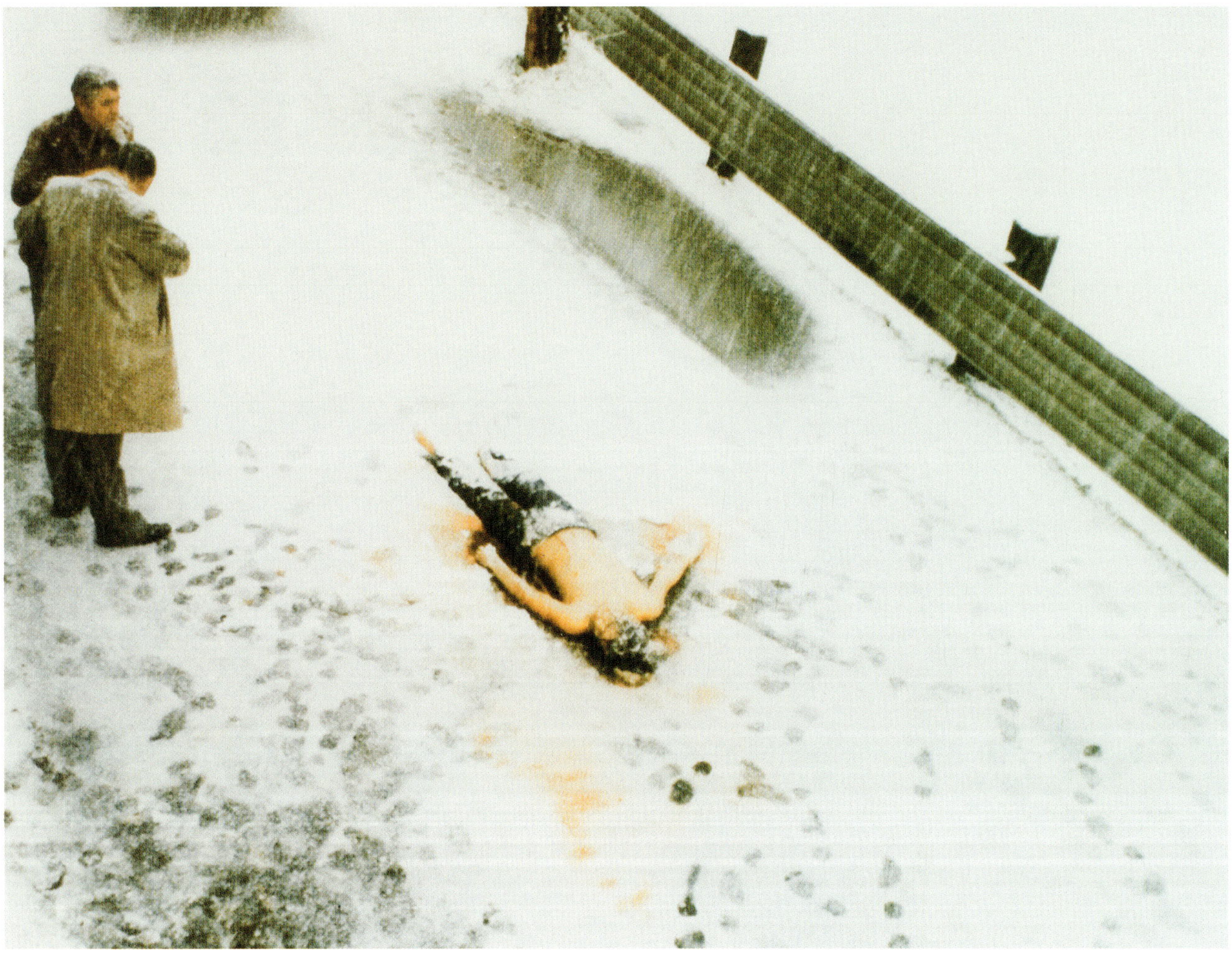

Clockwise from top left

Kate Craig, still from *Delicate Issue*, 1979

Ken Lum, still from *Entertainment for Surrey*, 1978

Paul Wong with Kenneth Fletcher, *Murder Research*, 1977, detail

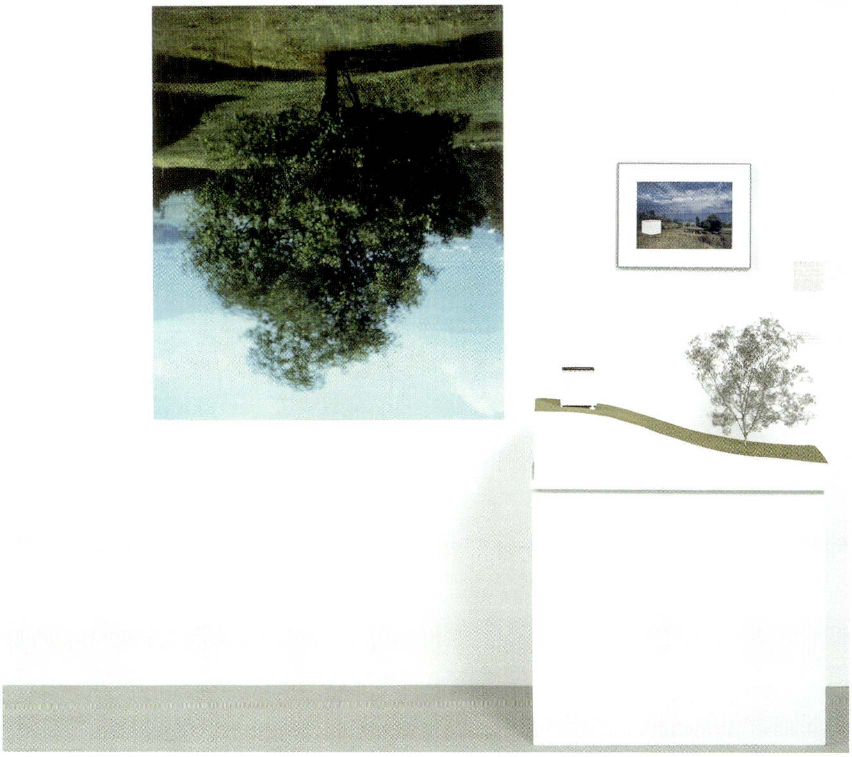

Rodney Graham, *Camera Obscura*, 1979

easily have been made in "Chicago, Edmonton, Toronto or anywhere,"[22] sharply distinguished Dikeakos, Lunden, Wall and Wallace from artists such as Image Bank, Itter, Kiyooka and Lewis. The late 1970s brought a distinct shift in the dynamics of the West Coast art scene. After the departure of Tony Emery from the Vancouver Art Gallery in 1974, the institution began to place greater emphasis on object-oriented modes of art making. NETCO ended with the separation of the Baxters in 1978. Iain Baxter left Vancouver, Michael Morris and Vincent Trasov moved to Berlin, Duane Lunden and Dean Ellis stopped making art. By 1977 Jeff Wall was working with the large-scale light boxes for which he would become widely known and, together with Ian Wallace, began to pursue interests that extended the pictorial tradition of European Modernism. By the late 1970s and early 1980s, the aesthetics of punk, with its emphasis on emotional intensity, inflected much of the new work produced in Vancouver, including the neo-expressionist painting of the *Young Romantics*.[23] If the prominence of conceptual art was temporarily diminished on the West Coast, it did not disappear. It persisted in work by younger artists, including Paul Wong's *Murder Research* (1977), Ken Lum's *Entertainment for Surrey* (1978), Rodney Graham's *Illuminated Ravine* (1979), Kate Craig's *Delicate Issue* (1979) and Theodore Wan's *Only the mind is allowed to wander* (1981), and its legacy would inform a great deal of the art produced in Vancouver over the following thirty years.

[23] *Young Romantics* was an exhibition presented at the Vancouver Art Gallery in 1985. Curated by Scott Watson, it included the work of eight young Vancouver painters who produced large-scale figurative paintings in a neo-expressionist idiom: Graham Gillmore, Angela Grossman, Attila Richard Lukacs, Vicky Marshall, Philippe Raphanel, Charles Rea, Derek Root and Mina Totino. In his catalogue essay, Watson situated the work of these artists as a challenge to aesthetics of high Modernism, with its emphasis on "unity of surface" and "flatness," rather than a break from the intellectual character of conceptual art.

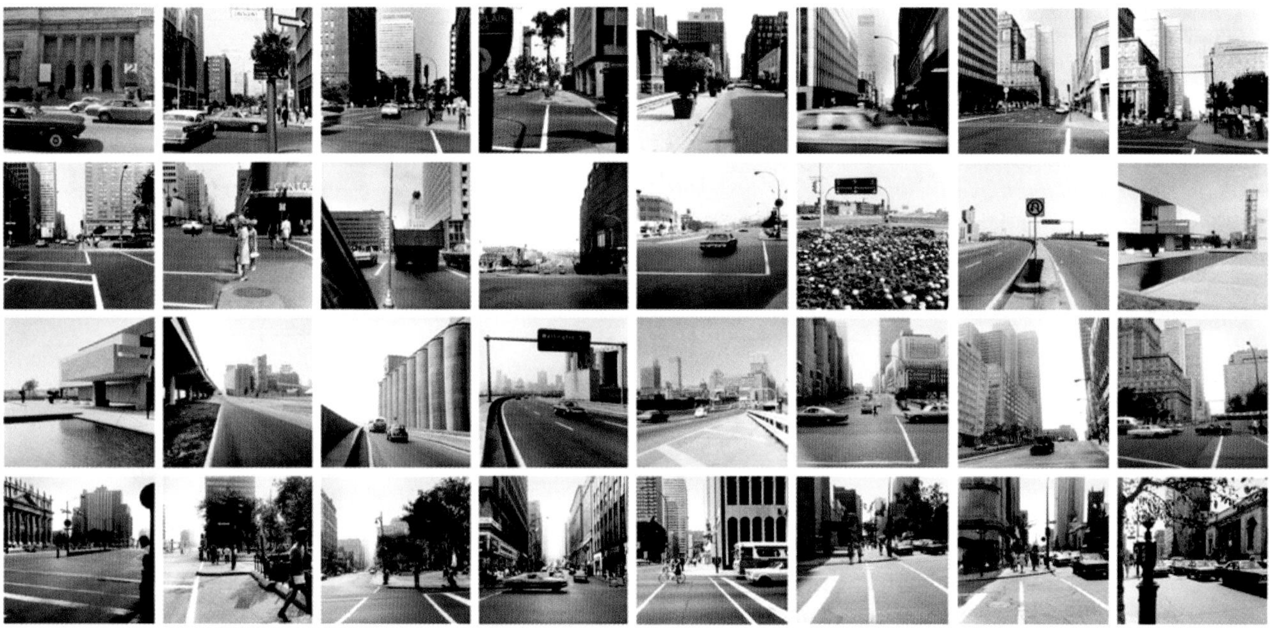

Françoise Sullivan, *La promenade entre le Musée d'art contemporain et le Musée des beaux-arts de Montréal*, 1970.

Early Conceptual Practices in Context: A Conversation

Participants:
Blair French
Lucy Lippard
Chantal Pontbriand
Mari Carmen Ramírez
Charlotte Townsend-Gault
Jeff Khonsary, Moderator

JEFF KHONSARY: As much of our discussion on conceptual practices in the mid-1960s to late 1970s in Canada and beyond will need to address the specific, diverse contexts within which this work was produced, I wanted to begin by asking about the ways economic and sociopolitical conditions helped shape the form and content of this body of work. This is a question about the ways conceptual artists responded to (or opposed) the institutional contexts within which their work could be shown, but also, and perhaps more interestingly, how conceptual practices helped create new institutional models and audiences.

BLAIR FRENCH: Certainly developments in conceptual art during the period we are discussing occur concurrently with significant growth and recalibration of what we might term the institutional frameworks and structures for contemporary practice. The action of artists moving beyond the institutions of art into other open forms—public and social spaces, for example—or into direct relationship to specific environments—from the city street to volcanic craters—are met by rapid mutation of "the institution" in order to join in or accommodate this changing approach.

There is a general temptation, perhaps a desire of art history, to ascribe a strong element of institutional critique to conceptual practices. While this exists in often quite potent forms, it is not always as clearly focused upon an examination of the particular institutions of commodity modernism within art as it is on a critique of wider power structures established within social, political and economic institutions. These range from the structures of language in conventional usage to overt manifestations of political power. Perhaps perversely, forms of the (art) institution, while complicit within these wider fields of power relations, served also as a location for such critique (whether self-reflexively or not, whether to the elision or neutralization of critique or not, is open to conjecture).

Indeed, within the Australian and New Zealand situations which I am most familiar with, the development of conceptual art practices was closely aligned to that of one particular institution—the art school either aligned with, or developing towards, a future association with the university. This developing model of a professional art education encouraged philosophical reflection, sociological inquiry and a general interdisciplinary approach that impacted greatly on approaches to art making as a process of intellectual inquiry. The sculpture program at Elam School of Art, University of Auckland, is a key example. It was utterly revamped into an interdisciplinary program by its head, artist Jim Allen. Between 1969 and Allen's departure in 1976, much of the most sophisticated conceptual practice in the region was being produced within or in association with this program—particularly in the area of performance work now extant in video or photographic form. (This is the case, for example, with the early to mid-1970s performance works of then Elam student Bruce Barber, who moved to Canada later in the decade where he has remained ever since, for some time now teaching at NSCAD University.) It might be argued, therefore, that the art school environment of much conceptual artwork became crucial for reshaping an understanding of work as exploratory process and of the gallery as studio (and vice versa). Associated with this, of course, was the often crucial role of the university-located gallery.

The educational institution also played some part in the partial realignment of the audience as participant within conceptual art. For example, as has been observed by artists involved with Elam at the time, audiences were primarily composed of peers, not uncommonly as participant audiences within performance actions or systems, many of which took place or were established in outdoor environments. Indeed, a key critic of and within this work, Wystan Curnow, has characterized 1970s performance in Auckland as "focused on the structure and consciousness of the group rather than the individual."[1] Audiences were necessarily small in number, but the almost workshop sensibility fostered in this environment carried over into other, more overtly public manifestations of work. The audiences these conceptual practices constituted for themselves were informed and drawn into the structures of work in new manners. On occasion it was exactly this expectation of the audience as participant—whether within actions, or the movement through constructed environments, or the necessarily active intellectual decoding of communication acts—that drew more mainstream media attention to the works when presented in larger public institutional settings, as much as it was the apparently baffling intentions and actions of the artists.

Of course the art school environment would never sate the ambition apparent within early conceptual art. In New Zealand there was the interesting situation of post-object practices being immediately foregrounded within at least a couple of major public art galleries. Under young founding director John Maynard (now a highly respected feature film producer in Australia), the Govett-Brewster Art Gallery in the remote, provincial North Island centre of New Plymouth opened in 1970 with a major kinetic and light environment work by Elam graduate Leon Narby. Back in Auckland, in the mid-1970s, Maynard subsequently ran a series of artist projects at the otherwise conventionally conservative Auckland Art Gallery that included such works as Bruce Barber's *Stocks and Bonds* (1975), involving the artist being restrained within a set of stocks for a 48-hour period, connected to his audience via a closed-circuit television loop, and David Mealing's *Jumble Sale: A Market Place* (1975), in which the gallery space was turned into a week-long charity fundraising event.

In Australia there appear to have been fewer opportunities in the early part of the 1970s for conceptual art to slip into the body of the institution. However, in the first half of the 1970s in particular, conceptual artists constructed their own spaces of practice—simultaneously studios and galleries—places of working life. Perhaps most notable were Inhibodress in Sydney and Experimental Art Foundation (EAF, now Australian Experimental Art Foundation) in Adelaide. Established in 1970 and closing in 1972, Inhibodress was the site of a number of key performance actions, including some of Mike Parr's earliest public works, and lingers as a key model of a set of artists creating their own contexts and, to an extent, their own publics.

The EAF was established by artists and theorists in the small South Australian capital city of Adelaide in 1974 with a very clear intent to foreground and support the development of

---

[1] Wystan Curnow, "Writing and the post object." In Christina Barton et al, (Eds.), *Action Replay: Post-script* (Auckland: Artspace and New Plymouth: Govett-Brewster Art Gallery, 2002), 42.

conceptual and experimental practices—to quote its website, to "encourage new approaches to the visual arts and to promote the idea of art as radical and only incidentally aesthetic." This was pursued with some vigour under founding director Noel Sheridan, with particular emphasis placed upon forging an international framework for Australian practice (or simply fostering international networks for Australian artists and audiences). The EAF was the first of what is now a nationwide network of publicly funded independent contemporary art spaces—a whole infrastructure for contemporary practice that to a certain extent emerged directly from the conceptual art period.

There are other key points of connection between practice and institutional structures that warrant mention here, including the relationship of conceptual art as fundamentally ephemeral in manifestation and the rise of the contemporary art "event," from the series of temporary international artist projects initiated privately by patron John Kaldor in Australia, beginning with Christo and Jeanne-Claude's *Wrapped Coast* (1969), to the Sydney Biennale (launched in 1973), the Mildura Sculpture Triennials of the 1970s and the ANZART artist exchange projects of the early 1980s; the development of an embedding, witnessing, participatory mode of reflective art writing; or the importance of new communication networks and platforms central to conceptual art as an international practice.

LUCY LIPPARD: In the US, in any case, and probably similarly in Canada, the sociopolitical zeitgeist was a major influence on the conceptual artists I knew. Opposition to the Vietnam War and the countercultural rejection of capitalism, authority and patriarchy made younger artists working zealously in their studios want to break out too. If you left the studio, you couldn't take all those bulky canvases and sculptures with you. This was a trip to be travelled with little baggage. The anti-object stance of this branch of the 1960s avant-garde also rejected the stance of the reigning Greenbergian abstraction, which was conservative, anti-intellectual and elitist. If Pop and Minimalism had shown a way out of the obsession with paint and surface, Conceptualism offered freedom to step out into the world and (so it seemed then) gain independence from the incestuous art market. Who would buy blurry snapshots, deadpan artists' books, photocopies of bright ideas or dictionary definitions? Could they be disseminated into the "real world" cheaply and easily? The populism of the medium clashed with the complexity of the messages, which were often aimed at the art world itself rather than toward any new audiences.

I wouldn't call anything that came out of this situation an "institution," but alternative mediums of exchange did develop, and they were sometimes welcomed into more open institutions like NSCAD, which became a showcase for conceptual art around 1969–70 and supported talks and performances and artworks that would have been spurned by most schools at the time. Seth Siegelaub's "businesslike" shows (or ironic parodies on the art business) that could take place all over the place at the same time, and artists' books, provided new networks with which to distribute new kinds of work.

CHANTAL PONTBRIAND: Coming out of Montréal, having inherited a mixture of American, Canadian and French culture and feeling the urge to participate in the creation of a new world, I must say that, as a young adult, I personally jumped into conceptual art as being a necessary and fantastic exploratory tool. For me as well as others, it sort of became a revolutionary disposition, even. I sensed the transformative power of the new modes of thinking and making that were coming along and immediately felt a kinship to the emerging practices.

Conceptualism marked a time in history where ideals and values were being shaken by a post–World War Two crisis. The enthusiasm created by the end of the war, which affected the entirety of the globe, and the forward-looking attitude that had followed the end of the war came to an end. American triumphalism had been emblematized by painting and heralded by the media (*Time* and *Life* magazines regularly gave American art coverage in an unprecedented manner). Art, in this period, had become a symbolic and collective value for the American people and politics. Being an artist had finally become a heroic position, as America seemed to rule the world. Andy Warhol, following the heroic generation of painters (Pollock, Morris, Still, etc.), quickly seized the opportunity to exploit the glamour and prominence that post-war art in America had gained.

The dreams put forth in this period started to be shattered as America faced new developments, with the Cold War getting nearer to home with the Cuban Missile Crisis and simultaneously with the escalation of the war in Vietnam. The new psychic environment created by the emancipation from a century of Modernism went to extremes that would culminate in the worldwide demonstrations of the sixties. The sixties generation was keen on making a new world that would finally emerge from Old World values and be carried to other continents by an already increasing level of immigration. Centred on the "peace and love" idiom, the demonstrations questioned racism, nationalism and sexism, as much as they fought bureaucratization, Taylorism and capitalism (and in other countries, communism).

In this context, centring art on concepts meant steering practices and concerns toward "the Real." Autonomous art practices, such as those supported by Abstract Expressionism, could no longer fulfill the needs of the sixties. The larger world became the territory to invest oneself in and investigate as an artist. The disconnection of art from life was no longer possible as new and very complex realities emerged. Art was to have a different agenda and concern itself with time as well as space, with the whole sensory organism rather than the dominant visuality, and with language. Language in this context had to be deconstructed as a material in itself, and this was done, paradoxically, by making it appear as a visual construct, and often by putting words on the wall, or appropriating words and photographic images in the form of self-published artists' books.

Although the history of conceptual art is by now well documented, there is still much to be explained as to how it came about, and especially so as there is more and more curiosity for how it may have developed in different parts of the world. Montréal is a cultural metropolis of a unique kind in North America. It is the second-largest primarily French-speaking city in the world. By 1960 there had been an influx of immigrants from Europe (Italian, Greek, Portuguese, German, as well as East European) that blended into the population of French, English, Irish and Scottish descendants, not to forget the ongoing presence of the Amerindians. Montréal became a cosmopolitan city, but not without lingering tensions that came in the aftermath of first the French and then English colonization (1759). By 1960, Canada was a well-established confederation of provinces, a country on its own, but the relationship between the two "founding" peoples was still uneasy, a situation described as the "two solitudes" in the book of that title by Hugh MacLennan.[2] The strong wind that blew in the post-war years and complicated questions of nationhood and identity, as well as affirmation and self-determination in the midst of modernity, also affected Québec and manifested itself in a major art movement led by Paul-Émile Borduas, a painter who brought together a group of artists from different disciplines to form the Automatistes. Although the group's manifesto *Refus global* appeared in 1948, its influence can be perceived in the very active artistic community that developed in Montréal in

---

[2] Hugh MacLennan, *Two Solitudes* (Toronto: Macmillan, 1945).

the aftermath of its publication. *Refus global* was only the beginning of a movement of cultural emancipation that would culminate in the election of a new social-democratic government of Québec in 1962. This government instigated the Quiet Revolution (*la Révolution tranquille*), which led the people of Québec to quickly adopt new values and modes of being. Dramatic transformations occurred in the field of universal health insurance, universal education, a separation of the state from the church, the institution of civic marriage, the recognition of the Amerindian as well as women's rights, to name only a few of the major changes that followed. To understand how important this opening up actually was, one must recall the Duplessis years (named for a premier who maintained power over Québec for the three decades that preceded the Quiet Revolution). These were years of stagnation and political withdrawal from the larger modern world, except for the activities of a persistent, liberal-minded elite.

The revolutionary spirit that animated *Refus global* was rekindled by these changes. In Québec also, a need to resort to art practices that differed from the traditional (although modernized) activity such as painting and sculpture, or ballet and classical music, became apparent. The art galleries, magazines and museums, all the existing institutions, were soon to be challenged by new ones. By 1970 sufficient changes were in the air for a new generation of art practitioners to emerge with new agendas. In Montréal, organizations such as Vidéographe and Véhicule Art were founded in order to support emerging practices such as video art, mail art, conceptual art, etc. I would say that the main focus of these organizations was to support social involvement as well as the internationalization of the situation. A need for increasing local as well as international exchange and development was at the heart of what was moving and shaking Montréal.

In this context, it became a personal necessity to found a magazine such as *Parachute*. Published in English as well as in French (a decision considered by many as heresy in the context of a growing separatist movement in the French-speaking province of Québec), *Parachute* set out to open doors internationally as well as to open minds to new art practices closely related to the new technologies available in the fields of image production (photography, film, video), sound and print, as well as in the world of information. All communication technologies, be they in telephone, radio, television or print, due to their increase in availability and speed, helped to bring about the new art. Conceptual art flourished in this context of art and life and the dialogue with artists in the rest of Canada and internationally.

MARI CARMEN RAMÍREZ: I will attempt to answer Jeff's question about the ways economic and sociopolitical conditions helped shape conceptual practices from the perspective of Latin America. However, I should note from the start that this is a difficult task given the complexity of the region. Unlike Australia, Canada or the United States, Latin America is not a single country but an operative concept that stands for more than twenty countries with diverse political, economic, ethnic and racial makeups, even within their own borders. In this context, no artistic movement or trend can claim to be continentally broad or, least of all, homogeneous.

Since the early sixties, Conceptualism not only played a major role in key countries of the region but, one could argue, produced highly original manifestations that in some cases anticipated developments elsewhere. In order to avoid confusion, it is important to distinguish three distinct moments in the emergence of conceptual practices in Latin America. The first encompasses the period 1960–74 and was largely restricted to Brazil (Rio de Janeiro), Argentina (Rosario and Buenos Aires) and the community of South American artists living in New York. This phase not only coincides with the emergence of Conceptualism worldwide, but also registered some of the most groundbreaking proposals coming from Latin America. The second stage took place between 1975 and 1980, a period when conceptual-based artists' collectives appeared in Chile, Colombia, Venezuela and Mexico, signalling the broader assimilation of Conceptualism in the region. It is emblematically represented by the Mexican phenomenon of *Los Grupos*. A third moment would apply to the emergence of neo-conceptual practices in almost every country of Central and South America and the Caribbean in the late 1980s and '90s. In stark contrast to the earlier manifestations, the recent explosion of conceptual-based practices as the *lingua franca* of the global art circuits can be linked to globalization and its demands for strategic economic assets from previously marginalized regions. Given the thrust of this conversation and the exhibition project that is grounding it, most of the comments that follow refer to the first stage outlined above.

What is interesting, in light of the responses to Jeff's question from Blair, Chantal and Lucy, is that in the case of Latin America, institutional critique, while present to some extent, did not play as critical a role in these countries in the 1960s and early '70s as it did in Australia, Canada, Europe and the United States. This is largely due to the institutional lag that has characterized Latin American countries since the colonial period. Art institutions—museums, schools, galleries and other emblematic spaces for the visual arts—not only lagged behind in resources but never achieved the degree of maturity and autonomy that they enjoyed in the First World. In this context, what triggered the emergence of conceptual practices in the early sixties was the ascendancy of authoritarian regimes in the main countries of the region. Between 1964 and 1976, six major countries fell under repressive military rule, including Brazil, Argentina, Uruguay, Peru and Chile. In these conditions, artists turned to conceptual tactics as a vehicle for understanding and conceptualizing "the Real" as well as communicating messages to their audiences. The Brazilian artist Cildo Meireles' *Insertions into Ideological Circuits: Coca-Cola Project* (1970) emblematically summarizes the interventionist, meaning-oriented thrust of these practices. In a move that anticipated the conceptual-based guerrilla tactics of US artists' groups—including women—Meireles provided messages for the viewer to affix to glass Coke bottles before returning them to the redistribution system. These works turn attention away from art and its institutions and redirect it toward the social sphere. In this context, ideology itself became the fundamental material identity of the conceptual proposal.

As a result of these contextual factors, the notion of dematerialization coined by Lucy in 1969 and its substitution by a linguistic mechanism never really took hold in Latin American conceptual practices. Instead, one could argue that the opposite took place: that is, artists reclaimed the object in the form of the mass-produced or assisted readymade as the preferred vehicle to articulate their conceptual proposals and convey messages to audiences. The notion of the readymade as a "package in which to communicate" ideas (*cf.* Luis Camnitzer) involved questioning the object's visual and semiotic functions within a larger social circuit or context. In other cases, exemplified by the late work of Brazilians Lygia Clark and Hélio Oiticica, the body itself—in all its sensorial dimensions—takes centre stage as the vehicle for the conceptual proposal. In other cases, paradigmatic groups like Tucumán Arde (Rosario and Buenos Aires, Argentina, 1968) appropriated the existing structures of mass media in order to denounce conditions of oppression and subordination, such as those that subjugated the workers of the Tucumán region. In all, Latin American conceptual artists integrated readymade objects, language, the body, communication and information theory as well as vernacular traditions in order to counter-circulate messages and communicate new values to audiences.

Going back to Jeff's initial question, there is no doubt that all of these tactics not only produced new audiences but ultimately redefined the very notion of the audience as a key component of the conceptual proposal. This participatory dimension of Latin American Conceptualism is the opposite of what happened with North American conceptual art, where the proposal is not only hermetic but resists producing an audience.

JK: Chantal, you bring up the new importance of language within early conceptual art. This was a shift that had a profound impact on the ways these new practices spread worldwide—helped, no doubt, by new (and newly refashioned) material forms like artists' books and mail art. And yet, as you rightly allude to, these processes were quite fraught—especially in regions of the world where English was not the primary language. How did the new dissemination of language-based art from (primarily) Anglo-American art centres play out in the non-English-speaking communities of the Americas, Asia and Europe? Is there a strong counter-history of non-English language-based conceptual practices? And if so, what impact did these have on English-speaking artists?

CP: In order to elaborate somewhat more about the question of language in conceptual art, one has to see how language constituted the main axis, the pivot of the thing. A concept is a figure of the mind. It is a form in which content manifests itself in a direct, open manner. The concept reveals the discrepancy of the mind/body problem. How is an idea incarnated, how does an idea, immaterial as it is, become a material body? In the language of art, one would say that the idea becomes an object. Conceptual art questions the nature of the object. Before the concept was put forward in the twentieth century in the history of art practices, art materialized itself in the form of painting, sculpture, architecture, etc. It necessarily took a form other than language itself. There was a moment, though, at the end of the nineteenth century when language itself became an object of plasticity, and of pure visuality. One thinks of Stéphane Mallarmé or Raymond Roussel, in poetry, or else Erik Satie in music. These artists were very influential to Marcel Duchamp, as they were to several Canadian conceptual artists such as Rodney Graham, Raymond Gervais and Rober Racine.

So language plays the main part in the development of what we now refer to as conceptual art. Mostly, one thinks of language as the ability to express ideas in the form of words. The articulation of ideas or concepts in the form of words gives language the possibility of communicating ideas that are nurtured in the self to others. Language has a social function. It is a mark of identity, but also that of a shared notion of identity. Language is one of the main bonds of community. Community is a shared-being, one that is never fixed and always in transformation. It begins with the sharing of concepts, it brings up differences, and ends up developing, morphing, into an unprecedented form of this shared-being. Chantal Mouffe in her philosophical essays has developed this recognition of antagonism being linked to agonism in community building. Conceptual art has dealt with these divergent forces in the social world—the work of Jenny Holzer or Barbara Kruger in what can be called the post-conceptual period has pointed out this phenomenon. Conceptual art has also given us a different view of history in the reenactment of historical tropes or moments. In the visual world, it has mapped out new territories of learning, of interpretation and of criticality. These tend to be recognized today as being much more diversified and non-linear in their development than they were in art history as it was practised before the sixties.

From this perspective, is it still possible to say that conceptual art was and still could be dominated by one language—that is, the English language—or even that conceptual art originated in the Anglo-Saxon world and hence dominated the history that followed? I find this way of putting things quite antiquated in view of the current evolution of theory (to use a word that brings together philosophy, sociology, history, as well as art history). One must at this point place the development of conceptual art in the context of local/global cultures that are varied and disparate throughout the world. Fluxus, as a movement, quickly realized that new practices and attitudes in art were emerging internationally and that these were not an essentially American phenomenon. A good number of the new artists working in New York and now associated with conceptual art were Americans whose forefathers had recently immigrated mostly from Europe after the great wars or were immigrants in their own right from different parts of the world. English became a working language, a bonding device for a new international community of artists whose practice was based on ideas and took innovative material incarnations.

Ideas travel through regions of the world and through time. They create hybridization and signify change, which affects attitudes, modes of being as well as modes of working, and eventually modes of government and sharing of public space. Conceptual art has tapped into this specific phenomenon in many instances. It has identified time as being a substrate of visual art, in the same respect as space. On Kawara's date pieces are emblematic of this moment in art history where the notion of time took a leap forward in art. The migration of ideas, as well as that of people themselves, is a determining factor in the development of conceptual art throughout the world. It cannot be interpreted in the linear mode still too endemic to art history. In a more complex way, conceptual migrations work through social fabric as a kind of weaving of opportunities and encounters, influenced by the material as well as the social world. The question of technologies, closely linked to the material work, as they give it form, was also a determinant field for conceptual art. Technologies, including communication technologies and modern transportation, eventually contributed to lifting the word off the page and spatializing it, putting it into space. The dematerialization of art was made possible by this new environment, which World War II greatly enhanced, as an unprecedented global war.

Although conceptual art in Montréal is mainly associated with Véhicule Art, the artists' centre that was founded in 1972 in order to support emerging practices, it is interesting that those artists we mostly associate with conceptual art (and its emphasis on language) in this city were only peripherally associated with the gallery, that is Raymond Gervais and Rober Racine. The main artists working in a conceptual mode at Véhicule were Bill Vazan; Suzy Lake, working in photography; Roland Poulin and Henry Saxe, in sculpture; and Françoise Sullivan, a multidisciplinary artist, to name only a few of the dozen artists involved in exhibiting their own work as well as in bringing artists from Europe as well as the United States or Canada (Les Levine, Sol LeWitt, Vito Acconci, Franz Erhard Walther, Cioni Carpi, etc.). Gervais and Racine both worked on historical data that they reprocessed in a conceptual mode. Raymond Gervais' influences came very much out of his interest in and knowledge of jazz and new music, especially John Cage, as well as world literature, music and the development of contemporary practices in Europe as much as in America. Rober Racine studied literature and film, and was also influenced by the history of modern literature and music. His first works dealt with Gustave Flaubert and Satie, and he went on to develop multiple variations of works on the French dictionary *le Petit Robert*. As much as Gervais was involved in a deconstruction of music, its history, its technologies, Racine was involved in that of the French language and the forms that time had given it, such as the novel or the dictionary. Both oeuvres are very complex and difficult to summarize here, but they do help us understand the inner workings of the question of language and conceptual art as they are related to time, place and history. Both are as very much infused by their knowledge of world history as they are by their curiosity for the avant-garde in art, as it could still be called in the seventies. I would think that this observation can translate into other contexts, whether American or English, German, Brazilian or Korean. Conceptual art, precisely because of the fact that it is closely linked to language, to the formation and circulation of ideas, to shared and developing identities and communities, cannot be traced to an easily identifiable origin or place.

In fact, its critical edge, its meaning, is to be found in analyzing, from today's perspective, how different this practice could be as it emerged in different individuals and different locations. To evaluate things in this manner gives us a better understanding of how powerful the turn brought about by conceptual art in the history of art actually is. For the generation of artists such as

Gervais or Racine, or Vancouver artists who came out of conceptual art—Rodney Graham, Iain and Ingrid Baxter (N.E. Thing Co.), Mr. Peanut, Ian Wallace, Jeff Wall, Ken Lum and Roy Arden—or, in Toronto, General Idea, conceptual art had the effect of a time bomb. Minds could explode and search out new ways of working, and especially new modes of apprehension in a very different world than the one that had been inherited from the recent past.

JK: Mari, how does this relate to the situation in Latin America?

MCR: I would say that in Latin American Conceptualism there is not so much a counter-history of language-based conceptual practices but an inversion of these practices. In other words, the self-reflexive quality of these central practices is turned on its head exposing the instrumental nature of language itself. Latin America, for example, produced one of the earliest examples of language-based conceptual art. I refer to León Ferrari's *Cuadro escrito* [Written Painting] (1964), a work that consists of a calligraphic rendering of a baroque text describing a nude painting, something inconceivable for North American conceptual artists. *Carta a un general* [Letter to a General] (1964), another paradigmatic work by Ferrari, uses a similar calligraphic technique to create a nonsensical message that calls into question the authority of the military. Despite these early incursions into language-based art, artists from Latin America did not limit themselves to exploiting the empirical properties of language in the same way as their North American counterparts. Clearly, the urgency of intervening in "the Real" in order to expose pressing, life-threatening issues precluded the type of highly abstract, self-reflexive propositions embodied in language-based Conceptualism. The notion of the artist as an encoder rather than administrator of meaning is present in all these propositions that seek to actively communicate messages to their audiences. In the works of those artists who based their early proposals on language, tautology became a vehicle for irony (Luis Camnitzer) or for exploiting the links between words and social structures (Antonio Dias). In most of these cases, as well as many others, the referent takes the place of tautology, and the subject becomes reinserted in the conceptual proposal.

JK: Discussions of early global conceptual practices are often framed by an opposition between centre and periphery. The underlying assumption being that countries or regions on the periphery—as in Canada's case—drew and benefitted from the activities and innovations made at the centres. Given the expansion of cultural networks from regional to new international contexts, as well as a new mobility of artistic and curatorial practice that came with what Lucy has described as the dematerialization of the art object, does this construction hold up? In many ways, it raises questions as to what extent the centres benefitted from or depended upon the existence and activities of the peripheries.

DF: From where I sit, it's very difficult to respond to this question without referencing Terry Smith's essay "The Provincialism Problem,"[3] an essay aptly so much more influential in its "provincial" context—Australia—than its place of publication—New York. In retrospect, the act of its intervention into this context appears almost as significant a commentary as the text itself. Smith set out the conditions of what he termed the "provincialist bind" of art in Australia in particular, but also of almost any art-making context outside of New York. For Smith, writing in the early 1970s, "cultural transmission is one way," the system of power reinforced in fact by its exceptions. "As the system stands . . ." Smith wrote, ". . . the provincial artist cannot choose not to be." Yet, and here Smith is clear, this condition is effectively a collective cultural projection, actively generating its own agency.

---

[3] *Artforum* 13, no. 1 (September 1974): 54–59.

An extraordinary amount of work on this subject has been undertaken in the thirty-five-plus years since publication of this text. From the present day, the essay reads as both freshly urgent (just update some of the reference points) and somehow deeply outdated in terms of both contemporary migration and cultural diaspora and the conceptual tools and material processes by which artists respond to and interrogate each other's work. Twenty-five years later, writing in the *Global Conceptualism* catalogue, Smith claims Conceptualism of the mid-1960s "was produced in cities such as London and New York by artists such as Ian Burn from Melbourne and Billy Apple from Auckland, that is, by individuals striving to define an art practice distinctive for travelers between the peripheries and centres of cultural power." Conceptualism could be, was, "international in form" yet "local in content." The time-lag effect of distance remains, however. On the peripheries, Conceptualism occurred simultaneously with the institutionalization of conceptual art as a style. Nevertheless, writing in the late 1990s, Smith views Conceptualism as the practice through which the condition of the centre/periphery relationship in all its complexities could be subjected to critical analysis within a newly self-reflective practice.

The phenomenon described by Smith in 1974 is at least stretched and tested by conceptual artists in the 1970s, but even within such work, specificity of context—the political and economic conditions within which the work is generated—necessarily inscribes its presence.

As for speaking back to the centre, under Smith's 1974 model the centre is necessarily sustained by the very existence of the periphery, without ever allowing it a form of affective agency. At the micro-level of artist networks, new forms of dispersed artist communities certainly formed at the heart of conceptual practices, and these would necessarily have had some shaping influence at the centre, but more overtly? Perhaps that's the efficacious function of present day art history and curatorship. Last year, forty-six years after his first major London exhibition, forty-three after his first major New York showing, New Zealand conceptualist Billy Apple finally had his European institutional survey at Witte de With.

LL: Writing from the centre, I obviously have a kind of different take on this. Keep in mind that New York itself was wildly provincial in its ignorance of art from "elsewhere," at least until the conceptual days, when things did improve thanks to the portable nature and easy transmission of conceptual art (nothing like email, but it seemed rapid at the time). I was not alone in finding it really exciting to hear about similar ideas that were in the air all over the place, though years later, after the *Global Conceptualism* show/catalogue, I realize I was not as much in the loop as I thought I was when writing *Six Years*. (It should also be said that a lot of work in *GC* was made later than 1973 . . .) Iain Baxter was my closest extra-US connection and his unbounded enthusiasm for all things conceptual was contagious. I travelled very little to Europe and depended on my peripatetic artist friends to inform me, which they did, but only about artists they approved of. I was in Australia and New Zealand at separate times in the mid-seventies and maintained connections with some of the artists Blair mentions. I think the peripheries concocted their own conceptualisms that in turn did reinvigorate the centres (although I'm not sure centres were, as Blair puts it, "necessarily sustained by the very existence of the periphery")—primarily because some of the artists were so committed to dematerialized work as a means of communication. That was half the fun, and a certain intentional decentralization came along with it.

Opposite
Greg Curnoe, *Map of North America*, 1972.

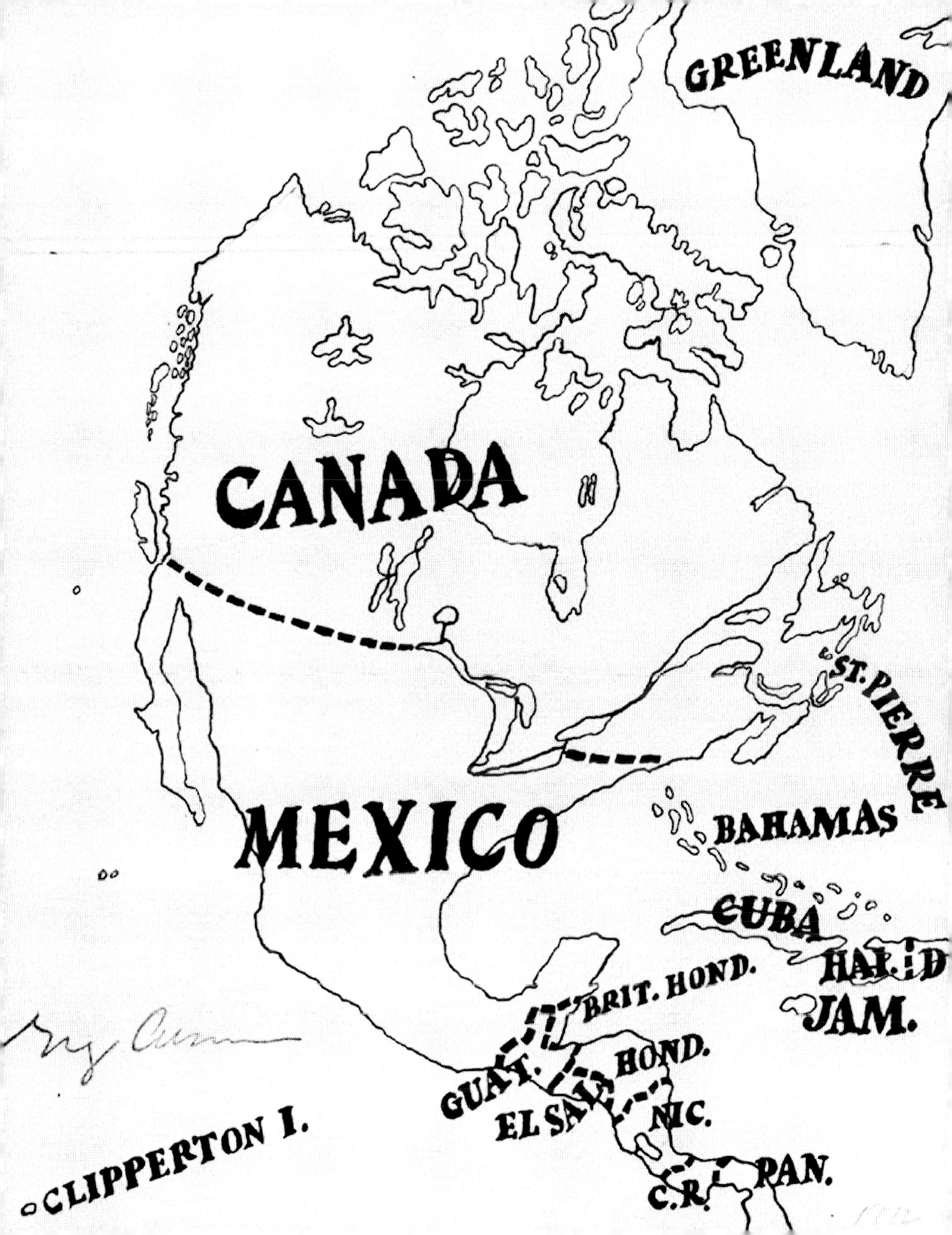
GREENLAND
CANADA
ST. PIERRE
BAHAMAS
MEXICO
CUBA
HAI. D
JAM.
BRIT. HOND.
HOND.
GUAT.
EL SAL.
NIC.
C.R.
PAN.
CLIPPERTON I.

I might argue with Terry Smith's "the provincial artist cannot choose not to be provincial." Those with the confidence to be where they were could, as I said, do their own thing. Those dying to get into the international art world could do a more homogeneous thing and were often very good at it.

Latin America was really another centre, in that artists there were making early innovations and expanding early ideas, though I know the Latino artists didn't feel that way; they were working under dictatorships, and when they got to NYC they were ignored by the hierarchy. Luis Camnitzer was one who managed to be a conceptual activist in Uruguay, from NYC.

Time lag was definitely a problem. (My partner says I'm always saying "we did that X years ago in New York.") Despite the more rapid than usual transmittal of conceptual art through magazine pieces, catalogues, etc., "I did it first" has always been a big deal in the commercial art world and instant obsolescence worked against "provincials."

To go back to responses to the first point, I learned a lot about local details from Blair's and Chantal's texts. The academic connections prevalent in Australia didn't even exist in the US, at least not until later. Since I didn't teach, I may have missed something, but it was young rebellious artists who did it all in NY. Kosuth did disseminate a lot of his own ideas through the School of Visual Arts, but that was an art school. I don't remember any academic support whatsoever for these ideas. If there was a professor, it was Sol LeWitt, who was older than the others, or Siegelaub with his distribution strategies.

MCR: I agree with Lucy that Latin America operated as a centre for new ideas and approaches to Conceptualism from very early on. To the extent that these ideas migrated to the centres, they served to expand or refuel conceptual practices active in these hegemonic enclaves. However, this only happened if the art under consideration was recognized and legitimized, which was not frequently the case. Indeed, it has taken a long time for the mainstream to recognize the authenticity and originality of the Latin America–based conceptual artists and groups. León Ferrari, for example, only achieved his due recognition in 2007 at the age of eighty-seven. Until very recently, these artists were completely marginalized, a situation that led, in many cases, to the loss of significant aspects or even the entirety of their production. And, despite the fact that today conceptual artists like Gabriel Orozco (Mexico) or Jorge Macchi (Argentina) are enjoying the benefits of expanded visibility in global circuits, I would strongly argue that the uneven axis of exchange that until now has characterized the relations of Latin America to the First World has not significantly changed. Globalization has done nothing to erase this unequal relationship; in any case, it has accentuated it. The increased demand for conceptual-based Latin American art is nothing but the demand for strategic assets from this region to satisfy the taste of global collectors and their local counterparts.

JK: Charlotte, I wonder if you could touch on your experience with the Mezzanine at Nova Scotia College of Art and Design, where you were director from 1970 to '73. Under Garry Neill Kennedy, the NSCAD program really developed through its close relationship with visiting artists and curators (including Vito Acconci, John Baldessari, Dan Graham, Sol LeWitt and many others). The school's Lithography Workshops and artist book publication series seem especially interesting here in that this shifted the site of production away from the centre to a periphery.

CHARLOTTE TOWNSEND-GAULT: Part of the trick now, for me, is contending with what must be called youthful idealism, naïveté and the assurance that came from a sense of belonging to something that had no particular place. As I remember, that's how many people I knew felt in the late sixties: a kind of dazed commitment. (What I might now think about small-group cohesion, discursive realms, bureaucratization of knowledge, charismatic manipulation, social rules and the rules of art, power differentials . . . came later.) A memoir is not required here, but I found Chantal's thumbnail of the mood into which she was personally caught prior to *Parachute* very telling, and helpful. Anyway, that's more or less how I would characterize myself, newly arrived in Canada, exposed as an arts reporter to what was happening in Vancouver from 1968 to '70, and then, with a significant push from Lucy (whom I first met when I was living in the N.E. Thing Co. headquarters in North Vancouver) and a pull from Garry Kennedy and Jerry Ferguson, arriving at the Nova Scotia College of Art and Design in Halifax, to do a job that was simultaneously focused and inchoate. Focused, that is, on a kind of art that seemed, excitingly, to be making itself up as it went along, but that was instantly recognizable as conceptual art. Inchoate because none of us really understood what would be involved in having a space in an institution that was conceived of as a non-space, with a brief to "solicit," "respond to," "enable" this kind of work, essentially de-institutional. This operation was called the Mezzanine (not the Mezzanine Gallery), being on the half-floor above the Anna Leonowens Gallery. The name then, and now, recalls for me the stops of an elevator through a department store—but the space, like what happened in it or through its agency, was supposed to be shorn of such references. It is what it says it is: display modes, modes of address, of circulation—taken as a phenomenological square one.

If there was doublethink it didn't seem too troubling at NSCAD just then. The artists we were working with were set on evading the traditional framing devices for art, were against institutions, centralization, commodification and forms of established advantage. The letters I sent out from the Mezzanine invited ideas, or instructions, or projects that were, mostly, mailable (email obviously didn't exist), could be evanescent, or physically non-existent. They often needed to be executed by students, a convenient institutional by-product.

Of the assorted critiques inherent in conceptual art, as initially understood, that of the institution as classification machine would have been primary, and as validation machine a close second. Nevertheless, It Is evident that an audience is required—for validation, if not classification, purposes. NSCAD, the institution, was prescient on this. The Mezzanine existed primarily to put its projects into circulation, for audiences elsewhere, from an institutional address that intended to bring *réclame* to the work and to itself. The address list was stellar; Seth Siegelaub, for one, loaned me his contact books. This opens into the next question: circulation.

All the Mezzanine works and materials were displayed, or variously made available to students and visitors—but still a limited audience. Did it seem important to enlarge it locally? Not really. In retrospect it would seem that ideals of accessibility and communication were both far-reaching and exclusive from the vantage point of NSCAD and the Mezzanine. Among groups, individuals and sites with which we were actively connecting (sending and receiving notices and materials) in the late sixties and early seventies were Art & Project in Amsterdam, Art & Language and Gilbert and George in the UK, Ian Burn and others in Australia, Alan Sondheim, the N.E. Thing Co., then a bit later A Space and General Idea in Toronto and Bill Vazan in Montréal. They led inevitably to others. Considering the modes of connecting—some of which we were naïvely keen enough to think that we were inventing—they seemed more like connections between scattered hubs; this would have been closer to Latourian networking than international idealism, and globalization came later.

Among formative influences from elsewhere: Kosuth and LeWitt in terms of ideas and Dan Graham in terms of technology. From Vancouver: N.E. Thing Co., with its obsession with the levelling materiality of plastic, ordinary manufacturing processes and the connectivity enabled by telex technology, was an important exemplar. Les Levine's comparable directions also drew in some senses on Warhol. More knowingly cerebral, giving themselves art historical lines of descent, Ian Wallace and Jeff Wall and Duane Lunden produced the *Free Media Bulletin*—critical in its open, but controlled, distribution of the thinking that seemed essential at the time. Wall's *Landscape Manual* and Duane Lunden's *Locator* project both confirmed the levelling serendipity of that late-sixties moment, the evening out, the equal, undifferentiated, access that an interest in phenomenology, the capacity of the camera, and their, our, left politic seemed to enable. (*Flatland* was a cult read, not incidentally.)

These ideas informed the direction taken by the Mezzanine. Artists' co-ops and artist-run centres were starting up everywhere—some of them at least untrammelled by the contradiction of being both part of, and against, the institution, or that other unexamined disjuncture between phenomenologically given and political idealism. They were cemented by visits to Vancouver by Smithson, Lippard and Dan Graham—the last two in particular continuing their influence on to NSCAD. At the same time, the Lithography Workshop was working with some of the same artists who visited David Askevold's Projects Class and did work in or for the Mezzanine. Although they were extending the meaning of print and its distribution norms in various ways, I thought then, and still do, that these practices were something else, distinct from the institutional critique, object-phobia and counter-commoditization.

From what I remember, from the evidence in the Mezzanine archive, and from what I have gathered subsequently, the artists we worked with, most at nascent stages in their careers, welcomed the opportunity not just to show their work—that would be obvious—but to get it out in ways that were free, in every sense, and unencumbered, in some senses. Cyberspace has made this normal. Back then it was not. (For the record, in some parts of Canada there was resistance to what was happening at NSCAD, driven, inter alia, by a vituperative anti-Americanism.) The disjuncture between the utopian desires attached to the unprecedented extended reach for ideas and projects that seemed to bypass the flawed art world and the speed with which it all became business as usual, has been remarked upon by cynics and idealists alike.

JK: It's interesting that you come back to the issue of circulation. As has already been mentioned earlier in the discussion, the circulation of both bodies and artwork was quite important in forming the character of earlier conceptual practices. More recently, this early work is made visible primarily in the form of exhibitions and their accompanying publications. According to at least one scholar (William Wood), these have been largely driven by a revisionist agenda that obscures the actual geographic and cultural diversity of conceptual art while affirming an orthodox canon that favours those artists working at the centres of the art world in Europe and North America.[4] Do you think this argument is valid? If so, to what extent might the revisionist agenda of such exhibitions have been driven by the interests of enhancing the economic value of historical conceptual art for the purposes of commercial dealing and collecting today?

CTG: It now seems as predictable that ways would be found to commodify the consequences of these moves—wherever they were made—as it should have been predictable at the time that this is exactly what would happen. Even the flimsiest and most ephemeral, and so potentially the most surprising, works proved marketable. But who really was surprised? Did we actually think that these works were, per se, market resistant because of these qualities, and that these artists, in the end, would not acquire some renown?

---

[4] William Wood, "The insufficiency of the world." In *Intertidal: Vancouver Art and Artists* (Antwerp: Museum van Hedendaagse Kunst and Vancouver: Morris and Helen Belkin Art Gallery, 2005), 63–76.

Nevertheless, significant inroads were initiated then into the perceived hegemony of Modernism: the recovery of individual performative modes linked to collaborative production styles, a particular attention to materiality, focus on the body, enthusiasm for new forms of technologically enabled communication, and yes, the moving around of the artist as opposed to the shipping of art objects. All of which were prescient. This is not to say that other hegemonies, or versions of the same, have not taken over, or that there are not new attempts at resistance.

Could it be that the history, and consequences, of Conceptualism extend into the upper reaches of ideology—proof, if proof were needed, of its significance—thus demanding close attention and more time?

LL: I don't know the Wood essay, but I have no doubt whatsoever that the revisionist promotion of conceptual art (which I haven't followed that closely) has been partly market driven. So what else is new? And when I look back at *Six Years* I realize how few of those artists are still in the canon. Just as (I think I said before) the *Global Conceptualism* show contained some surprises (not least among them the ongoing flourishing of conceptual art much later than in the centres). And of course it continues. As does interest in it. Someone is trying to do a show of *Six Years*; if it happens I trust it will be inclusive and not just stars. Perhaps more interesting would be an update on those and younger artists' work?

BF: I can only assume that the exhibitions and publications that Wood refers to are produced and appearing in Europe and North America and thus are in a sense protectionist and isolationist vis-à-vis a canonical history? If I look at similar projects that might be labelled revisionist in this part of the world, they have tended toward an overt assertion of the particularity of locality. For example, they have often asserted alternative lineages through which to trace the particular trajectories of contemporary practice in Australian and New Zealand art than those offered by dominant threads of 1980s appropriationist and 1990s identity art. So they are revisionist, or perhaps better, recuperative in relation to local histories. Frequently at the heart of such curatorial/critical projects lies a complex claim to both the international traffic in ideas at the heart of conceptual or post-object practices, and their specific local dimension—a claim that the former inscribes the latter in ways differently accounted for in other art-historical explanations of the development of contemporary art.

While we may see the recent or current carving out of international profile for certain of these artists—I think here of Billy Apple or Mike Parr, for example—insomuch as new market influence is being developed, it is local, and the local commercial market is small. Even within a small market, economic influence is relative, and in this sense the art institutional and critical interest in conceptual and post-object practices over the past ten to fifteen years in Australia seem to me to have more created a receptive critical and economic environment for subsequent generations of post-conceptual artists than to have consolidated a blue-chip conceptual canon. Jim Allen's remaking of some of his own key 1970s performance and environment works (a process supported in part through a private gallery) has enhanced the profile to his work of course, but more broadly has enacted (performed) a recuperative art history in the field of the contemporary shared by many far, far younger peers for whom the work—or example of process—has become a new touchstone. Maybe I'm overly shaped by my position within a not-for-profit gallery sector and my academic perspective, but it seems to me that much focus here is being given to processes of archive formation and interpretation on one hand, and restaging of work in less than canon-building institutions on the other.

I might end with a note on the archive. In the latest issue of the Auckland Art Gallery journal *Reading Rooms* (issue 4, 2010)—which always contains some component focused on interpretation of its own archival holdings—there is a commentary by artist Stella Brennan on the process of working through some boxes of personal archives given to the gallery library by Bruce Barber. Brennan quite beautifully articulates something I imagine we've all felt.

> The continuing re-examination of post-object works often preserved only as instruction sheets, photographs or tapes, leaves me thinking of the increasing evanescence of our everyday communications, of art projects that leave trails of bytes, broken web links and defunct hard drives, and I wonder what a similar archival trawl will feel like in another 20 or 30 years. I'm not so naïve as to suggest a paperless future, but great portions of our discourse and exchanges are, for better or worse, no longer localized (perhaps stored in a Google server farm in Oregon or Eemshaven) nor so cleverly material (though most certainly embedded in physical stuff). What kind of nostalgia will there be in ancient email logs and discs of images, navigated by tags and filenames, when high definition video projections seem as redolent of a particular past moment as the blurry black and white of a Sony Portapac? What will form the evocative marginalia—in this collection, the venerable letterheads, the crinkly onionskin writing paper, the advertisements in the yellowed newspaper clippings—the things that give history weight and grit?

Indeed.

Opposite
Garry Neill Kennedy, invitation to *Garry Neill Kennedy*, Eye Level Gallery, 1980

GARRY NEILL KENNEDY

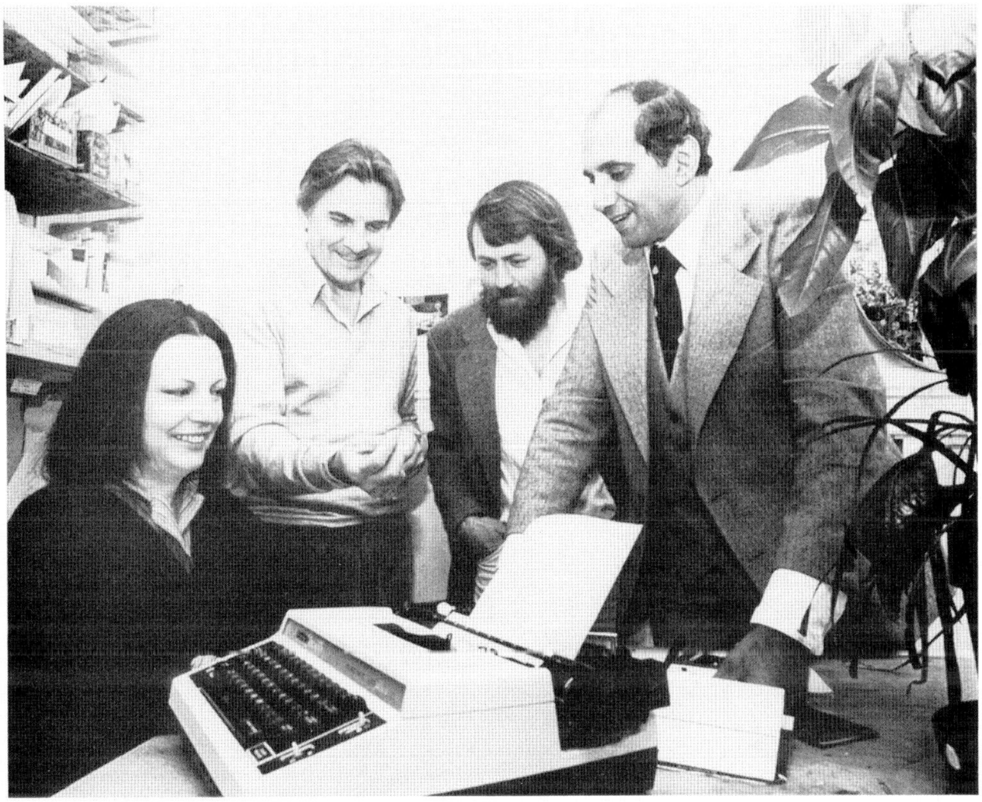

ATTEND PREVIEW—At a preview of his forthcoming exhibition at eye level gallery (June 23 - July 1, 1980) Garry Neill Kennedy is seen examining the bottom half of the lower case e which he has removed from the gallery typewriter. This portion of the e will remain removed for the duration of the exhibition and as it is completed a copy of each piece of typed correspondence during the term of the exhibition will be placed on the gallery wall.

Looking on from the left are Marina Stewart, eye level gallery director, and representatives of the exhibition's sponsors, John Greer, regional representative of the Canada Council and Louis Stephen, deputy minister, Department of Culture, Recreation and Fitness, Nova Scotia.

(Wambolt-Waterfield)

EYE LEVEL GALLERY
JUNE 23 - JULY 1, 1980
HALIFAX, NOVA SCOTIA

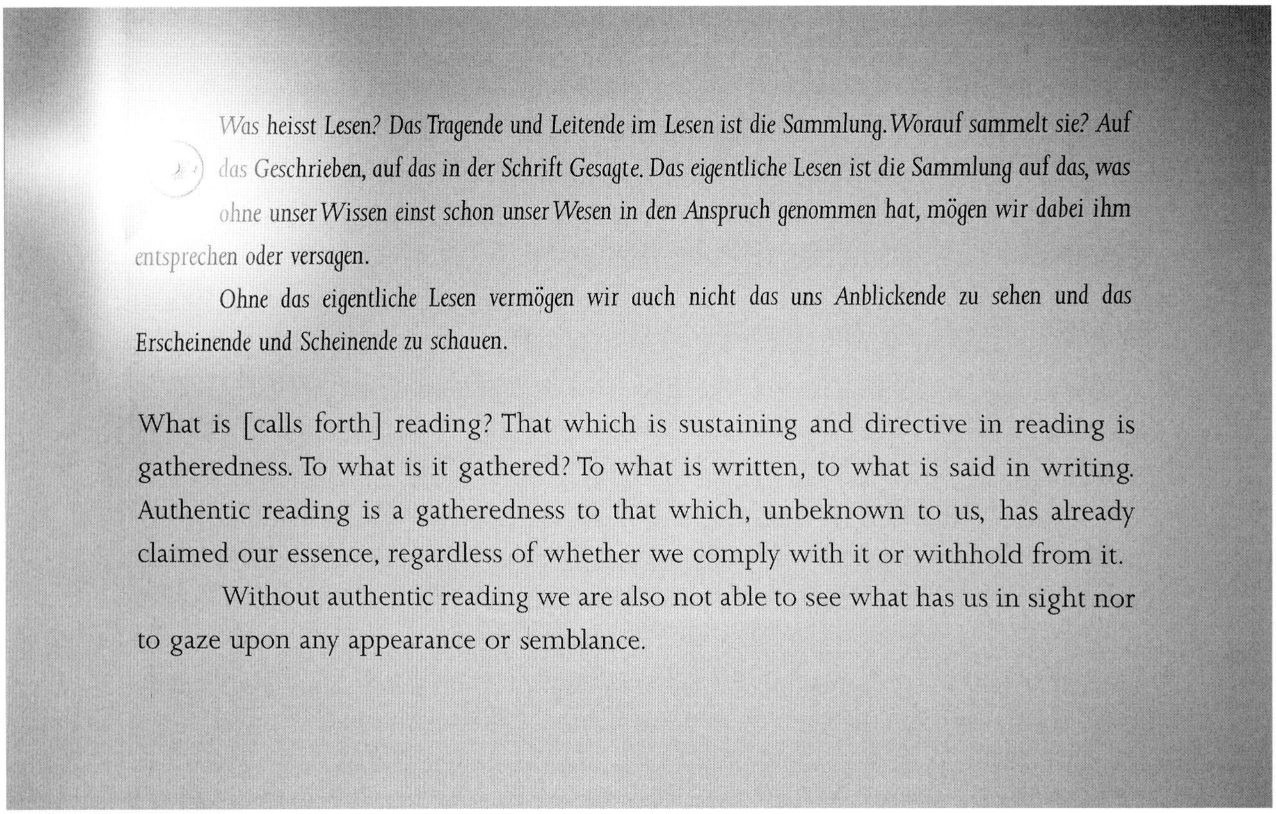

Gordon Lebredt, *Text with Warning Light*, based on a drawing from1977 (reconstructed 2010)

Conceptual Art in Canada 1965–1980: An Annotated Chronology

Compiled by Vincent Bonin (1965–1969) and Grant Arnold (1970–1980)

1965

JANUARY

Co-founded by art historian Yves Robillard and printmaker Richard Lacroix, the Fusion des arts group seeks to redefine the role played by artists as key players in effecting radical social change during the Quiet Revolution. Robillard, the group's spokesperson, submits a project to the general commissioner of the Canada Pavilion of Expo '67 entitled *Project for the creation of a space for the fusion of the arts*.

It was during a trip to Ottawa to negotiate with the commissioner that we found the term Fusion des arts, a term implying more than just synthesis, more than just integration; [it denotes] a real fusion, the refusal of isolation.

The term Fusion des arts . . . has various meanings. It is the name of a group of people who have founded a non-profit organization incorporated in 1965. It is also the name of an activity centre that aims to re-evaluate the relations between art and society . . . We live in America, but in an America that is not as rich and as "cultivated" as the United-States . . . We founded Fusion des arts . . . for it seemed indispensable that persons from different disciplines should meet and work to broaden the boundaries within which artistic activity was then confined.[1]

FEBRUARY

The fifth edition of the Festival of the Contemporary Arts, entitled "The Medium Is the Message," is held on the campus of the University of British Columbia in Vancouver. Since its inception, the festival has showcased examples of almost every manifestation of American avant-garde art. The Anna Halprin dance company performed in 1961. The following year, the festival hosted a performance by John Cage and Merce Cunningham. The 1965 version is based on Marshall McLuhan's concept of the "sensorium" to describe the festival's programming as a total environment that blurs the boundaries between audiovisual phenomena, artistic interventions and the gestures of spectators, who are invited to take part in an active way. Conceived by Iain Baxter, Arthur Erickson, Helen Goodwin and Takao Tanabe, and organized by architect Abraham Rogatnick, this edition lays the groundwork for the future interdisciplinary collaborations that distinguished Vancouver's arts scene in the second half of the 1960s and early 1970s.

The presentation in the Armouries (we have been calling it "The Armouries Show of 1965") was also certainly influenced by "happenings" that have been staged by artists in New York, San Francisco, Paris and elsewhere in recent years. These have characteristically involved a great deal of audience participation—not in the sense of sing-along, but in the sense of spontaneous, unselfconscious activity, which, in its simplest aspect, results from the audience having to walk amongst the events which are occurring around them . . . But since the audience is "on stage," its very presence makes it an integral part of the show, and part of the whole complex of events. McLuhan has said of our age ". . . a re-focusing of aims and images to permit ever more audience participation has been inevitable."[2]

[1] Yves Robillard, "Fusion des arts: historique." In Yves Robillard (Ed.), *Québec Underground 1962–1972*, Vol. 1 (Montréal: Les éditions Médiart, 1973), 179–185.

[2] Press release, "The medium is the message," 1965. Morris and Helen Belkin Art Gallery fonds, Morris and Helen Belkin Art Gallery, University of British Columbia, Vancouver.

1966

FEBRUARY

For the sixth Festival of the Contemporary Arts, Iain Baxter creates the *Bagged Place* environment at the Fine Arts Gallery, UBC, Vancouver.

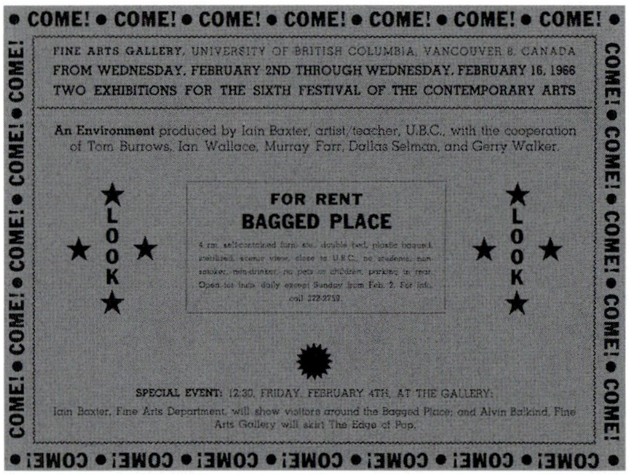

"FOR RENT: BAGGED PLACE
4rm self-contained furn. ste., double bed, plastic bagged, sterilized, scenic view, close to U.B.C., no students, non-smoker, non-drinker, no pets or children, parking in rear. Open for insp. daily except Sunday from Feb. 2. For info, call: 228-2759."

The announcement heralded the exhibition of Iain Baxter's extraordinary four-room apartment, in which not only the rooms themselves, but every object in them—mops, brooms, towels, cans, compacts, clocks, pictures, vegetables, chairs, tables, beds—were carefully bagged in plastic. (The phrase in the announcement "close to U.B.C." is especially piquant: the Fine Arts Gallery is located in the basement of the library building).[3]

NOVEMBER

N.E. Thing Co. is founded in Vancouver by Iain and Ingrid (then Elaine) Baxter. It is predated by IT, a collaboration between Iain and Elaine Baxter and John Friel, one of the first artistic undertakings in Canada to function in collective terms. IT's members chose to operate anonymously; they did not attend the opening of their exhibition at the Albert White Gallery in Toronto. When Friel leaves the group, Baxter conceives N.E. Thing Baxter Co. while he is artist in residence at the Centre for Communications, Simon Fraser University, Burnaby. This shortly becomes N.E. Thing Co., in order to distance their activity from the conventional understanding of art as a form of personal expression and to include a wide range of activities normally unrelated to art (research, communications, advertising, accounting and consulting).

1967

APRIL

The 1967 International and Universal Exposition—Expo '67—opens in Montréal. Although conceptual art is not showcased, the exposition's technological infrastructure—including the globalized telecommunications systems it heralds—influences the program of cultural decentralization that would later characterize the so-called "dematerialized" practices of the following decade. Aside from the exposition's impact in symbolically consolidating Canadian unity (1967 was the Confederation's 100th anniversary), in Québec the event is one of the Quiet Revolution's turning points. Members of the Fusion des arts group create immersive environments in the Youth Pavilion, where they also hold performances. Painter Charles Gagnon designs the interior of the Christian Pavilion, where he projects his film *The Eighth Day*, which narrates key events of the twentieth century's social and political history through a montage of scenes taken from newsreels. Michael Snow presents *Expo Walking Woman* in the Ontario Pavilion; the work functions as a sign system designed to manage the crowd of visitors.

In future, artworks will not only be shown in museums but in our surroundings as well; the environment itself becomes one with the museum, which thus becomes "a popular communication mechanism." Montreal's 1967 Universal Exposition has shed some light on the global environment that tends to integrate all media [within itself], and in which all the arts are themselves media.[4]

Above
Iain Baxter, invitation for *Bagged Place*, 1966

[3] Philip Leider, "Vancouver: Scene with no scene," *artscanada XXIV* no. 6/7, issue no. 109/110 (June/July 1967): 6.

[4] Marcel Rioux, "La société, la culture et l'éducation. Rapport Rioux (1968)." In *École et Société au Québec. Éléments d'une sociologie de l'éducation* (Montréal: Éditions Hurtubise HMH, 1975), 47.

MAY

Michael Snow completes his film <u>Wavelength</u>. At the beginning of the 1960s, Snow and Joyce Wieland had moved to New York and become acquainted with New York's experimental cinema milieu.

Wavelength *was shot in one week in Dec[ember] 66, preceded by a year of notes, thoughts, mutterings. It was edited and [the] first print [was] seen in May 67 . . . The film is a continuous zoom, which takes 45 minutes to go from its widest field to its smallest and final field. It was shot with a fixed camera from one end of an 80-foot loft, shooting the other end, a row of windows and the street. This, the setting, and the action which takes place there are cosmically equivalent. The room (and the zoom) are interrupted by 4 human events including a death. The sound on these occasions is sync sound, music and speech, occurring simultaneously with an electronic sound, a sine wave, which goes from its lowest (50 cycles per second) to its highest (12000 c.p.s) in 40 minutes. It is a total glissando while the film is a crescendo and a dispersed spectrum which attempts to utilize the gifts of both prophecy and memory which only film and music have to offer.*[5]

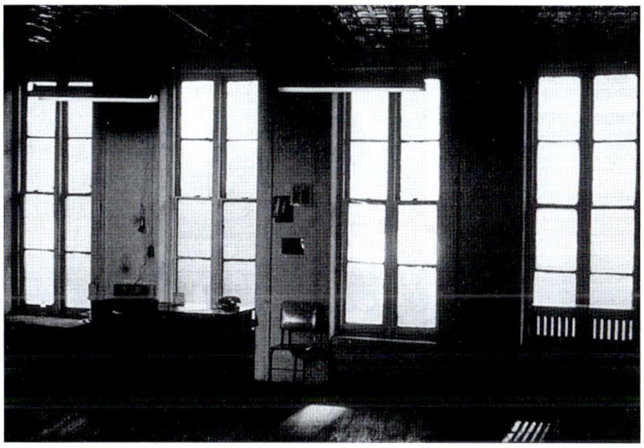

JUNE

<u>Sculpture 67</u> is held at City Hall, Toronto. Michael Snow presents <u>First Last</u> (1967).

First Last *(1967) is a kind of absolute that frames things that are fortuitous. It is totally symmetrical, a perfect square in middle-grey, turned in on itself . . . When you look through the slots, first you see the shiny aluminum that is the inner basis of the work, and then you realize you are seeing a prism of some kind itself . . . The sculpture is internal (but) it feeds on what is external . . . Art is often a limitation, a focusing-in on things itself . . . For the last 3 or 4 years I have been influenced by films and by the camera. When you narrow down your range and are looking through just that small aperture of the lens, the intensity of what you see is so much greater.*[6]

The Board of Governors of the Nova Scotia College of Art and Design (NSCAD), Halifax, hires artist Garry Neill Kennedy as the college's president. Kennedy subsequently teams up with Gerald Ferguson, David Askevold, Jack Lemon, Bill Nolan, John Pearson, John Greer and Pat Kelly to familiarize students with the most experimental trends in international contemporary art, thereby radically changing the school's curriculum. By relying on a flexible administrative structure and on several grants awarded by the Canada Council for the Arts, Kennedy affords emerging New York artists the chance to teach for one semester. From 1969 to 1975, NSCAD brings representatives of the American conceptual art movement into contact with some of their Canadian peers.

JULY

Influenced by the theories of Marshall McLuhan, a group of Vancouver-based artists, media theorists, scientists and architects found the Intermedia Society with a view to providing access to information technology. Many important members of Vancouver's contemporary art milieu take part in the organization's technical workshops, meetings and performances (Werner Aellen, Iain Baxter, Michael de Courcy, Kate Craig, Arthur Erickson, Gary Lee Nova, Glenn Lewis, Eric Metcalfe, Michael Morris, David Orcutt, Al Razutis, Jack Shadbolt, Vincent Trasov, Ed Varney and more). The cooperative is incorporated as a non-profit company on 6 July 1967.

INTERMEDIA WILL BE ENVIRONMENTALLY ORIENTED: There will be an emphasis on environmental creation,

---

[5] Michael Snow, "A statement on Wavelength for the experimental film festival of Knokke-le-Zoute," *Film Culture*, no. 46 (Fall 1967): 1.

[6] Michael Snow, interview with Dorothy Cameron, 23 May 1967, published in the catalogue of the *Sculpture 67* exhibition (Ottawa: National Gallery of Canada, 1967), 12.

Above
Still from Michael Snow, *Wavelength*, 1960

simulation and manipulation. Because of this, there will be an exchange with those social scientists who are interested in behavioral problems. In addition to environmental orientation, it is part of the outlook of the individuals connected with Intermedia to see things in terms of interrelationships. The traditional barrier between artists and scientists, besides having tragic consequences, doesn't make sense and it will be one of the purposes of Intermedia to facilitate fruitful exchange.[7]

1968

FEBRUARY

Random Sample, N-42, "an exhibition organized by Arnold Rockman of randomly selected and randomly displayed contemporary artifacts," is held at the Fine Arts Gallery, UBC, Vancouver. Twelve objects taken from the plane of everyday life are arbitrarily designated as sculptures; by default all other objects in the selection are classified as paintings.

The Random Sample show is growing in my mind all the time. As I conceive of it now, I shall make it an assignment for my students in the communication course I teach at York University. I shall ask them to supply photos of rooms in their own homes, plus photos I shall take in my own home and in the street downtown. Then we shall enlarge the photos, place a plastic grid around them, and select squares from a table of random numbers. The objects in the square then become the objects in the show. You will get a list of the objects divided into "inside objects" and "outside objects".[8]

N.E. Thing Co. exhibits *Piles* for the eighth Festival of the Contemporary Arts at UBC, Vancouver.

Piles are not pretentious—they are just there being beautiful and doing their thing. Why piles? Their structure is usually determined either by the object alone or the object plus the pile's imagination or lack of it. Naive piles usually are the greatest. It's the molecular structure and physical characteristics that give pile materials their nuances of stackability.[9]

MARCH

Udo Kasemets organizes *Technology Week* in various locations throughout Toronto.

One day Udo Kasemets asked if he could come and see me about an idea he had. Once again, God bless the Canada Council. We received a grant, and began what was to be for me a puzzling, exciting and astonishing series of "Mixed Media" presentations which culminated in producing a concert/performance of John Cage playing chess against Marcel Duchamp while electronic sound was being created by Gordon Mumma. The chess board was wired so that every time a piece was moved it would affect the nature of the sound. This performance took place in the Theatre at Ryerson (University) and it produced a good sized crowd. As the matches went on and on, our audience began to thin out. Finally, at about 11 o'clock we called it quits.[10]

Dennis Young founds a Toronto-based chapter of Experiments in Art and Technology under the administrative responsibility of the education department of the Art Gallery of Ontario, where Young is employed as a curator of contemporary art. E.A.T. was founded in 1966 in New York by engineers Billy Klüver and Fred Waldhauer from the Bell Telephone Laboratories and artists Robert Rauschenberg and Robert Whitman. E.A.T. functions by matching scientists and artists to foster interdisciplinary collaborations. The organization has over 300 members in North America, Europe and Asia.

Michael Goldberg is responsible for the Montréal wing of E.A.T.

APRIL

Les Levine produces "Disposable" for an issue of *artscanada* devoted to the ephemeral in artistic practice. The article contains instructions for constructing several "by-products" of Levine's project that make use of inexpensive materials. The artist allows his readers to become co-authors of these works provided they keep him informed in writing as to where such "by-products" were produced and send him photographic

---

[7] *INTERMEDIA, A Survey of Intended Project Areas*, 1967. Intermedia Society fonds, University of British Columbia Library, Rare Books and Manuscripts, Vancouver.

[8] Arnold Rockman, letter to Alvin Balkind, director of the Fine Arts Gallery, UBC, October 1967. Quoted in Lucy R. Lippard, *Six Years: The Dematerialization of the Art Object from 1966 to 1972* (New York: Praeger, 1973), 39.

[9] N.E. Thing Company, "Piles," *artscanada* XXV, issue 120/121 (August 1968): 44.

documentation. According to Levine, failure to comply with these rules results in an infringement of intellectual property and deprives the projects of all artistic value.

With disposable art you are free from any historical or monetary values. The concern becomes a completely conscious one. The viewer becomes involved only in the visual stimuli and awareness transmitted by the work. All other values become redundant, thereby making the art a pure experience, as it becomes a totally conscious expanding device. There are no heroics or nostalgia in disposable art. The mind absorbs various data and knowledge. If one can extract the consciousness from this knowledge and throw out the redundant matter, then a greater degree of intellectual activity is possible.[11]

MAY

Michael Morris' painting *The Problem of Nothing* (1966) is reproduced in *Artforum*; the image influences Ray Johnson, who was then in the process of creating his *Nothings*, fictitious meetings or non-happenings organized under the aegis of his New York Correspondance School. After initial contact, both artists engage in a long-distance dialogue that catalyzes the creation of Image Bank in Vancouver in 1969.

NOVEMBER

Opération Déclic at the Bibliothèque nationale in Montréal is a group of artists who hold meetings to discuss the role of cultural workers given the social changes that sweep Québec society at the end of the 1960s.

Please post
"OPERATION DÉCLIC"
TO:
To allow socially engaged artists of all disciplines to convene in order to make their current preoccupations heard and thereby to situate themselves in the socio-economic context.
...
To draft a manifesto or a "collage of testimonies" [collage-témoignage] *based on facts and experiences, grievances, and the outcome of various research groups.*
To redefine the situation of creative activity in Québec society.
...
It is high time that collective gestures be performed, to immolate our fear.[12]

1969

JANUARY

NSCAD inaugurates its Lithography Workshop, which operates until 1976. The studio allows seventy-nine artists to produce 290 works that explore the possibilities of lithography in innovative ways. Vito Acconci, John Baldessari, Dan Graham, Sol LeWitt, Les Levine, N.E. Thing Co. and Michael Snow are some of the artists who use the workshop during its first few years.

N.E. Thing Co. is incorporated. American curator and art dealer Seth Siegelaub compares the company's eleven departments to an intellectual mapping of operations that are usually linked in a fluid way in the process of making artworks. Excerpt of N.E. Thing Co.'s incorporation certificate issued on 16 January 1969 reads:

(i) To produce sensitivity information
(ii) To provide a consultation and evaluation service with respect to things
(iii) To produce, manufacture, import, export, buy, sell, and otherwise deal in things of all kind.

FEBRUARY

N.E. Thing Co.'s *Building Structure* is held at the Carmen Lamanna Gallery, Toronto. The collective installs a network of wooden beams onto the walls, floors and ceilings of the exhibition space. The resulting structure undermines the border between the gallery's perimeter and the fictitious environment it contains, which the company regards as its new field of operations.

---

[10] Avrom Isaacs quoted in John Parry (Ed.), *Isaacs Seen: 50 Years on the Art Front: A Gallery Scrapbook* (Toronto: University of Toronto Art Centre, Textile Museum of Canada, The Art Gallery of Ontario, 2005), 69.

[11] Les Levine, "The disposable transient environment," *artscanada* XXV, issue 116/117 (April 1968): 27–28.

[12] "Opération déclic (1968)," quoted in Yves Robillard (Ed.), *Québec Underground 1962–1972*, Vol. 1 (Montréal: Les éditions Médiart, 1973), 357.

MARCH

Survey/Sondage 69 is held at the Montreal Museum of Fine Arts. This exhibition is intended as a survey of the most important trends of contemporary art in Canada. The selection jury is composed of Andrée Paradis, editor of Vie des arts, artist Ron Bloore and New York art critic Lucy Lippard. Bill Vazan presents Twisted Plane, one of his first projects to make use of adhesive tape. The exhibition also includes works by Karl Beveridge, N.E. Thing Co., Michael Snow, Joyce Wieland and Ian Wallace.

Les Levine operates a restaurant called Levine's in New York. Levine describes the restaurant as the only place in New York City that serves Canadian cuisine (the menu also includes typical American dishes and certain Irish specialties). A closed-circuit video system allows clients to watch themselves from different spatial configurations.

Concrete Poetry, An Exhibition in Four Parts is held at the Fine Arts Gallery, UBC, Vancouver. At the end of the 1960s, many Vancouver-based artists and writers regard their works as concrete poetry, an idiom that foregrounds the (graphic, typographic) ways in which text occupies the printed page in order to create effects that are independent of literary content per se. In view of establishing a critical survey of this approach that draws on various artistic disciplines, curator Alvin Balkind collects, among others, collages by Ray Johnson, letters/drawings by Michael Morris, texts by bill bisset, and "Computer Poems" by Stephen Scobie. The resulting exhibition also includes a sample of slides, films and audio recordings produced by American and European artists whose work belongs to an expanded field of concrete poetry. Thus, exceptionally, the work of Joseph Kosuth is also included.

Language is liquid. It does not provide the shape of its own container. Literature gives language "something to say," a shape, a content wherein lies the power to tease. The power of literature as a creative activity has traditionally treated language as a transparent medium so that the content is revealed in a direct reading of "what is said." Recent movements in literature, concrete poetry explicitly, treat language as an opaque medium, which throws content back into the realm of literature as "something to say" rather than "what is said." A sense of historical context will clarify the rationale of this redirection.[13]

The exhibition included things I would have omitted. I should prefer to think that Concrete Poetry is something made (or discovered) by poets—that it has something to do with intention. Kosuth's (Art-as-Idea-as-Idea) intention is anti-objectness which is contrary to the concrete.
. . .
As art dematerializes, poetry materializes.
Words as material entities rather than references non-representational word/objects.[14]

APRIL

The Anna Leonowens Gallery, NSCAD, presents 5 Works, the first solo exhibition of conceptual art by Lawrence Weiner.

MAY

May 19, 1969–June 19, 1969 (untitled) is held on the campus of SFU, Burnaby. In his capacity as teacher and artist in residence at the Communications Department, SFU, Iain Baxter invites Seth Siegelaub to conceive the exhibition, which is part of a series of similar events the New York art dealer organizes in 1969. Although a poster was printed in conjunction with the exhibition, *May 19, 1969–June 19, 1969* is not accompanied by didactic materials, and thus conflates some of the works with the sites and contexts in which they appear. Since some works exist only as proposals (which are in some cases circulated by means of the local media), they remain entirely invisible to the Vancouver public. The publication is launched a few days before the end of the exhibition. It contains descriptions of the proposals Siegelaub received and, in cases in which such information was lacking, documentation on the works' material instantiation. A round table is held in the university's auditorium; all participants take part by means of a telephone network linking Vancouver, New York (Joseph Kosuth, Robert Barry, Sol LeWitt, Lawrence Weiner, Douglas Huebler) and Ottawa (Iain Baxter).

Opposite
Willoughby Sharp, unidentified man and Bill Kirby at the Edmonton Art Gallery for *Place & Process*, 1969

[13] Ian Wallace, "Literature—transparent and opaque." In *Concrete Poetry* (exhibition catalogue) (Vancouver: O'Brien Press Limited, 1969), n.p.

[14] John Noel Chandler, "Incoherent thoughts on Concrete Poetry," *artscanada* XXVI, issue 134/135 (August 1969): 11–13.

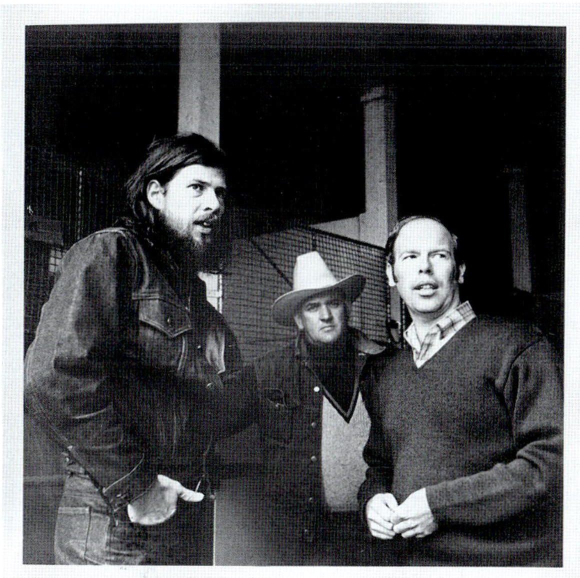

JUNE

The *N.E. Thing Co./La compagnie N.E. Thing* exhibition is held at the National Gallery of Canada, Ottawa. In May 1968, the National Gallery of Canada decided to organize an exhibition showcasing the work of an emerging artist to inaugurate the National Arts Centre's new building, designed in the then fashionable Brutalist style. Iain Baxter is selected. Baxter's project consists of opening a "branch" of N.E. Thing Co. on the ground floor of the Lorne Building on Elgin Street. The project thus temporarily recalls the building's original function, which was to house public servants. In the N.E. Thing Co. project the space is altered to look like the administrative offices and showrooms of an average-sized business. Iain and Ingrid Baxter conceive the environment as an "information centre" in which the company's own strategies of mimicking administrative functions meet the organizational infrastructure of the Canadian government apparatus. During the exhibition, the Baxters fax messages to the Paula Cooper Gallery, New York; the Communications Department at SFU, Burnaby; and NSCAD, Halifax. Iain Baxter also organizes a round table whose speakers include dealer Seth Siegelaub and art critic Lucy Lippard. In 1971, N.E. Thing Co. and Pierre Théberge publish a report of the company's activities at this second head office.

AUGUST

Bill Vazan and Ian Wallace produce *Canada in Parentheses/Canada entre parenthèses*. After becoming friends during the *Survey/Sondage 69* exhibition held at the Montreal Museum of Fine Arts, on 13 August, Vazan and Wallace open and then close virtual parentheses by drawing diagonal lines on the beaches of Paul's Bluff, PEI (Vazan) and Spanish Banks, Vancouver (Wallace). The resulting work comprises a series of photographs documenting each of the two sites and a telegram.

SEPTEMBER

The *Projects Class* becomes part of the curriculum of NSCAD. This course is coordinated by David Askevold from 1969 to 1970. Askevold invites James Lee Byars, Rex Lau, Dan Graham, Lawrence Weiner and others to organize events, exhibitions and symposia at the college, which he then integrates into the curriculum. According to the description in the 1969 NSCAD calendar, the *Projects Class* aims to familiarize students with a range of practices that do not subscribe to the "assumptions" of traditional disciplinary boundaries within the fine arts. In keeping with this program, the college leaves certain teaching positions open so as to accommodate artists who are in transit through Halifax. Each guest professor is asked to conceive a "conceptual" proposal or score to be executed by the students on site. Although some artists do come to Halifax, many send their instructions by mail or telephone.

Place & Process: An Exhibition of Outdoor Sculptural Projects is held at the Edmonton Art Gallery. Bill Kirby, gallery director, hires art critic Willoughby Sharp as the project coordinator. As part of the exhibition, N.E. Thing Co., Harry Savage, Lawrence Weiner and Lucy Lippard leave Edmonton, Alberta, and travel to Inuvik, Northwest Territories. Savage, Weiner and the Baxters produce site-specific works that are documented by Lippard through photographs and texts. Professor Virgil Hammock also takes part in the excursion and documents the group's activities.

Place & Process is divided into two parts. "Place" is composed of propositions presented in the gallery, mostly in the form of documentation. It includes a visual and textual account of the Inuvik excursion by N.E. Thing Co., Weiner, Savage and Lippard. It also includes works by Carl Andre, Joseph Beuys, Walter De Maria, Jan Dibbets, Barry Flanagan, Hans Haacke, Michael Heizer, Les Levine, Richard Long, Bruce McLean, Preston McClanahan, David Medalla, Robert Morris, Dennis Oppenheim, Klaus Rinke, Robert Smithson, John Van Saun, William Wegman and Larry Weiner. "Process," the exhibition's second part, presents six site-specific sculptural interventions made in Edmonton by Les Levine, Robert Morris, Dennis

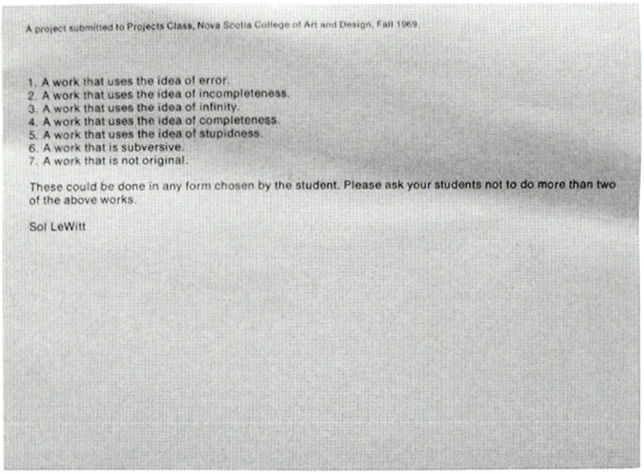

A project submitted to Projects Class, Nova Scotia College of Art and Design, Fall 1969.

1. A work that uses the idea of error.
2. A work that uses the idea of incompleteness.
3. A work that uses the idea of infinity.
4. A work that uses the idea of completeness.
5. A work that uses the idea of stupidness.
6. A work that is subversive.
7. A work that is not original.

These could be done in any form chosen by the student. Please ask your students not to do more than two of the above works.

Sol LeWitt

Card describing artwork by Sol LeWitt for David Askevold's Projects Class, NSCAD

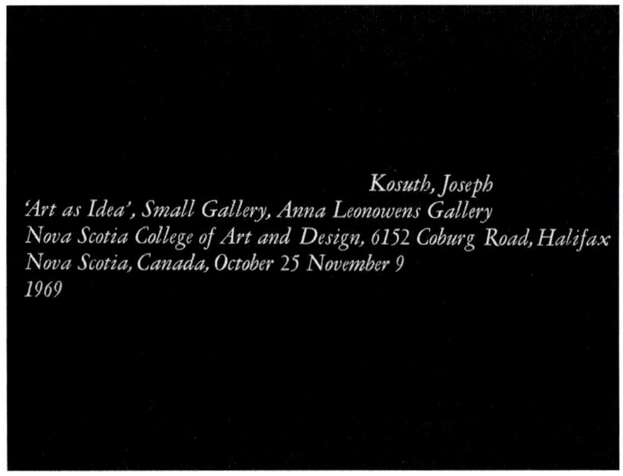

Kosuth, Joseph
'Art as Idea', Small Gallery, Anna Leonowens Gallery
Nova Scotia College of Art and Design, 6152 Coburg Road, Halifax
Nova Scotia, Canada, October 25 November 9
1969

Joseph Kosuth, invitation for *Art as Idea*, Anna Leonowens Gallery, 25 October–9 November 1969

Oppenheim, John Van Saun and Hans Haacke. The Baxters' contribution for the "Process" component involves retiring to an Edmonton hotel room for an indeterminate amount of time as a manifestation of what they call "non-activity." Willoughby Sharp asks Robert Fiore and Evander Schley of New York's Great Balls of Fire, Inc. collective to produce a 35 mm film to document the entire event. In November the film is screened at Sharp's New York office. Between 4 September and 26 October, the *AIR ART* exhibition organized by Sharp for the Lakeview Center for Arts and Sciences is also on view at the Edmonton Art Gallery. The work of several artists (Hans Haacke, Les Levine, Robert Morris) is shown in each of the exhibitions.

Joyce Wieland completes *Reason Over Passion/La raison avant la passion*, a film she began shooting in 1967. The film partly comprises scenes shot from the windows of a train as it travels across Canada from east to west. Wieland asks filmmaker Hollis Frampton to devise a mathematical equation that allows her to permutate the letters of the statement "Reason over passion" 537 times on the bottom of the screen. The statement's reiteration progressively unhinges its meaning from its source, namely, a phrase attributed to then Prime Minister Pierre Elliot Trudeau to describe his theoretical work ("Reason over passion; that is the theme of all my writings.").

I started working with that material as though it were a propaganda film, Triumph of the Will and Reason Over Passion. There was a dialogue between Trudeau and myself. But speaking to (and working for) Canada. The whole thing is a very high, far-out fantasy, I admit, and to the power figure, the father figure.[15]

OCTOBER

Joseph Kosuth produces *15 Locations 1969/70 (Art As Idea As Idea)* as part of the Projects Class at NSCAD, Halifax. This project is part of Kosuth's "Second Investigation." To produce this work, the artist asks fifteen international institutions to buy advertising space in local newspapers, thereby enabling the artist to publish excerpts from Ludwig Wittgenstein's thesaurus. Kosuth thus attempts to create new contexts of enunciation for Wittgenstein's propositions, which can be manipulated by a third party.

[The work] can be dealt with by being torn out of its publication and inserted in a notebook or stapled to the wall—or not torn out at all—but any such decision is unrelated to the art. My role as an artist ends with the work's publication.[16]

[15] Joyce Wieland, interview with Hollis Frampton, 1971, "I don't even know about the second stanza," in Kathryn Elder (Ed.), *The Films of Joyce Wieland* (Toronto: Cinematheque Ontario, 1999), 178.

[16] Joseph Kosuth quoted in Arthur R. Rose (pseud.), "Four interviews with Barry, Huebler, Kosuth, Weiner," *Arts Magazine* 43, no. 4 (February 1969): 22–23; reprinted in Gregory Battock (Ed.), *Idea Art: A Critical Anthology* (New York: E.P. Dutton, 1973), 145–146.

For the Halifax project, the propositions appear between 25 October and 9 November in the *Mail-Star T.V. Guide*, on billboards, inside city buses and in other sites, and are exhibited along with ephemera at the Anna Leonowens Gallery, NSCAD. Kosuth's exhibition is also shown at the Art Gallery of Ontario and at the Douglas Gallery in Vancouver, as well as in the United States (Pasadena Art Museum; Leo Castelli Gallery, New York) and at the National Gallery of Victoria, Melbourne.

New Alchemy: Elements, Systems, Forces/Nouvelle alchimie : éléments, systèmes, forces is held at the Art Gallery of Ontario, Toronto, and travels to the Musée d'art contemporain, Montréal. Curator Dennis Young presents Hans Haacke's conceptual and minimalist works in Canada for the very first time, including, among other works, *Condensation Cube* (1963–65). In the catalogue, Young quotes American art historian Jack Burnham, who endorses a systemic view of art exemplified by Haacke's practice. *New Alchemy* also contains works by John Van Saun, Charles Ross and Takis.

The collaboration that will come to be known as General Idea is founded by Winnipeg artists Michael Tims, Ronald Gabe and Slobodan (Jorge) Saia-Levias. The three artists share an apartment located at 78 Gerard Street West in Toronto. The group's members organize various impromptu events within that space; progressively, it becomes a meeting place for Toronto's alternative arts scene. Designed by Jorge Saia and John Neon, the *Belly Store* sells generic merchandise (such as plastic bottles filled with cotton) and operates a cash register. This environment foreshadows General Idea's later use of multiples and the metaphors of the store, the pavilion and the showroom.

Image Bank is founded by Gary Lee-Nova, Michael Morris and Vincent Trasov in Vancouver. The artists hope to circumvent the power of commercial rights holders over the visual culture of the 1950s and '60s. Their project relies on several strategies developed by the historical avant-gardes (Dada in particular) and Fluxus, but Ray Johnson is their main influence. In similar fashion, Image Bank appropriates the postal system as an ad hoc tool to consolidate a space for exchange that lies beyond the reach of the art market and the hegemony of the media.

The *Free Media Bulletin no. 1* is published by Duane Lunden, Jeff Wall and Ian Wallace (Vancouver: Intermedia Press, 1969). The publication comprises interventions (texts, works) signed by the artists as well as articles reproduced without the consent of their respective authors that coalesce into a field of references common to all three artists. The *Bulletin* includes, among other things, a portion of Marcel Duchamp's "Notes on the Readymade" (taken from *The Green Box*); a text by Richard Huelsenbeck in defence of the contemporary relevance of Dadaism (written in 1936); and excerpts from essays by Ad Reinhardt, Arturo Schwarz and Situationist Alexander Trocchi.

"All that stuff," conceptual art, idea art, documentary earthworks, etc., make more sense when it is read as a literature of images rather than confronted as works of art to be gallery promoted, even magazine promoted through gallery devices. The most important differences between art and literature lie in the effect or vulnerability as media. Its immediate inception and intention re the artist is not the point of interest here. We are now thinking of the public location of this art. I think that it is being publicly misled and misread. It is essentially "page" stuff that is plugging into the media power of the present gallery (commercial and institutional) setup and thus through the name-gathering (names as a commodity valued for their drawing-power, the "star" system of the art world) critics to the art magazines.[17]

NOVEMBER

Lucy Lippard lectures at NSCAD, Halifax (29 November). She previously lectured at the Vancouver Art Gallery, Vancouver (2 July).

Since you've already had as guest speakers, Larry Weiner, Iain Baxter, Joseph Kosuth, Dan Graham, James Byars and so on, you really should be more up to the kind of thing I'll be talking about than a hell of a lot of people in New York are. And that's one of the points of this kind of work. Anyway, as a critic, I'm just as prejudiced

[17] Ian Wallace, "A literature of images," quoted in *Free Media Bulletin no. 1, unpaginated.*

as the artists are, although I'm not supposed to be. I don't happen to think a good critic could be anything but prejudiced. Or at least committed, to put it more politely. I'm going to emphasize the physical aspects of a trend toward a de-materialized or non-object art. Mainly because I've got slides of them, and because I like slides for lectures. Afterward, I'd like the questions to be aimed more at the things that can't have pictures taken of them. Your questions can be specific, arising from my generalizations.[18]

Sculpture 69 is held at Hart House Gallery, University of Toronto. Organized by Paul Russell, this exhibition includes works by Karl Beveridge, Robin Collyer, Stephen Cruise, Les Levine and Michael Snow.

DECEMBER

Photo Show is held at the SUB Gallery, UBC, Vancouver. Organized by Christos Dikeakos, the exhibition includes works by Vito Acconci, Christos Dikeakos, Dan Graham, Douglas Huebler, Duane Lunden, Bruce Nauman, N.E. Thing Co., Illya Pagonis, Ed Ruscha, Bill Vazan, Jeff Wall and Ian Wallace, among others.

The commonness of the medium, its ability to "take" everything, its unique, but uniform, appearance as the great equalizer, whereby everything is reduced to the celluloid or printed surface, these qualities are the ones that interest the artists concerned rather than any "fine photography" tradition . . . To call theirs "bad" photography misses the point (though in some cases there is a deliberate and witty attack on the "good" photograph). Every snap is one possible realization of the infinitely available potential material for the camera. Jeff Wall's analogy between the photographer and the gun-fighter links this fact with a lot of the work in the show.[19]

1970

JANUARY

Jeff Wall's Landscape Manual (1969-70) is published by the Fine Arts Gallery, UBC, Vancouver.

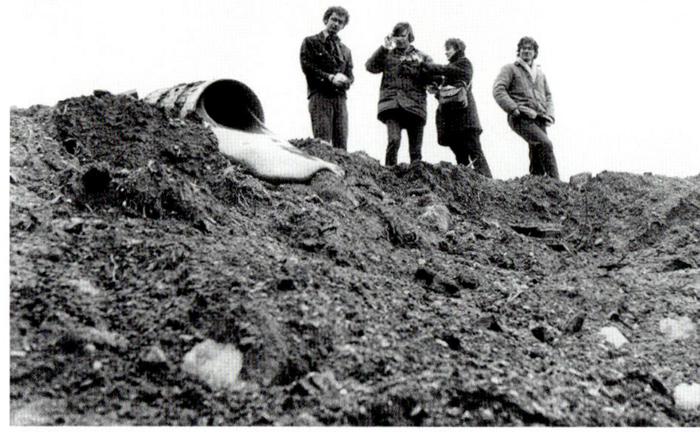

In Vancouver, Robert Smithson executes Glue Pour for the exhibition 955,000.

955,000, curated by Lucy Lippard, opens in Vancouver with work by sixty-two North American and international artists, including Vito Acconci, Terry Atkinson, John Baldessari, Rosemarie Castoro, Dan Graham, Eva Hesse, On Kawara, Bruce Nauman, Adrian Piper, Ed Ruscha, Robert Smithson and Lawrence Weiner, among others. Canadian artists include Greg Curnoe, Christos Dikeakos, Duane Lunden, N.E. Thing Co., George Sawchuk and Jeff Wall. The title refers to the population of Vancouver and the surrounding suburbs. Venues include the Vancouver Art Gallery, UBC SUB Gallery, Simon Fraser University Gallery and various public spaces. The exhibition follows 557,087, also curated by Lippard, at the Seattle Art Museum during the fall of 1969.

Idea or conceptual art, like that of Darboven, Atkinson, Baldwin, Borofsky, Kawara or Kosuth, and physically extant but imperceptible art like Barry's, share basic conditions with all previous art. What is radically new is its context, the exhibition and dissemination possibilities.[20]

FEBRUARY

Gar Smith: Notes on Light opens at the Isaacs Gallery, Toronto, and later at the Vancouver Art Gallery in April.

At each of 30 points at equal intervals from St. John's

---

[18] Lucy R. Lippard, "Toward a dematerialized or non object art" (transcript of a conference given in the course Art Now at the Nova Scotia College of Art and Design, Halifax, 29 November 1969).

[19] Charlotte Townsend, "Photo Show, SUB Art Gallery, University of B.C., December 1969–January 1970," *artscanada* XXVII no. 3, issue no. 144/145 (June 1970): 49.

[20] Lucy R. Lippard, unpaginated cue-card catalogue for *955,000*.

[21] Artist's statement accompanying *Notes on Light*, as quoted in Barry Lord, "Sun's innocence captured," *Toronto Daily Star*, 6 March 1970, 27.

Nfld. to Tofino BC on thirty successive days, I took 20 photographs beginning at sunset facing west and twenty photographs ending at sunrise, facing east.[21]

In British Columbia, execution of Robert Smithson's *Island of Broken Glass* is blocked when the Society Promoting Environmental Conservation (SPEC) argues the project is harmful to the environment. Smithson proposes *Island of the Dismantled Building* as an alternative, but the provincial government refuses to allow him to use the islet chosen for the work.

APRIL

In Halifax, Greg Curnoe's *Homage to Sam Langford* is published by the NSCAD Lithography Workshop. This suite of 10 lithographs, produced in an edition of 50, mimics a campfire notebook with a diary of Curnoe's visits to Halifax. Sam Langford was a black Canadian boxer in the late nineteenth and early twentieth centuries, who was originally from Weymouth Falls, Nova Scotia.

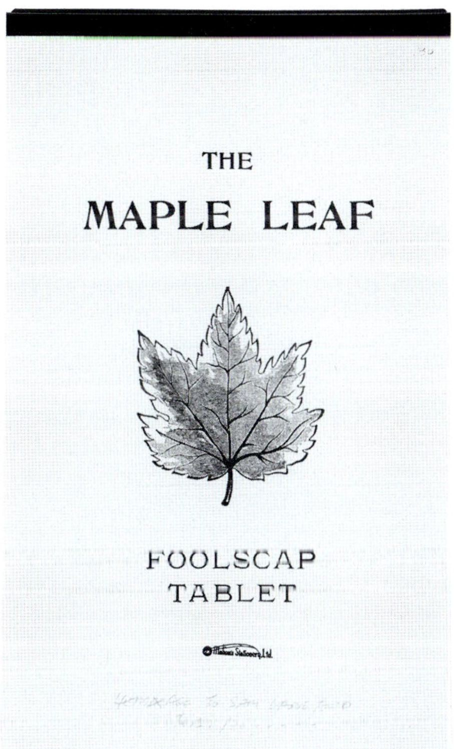

MAY

Survey/Sondage 70: REALISM(E)S opens at the Montreal Museum of Fine Arts. Included are *Did You Ever Milk a Cow?* (in which a live cow is exhibited in the same gallery as paintings of cows from the Musée's collection) by Glenn Lewis and Michael Morris; *Subway Rides* by Bill Vazan; 5 light boxes by N.E. Thing Co.; *Sink Color Photo* by Michael Snow; and Joyce Wieland's quilt work *I Love Canada - J'aime le Canada*.

JUNE

Along with IBM, UNIVAC and National Cash Register, N.E. Thing Co. sets up a booth at Session '70, a conference on information technology at the Bayshore Inn, Vancouver. The booth is staffed by Co-presidents Iain and Ingrid Baxter and Director of Special Projects Paul Woodrow. Among other activities, NETCO dispenses buttons marked GNG (Gross National Good). As a result of contacts made during the conference, NETCO participates in a data processing and business exposition in Seattle later in the month.

JULY

Information, curated by Kynaston McShine, opens at the Museum of Modern Art (MOMA), New York. Canadian artists in the exhibition include David Askevold, Gerald Ferguson, N.E. Thing Co. and Jeff Wall.

Gerald Ferguson initiates *Relational Sculpture* at NSCAD. The work consists of

1/a point in Halifax, Nova Scotia, 44° 38' 47.41" north latitude, 63° 34' 48.21" west longitude
2/a point on Gerald Ferguson, tattoo left forearm
3/a point as yet to be determined
Upon initiation the sculpture exists as an indeterminate relationship; upon the artist's death the sculpture exists as a determinate relationship.[22]

AUGUST

General Idea performs *What Happened* as part of the Festival of Underground Theatre at the St. Lawrence Centre for the Arts and Global Village Theatre in Toronto. The components include *The 1970 Miss General Idea Pageant* in the lobby of the St. Lawrence Centre.

---

[22] Lucy R. Lippard, *Six Years: The Dematerialization of the Art Object from 1966 to 1972* (Berkeley/Los Angeles: University of California Press, 1997; first published New York: Praeger, 1973), 179.

Opposite
Christos Dikeakos, *Robert Smithson executing* Glue Pour, 1970

Above
Greg Curnoe, *Homage to Sam Langford*, 1970, detail. © Estate of Greg Curnoe / SODRAC (2012)

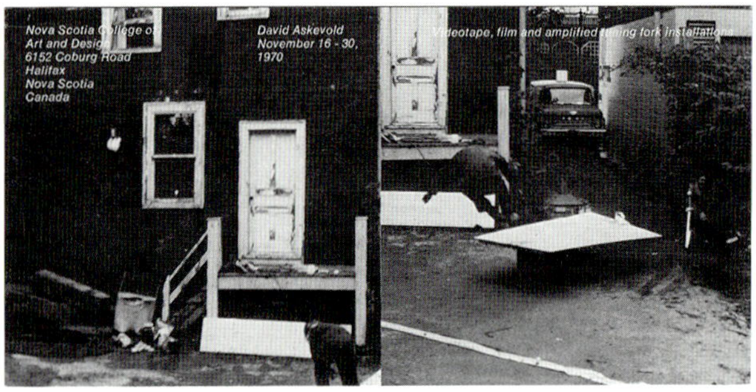

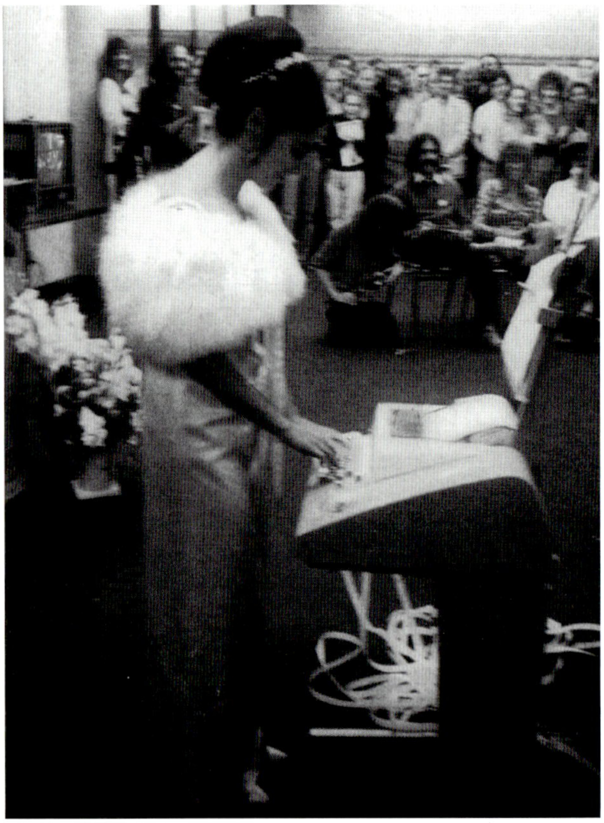

SEPTEMBER

In Halifax, the Mezzanine is established at NSCAD with Charlotte Townsend as director. The space opens in October. Conceived as "a facility" rather than a gallery, it focuses on disseminating ephemeral and conceptual art projects during its three-year lifespan. Artists who exhibit include Vito Acconci, Eleanor Antin, Art & Language, John Baldessari, Jan Dibbets, Lee Lozano, N.E. Thing Co., Bill Vazan and Tim Zuck, among others.

The Nightingale Arts Centre is founded in Toronto by Chris Youngs with artists Robert Bowers, Ian Carr-Harris, Stephen Cruise and John McEwen, and businessman Bill Graham. The Nightingale Gallery, run by Youngs since 1968, is renamed A Space and will become an important centre for the dissemination of conceptual and socially critical art.

OCTOBER

NSCAD hosts *The Halifax Conference*, initially conceived by Gerald Ferguson and Lawrence Weiner and organized by Ferguson and Seth Siegelaub. Participants include Carl Andre, Daniel Buren, Mario Merz, Robert Morris, Robert Murray, N.E. Thing Co., Richard Serra, Robert Smithson, Michael Snow and Weiner, among others. Conflict arises over the hierarchical format of the event, in which the participating artists are inside a conference room and the audience of mostly students is in the Mezzanine watching via a video feed. Some participants object to NSCAD's intention to profit by producing a publication from transcripts and to the role of Benson & Hedges as conference sponsor. While the college agrees not to publish a transcript, the issue of the conference format cannot be solved and Morris, Serra and Smithson leave.

N.E. Thing Co. launches *Global Trans-VSI Network*. The project involves the transmission of "art information" between NETCO's "central station" in North Vancouver and locations such as MOMA, New York; California Institute of the Arts, Los Angeles; and NSCAD, Halifax, using telecopier and telex machines. Many of the transmissions from NETCO consist of instructions for projects to be carried out by art students at network locations.

Above, from top

Invitation for David Askevold, *Videotape, Film and Amplified Tuning Fork Installations*, Mezzanine, 16-30 November 1970

General Idea, photograph from *The 1970 Miss General Idea Pageant*, 1970

[23] Claudine Roger, "Selective bio-bibliography." In *Bill Vazan: Walking into the Vanishing Point* (Montréal: VOX, centre de l'image contemporaine, 2009), 187.

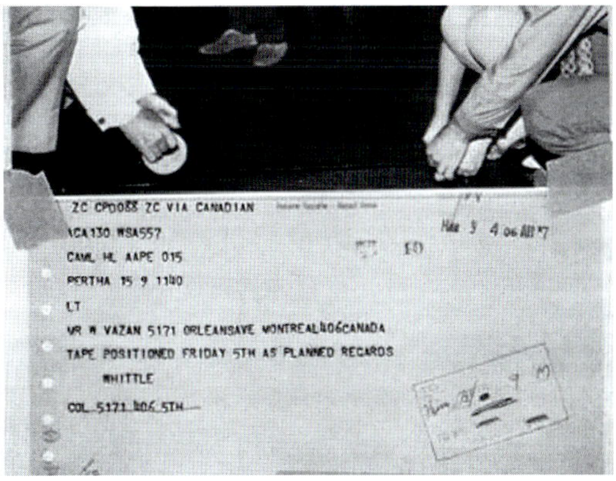

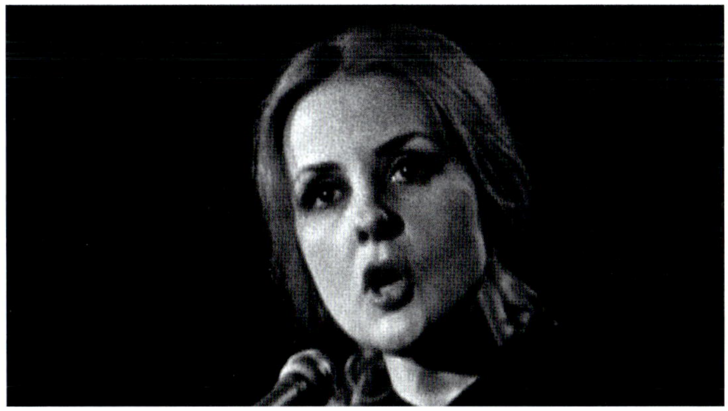

Dan Graham first exhibits *TV Camera/Monitor Performance* in *7 Performances, 16 Presentations, Obverse* at the Anna Leonowens Gallery, NSCAD, Halifax. The work involves the artist rolling across a table and along the floor while videotaping the audience, situating the audience as the primary subject of the work.

DECEMBER

Gerald Ferguson performs *Four*, a reading of four-letter words from his project *The Standard Corpus of Present Day English Language Usage*, in which words from the English language are arranged by length, at the Anna Leonowens Gallery. Ferguson's *The Standard Corpus of Present Day English Language Usage arranged by word length and alphabetized within word length* is published earlier this year.

1971

FEBRUARY

45°30' N—73°36' W opens at Sir George Williams University Art Galleries and the Saidye Bronfman Centre, Montréal. Organized by Arthur Bardo, Gary Coward and Bill Vazan, the exhibition includes work by David Askevold, Robert Barry, Greg Curnoe, Tom Dean, Jean-Marie Delavalle, François Déry, Mervyn Dewes, Christos Dikeakos, Gerald Ferguson, Douglas Huebler, Sol LeWitt, N.E. Thing Co., Harold Pearse, Michael Snow, Françoise Sullivan, Ian Wallace and Lawrence Weiner, among others. A conference titled "Art and Its Social Responsibilities" is organized in conjunction with the exhibition.

MARCH

Bill Vazan executes *World Line*.

The imaginary line circles the planet in 25 physical segments, passing through 18 countries. The Montreal Museum of Fine Arts is where the line "touches down" in Montreal. People in each location . . . are instructed to simultaneously lay a piece of adhesive tape on the ground using data calculated by civil engineer Ahmad Salahuddin.[23]

N.E. Thing Co. presents a solo exhibition at Simon Fraser University Gallery, Burnaby, in which the artworks are installed, recorded on video and then removed from the gallery. After the exhibition opens the works are visible only on a video monitor.

The attractiveness of video is twofold: it allows the artist to control the way his work is presented on a mass medium and, by outflanking the gallery system, it enables him, in Baxter's words, "to really get to the people."[24]

Image Bank and General Idea collaborate on *Fire/Mirror/Video*, a video project on Spanish Banks in Vancouver. Mirrors are placed in a circle on the beach, gunpowder is poured between them and then ignited. In an essay on art in Vancouver by John Buckley, published in *artscanada*, images of the work are combined with an excerpt from William S. Burroughs' *Nova Express*.

. . . AND HE BREAKS OUT ALL OF THE UGLIEST PICTURES

---

[24] Joan Lowndes, "Iain Baxter (N.E. Thing Co. Ltd.)," *artscanada* XXVIII, no. 3, issue 156/157 (June/July 1971): 79.

Above, from left
Bill Vazan, documentation from *World Line*, 1971

Jean-Claude Labrecque and Jean-Pierre Masse, still showing Michèle Lalonde reciting her poem "Speak White", 1970, © National Film Board of Canada. All rights reserved

IN THE IMAGE BANK AND HE PUTS IT OUT ON THE SUBLIMINAL SO ONE CRISIS PILES UP AFTER THE OTHER RIGHT ON SCHEDULE.[25]

Martha Wilson exhibits Chauvinistic Pieces at the Anna Leonowens Gallery, Halifax. The works incorporate texts based on gender, identity and reproduction. They include Determined Piece, which states, "A woman selects a couple on the basis of IQ test scores high or low and raises their baby."

APRIL

John Baldessari's I Will Not Make Any More Boring Art is presented at the Mezzanine, Halifax. In a letter to director Charlotte Townsend, Baldessari refers to the work as a "Punishment Piece."

I've got a Punishment Piece for you. It will require a surrogate(s) since I can't be there to take my self-imposed punishment but that's o.k. . . . The piece is this: from ceiling to floor should be written by one or more people, one sentence under another the following statement - - "I will not make any more boring art." At least one column of sentences should be done ceiling to floor before the exhibit opens and the writing of the sentences should continue every day if possible for the length of the exhibit.[26]

Baldessari's sentence is also produced as a print, in an edition of 50, by the NSCAD Lithography Workshop.

JULY

True Patriot Love, a solo exhibition of the work of Joyce Wieland, opens at the National Gallery of Canada. It is the first survey exhibition of a living female artist to be organized by the gallery.

OCTOBER

General Idea presents The Miss General Idea Pageant at the Art Gallery of Ontario with participants from across Canada. The pageant is conceived and recorded as a television event, with a studio audience numbering in the hundreds. An exhibition at A Space that precedes the pageant includes "entries" from the contestants: gowns, photographs, text and related paraphernalia.

Image Bank Postcard Show opens at the UBC Fine Arts Gallery in Vancouver. A catalogue consisting of a small box and about 100 postcards is printed by Coach House Press. The exhibition includes postcards by Ant Farm, Eleanor Antin, Dr. Brute (Eric Metcalfe), Lowell Darling, Christos Dikeakos, General Idea, Jochen Gerz, Gary Lee-Nova, Flakey Rose Hips (Glenn Lewis) and Bill Vazan, among others. The exhibition is circulated across the country by the National Gallery of Canada Extension Services.

1972

JANUARY

Clive Robertson performs The Bat Becomes a Real Flyer at the Workshop in Calgary. A recent arrival to Canada from the United Kingdom, Robertson is well acquainted with European artists involved in Fluxus. The performance employs a variety of electronic media as well as toy musical instruments, voices and traditional musical instruments.

Michael Snow's La Région Centrale premieres at the Anna Leonowens Gallery, Halifax. Shot in the wilderness of northern Québec, La Région Centrale was made using an apparatus that allowed the camera to move 360 degrees in any direction.

I only looked in the camera once. The film was made by the planning and by the machinery itself . . . The single rectangle can contain a lot. In La Région *the frame is very important as the image is constantly flowing through it . . . It can seem sad that in order to exist a form must have bounds, limits, set and setting. The rectangle's content can be precisely that. In* La Région *the frame emphasizes the cosmic continuity which is beautiful but tragic: it just goes on without us.*[27]

FEBRUARY

In Montréal, the journal Médiart, which focuses on issues related to visual art in Québec and abroad, is founded by the Groupe de recherche en administration de l'art. Participants include René Blouin, Claude Gosselin, Chantal Pontbriand and Normand Thériault, among others.

---

[25] William S. Burroughs, as quoted in John Buckley, "Keeping it together in Vancouver: The search for alternatives," *artscanada* XXVIII, no. 3, issue 156/157 (June/July 1971): 39–43.

[26] John Baldessari, letter to Charlotte Townsend, 1 February 1971. NSCAD University, Gallery Archives, Mezzanine Fonds, Halifax.

[27] Michael Snow, "Converging on *La Région Centrale*: Michael Snow in conversation with Charlotte Townsend," *artscanada* XXVIII, no.1, issue 152/153 (February/March 1971): 47.

Process Paintings, a solo exhibition of work by Eric Cameron, opens at Mount Saint Vincent University Art Gallery, Halifax. The process for the paintings is *a rationalization of the use of masking tape . . . Strips are laid out vertically and horizontally over prepared rectangular panels, leaving intervals equal to the width of the tape itself. Paint is applied through the grid with a cloth stamp . . . However hard one tries it is never possible to lay out the tape exactly straight. The result is the "squares" are in fact never exactly square, and the theoretically regular system of squares is very evidently irregular in detail.*[28]

MARCH

The Halifax/Vancouver Exchange is initiated by Roy Kiyooka. Participants include, from Vancouver, Don Druick, Gathie Falk, Gerry Gilbert, Image Bank, Carole Itter, Glenn Lewis, Mr. Peanut and David Rimmer, and from Halifax, Gerald Ferguson, David Hellyer, Alastair MacLennan, Toby MacLennan, Anita Martin, David Martin, Ian Murray, Bruce Parsons and Ellison Robertson. Works presented in Halifax by Vancouver artists include Glenn Lewis' *Forest Industry—Movie Event*, Image Bank's *March Statements—A Screening*, Gathie Falk's performance *Some Are Egger Than I* (first performed in 1969) and Carole Itter's *Personal Baggage*. The last consists of a red cedar log from Roberts Creek that is sawed into sections, packed into canvas bags and transported as Itter's baggage during the train trip from Vancouver to Halifax. The log is eventually fitted back together and placed on the beach near the community museum in Lockeport, Nova Scotia.

Works presented at the Vancouver Art Gallery by Halifax artists include *Nude as Negative Space* by Bruce Parsons, *144 Cards* by David Hellyer and *CHORAL READING—An Abridged Choral Reading of The Standard Corpus of Present Day English Language Usage arranged by word length and alphabetized within word length* by Gerald Ferguson. A symposium is held in Halifax, with Lawrence Weiner and James Lee Byars as additional participants.

"Two sensibilities; two life rhythms, two feelings of superiority. Knock them together," said Roy Kiyooka to the Canada Council . . . Halifax comes well prepared. Eight participants of whom three are connected with the Nova Scotia College of Art and Design: Bruce Parsons, faculty; Ellison Robertson and Ian Murray, graduates . . . First contacts abrasive. "We think West Coast art is mushy and emotional. Our work is cool, more scientific." We think it introverted. Video used as narcissistic reflection rather than for community involvement. Boring "real time." No work in groups as with us.[29]

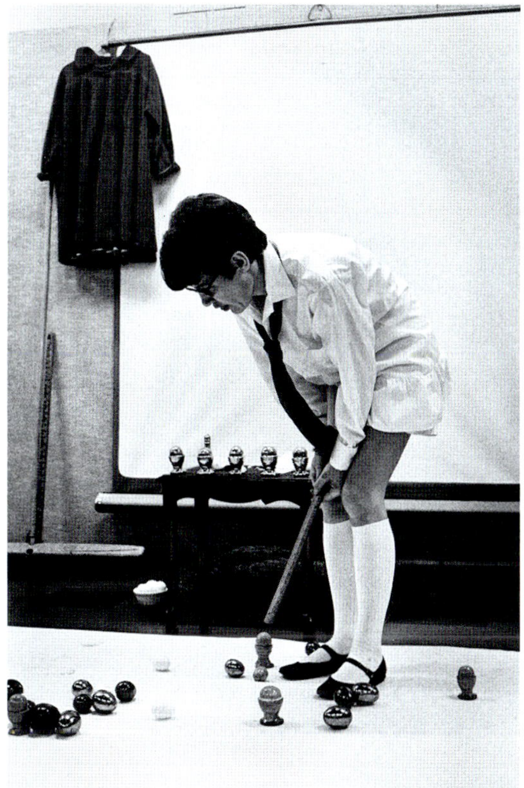

APRIL

The first issue of *FILE Magazine* is published by General Idea with funding support from the Local Initiatives Program of the Canadian government. The cover features a photograph of Mr. Peanut (Vincent Trasov) with the Toronto skyline in the background. Conceived as a link between artists from across the country, *FILE* is an early example of General Idea's methods for appropriating

[28] Eric Cameron, "Production process." In *Eric Cameron Process Paintings* (Halifax: The Art Gallery and Museum, Mount Saint Vincent University, 1972), unpaginated.

[29] Joan Lowndes, "Halifax-Vancouver Exchange, The Vancouver Art Gallery, March 26–30, 1972," *artscanada* XXIX, no.2, issue 166/167/168 (Spring 1972): 99.

Above
Gathie Falk, *Some Are Egger Than I*, 1969

the vehicles of mass culture. In 1974 the journal is sued by *LIFE* magazine, which alleges its logo was improperly appropriated by *FILE*.

Vancouver writer Dennis Wheeler publishes (anonymously) a caustic response to the first issue of *FILE* in *Grape*, a leftist Vancouver newspaper.

As a substitute for genuine criticism and confrontation wherein the actual interdependence of phenomena will be exposed so that real growth might occur, this magazine full heartedly supports the proliferation of bullshit, obsessions, private reveries, and facile fantasies . . . Shitting on their homosexuality they have done an inestimable disservice by re-repressing what remains for many a serious and actual struggle within our society. They have paraded their homosexuality as though that in itself gave the mag. some bizarre status within the enigma of the alternative society. Instead the problems of homosexuality as an actual way of life recede into pageantry camp parody.[30]

In response to Wheeler's rejection of General Idea's tactics, torn copies of the article and packages of human feces are sent to "Dee Dee Wheeler" at the National Gallery of Canada, where he works.[31]

JULY

The Press of the Nova Scotia College of Art and Design is established with Kasper Koenig as the first editor. *The Architecture of Ludwig Wittgenstein* by Bernhard Leitner and *Raw Notes* by Claes Oldenburg are the first books to be published, in 1973.

OCTOBER

Martha Wilson's *Art of Incarnation* opens at the Mezzanine in Halifax. The work addresses identity and gender relations through performance, video and image/text works.

NOVEMBER

The artist-run cooperative Véhicule Art opens on rue Ste. Catherine in Montréal. It becomes an important venue for conceptually based work using performance, video and photography. Founding members include Gary Coward, Tom Dean, François Déry, Andrew Dutkewych, Suzy Lake, Jean-Marie Delavalle, Dennis Lukas, Kelly Morgan, Gunter Nolte, Henry Saxe, Milly Ristvedt, Serge Tousignant and Bill Vazan.

DECEMBER

Dean Ellis' exhibition *Landscape Morphology and Perceptual Tools* opens at the Vancouver Art Gallery and then travels to the Mezzanine at NSCAD.

Although earthworks and conceptual art can be seen as simply one more revolution of the merry-go-round of style, they manifest a demand for meaning and a critical self-consciousness that had all but disappeared from much traditional painting and sculpture of the region. It was in this regard refreshing to see an exhibition at the Vancouver Art Gallery by Dean Ellis titled Landscape Morphology and Perceptual Tools, *where the significance of process-oriented art has been taken in its full responsibility . . . It is an attempt to integrate aspects of the cultural-historical landscape, of which the artist's work is but one part, with the spatial contingencies involved in any viewing of the physical landscape.*[32]

1973

JANUARY

Blurting in Art & Language: An Index of Blurts and Their Concatenation (The Handbook) . . . by Mel Ramsden and Michael Corris is co-published by Art & Language Press, New York, and the Mezzanine, Halifax.

MARCH

The artist-run Western Front opens in Vancouver. Founded by Martin Bartlett, Kate Craig, Glenn Lewis, Eric Metcalfe, Michael Morris, Vincent Trasov and Mo Van Nostrand, the Western Front will become an important laboratory for the production, exhibition and performance of contemporary art, especially work with Fluxus affinities.

JUNE

Ian Murray's *Keeping On Top of the Top Song* (completed in 1970) is exhibited at the Mezzanine, Halifax. It features

---

[30] Dennis Wheeler, unattributed article in *Grape* (24–30 May 1972), as cited in Robert Ballantyne, *Glamour, Pageantry and Knives: Gay Identity in FILE Megazine* (unpublished master's thesis, University of British Columbia, Vancouver, 1994), 1.

[31] See Ballantyne, *Glamour, Pageantry and Knives.*

[32] Dennis Wheeler, "Dean Ellis: Landscape morphology and perceptual tools," *artscanada* XXX, no. 1, issue 176/177 (February/March 1973): 23.

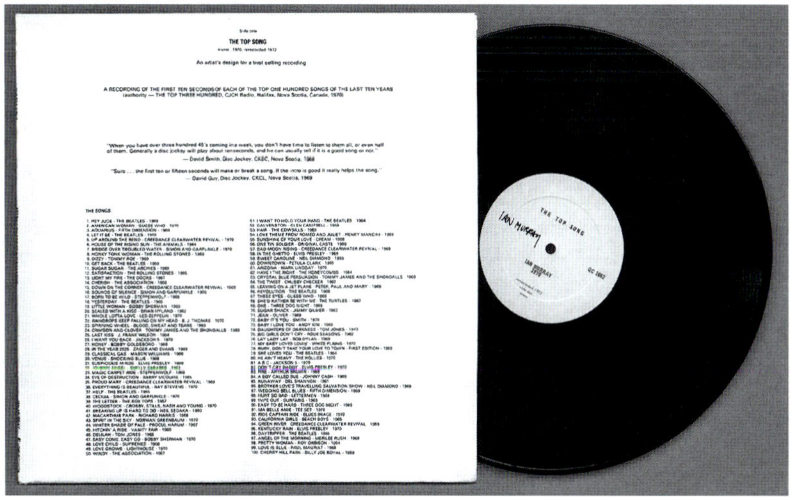

Ian Murray, *The Top Song: An Artist's Design for a Best-selling Record*, 1970/1973

a 12-inch vinyl record, released in an edition of 250, with "The Top Song" and "Keeping on Top of the Top Song" on recto and verso sides. "The Top Song" was originally produced in 1970 as a tape recording of the first ten seconds of the top 100 songs from the past ten years. "Keeping on Top of the Top Song" was a seventeen-minute performance at the Dalhousie University Student Union Auditorium in which a professional drummer was hired to play along with the tape of "The Top Song," which he had not previously heard. "Keeping on Top of the Top Song" is an audio recording of that performance.

OCTOBER

Founded by General Idea, Art Metropole opens its doors in Toronto. The editorial in the December 1973 issue of *FILE Megazine* states:

Art Metropole intends to keep abreast of the tide, housing and distributing evidence of activity and imagery: magazines, publications, videos, correspondence, snapshots, memories, and the ephemeral flood.[33]

artscanada publishes "W.O.R.K.S.—A Conceptographic Reading of Our World Thermometer." Written by Paul Woodrow, the article describes a project, conceived by Clive Robertson, for which fifty-six artists from seventeen countries contributed material ranging from postcards to videotapes for a television series broadcast over Calgary's Community Antenna Television.

1974

JANUARY

Organized by Image Bank, General Idea, Ant Farm, Lowell Darling, Willoughby Sharp and the Western Front, the *Hollywood Decca Dance* and celebration of art's 1,000,011th birthday is held in the ballroom of the Elk's Lodge at MacArthur Park in Hollywood. Radiating a Fluxus sensibility, the stage show is a parody of the Academy Awards and features performances by General Idea, Michael Morris, Glenn Lewis, Hank Bull, Eric Metcalfe and Kate Craig, among many others.

Investigations, an exhibition of work by Ian Carr-Harris, John Greer and N.E. Thing Co. opens at the Owens Art Gallery in Sackville, NB. The exhibition includes NETCO's *Color Language Research—Food*, which involves the display of food purchased in a Sackville grocery store. A symposium with the artists, National Gallery of Canada curator Pierre Théberge and Owens Art Gallery director Chris Youngs is presented in conjunction with the exhibition.

[33] *FILE Megazine* 2, no. 4 (December 1973): 10.

Pierre Théberge: *Another question I've been wondering about is, does it bother you that your work is incomprehensible if you don't speak English?...*

Iain Baxter: *Just a curiosity thing, all that food is in French.*

Ingrid Baxter: *But we haven't checked to see if our concept works in French.*[34]

FEBRUARY

Organized by Kitty Byrne, *Ian Wallace: The Summer Script* opens at the UBC Fine Arts Gallery, Vancouver. *The Summer Script* grew out of an uncompleted film project in collaboration with Rodney Graham and Jeff Wall. The work comprises 12 large-scale, hand-coloured photographs made by photographing a black and white video monitor displaying video studies for the film. Eric Cameron later writes of *The Summer Script*:

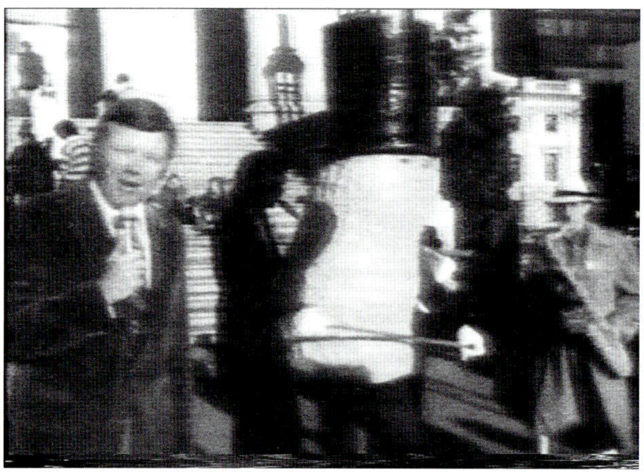

Wallace has been much influenced by writers like Jacques Lacan who attempt to effect a union of linguistics and psychoanalysis. According to Lacan the unconscious is "structured as a language," or, more strongly, "the material of the unconscious is language." Wallace, convinced that our lives are constructed from an imaginary text, a condensation of experience, points to Mallarmé in asserting that the text is the space of the page as well as the words...[35]

OCTOBER

In Vancouver, Mr. Peanut (Vincent Trasov) files nomination papers to run as a candidate for mayor in the upcoming civic election. The project was devised by Trasov and John Mitchell, who acts as campaign manager. While Mr. Peanut never speaks, he attends candidate meetings, responds to press interviews and engages in debate through the voice of Mitchell. The campaign is covered extensively in the local press and in magazines such as *Esquire* and *Interview*, and Mr. Peanut's candidacy is endorsed by William S. Burroughs. Mr. Peanut receives 3.4 percent of the vote, which is sufficient for his campaign deposit to be refunded.

A solo exhibition by David Askevold, titled *A Completion of Works*, opens at the Anna Leonowens Gallery, Halifax.

The recent exhibition of graphic work and films by David Askevold at the Nova Scotia College of Art and Design was proof that important new art has been spawned by [the current] emphasis on language and philosophy in a visual art context. Askevold has managed to create art that is highly personal while drawing on numerous aspects of knowledge and experience.[36]

DECEMBER

Camerart opens at Galerie Optica in Montréal. It includes work by twenty-four Montréal artists, including Pierre Boogaerts, Tom Dean, Jean-Marie Delavalle, Charles Gagnon, Suzy Lake, Les Levine, Gunter Nolte, Françoise Sullivan, Serge Tousignant, Robert Walker and Bill Vazan, among others. Conceived by Robert Walker, the exhibition attempts to erode the "strange barrier" that separates "the artist and the photographer... by bringing into a gallery of photography a number of artists who incorporate photographic ingredients, yet do not consider themselves to be photographers."[37] The catalogue also includes essays by Les Levine, Paul Hayer, Chantal Pontbriand and Pierre Vallières.

If President Ford says he's appalled by the cost of living, the pre-camera artist assumes that he's telling them that he is appalled by the cost of living. The camera artist... looks at the shirt he is wearing, the color of his tie, the texture of his face and comes up with the aggregation:

Above
Image Bank, still from *Off the Air Coverage of the Peanut Campaign*, 1974

[34] Transcript of *Investigations/The Owens Art Gallery* (Sackville: Owens Art Gallery, 1974), unpaginated.

[35] Eric Cameron, "Semiology, sensuousness and Ian Wallace," *Artforum* XVII, no. 6 (February 1979): 32.

This texture and that image in that form is saying, "I am appalled at the cost of living." What has been said for the camera artist lies somewhere in between the phenomenology of striped silk ties, blue serge suits and the cost of living.[38]

1975

David Tomas makes *Works on the History of Physics, "Physical Review, The Positive Electron, Carl D. Anderson, California Institute of Technology, Pasadena, California (Received February 28, 1933)"*. Tomas' first works, produced from 1974 to 1975 while the artist was still a student at Concordia University, address the way in which meaning is either lost or supplemented as one shifts from one specialized discursive field to another. The Super 8 film *1000 Seconds: five permutations on the theme of the last 200 seconds before 7:30 am, July 1916, The First Battle of the Somme* (1974), juxtaposes the linguistic representation of a historical event to the perception of real time as visualized by a quartz time counter (capable of counting to thousands of a second). In the bookwork *Works on the History of Physics* (1975), the content of a 1933 article on the positive electron is handwritten by the artist onto another surface to create a meeting point between two incompatible registers of knowledge (the scientific paper and the enunciative space underpinning the field of art).

The Parachute Center for Cultural Affairs is founded in Calgary by Marcella Bienvenue, Don Mabie and Clive Robertson. The Center provides audio and video production and performance spaces and hosts the production of *Centerfold* magazine.

JANUARY

Karl Beveridge's *Window Installation* opens at the Anna Leonowens Gallery, Halifax. The work consists of black paint applied to the two windows of the gallery's facade. Half of each window has paint applied to the interior, the other half has paint applied to the exterior.

OCTOBER

Founded by Chantal Pontbriand and France Morin in Montréal, *Parachute* is the first Canadian art journal

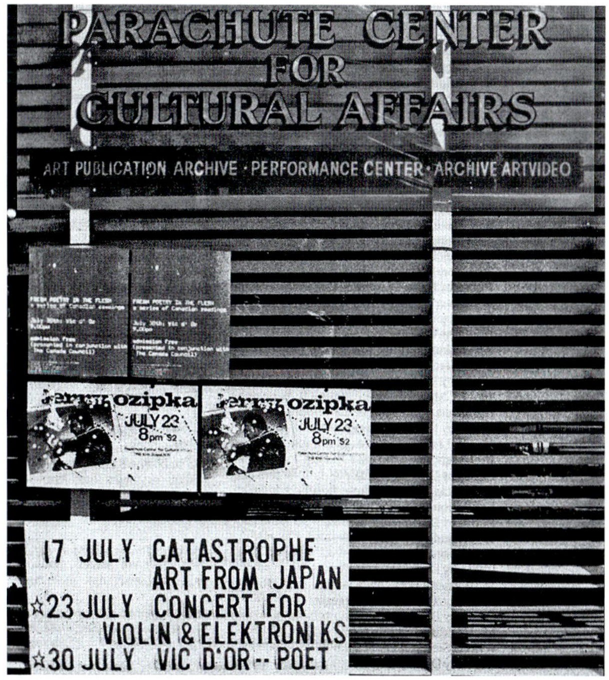

to have an international outlook rather than primary emphasis on Canadian artists and writers. Publishing in French and English, it becomes noted for its high standard of writing, an impressive roster of contributing writers and a focus on conceptually based art.

Québec 75, a large exhibition in three parts (art, film and video), opens in Montréal at the Musée d'art contemporain, Cinémathèque québécoise and Bibliothèque nationale du Québec. Organized by the Institut d'art contemporain de Montréal, with director Normand Thériault as the principal curator, the exhibition attempts to identify the most vital areas of activity in contemporary art in Québec. Thériault argues that "Québecois art doesn't exist: only Québecois artists exist," and asserts that the work presented in the exhibition affirms

the existence of a new situation. Art is not simply an ensemble of objects which are given meaning by their aesthetic or moral principles. A work of art is an object and as an object its meaning is the product of a process of communication with the spectator . . . An object is an

[36] Ron Shuebrook, "David Askevold." Review in *artscanada* XXXI, no. 3/4, issue 192/193/194/195 (December 1974): 124.

[37] William A. Ewing, "A point of view." In *Camerart* (Montréal: Galerie Optica, 1974), 2.

[38] Les Levine, "Camera art." In *Camerart* (Montréal: Galerie Optica, 1974), 7–8.

Above
The Parachute Center for Cultural Affairs, Calgary

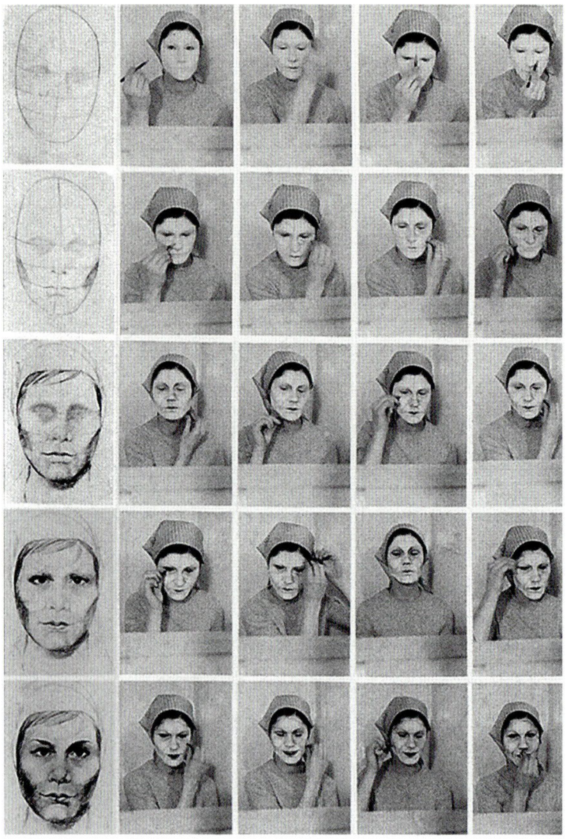

art work because it reveals a pattern of significations and because it is generating a new perception of reality, not because it is presented in a museum.[39]

The exhibition includes Suzy Lake's The Natural Way to Draw in photographic and video formats. Referring to Kimon Nicolaides' well-known manual on drawing, Lake produced the work by painting her face white and then drawing her portrait on the "blank" surface.

Other artists in the exhibition include Melvin Charney, Gunter Nolte, Serge Tousignant, Bill Vazan and Robert Walker, among many others. The exhibition generates heated debate concerning the unconventional nature of much of the work and the fact that many of the artists are from Montréal's Anglophone art community.

NOVEMBER

Language & Structure in North America, "the first large definitive survey of North American Language Art," opens at the Five Six Seven Gallery in Toronto. Coordinated by Beth Learn of the Kensington Arts Association and curated by the American artist and historian Richard Kostelanetz, the exhibition includes more than 200 artworks in which language is the primary aspect. Artists represented include John Baldessari, bill bissett, Gerald Ferguson, Vera Frenkel, Eldon Garnet, Glenn Gould, Dick Higgins, Beth Learn, Garry Neill Kennedy, Kostelanetz, Don Mabie, Bruce Nauman, bp nichol, Steve Reich, Clive Robertson, Michael Snow and Lawrence Weiner, among many others. The exhibition is accompanied by Language Art, a performance series including work by Vito Acconci, Vera Frenkel, bill bissett, Yvonne Rainer and many others. The two events provide an example of "the conjunction of theory and practice" that will become a hallmark of CEAC (The Centre for Experimental Art and Communication), an organization that grows out of the Kensington Arts Association over the following months.[40]

1976

JANUARY

Ian Carr-Harris: . . . the Right Decision opens at the Carmen Lamanna Gallery, Toronto.

What the 34-year-old sculptor has done is to turn out a number of handsomely made pieces of near-furniture that, when arranged in a certain order, make up a Lilliputian movie theatre right there in the gallery . . . Carr-Harris has produced a two minute film in 16 mm to be shown within this handmade cinema. It opens to a still shot of a red lotus blossom, then focuses on the head and shoulders of a young woman named Wendy Sage who, after staring back at us in silence for a few seconds, finally says "It's simply a matter of making the right decision." That accomplished, Miss Sage walks out of camera range, leaving the screen empty for the remainder of the film.[41]

Carole Condé and Karl Beveridge: . . . It's Still Privileged Art opens at the Art Gallery of Ontario, Toronto. For Condé and Beveridge, who have affiliations with Art

Above
Suzy Lake, storyboard for *The Natural Way to Draw*, 1975, detail

[39] Normand Thériault, "An exhibition." In *Québec 75 Arts* (Montréal: Institut d'art contemporain de Montréal, 1975), 10.

[40] See Dot Tuer, "The CEAC was banned in Canada," *C Magazine*, no. 11 (1986): 22–37.

[41] Gary Michael Dault, "A complex view of art success," *Toronto Star*, 23 January 1976.

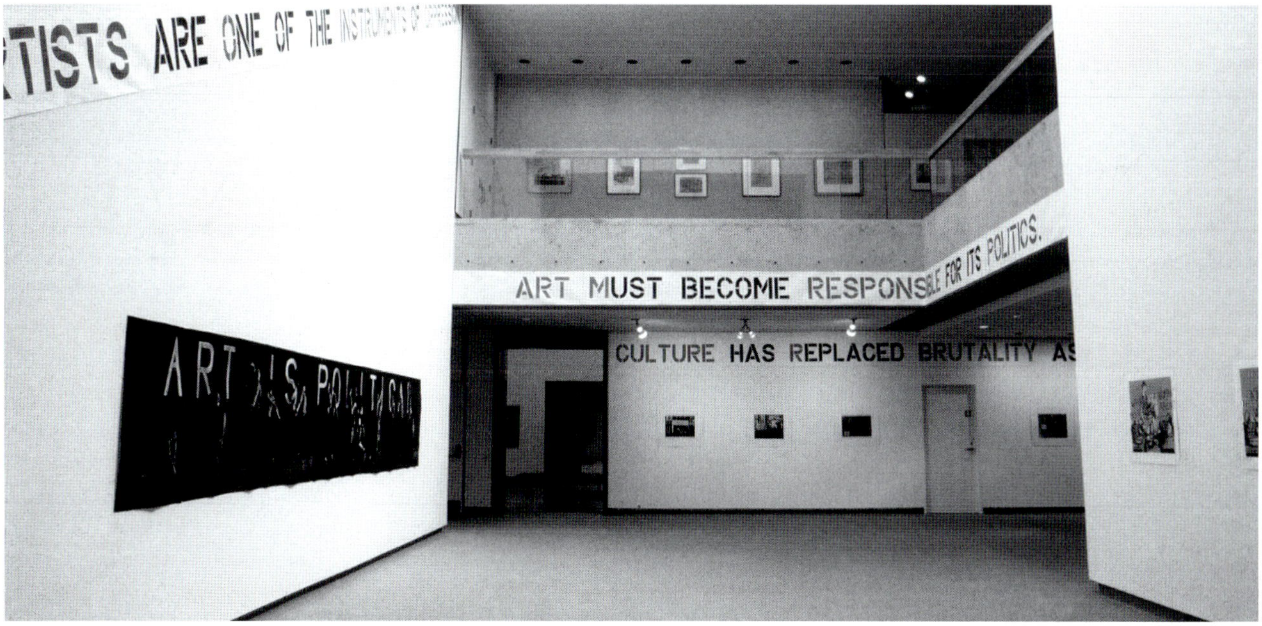

& Language and the journal The Fox in New York, the exhibition marks a move away from conceptual work with connections to Minimalism toward overtly polemical, photographic imagery that addresses the role of culture in the larger social order.

The exhibition . . . is the first showing of new, exploratory work by these artists, formerly known as minimalist sculptors. Through five large photographic and print works, with banners and written and recorded commentary, Beveridge and Condé explore issues such as the political responsibility of artists, the role of social institutions and alternatives to existing art practices. Condé and Beveridge hope to raise provocative questions . . . relating to our society's need for a radical transformation of life and culture. "Our culture emphasizes the individual's self expression," says Beveridge, "and prevents people from acting communally."[42]

The exhibition creates internal tension in the AGO. It's later reported that several trustees resign in protest over the exhibition.

MARCH

Rodney Graham and Robert Kleyn opens at the Pender Street Gallery, Vancouver. Graham exhibits *75 Polaroids*, his first photographic work, consisting of 75 Polaroid photographs made with a flash at night in a forested area on the fringes of Vancouver. Graham later notes that the work is based on

the contemplation of two simultaneous processes: the fading away of the negative retinal after-image caused by the intense flash of light which brought the objects and sites before my vision for the first time, [and] the coming into being of the positive photographic image, eventually fixed on the Polaroid film.[43]

Kleyn's work consists of photographic sequences including *Blue Cards Thrown Into a Fountain* (depicting blue index cards with words such as "trace" and "evade" accumulating in a fountain), *Cards Thrown Into a Fountain* (with the same words on yellow cards) and *The Dream Is Completed—The Words Are Erased* (in which the words are "erased" or made invisible through the rapid up-and-down shaking of the cards as they are photographed).

[42] Art Gallery of Ontario press release for *. . . It's Still Privileged Art*, January 1976.

[43] Rodney Graham, "Artist's notes." In *Rodney Graham: Works from 1976 to 1994* (Toronto, Brussels and Chicago: Art Gallery of York University, Yves Gevaert and the Renaissance Society at the University of Chicago, 1994), 100.

Above
Installation view of Carole Condé and Karl Beveridge, *. . . It's Still Privileged Art*, Art Gallery of Ontario, 1976

JUNE

In Vancouver, Michael de Courcy's Greetings from the Urban Wilderness, Vancouver, BC opens at the Artists' Gallery. The exhibition is a component of a project in which de Courcy, assisted by Sheera Waisman and Scott Plear, construct three "trails" through public space in the city's core. The trails are marked by laminated photographs of mundane material—debris, puddles, pebbles, pavement—found on the sites at which the photographs are posted, painted signs and other components. Aerial views indicating the route of the trails through the city are also included, "so people will get an idea of where they are on the trail." The project is timed to coincide with Festival Habitat, an international conference addressing issues of housing and the urban environment.[44]

JULY

Raymond Gervais presents the installation 12+1= at galerie Média, Montréal (7–9 July). Described as a sound environment on the poster that announces it, 12+1= comprises thirteen turntables that simultaneously play different sound samples from various world music styles over three days. The resulting configurations each represent an improbable encounter between geographically disparate recording contexts and emphasize the sonic tensions produced by these juxtapositions as well as the narrative possibilities they trigger.

NOVEMBER

CEAC hosts a two-day conference on contextual art. The term *contextual art* is based on the writing of Polish artist/philosopher Jan Świdziński, first encountered by members of CEAC while in Europe earlier in the year. Świdziński proposes an understanding of art

not as the syntactic proposition of conventional art or as the analytical proposition of conceptualism, but as the indexical proposition/the occasional sentence/of naturally contextual meanings.[45]

Participants in the seminar include Jo-Anne Birnie-Danzker, AA Bronson, Sarah Charlesworth, Carole Condé and Karl Beveridge, Hervé Fischer, Vera Frenkel, Joseph Kosuth, Amerigo Marras, John Bentley Mays, Anthony McCall, John Scott and Świdziński, among others.

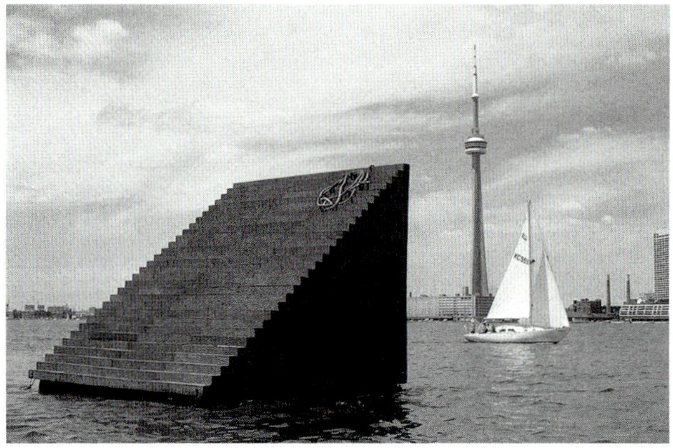

1977

Tom Dean begins work on Floating Staircase, a massive wooden staircase floated on Lake Ontario that is unrelated to any exhibition or institution. Dean later installs a steering device and motors with the idea of taking the staircase through the Welland Canal. The project eventually becomes unmanageable and the staircase is burned on the lake near Toronto in the fall of 1981.

APRIL

In Halifax, Theodore Wan realizes his work Name Change, which involves legally changing his name from Theodore Fu Wan to Theodore Saskatche Wan, after a small town in Saskatchewan. He publicizes the work through announcements in newspapers.

N.E. Thing Co. opens the Eye Scream Restaurant in Vancouver.

MAY

Murder Research, a multi-part photographic/text/video work by Paul Wong and Kenneth Fletcher, opens at the Western Front in Vancouver. The impetus came from an incident in which Wong and Fletcher saw the body of a murder victim from a window in Wong's residence in East Vancouver. The work reflects the artists' research

Above
Tom Dean, *Floating Staircase*, 1977

[44] See Ralph Maurer, "They blazed a trail in city jungle," *The Province*, 7 June 1976.

[45] Jan Świdziński, cited in Dot Tuer, "The CEAC was banned in Canada," *C Magazine*, no. 11 (1986): 30.

[46] Unattributed description of *Drawing Event* in *Sculpture on the Prairies* (Winnipeg: Winnipeg Art Gallery, 1977), 75.

into the murder and addresses the gap between the clinical terms in which such events are analyzed and presented to the public, and the personal context that surrounds them.

JULY

Max Dean performs _Drawing Event_ at the Winnipeg Art Gallery.

The event involved two people trying to execute drawings on opposite walls of a room. A partition divided the room in half and inhibited the participants from seeing each other at work. They were joined by a rope which was secured to their waists and passed through a hole in the partition. The rope was only long enough to allow one person to draw at a time. The event, which took place on July 26, lasted six hours.[46]

1978

In Toronto, Andy Patton begins a body of anonymous street works, initially posters on which a written text describes the site where the poster is installed, without identifying the artist or any gallery with which the work might be affiliated. He also installs posters with written statements over top of posters promoting candidates in the 1978 Toronto civic election. He later produces posters with photographic images.

JANUARY

The Centre for Art Tapes opens in Halifax, with Brian MacNevin as founding director. During the first year of operation, the centre presents work by Dara Birnbaum, Susan Britton, David Craig, Nancy Holt, Ian Murray, Ed Slopek, Theodore Wan, Douglas Waterman and John Watt.

Two Audio-Visual Constructs, with work by Eric Cameron and Noel Harding, opens at the Vancouver Art Gallery. Cameron's work is a video installation titled _Keeping Marlene Out of the Picture_.

The images in question are all separate closed-circuit video loops, shot on location in the Vancouver gallery precisely from the spot in which they are now placed, and on first glance one can suppose that the views are "live" . . . This is not the case, however, for the images are not real-time at all, but instead are highly edited assemblages showing a woman, elegant in dress and high heels, walking across the floor, through the doors, back and forth in front of the (once present) camera. But as soon as the model (Marlene) reaches the camera's view, she is cleanly and promptly edited out of the picture.[47]

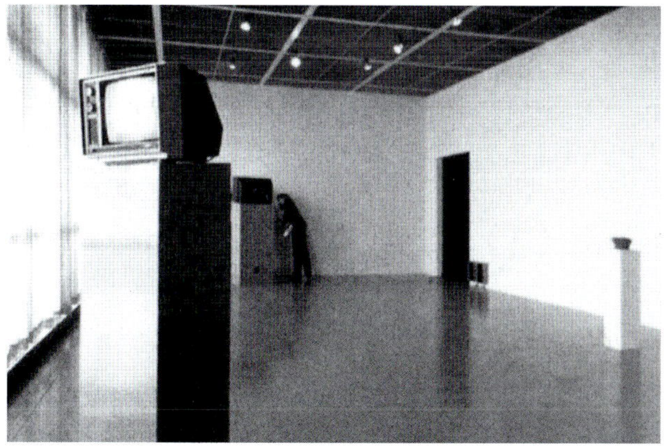

Above
Installation view of Eric Cameron, *Keeping Marlene Out of the Picture*, 1973–76, Vancouver Art Gallery, 1978

FEBRUARY

Greg Curnoe: A Proposed Referendum and Five Series opens at the Isaacs Gallery, Toronto. The exhibition includes watercolour paintings with stencilled texts addressing themes of music, song, bicycle racing, modern technology and events of personal significance, together with an overtly political work titled _The National Question_.

Unquestionably didactic, political and militant, The National Question *asks, "Which nation do you want to be separate from—Quebec or the United States?" By deliberately articulating a "complex question" (a fallacy of relevance), Curnoe raises multiple questions, for the stated question has the effect of ratifying the implied answer to the unasked question or implying that the same answer must be given to both questions. Only as we logically analyze the component parts of the several questions rolled into one do their meanings unfold.*[48]

APRIL

Lies & Truths by Vera Frenkel opens at the Vancouver Art Gallery. The exhibition includes a group of works titled

[47] Peggy Gale, "Temporal realities: Eric Cameron and Noel Harding," *Parachute* 10 (Spring 1978): 12.

[48] José Barrio-Garay, "Greg Curnoe, The Isaacs Gallery," *artscanada* XXXV, no. 2, issue 220/221 (April/May 1978): 47.

No Solution—A Suspense Thriller for which Frenkel uses the format of the detective novel as a way of assembling visual material.

In this group of works [Frenkel] takes as her theme the transforming instances . . . in which the searcher experiences a shift of meaning following new information. Frenkel . . . sets up fields of possibilities, rather than set answers. This permits the viewer to explore an arena of possible connections and changes of point of view and therefore a change in what is experienced as real.[49]

JULY

The symposium Women in Art is held at NSCAD in Halifax. Participants include Peggy Gale, Martha Wilson, Helene Winer and Elizabeth Weatherford.

Ken Lum performs Entertainment for Surrey. For four days he stands beside an overpass on the highway that links the suburbs surrounding Vancouver to the city per se during the morning rush hour. On the fifth day, a full life-size white outline of Lum takes his place in the suburban landscape.

SEPTEMBER

After two years of inactivity, The Press of the Nova Scotia College of Art and Design resumes publishing with Benjamin H.D. Buchloh as the new editor.

OCTOBER

The first exhibition of Jeff Wall's large-scale light boxes opens at the Nova Gallery in Vancouver. The exhibition includes 2 works, The Destroyed Room (1978), which is installed in the gallery's window so it can be seen from the street, and Faking Death (1977), which is presented inside the gallery.

Joseph Kosuth: Text/Context is presented at the Carman Lamanna Gallery, Toronto. The work consists of a notice placed in the gallery's window that indicates meaning lies not only in the text itself, but in the way it is framed by the social, cultural and political space of the gallery. The work receives a scathing review from another Lamanna artist, Karl Beveridge, who calls into question the political efficacy of a practice such as Kosuth's.

Mr. Kosuth, described in the current issue of New York Magazine *as the last conceptual artist (!), and a self-proclaimed feminist-anarchist (?!?), intends these statements to be searing critiques of the system he has so well serviced. But Joseph has simply utilized an already worn critique as a formal device which may have seemed interesting 10 years ago . . . Politics in this guise consists as a "word" in the formal fabric of a questionable career. Politically the work reinforces the apologetics of capitalist aesthetics. Politics and therefore culture, to be effective, have to do more than simply (and simplistically) nominate their context. In its social practice, as well as its production, it has to align itself with the social forces that seek its overthrow.*[50]

Curated by Roald Nasgaard, a solo exhibition of recent paintings and drawings by Garry Neill Kennedy opens at the Art Gallery of Ontario. The exhibition includes a painting for which the size was determined by averaging the size of the paintings on view in the AGO's Signy Eaton Gallery, as well as a monochrome wall painting for which the colour was determined by averaging the colours of the 32 paintings on view in the AGO's "upstairs collection."

NOVEMBER

On 4 November, Rober Racine performs Erik Satie's Vexations (1893) at Véhicule Art. Vexations is a score in which the performer plays a very short musical passage 840 times without interruption. Much like the works Raymond Gervais produces during the same period, Racine's practice explores interconnected references to the histories of musical, literary and artistic avant-gardes. With the installation of Le Terrain du dictionnaire A/Z (1980), the artist systematically separates words from their definitions in the French dictionary Le Robert, thereby forming a new "text" articulated according to spatial parameters. Thus, the artist's identity as reader becomes inscribed within the vacant, interstitial spaces he creates throughout the French-language lexicon.

1979

MARCH

Carole Condé and Karl Beveridge: Maybe Wendy's Right opens at the Carmen Lamanna Gallery, Toronto.

---

[49] Unattributed note in *Lies & Truths by Vera Frenkel* (Vancouver: Vancouver Art Gallery, 1978), 28.

[50] Karl Beveridge, "The last conceptual artist," *Centerfold* (Feb/March 1979): 127. First published in *Artists Review* 2, no. 6 (December 6, 1978).

The exhibition includes a narrative sequence of 15 photographs that depict a crisis generated by the social relations implicit in capitalism as they play out in a working-class family. The political potential of Condé and Beveridge's art is called into question by several critics, including Philip Monk.

Condé and Beveridge may wish to take control of the signs usurped by media in the service of capitalism. By remaining within representation, however, the effectiveness of the action is neutralized. Moreover, they are still contained within the limits of control: the control of signs, the control of meaning.[51]

Tim Clark presents his first installation *Some Thoughts on the Question of Limits in Art* at Optica in Montréal. Later in the year he performs *A Reading of "On Obedience and Discipline" from* The Imitation of Christ *by Thomas à Kempis* at station Cable T.V.P., Montréal. Clark's practice appends theoretical references to the pragmatic methodologies developed by the first conceptualists when they challenged the art object's status and definition. At the end of the 1970s, Clark broadens performance as a genre by reading out loud philosophical and literary texts addressing social discipline while his body is subjected to various tests of strength. In *A Reading of "On Obedience and Discipline"*, Clark wears a leather gauntlet and screams, syllable by syllable, a declarative text expressing the total submission of the devotee to mystic powers. The publication *Some Thoughts on the Question of Limits in Art* accompanies a double-screen film installation of the same title. Clark is seen writing an excerpt of a text by Wittgenstein on a transparent plastic sheet while its printed source is projected on the second screen. The incapacity of the reader to decipher the two versions of the text (because the camera is on the opposite side of the sheet, thus presenting the text in reverse) echoes the content of the text, in which Wittgenstein defines ethics as "the running up against the limits of language."

AUGUST

On the evenings of 1–3 August, Rodney Graham stages *Illuminated Ravine* near the campus of Simon Fraser University in Burnaby. To encounter the work, viewers

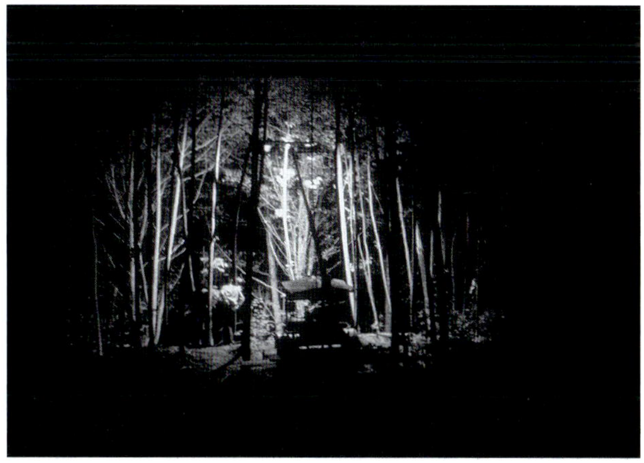

must walk down a forested path to the verge of a ravine. Diesel-powered lighting units are positioned to illuminate the ravine from high up in the surrounding trees. The work is turned on from 9:30 to 11:30 each evening. During this time, the light throbs perceptibly with fluctuations in electric power and the intense din of the generators restricts the possibility of conversation with other viewers.

SEPTEMBER

Ian Wallace: Work 1979 opens at the Vancouver Art Gallery. The exhibition includes *Lookout* and *Image/Text*, both large-scale, multi-part photographic works accompanied by video "studies" used to determine the gestures and poses of the figures in the completed work. Both works are later exhibited at Galerie Optica in Montréal.

NOVEMBER

13 Cameras/Vancouver opens at the Vancouver Art Gallery and includes work by thirteen Vancouver-based artists with markedly different relationships to the photograph as a medium. The artists represented include Marian Penner Bancroft, Iain Baxter, Michael de Courcy, Chris Gallagher, Barrie Jones, Roy Kiyooka, David Rimmer and Paul Wong, among others.

1980

JANUARY

Allan Sekula's *School is a Factory* (1978–80) and Martha Rosler's *The Bowery in Two Inadequate Descriptive*

[51] Philip Monk, *Parachute* 16 (Fall 1979): 50.

Above
Rodney Graham, *Illuminated Ravine*, 1979

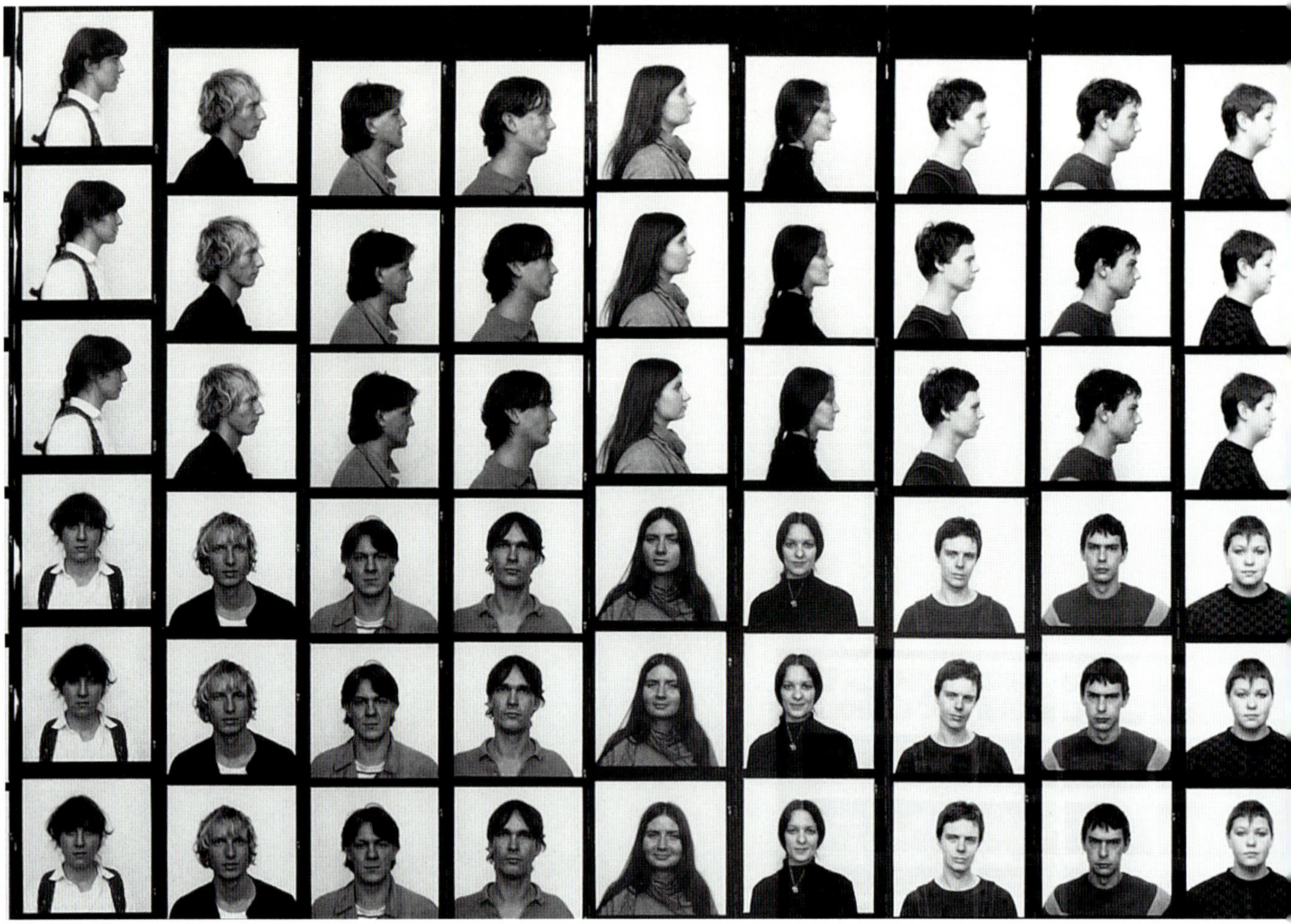

Systems (1974-75) are exhibited at the Anna Leonowens Gallery, Halifax.

FEBRUARY

Site Lines opens at Galerie Optica, Montréal. The exhibition includes work by Colin Lochhead, Robert McNealy, Renée Van Halm and Bill Vazan developed specifically in response to the site and physical structure of the gallery.

MAY

Jamelie Hassan's _BEYROUTH...IS WAR ART?_ is presented at the Forest City Gallery, London. The exhibition includes photographs of Beirut, devastated by war. Hassan also has a gallery wall demolished so that bricks are strewn on the floor and the interior of the gallery is open to the outside world.

A Space presents a series of commissioned television programs by artists on Rogers Cable. Included are works by Dan Graham, Ian Murray and Tom Sherman, among others.

JUNE

Eye Level Gallery, Halifax, presents a solo exhibition by Garry Neill Kennedy. Kennedy's work involves removing the bottom half of the lower case "e" on the gallery's typewriter for the duration of the exhibition. Each typed document produced during the run of the exhibition is placed on the gallery's walls.

Above
Arnaud Maggs, *Kunstakademie*, 1980, detail

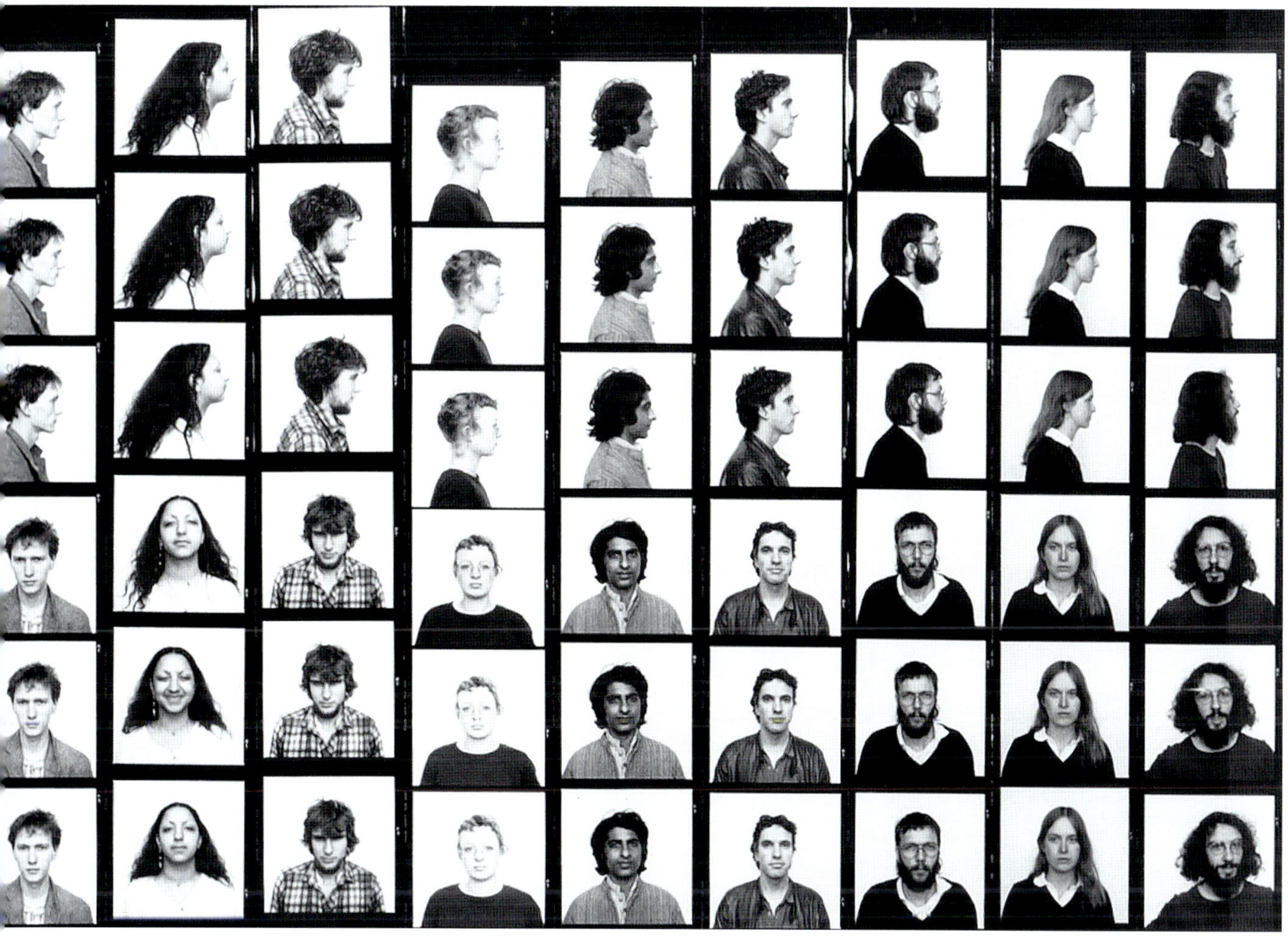

NOVEMBER

Arnaud Maggs opens at the Canadian Cultural Centre in Paris.

Sixty-Four Portrait Studies . . . *has a clear sense of personal, yet universal authority. The complete piece, thirty-two unidentified portraits, mounted in four rows of sixteen photographs, appears somewhat official, like documentation. Maggs* [sic] *use of the vernacular "mug shot" genre of frontal and profile views further heightens their authority. The form is in fact designed to reveal individual differences, and it is with the diversity of each individual's appearance with which one is impressed.*[52]

DECEMBER

Gerald Ferguson's 1,000,000 Pennies is exhibited for the first time at the Glenbow Museum in Calgary. The installed work exists as a mound of 1,000,000 pennies. When not exhibited it can be deposited in a bank, where it will generate interest.

[52] David McWilliam, untitled essay. In *Arnaud Maggs* (Paris: Canadian Cultural Centre, 1980), unpaginated.

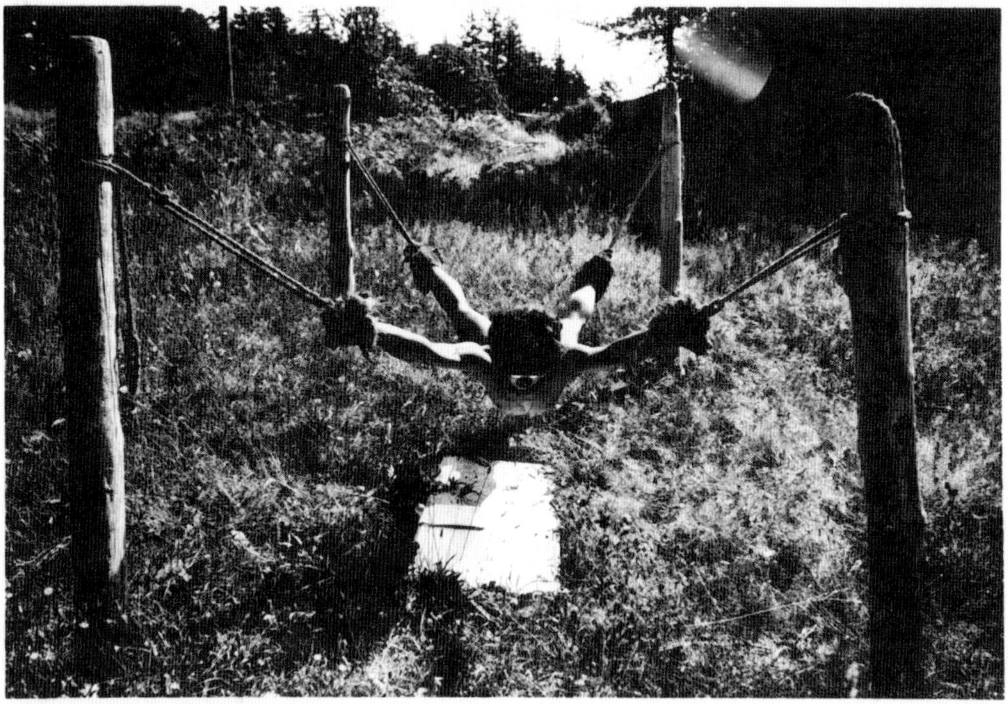

What was will be again. What has been done will be done again, and there is nothing new under the sun....

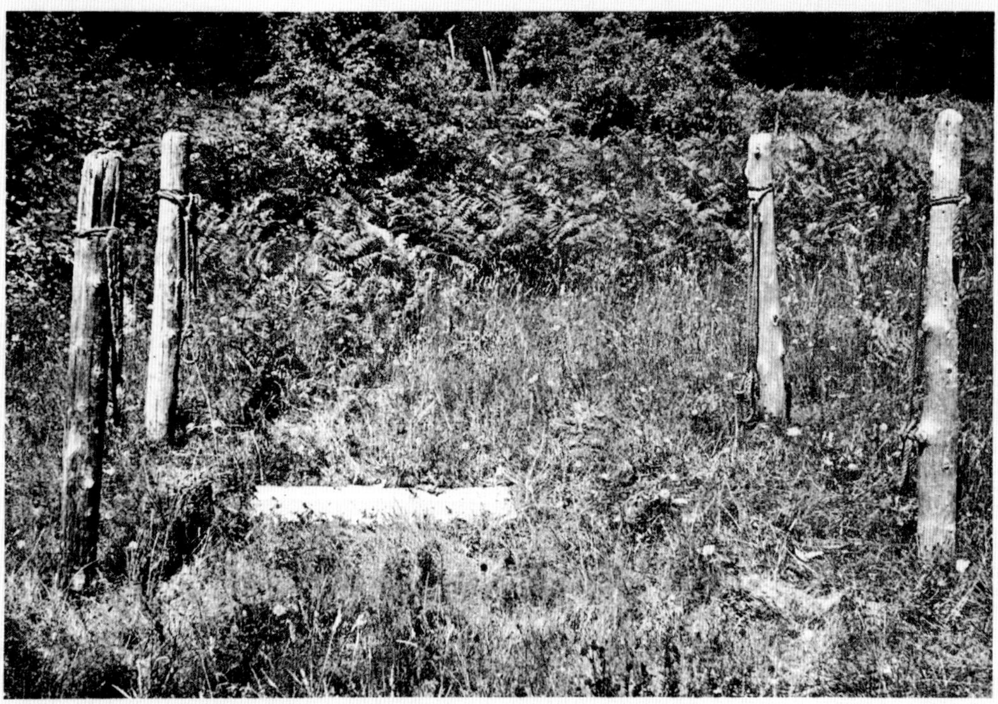

Performed by Theodore Wan on Hornby Island, July 1975
Reading the book of Ecclesiates.
Duration; as long as I could stand the pain.
Assistants; Tom Burrows, Jerry and Margaret Pathick.

Artists and Works in the Exhibition

Dimensions are provided for artworks but not for ephemera. All dimensions are in centimetres; height precedes width precedes depth. Artworks are in order by date and then grouped by collection, noted in the last work in the series.

Theodore Wan, *Untitled (Hornby Island Performance)*, 1975, details

03 23 03 Premières rencontres internationales d'art contemporain, 1977
publication documenting the event in March 1977, including conferences, performances, discussions and exhibition
Courtesy of the Leonard & Bina Ellen Art Gallery, Concordia University, Montréal

Vito Acconci

b. 1940, New York, NY; lives and works in New York, NY

Private Piece for David Askevold, 1970
typewritten instructions on single sheet of paper
28 x 21.6
National Gallery of Canada Library and Archives, Art Metropole Collection, Ottawa; Gift of Jay A. Smith, 1999

Accessibilities, 1–15 December 1971
sheet of paper with text describing works in exhibition at the Mezzanine (facsimile)

Untitled, 1971
card with text "1. on February 8, 1971, I will fly, Air Canada, to Halifax . . ." (facsimile)
NSCAD University, Gallery Archives, Mezzanine Fonds, Halifax

Kiss Off, 1971
lithograph on Arches paper
76.3 x 56.3

Trademarks, 1971
lithograph on German Etching paper
50.9 x 50.8
Lithography Workshop, Collection of NSCAD University, Halifax

Sounding Board, 1971
single-channel video transferred to DVD
22:00
Courtesy of the Artist and Electronic Arts Intermix, New York

Bas Jan Ader

b. 1942, Winschoten, The Netherlands; d. 1975, lost at sea between Cape Cod, MA, and Falmouth, England

Thoughts Unsaid, Then Forgotten, 1–7 April 1973
three-page letter to Charlotte Townsend plus diagram dated 1 March 1973, with instructions for installing the work

(all facsimiles)
NSCAD University, Gallery Archives, Mezzanine Fonds, Halifax

Eleanor Antin
b. 1935, New York, NY; lives and works in San Diego, CA

Library Science, 1–9 February 1972
one-page letter, one-page description of the work (facsimile), exhibition invitation
NSCAD University, Gallery Archives, Mezzanine Fonds, Halifax

Art & Project (Adriaan van Ravesteijn and Geert van Beijeren, publishers)
Bulletins 1–65 Exhibition, 19 February–5 March 1973
exhibition invitation
NSCAD University, Gallery Archives, Mezzanine Fonds, Halifax

Art Metropole
Archive Privileges (business card), 1974
Art Metropole letterhead, 1974
Catalogue No. 1 CANADA. Artists Publications and Materials, 1974
Editions by Artists (business card), 1974
Official opening party invitation, 1974
Information on Joseph Beuys (exhibition invitation), 1976
Lisa Steele—Colin Campbell (exhibition invitation), 1976
Rodney Werden (exhibition invitation), 1976
Video by Artists, Peggy Gale (Ed.), 1976
Catalogue No. 4/Editions by Artists, Spring 1977
Performance by Artists, AA Bronson and Peggy Gale (Eds.), 1979
Collection of Art Metropole, Toronto

David Askevold
b. 1940, Conrad, MT; d. 2008, Halifax, NS

Projects Class (with Robert Barry, Mel Bochner, James Lee Byars, Jan Dibbets, Dan Graham, Douglas Huebler, Joseph Kosuth, Sol LeWitt, Lucy Lippard, N.E. Thing Co., Robert Smithson and Lawrence Weiner), 1969
12 cards
12 x 18 each
Collection of Bruce Barber

Halifax Travelogue, *March 69, Bus Route 12, Midway between Every Block*, March 1969
22 silver gelatin prints joined verso with Scotch-type tape and laminated in plastic
10.1 x 15.2 each; 15.2 x 222.2 overall

Dashiell Hammett & Martin Shubik, 1970
photostat on paper, edition of 25
21.5 x 27.7
Collection of Garry Neill Kennedy

Air Mail Postcard, 1970
postcard
NSCAD University, Gallery Archives, Anna Leonowens Gallery Exhibitions Fonds, Halifax

Videotape, Film and Amplified Tuning Fork Installations, 16–30 November 1970
exhibition invitation (facsimile)
NSCAD University, Gallery Archives, Mezzanine Fonds, Halifax

Three Cameras Over a Double Sided Mirror and Back Again, Figure Smear, and Two Plant Perspectives Reacting to a Walking Dog, 7–14 August 1972
exhibition invitation

A Compilation of Works, 14–23 October 1974
exhibition invitation and envelope
NSCAD University, Gallery Archives, Anna Leonowens Gallery Exhibitions Fonds, Halifax

David Askevold: A Video Retrospective (excerpt), 2008
Nova Scotia Fires, 1969, 2:30
Fill, c. 1970, 8:20
Rubber Band, 1971, 3:18
It's No Use Crying, 1972, 3:30
Bliss D.F.2, 1979, 8:25
single-channel video transferred to DVD
Courtesy of VTape, Toronto

Askevold, Dube, Ferguson, Jarden, Kelly, McNamara, Murray, Robertson, Waterman, Young, Zuck, 1971
exhibition catalogue, A Space Gallery, Toronto
NSCAD University Library, Halifax

Alice Aycock
b. 1946, Harrisburg, PA; lives and works in New York, NY

Vectors of Inferred Magnetic Which is Reportedly Moving at the Approximate Rate of 5 Miles a Year, 26–31 March 1972
exhibition invitation
NSCAD University, Gallery Archives, Mezzanine Fonds, Halifax

John Baldessari
b. 1931, National City, CA; lives and works in Santa Monica, CA

I Will Not Make Any More Boring Art, 1–10 April 1971
exhibition invitation; letter from Baldessari to Charlotte Townsend, 1 February 1971; 2 photographs of students executing the work by writing title on gallery walls (all facsimiles)
NSCAD University, Gallery Archives, Mezzanine Fonds, Halifax

I Will Not Make Any More Boring Art, 1971
lithograph on Arches paper
56.9 x 76.5
Lithography Workshop, Collection of NSCAD University, Halifax

John Baldessari and Garry Neill Kennedy in Conversation, 1975
single-channel video transferred to DVD
12:00
NSCAD University Visual Resources Collection, Halifax

Bruce Barber
b. 1950, Auckland, New Zealand; lives and works in Halifax, NS

Whittler's Soliloquies, 1976
documentation of performance at NSCAD (photograph with text, booklet with text for the performance)
33 x 21.3 (photograph); 28.5 x 22.5 (booklet)

E, 1978
text for performance (ink drawing on vellum); poster for performance at Anna Leonowens Gallery, 30 March 1978
51 x 61 (text); 42.4 x 27.5 (poster)

E, 1979
video clips of performance at *The Living Art Performance Festival*, Vancouver, 29 September–1 October 1979
single-channel video transferred to DVD
10:00
Courtesy of the Artist

Arthur Bardo and Gary Coward
Coward b. 1940, Calgary, AB; lives and works on Galiano Island and in Vancouver, BC

45°30' N—73°36' W + Inventory, 1971
exhibition catalogue of 164 cards in plastic bag
10.8 x 13.3 each
Collection of Jean-Marie Delavalle

Installation views of *45°30' N—73°36' W*, 1971 (with Bill Vazan)
9 silver gelatin prints
20 x 25 each
Collection of Bill Vazan

Beaux-Arts, Spring and Summer 1972 and Special Pornography Issue 1973
magazine edited by Tom Dean
Collection of Jean-Marie Delavalle

Karl Beveridge
b. 1945, Ottawa, ON; lives and works in Toronto, ON

Window Installation, Black Paint on Glass (Interior-Exterior), 20 January–28 February 1975
exhibition invitation
NSCAD University, Gallery Archives, Anna Leonowens Gallery Exhibitions Fonds, Halifax

Marcella Bienvenue
b. 1946, Stettler, AB; lives and works in Calgary, AB

I Believe in Myself, 1979
video documentation of performance
Courtesy of the Artist

Dara Birnbaum and Jenny Holzer
Birnbaum b. 1946, New York, NY; lives and works in New York, NY
Holzer b. 1950, Gallipolis, OH; lives and works in Hoosick Falls, NY

Untitled (Holzer) and *Kiss the Girls: Make Them Cry* (Birnbaum), 24–28 March 1980
exhibition invitation (facsimile)
NSCAD University, Gallery Archives, Anna Leonowens Gallery Exhibitions Fonds, Halifax

Pierre Boogaerts
b. 1946, Brussels, Belgium; lives and works in Ulverton, QC

Par terre en l'air I—Par terre en l'air II (Version b), 1974
10 silver gelatin prints and 2 texts mounted on foamcore
29.9 x 24 (3 prints); 13.6 x 10.2 (7 prints); 70 x 100 overall
Canadian Museum of Contemporary Photography, Ottawa; Gift of the Artist

Robert Bowers
b. 1943, Albany, NY; lives and works in Toronto, ON

Kiss, 1971
single-channel video transferred to DVD
5:30
Courtesy of the Artist and Vtape, Toronto

Daniel Buren
b. 1938, Boulogne-Billancourt, France; lives and works in France and internationally

Permutations: 7 Days, 6 Placements, 7 Colours, 11–17 April 1973
exhibition invitation
NSCAD University, Gallery Archives, Mezzanine Fonds, Halifax

A Work by Daniel Buren . . . Fragment 1, Fragment 2, Fragment 3, 12–23 April 1973
exhibition invitation in three parts; black and white photograph of installation at the Mezzanine, NSCAD
NSCAD University, Gallery Archives, Mezzanine Fonds and Lithography Workshop Fonds, Halifax

Halifax: 7 Days—6 Placements—7 Colours, 1974
booklet of postcards plus cover
10 x 16
NSCAD University, Gallery Archives, Lithography Workshop Fonds, Halifax

Around a Block. A Sculpture in Situ by Daniel Buren, 5–22 June 1979
exhibition invitation, two-page description of work
NSCAD University, Gallery Archives, Anna Leonowens Gallery Exhibitions Fonds, Halifax

Victor Burgin
b. 1941, Sheffield, England; lives and works in London, California and Switzerland

All Substantial Things Which Constitute This Room, 14–21 October 1971
exhibition invitation
NSCAD University, Gallery Archives, Mezzanine Fonds, Halifax

Tom Burrows
b. 1940, Galt, ON; lives and works in Vancouver and Hornby Island, BC

Sand Pile (Sand to Pyramid to Sand), 1973
table, sand, single-channel video on continuous loop, monitor
dimensions variable
Vancouver Art Gallery, Vancouver

James Lee Byars
b. 1932, Detroit, MI; d. 1997, Cairo, Egypt

Events Week at the Anna Leonowens Gallery, 1–3 April 1969
exhibition invitation (with Rex Lau)
NSCAD University, Gallery Archives, Anna Leonowens Gallery Exhibitions Fonds, Halifax

The First Totally Interrogative Philosophy, n.d.
gold print on white tissue paper with red ink
61.3 x 41.6
Art Metropole Collection, National Gallery of Canada Library and Archives, Ottawa; Gift of Jay A. Smith

Camerart, 1974
catalogue for exhibition at Galerie Optica, Montréal
Collection of Jean-Marie Delavalle

Eric Cameron
b. 1935, Leicester, England; lives and works in Calgary, AB

Red, Yellow & Blue on White-Vertical (type IIK, ½" tape), 1968
oil on canvas over panel
304.8 x 213.36
University of Lethbridge Art Collection, Lethbridge

Black and White on Yellow, 1969
oil and tape on canvas laminated to wood
43.5 x 332.5
Art Gallery of Nova Scotia, Halifax

Insertion (My Mouth), 1973
single-channel video
30:00 (5:00 excerpt)
NSCAD University Visual Resources Collection, Halifax

Keeping Marlene Out of the Picture, 1973–76
single-channel video with 2 audio speakers
15:00

Lettuce, 1979
lettuce covered with 12,000+ coats of acrylic gesso
45.7 x 45.7 x 45.7 (lettuce); 91.4 x 91.4 x 45.7 (pedestal)
Courtesy of the Artist and TrépanierBaer, Calgary

Colin Campbell
b. 1942, Reston, MB; d. 2001, Toronto, ON

Video Tapes, 1–10 December 1972
exhibition invitation
NSCAD University, Gallery Archives, Mezzanine Fonds, Halifax

True/False, 1972
single-channel video transferred to DVD
9:00

Sackville, I'm Yours, 1972
single-channel video transferred to DVD
14:40
Courtesy of the Artist's Estate and Vtape, Toronto

Ian Carr-Harris
b. 1941, Victoria, BC; lives and works in Toronto, ON

Untitled (McLaren), 3–8 January 1972
exhibition invitation
NSCAD University, Gallery Archives, Mezzanine Fonds, Halifax

Nancy Higginson, 1949, 1972
painted wood construction, transcript of taped conversation on file cards, silver gelatin print
46 x 46 x 153

The Fully Clothed Body, 1972
Letraset on paper, dirty glass, frame
61 x 30.5

I thought I'd better not..., 1973
painted wood with silver gelatin print, Letraset on painted masonite in hinged frame
121.9 x 56.9

Mussurongo Types, 1973
2 chromogenic prints of published images, Letraset on painted masonite, frames
30.5 x 38 each

Wendy Sage Being Compared, 1973
2 silver gelatin prints, Letraset in double frame
30.5 x 61 overall

A Man Illustrating, 1973
2 silver gelatin prints (1 partially tinted), Letraset on painted masonite, frame
61 x 61 each
Collection of the Carmen Lamanna Estate

Centerfold Magazine
Vols. 1, 2 and 3, 1977–79
magazine
Collection of Clive Robertson

Melvin Charney
b. 1935, Montreal, QC, lives and works in Montreal

The Main...Montreal, 1965
29 silver gelatin prints mounted on 5 panels
44.5 x 357.1 (overall)
44.5 x 203.2 (overall)
Collection of the Musée d'art contemporain de Montréal

Tim Clark
b. 1945, Buckie, Scotland; lives and works in Montréal, QC

A Reading of "On Obedience and Discipline" from The Imitation of Christ *by Thomas à Kempis*, 1979
performance for single-channel video
3:03

Limits in Art, 1979
booklet accompanying the installation *Some Thoughts on the Question of Limits in Art* (facsimile), 1979
Courtesy of the Artist

Robin Collyer
b. 1949, London, England; lives and works in Toronto, ON

Shirley and Clint Eastwood (Newfoundland 7/73), 1973
silver gelatin print
36.6 x 50.8
Courtesy of the Artist and Susan Hobbs Gallery, Toronto

Something Revolutionary, 1978
6 chromogenic prints mounted on aluminum backing, text
36 x 168 overall
Collection of the Carmen Lamanna Estate

Untitled Magazine, 1979
22 silver gelatin prints mounted on plastic roofing stock
30.5 x 40.6 each
Courtesy of the Artist and Susan Hobbs Gallery, Toronto

Carole Condé
b. 1940, Hamilton, ON; lives and works in Toronto, ON

Two 12' x 8" x 8" Timbers. One 24' x 8" White Painted Line, 23 November–24 December 1974
exhibition invitation (facsimile)
NSCAD University, Gallery Archives, Anna Leonowens Gallery Exhibitions Fonds, Halifax

Carole Condé and Karl Beveridge

Cutural Signs, 1975
Art Gallery of Ontario, Toronto
Artists' loft, New York
Carmen Lamanna Gallery, Toronto (with Carmen Lamanna)
East 1st Street, New York
Loft of Leon Golub; Artists' Meeting for Cultural Change painting signs for protest at Whitney Museum, New York
Lower East Side, New York
Paula Copper Gallery New York Protest of Bi-centennial Exhibition (Rockefeller Collection) at Whitney Museum, New York
chromogenic prints
54.6 x 63.5 each

The Fox, Nos. 1, 2 and 3, 1975–76
journal, exhibition poster

Art Is Political, 1976
9 silver gelatin prints, framed together
33 x 180 overall

Avant-garde Artists Meeting for Cultural Change, 1976
exhibition poster

. . . It's Still Privileged Art, 1976
exhibition catalogue

Untitled, 1976
8 screenprints on paper
53 x 25

Untitled, 1976
Art Gallery of Ontario exhibition poster
Courtesy of the Artists

Michael de Courcy
b. 1944, Montréal, QC; lives and works in Vancouver, BC

A Vanishing View of the Lions, 1975
9 screenprints on paper
26.8 x 34.6 each
Vancouver Art Gallery, Vancouver

Sylvain P. Cousineau and Francis Coutellier
Cousineau b. 1949, Alvia, QC; lives and works in Lachine, QC
Coutellier b. 1945, Namur, Belgium; lives and works in Moncton, NB

Exzéo, 1975
paperbound book (58 pages)
33.1 x 27.3
Courtesy of Artexte, Montréal

Kenneth Coutts-Smith
b. 1929, Copenhagen, Denmark; d. 1981, Toronto, ON

Artext (RE=RECORD TO . . .), 1974
ink and graphite on paper
43.1 x 35.4

Spatial Poem #9, 1975
ink on paper
34.5 x 27.9
Morris and Helen Belkin Art Gallery, University of British Columbia, Vancouver; Gift of Helen K. Wright

Kate Craig
b. 1947, Victoria, BC; d. 2002, Storm Bay, BC

Delicate Issue, 1979
single-channel video with audio
12:33
Vancouver Art Gallery, Vancouver; Gift of the Artist

Stephen Cruise
b. 1949, Montréal, QC; lives and works in Toronto, ON

Putting a Bullet through ID, 1970
single-channel video transferred to DVD
6:30

Turn, 1971
single-channel video transferred to DVD
6:30
Courtesy of the Artist and Vtape, Toronto

Greg Curnoe
b. 1936, London, ON; d. 1992, London, ON

List of Names of Boys I Grew Up With, 1962
stamp pad ink on paper, graphite, mounted between Plexiglas
38 x 20.4
McIntosh Gallery, University of Western Ontario, London; Gift of Owen Curnoe

Row of Words on My Mind, 1962
stamp pad ink on paper
33.02 x 25.40

The Walk, 1962
stamp pad ink on paper notebook
20.5 x 18
Estate of Greg Curnoe, Courtesy of the Wynick/Tuck Gallery, Toronto

Calamity Corners, 1967
ink and acrylic on canvas
60 x 48
Hart House, University of Toronto; Purchased by the Hart House Art Committee

Homage to Sam Langford, 1970
lithograph on Arches paper (suite of 10)
31.4 x 18.7 each
Lithography Workshop, Collection of NSCAD University, Halifax

Map of North America, 1972
ink on paper
29.5 x 22.2
Dalhousie Art Gallery Permanent Collection, Halifax; Purchased from *The Third Dalhousie Drawing Exhibition*, 1978

Clocking D, 21 July 1969, 1972
stamp pad ink on leather, metal hanger with clips
67.95 x 57.47

Measurement No. 7, 1972
die-stamped leather, plastic and metal hanger
56.52 x 36.2
Estate of Greg Curnoe, Courtesy of the Wynick/Tuck Gallery, Toronto

Max Dean
b. 1949, Leeds, England; lives and works in Toronto, ON

No Crap Option, 1977
artist's book
23.5 x 19 x 12.7

Tool/Loot, 1977
lithographic printing plate, proof print
50.8 x 63.5 (plate); 49.5 x 64.8 (print)

You Made It, 1977
plastic tray, water/ice, Plexiglas, wood, light fixture, ice tray
64.8 x 64.8 x 25.4
Courtesy of the Nicholas Metivier Gallery, Toronto

Tom Dean
b. 1947, Markdale, ON; lives and works in Toronto, ON

Easy Cheap, 1971
artist's notebook in folder (63 pages)
dimensions variable
Collection of Jean-Marie Delavalle

Two Locations, 1971
16 leaflets in an envelope
27 x 12
Courtesy of Artexte, Montréal

Performance (Untitled), 1974
single-channel video documentation of performance
18:30
Courtesy of the Artist and Vtape, Toronto

Jean-Marie Delavalle

b. 1944, Clermont-Ferrand, France; lives and works in Montréal, QC

Une demi heure, 1973
vinyl record (33 rpm) and sleeve (audio transferred to CD)
60:00

Projecteur projeté, 1974
slide projector, slides, audio transferred to CD
dimensions variable
Courtesy of the Artist

Jan Dibbets

b. Weert, The Netherlands; lives and works in Amsterdam, The Netherlands

Untitled, May 1971
two-page handwritten letter to Gerald Ferguson rejecting first print and asking to do second print with the NSCAD Lithography Workshop (facsimile); sheet of black and white photographs of rejected (first) print
NSCAD University, Gallery Archives, Mezzanine Fonds, Halifax

Untitled, 1971
lithograph on Rives BFK paper
55.9 x 55.9
Lithography Workshop, Collection of NSCAD University, Halifax

Christos Dikeakos

b. 1943, Thessaloniki, Greece; lives and works in Vancouver, BC

Instant Photo Information, 1970
offset lithograph on paper, published in *BC Almanac* by the National Film Board of Canada
21 x 26.2 x 0.4
Vancouver Art Gallery Library and Archives, Vancouver

Brian Dyson

b. 1944, Leeds, England; lives and works in Oliver, BC

Companies Nameplate, 1977
etched lithographic plate, frame
23.8 x 21.3 x 1.9

I will not make any more art (after John Baldessari, 1971), 1977
archival inkjet print, scanned from original photograph
70 x 76

Remade Ready-made #3, A Periodic Chart of the Atoms, Phase 3. The artist laughs up his sleeve (l'artiste rit dans sa barbe), 1977
mixed media including found objects
dimensions variable
Courtesy of the Artist

Dean Ellis

b. 1948, Vancouver, BC; lives and works on Hornby Island, BC

Untitled, c. 1972
single-channel video transferred to DVD
19:35
Vancouver Art Gallery, Vancouver; Gift of the Artist

Gathie Falk

b. 1928, Alexander, MB; lives and works in Vancouver, BC

Performance documentation (restaged at the National Gallery of Canada in 1984)
Skipping Ropes, 1968, 7:28
A Bird is Known by His Feathers Alone, 1968 (revised 1972), 18:31
Some Are Egger Than I, 1969, 13:49
Cat Piece, 1970, 9:40
Landscape Painting, 1972, 7:17
Red Angel, 1972, 7:23
single-channel video transferred to DVD
Courtesy of the Artist

Gerald Ferguson

b. 1937, Cincinnati, OH; d. 2009, Halifax, NS

abcdefghijklmnopqrstuvwxyz, 1968–69 (book version published 1978)
paperbound book, copyright certification document
21 x 21.4 (book), 35.5 x 21.5 (document)
Collection of Jayne Wark

1-20 (prototype for *The Standard Corpus*), 1969–70
sheet of paper with diagram
19.4 x 21.5

Paste-Up for lithograph Length 4, 1969–70
single sheet of paper with diagram
46.4 x 61.6
Collection of Heather and Doug Ferguson

Length 4, 1970
lithograph on German Etching paper
46.4 x 61.6
Lithography Workshop, Collection of NSCAD University, Halifax

The Standard Corpus of Present Day English Language Usage arranged by word length and alphabetized within word length, 1970
unbound paper book with cover
28 x 21.6
Vancouver Art Gallery, Vancouver; Gift of the Artist

Four, 1971
announcement card for release of one-hour cassette recording from *The Standard Corpus of Present Day English Language Usage*

In Alphabetical Order, as Many Words by Word Length in Four Square Inches (from The Brown Standard Corpus of Present Day English Usage*)*, 1971
offset lithograph (poster)
28 x 21.7
NSCAD University, Gallery Archives, Mezzanine Fonds, Halifax

360° Rotation within a Space, 5 April 1971
single sheet of paper with text and diagram and 10 silver gelatin prints; all elements in plastic sleeves
28 x 21.7 (paper); 8.5 x 11 (each photo)
Collection of Garry Neill Kennedy

An Abridged Choral Reading of The Standard Corpus of Present Day English Language Usage arranged by word length and alphabetized within word length, 17 April 1972
publicity poster with instructions for reading and list of readers
28 x 21.7
NSCAD University, Gallery Archives, Mezzanine Fonds, Halifax

An Abridged Choral Reading of The Standard Corpus of Present Day English Language Usage (based on the 1970 bookwork, *The Standard Corpus of Present Day English Language Usage*), 1972/1986
audio recording of 9 March 1986, re-staging at Dalhousie Arts Centre Sculpture Court of the original *Choral Reading* held at Anna Leonowens Gallery, 17 April 1972
28:00

NSCAD University Visual Resources Collection, Halifax

1,000,000 Pennies, 1980 (conceived in 1979)
azo dye print
76.2 x 101.5
Courtesy of Heather and Doug Ferguson

Michael Fernandes

b. 1944, Trinidad; lives and works in Halifax, NS

(Remembering): Inner Dimensions Without Nap, 1977
paperbound booklet
22.8 x 15.3
NSCAD University Library, Halifax

Robert Fones

b. 1949, London, ON; lives and works in Toronto, ON

Leaf Collection, 1968
matchbooks mounted on board
110.1 x 65.4
McIntosh Gallery, University of Western Ontario, London; Gift of Zoe Curnoe

La Table Ronde, 1972
silver gelatin print
68 x 86
Canada Council Art Bank, Ottawa

Vera Frenkel

b. 1938, Bratislava, Czechoslovakia; lives and works in Toronto, ON

String Games: Improvisations for Inter-City Video, 1974
two-channel video, posters, catalogue, silver gelatin prints
dimensions variable
Courtesy of the Artist and InterAccess, Toronto

Jeff Funnell

b. 1940, Winnipeg, MB; lives and works in Winnipeg, MB

Sistine Tons, 1980
14 chromogenic prints, frames, single-channel video transferred to DVD
dimensions variable
Courtesy of the Artist

Charles Gagnon

b. 1943, Montréal, QC; d. 2003, Montréal, QC

Le son d'un espace/The Sound of Space, 1968
16 mm film transferred to DVD
27:00
Courtesy of the Estate of Charles Gagnon

Yves Gaucher

b. 1934, Montréal, QC; d. 2000, Montréal, QC

Transition, 1967
8 offset lithographs on paper
44.5 x 58.5 each
Private Collection

General Idea

AA Bronson b. 1946, Vancouver, BC; lives and works in New York, NY
Felix Partz b. 1945, Winnipeg, MB; d. 1994, Toronto, ON
Jorge Zontal b. 1944, Parma, Italy; d. 1994, Toronto, ON

Line Project, 1970
9 lengths of hemp rope with ID tags (recreation), textual records, photographs, map with ink drawing
dimensions variable
Courtesy of AA Bronson and Esther Schipper Gallery, Berlin

Light On, 1971
Elements from a larger installation

project documentation: 4 silver gelatin prints and 1 document (facsimile)
20.3 x 25.4 each (prints); 27.8 x 21.3 (document)

Light On (Footlight)
2 silver gelatin prints on masonite
20.3 x 25.4 each

Light On (General Idea's Headquarters, Toronto)
6 silver gelatin prints on masonite, 2 panels
20.3 x 25.4 each

Light On (Niagara Falls)
2 silver gelatin prints on cardboard, 2 panels
76.2 x 101.6 each

Light On (Toronto Dominion Centre, Toronto)
1 chromogenic print and 1 silver gelatin print on masonite
20.3 x 25.4 each

Light On (Toronto Dominion Centre, Toronto)
1 chromogenic print and 3 silver gelatin prints on masonite
20.3 x 25.4 each

Light On (Wipe Out, Frenchman's Bay)
2 silver gelatin prints on cardboard, 2 panels
76.2 x 101.6 each
Courtesy of AA Bronson

Double Mirror Video, 1971
single-channel video transferred to DVD
5:50
Courtesy of Electronic Arts Intermix, New York

FILE Megazine, 1972–75
Mr. Peanut Issue (with Image Bank), vol. 1, no. 1, April 1972
Morris/Trasov Archive at the Morris and Helen Belkin Art Gallery, University of British Columbia, Vancouver

Manipulating the Self Issue, Vol. 1, No. 2&3, May/June 1972
Eye of the Shadow Issue, Vol. 1, No. 4, December 1972
Special Double Issue, Vol. 2, No. 1&2, May 1973
Mondo Nudo Issue, Vol. 2, No. 4, December 1973
Annual Artists' Directory Issue, Vol. 2, No. 5, (including Image Bank International Image Exchange Directory), February 1974
Glamour Issue, Vol. 3, No. 1, Fall 1975
magazines
35.5 x 27 each

FILE Megazine business card, 1973
FILE: Bound to Please (postcard), 1977
Collection of Art Metropole, Toronto

Showcards, 1975
1-001 "General Idea"
2-001 "The 1984 Miss General Idea Pageant"
3-001 "Miss General Idea 1984"
4-001 "The 1984 Miss General Idea Pavilion"
5-001 "Frame of Reference"
offset lithographs and ink on paper
45.7 x 35.6 each
Private Collection

Luxon Louvre (Ambiguity Without Contradiction) from the *Pavilion Floor Plan* series, 1975
blueprint on paper, edition of 100 (20 produced)
20 x 19.2 folded; 58 x 112 unfolded

Proposed Seating Arrangement (Form Follows Fiction) from the *Pavilion Floor Plan* series, 1975
blueprint on paper, edition of 100 (20 produced)
20 x 18.2 folded; 44 x 83 unfolded
Courtesy of AA Bronson

Pilot, 1977
single-channel video with audio
28:56
Courtesy of Electronic Arts Intermix, New York

Raymond Gervais

b. 1946, Montréal, QC; lives and works in Montréal, QC

12+1=, 1976
five-page description of the work with list of music and composers, photograph, poster, sound transferred to CD
dimensions variable, sound 152:30
Courtesy of the Artist

Dan Graham

b. 1942, Urbana, IL: lives and works in New York, NY

Likes—A Computer-Astrological Dating-Placement Service, 1967–69
newspaper ad in the *Mail-Star* (Halifax), 11 October 1969
dimensions variable according to publication
Lisson Gallery, London, England

Two Correlated Rotations (rehearsal with Tim Zuck at NSCAD), 1969
single sheet of paper with 3 silver gelatin prints
25.4 x 20.7

7 Performances, 16 Presentations, Obverse, 8–15 October 1970 and 10–22 March 1971
exhibition invitation
NSCAD University, Gallery Archives, Mezzanine Fonds, Halifax

Homes for America, 1971
lithograph on Arches paper
56.8 x 76.5
Lithography Workshop, Collection of NSCAD University, Halifax

Like (rehearsal with Ian Murray at NSCAD), 1971
text card, 4 black and white photographs in plastic sleeves
28 x 22 each photograph
Collection of Ian Murray

Performance: New Piece, 17–24 January 1972
offset lithograph (poster) for exhibition at Fourth Floor Gallery, NSCAD, Halifax
NSCAD University, Gallery Archives, Mezzanine Fonds, Halifax

Nude Two Consciousness Projection(s), 1975
2 silver gelatin prints documenting performance, mounted on bond paper, with reproduction details for *Video-Architecture-Television*
20.4 x 24.6 and 19.7 x 24.3

Video-Architecture-Television, 1979
book published by The Press, NSCAD
21.6 x 28.9
NSCAD University, Gallery Archives, The Press Fonds, Halifax

Rodney Graham

b. 1949, Abbotsford, BC; lives and works in Vancouver, BC

Camera Obscura, 1979
chromogenic print, azo-dye print, architectural model, text
dimensions variable
Vancouver Art Gallery, Vancouver

Illuminated Ravine, 1979
offset lithograph (map indicating location of the work)
Vancouver Art Gallery Library and Archives, Vancouver

John Greer

b. 1944, Amherst, NS; lives and works in West Dublin, NS
Six Points of a Shadow, October 1969–November 1970
postcard and text document in Plexiglass and wood frame;
6 photocopied postcards mounted on mat board
29.3 x 63.8 overall

Tied Up, Tied Down, 1971
2 silver gelatin prints
51 x 41 each
Courtesy of the Artist

Somethings, 25 May–8 June 1972
exhibition invitation
NSCAD University, Gallery Archives, Anna Leonowens Exhibitions Fonds, Halifax

Ladder of Commitment, 1976
oak, maple and steel sculpture
75.4 x 49.2 x 8
Courtesy of the Artist

Hans Haacke

b. 1936, Cologne, Germany; lives and works in New York, NY

Untitled, 1969
documentation: letter from Alain Kirili to Hans Haacke, letter from Bill Kirby to Hans Haacke, letter to Hans Haacke from unidentified person, one page of instructions on Edmonton Art Gallery letterhead; plastic bottle; photograph of plastic bottles floating in the North Saskatchewan River
Collection of Bill Kirby

Framing and Being Framed, 1975
paperbound book published by The Press, NSCAD
NSCAD University, Gallery Archives, The Press Fonds, Halifax

The Halifax Conference, 5–6 October 1970

brochure
NSCAD University, Gallery Archives, Mezzanine Fonds, Halifax

Halifax/Vancouver Exchange, 6–11 March 1972 (Halifax), 26–30 March 1972 (Vancouver)

exhibition invitation, poster
NSCAD University, Gallery Archives, Anna Leonowens Gallery Exhibitions Fonds, Halifax

Noel Harding

b. 1945, London, England; lives and works in Toronto, ON
Birth's Child, 1973
single-channel video transferred to DVD
3:00
Courtesy of the Artist and Vtape, Toronto

John Heward

b. 1934, Montréal, QC; lives and works in Montréal, QC

Untitled 1 (Performance for the Camera) and *Untitled 4 (Performance for the Camera)*, 1976
2 silver gelatin prints (photography by Alex Neumann)
35.8 x 27.8 each
Courtesy of the Artist

Douglas Huebler

b. 1924, Ann Arbor, MI; d. 1997, Cape Cod, MA

Duration Piece #8, 1970
booklet
41 x 29
NSCAD University, Gallery Archives, Lithography Workshop Fonds, Halifax

Untitled, 12 November–5 December 1973
exhibition invitation
NSCAD University, Gallery Archives, Anna Leonowens Gallery Exhibitions Fonds, Halifax

Location Piece #25, 1973
lithograph on Arches paper
61 x 61
Lithography Workshop, Collection of NSCAD University, Halifax

Image Bank

Michael Morris b. 1942, Saltdean, England; lives and works in Victoria, BC
Vincent Trasov b. 1947, Edmonton, AB; lives and works in Vancouver, BC, and Berlin, Germany

Image Bank Mailings with Image of the Month, 1970–71
ink on paper
21.6 x 17.9

Fire/Mirror/Video (with General Idea), 1971
single-channel video with audio
5:50
Vancouver Art Gallery, Vancouver

Image Bank Postcard Show, 1971
boxed edition of 80 offset lithographs on card
15 x 10 x 4 (box)

Legal Tender, 1972
rubber stamp used to stamp title on annual report
2.5 x 10.7 x 7.1

Legal Tender: Image Bank Annual Report, 1972
book published by Poem Company, Intermedia Press
28 x 21
Morris/Trasov Archive at the Morris and Helen Belkin Art Gallery, University of British Columbia, Vancouver

Light-On (with Gordon Kidd and Martin Bartlett), 1970-71
16 mm black and white film transferred to DVD
3:54
Courtesy of the Artists

International Image Exchange Directory, 1972
book published by Talon Books
18.6 x 13.2

Off the Air Coverage of the Peanut Campaign, 1974
single-channel video with audio
20:00
Vancouver Art Gallery, Vancouver

A New Mayor for a New Era, 1974
offset lithograph on card
21.5 x 12.7

The Rise and Fall of the Peanut Party JOURNAL: 20 Days in November, by John Mitchell and Vincent Trasov, 1978
book
23 x 15.5

Image Bank Postcard Show, 1977
boxed edition of 48 offset lithographs on card
16 x 10.5 x 1.8 (box)

International Image Exchange Directory, n.d.
78 photo-mechanical transfers
51 x 41 each
Morris/Trasov Archive at the Morris and Helen Belkin Art Gallery, University of British Columbia, Vancouver

Information, 1970

catalogue for exhibition at Museum of Modern Art, New York
NSCAD University Library, Halifax

Investigations: Ian Carr-Harris, John Greer, N.E. Thing Co. Ltd., 1974

catalogue for exhibition at Owens Art Gallery, Sackville, NB
Courtesy of John Greer

Carole Itter

b. 1939, Vancouver, BC; lives and works in Vancouver, BC

Maquette for The Log's Log, 1973
mixed media
5 panels: 27.7 x 142; 27.7 x 177.7; 27.7 x 148.8; 27.7 x 213.1; 50.4 x 40.4
Collection of the Morris and Helen Belkin Art Gallery, University of British Columbia, Vancouver; Gift of the Artist

Richards Jarden

b. 1947, Philadelphia, PA; lives and works in New York

Facial Angle, 1970
card with text, 10 silver gelatin prints, manila envelope
7.5 x 11.5 each photograph

Falling, 1970
card with text, 6 silver gelatin prints, manila envelope
11.5 x 7.5 each photograph

High Tide (Simulation), 1970
card with text, 6 silver gelatin prints, manila envelope
7.5 x 11.5 each photograph

Traffic Jam, 1970
card with text, 6 silver gelatin prints, manila envelope
7.5 x 11.5 each photograph
Collection of Alan Cravitz and Shashi Caudill

Untitled (layout for *Avalanche* magazine), 1970
19 silver gelatin prints with text
4 x 5 each photograph; 39.5 x 63.2 overall
Collection of Garry Neill Kennedy

Untitled (mobius strip), 1–8 March 1971
exhibition invitation

Untitled, 2–11 February 1973
exhibition invitation
NSCAD University, Gallery Archives, Anna Leonowens Gallery Exhibitions Fonds and Mezzanine Fonds, Halifax

Bill Jones

b. 1946, Antioch, CA; lives and works in New York, NY

Landscape #1, 1970
silver gelatin print, glass
123 x 124 x 4.1
Vancouver Art Gallery, Vancouver

Donald Judd

b. 1928, Excelsior Springs, MI; d. 1994, New York, NY

The Complete Writings 1959–1975, 1975
paperbound book published by The Press, NSCAD
28.5 x 22.2
NSCAD University, Gallery Archives, The Press Fonds, Halifax

On Kawara

b. 1933, Japan; lives and works in New York, NY

One Million Years, 17–25 April 1972
exhibition invitation
NSCAD University, Gallery Archives, Mezzanine Fonds, Halifax

Mary Kelly

b. 1941, Fort Dodge, IA; lives and works in Los Angeles, CA

Post-Partum Document, 8–11 December 1981
black and white photograph of installation at Anna Leonowens Gallery (facsimile); exhibition invitation
NSCAD University, Gallery Archives, Anna Leonowens Gallery Exhibitions Fonds, Halifax

Pat Kelly

b. 1939, Steubenville, OH; d. 2011, Savannah, GA

A Shot in the Dark, 1971
lithograph on Rives BFK paper
50.8 x 51.4
Lithography Workshop, Collection of NSCAD University, Halifax

Garry Neill Kennedy

b. 1935, St. Catharines, ON; lives and works in Halifax, NS

Dedications, 1971
paperbound book in library binding
27 x 19.7
NSCAD University Library, Halifax

My Fourth Grade Class, 1972
lithograph on Arches paper
59.1 x 66.7
Lithography Workshop, Collection of NSCAD University, Halifax

Page 141, 1972
single-page magazine article for *Studio International*, October 1972, p. 141
30.4 x 24.2

6B Rub Off, 1975
3 sheets of paper with graphite
105.4 x 74.9 each

View from the Gallery Window, 1981
colour photograph
Courtesy of the Artist

View from the Gallery Window, 1981
exhibition invitation, offset lithograph on paper
10.2 x 15.2 each
Vancouver Art Gallery Library and Archives, Vancouver

Kensington Arts Association (Centre for Experimental Art and Communication)

(ephemera), 1973–77

Kensington Arts Association minutes, 1973
Kensington Arts Association brochure, 1975
Letter from Amerigo Marras to the editors, *The Fox*, 30 July 1975
Letter from Karl Beveridge to Amerigo Marras, 18 June 1976
Letter from Amerigo Marras to Anthony McCall, 16 July 1976
Body Art (exhibition brochure), 1976
Contextual Art Conference (transcripts of conference), 10–11 November 1976
Postcard from Lawrence Weiner to John Faichney, 12 December 1976
Letter from Joseph Kosuth to Amerigo Marras, 1977
Holiday card from Martha Rosler to the staff of the Centre for Experimental Art and Communication, 12 December 1977
Sketchbook by Amerigo Marras, *Faculty of Architorture*, 1976
The lumpen artist and everyone else, (handwritten note by Amerigo Marras), n.d
York University Libraries, Clara Thomas Archives and Special Collections, Toronto

Roy Kiyooka

b. 1926, Moose Jaw, SK; d. 1994, Vancouver, BC

Halifax Sea and Rock, 1971
72 silver gelatin prints
101 x 150 overall

Long Beach to Peggy's Cove, 1971
576 silver gelatin prints
41.5 x 551.25 overall

Untitled (Opposite Blue Mule Studio, Powell Street), 1978–80
16 silver gelatin prints
38.5 x 187 overall
Vancouver Art Gallery, Vancouver

Robert Kleyn

b. 1948, Amsterdam, The Netherlands; lives and works in Vancouver, BC

Island, 1972
dual 35 mm slide projections with audio
dimensions variable

Words Are Done With, 1973
9 chromogenic prints
20.5 x 25.5 each
Courtesy of the Artist

Joseph Kosuth

b. 1945, Toledo, OH; lives and works in New York, NY, and Rome, Italy

Opinion (Art as Idea as Idea), 1968
photostat
13.3 x 11.4
Collection of the Carmen Lamanna Estate

Insurance (Art as Idea as Idea), 1968
single sheet of paper with travel insurance policy signed to David Askevold as beneficiary
33 x 21.5
National Gallery of Canada Library and Archives, Art Metropole Collection, Ottawa; Gift of Jay A. Smith, Toronto, 1999

Art as Idea, 25 October–9 November 1969
exhibition invitation
NSCAD University, Gallery Archives, Anna Leonowens Gallery Exhibitions Fonds, Halifax

Sharon Kulik

b. 1951, Cleveland, OH; lives and works in Princeton, NJ

Standing from Noon to Dusk in the Sunlight, Exposing My Shadow to Observers, 31 May 1972
exhibition invitation (facsimile)

Untitled, 13–17 March 1972
exhibition invitation
NSCAD University, Gallery Archives, Mezzanine Fonds, Halifax

Jean-Claude Labrecque and Jean-Pierre Masse

Labrecque b. 1938, Quebec City, QC

La nuit de la poésie (excerpt with Michèle Lalonde reciting her poem "Speak White"), 27 March 1970
4:00 segment of 16 mm film transferred to DVD (111:18, full length)
National Film Board of Canada, Ottawa

Suzy Lake

b. 1947, Detroit, MI; lives and works in Toronto, ON

A One Hour (Zero) Conversation with Allan B., 1973
photomontage, 30 silver gelatin prints, felt pen
63.5 x 105.8 overall
Winnipeg Art Gallery, Gift of Dr. and Mrs. William F. Campbell

Suzy Lake as Gary William Smith, 1974
10 silver gelatin prints mounted on card
94 x 67 each
Courtesy of the Artist

Suzy Lake as Gilles Gheerbrant, 1974
4 silver gelatin prints
34.7 x 27 each
Canadian Museum of Contemporary Photography, Ottawa

Box Concert, 1974
single-channel video transferred to DVD
5:00
The Natural Way to Draw, 1975
single-channel video transferred to DVD
14:00
Choreographies of the Dotted Line, 1976
single-channel video transferred to DVD
13:00
Courtesy of the Artist and Vtape, Toronto

Gordon Lebredt

b. 1948, Winnipeg, MB; d. 2011, Toronto, ON

Get Hold of This Space, 1974
(reconstructed in 2010)
latex paint on wall
153 x 282

What's Behind It All, 1974–80
(reconstructed in 2010)
2 photostat panels
204.5 x 239

Text with Warning Light, based on a drawing from 1977, (constructed in 2010)
light, wall text, acrylic paint on existing wall
153 x 283.5
Collection of Lin Gibson

Les Levine

b. 1935, Dublin, Ireland; lives and works in New York, NY

Red Tape, (reconstruction of performance at Hart House), 1970
clay chimney flues, nylon rope, steel lathe
dimensions variable
Courtesy of the Artist

Archival materials related to *Red Tape*, 1970
Sculpture at Hart House, exhibition catalogue, 1969
"The installation was the message," newspaper article by Bernadette Andrews, *The Toronto Telegram*, 18 July 1970
"Levine's hangup never got up," newspaper article by James Bawden, *The Globe and Mail*, 28 July 1970
Correspondence between Paul Russell and J.S. Cunningham, 2 facsimiles, 1970
Letter from R.L. Brett to S.G. Hennessey, facsimile, 1970
Letter from S.G. Hennessey to Paul Russell, 1970
Monuments 70, Hart House exhibition catalogue and invitation card, 16 July–9 October 1970
Untitled (black and white photograph of Les Levine), 1970
"Sat. Ent. ART-LEVINE", typewritten document, n.d.
Collection of Paul Russell, Toronto

Les Levine Copies Everyone, unbound exhibition catalogue, 1970
Collection of Bill Kirby

Les Levine's "Peggy's Cove," 4–30 July 1973
exhibition brochure
NSCAD University, Gallery Archives, Anna Leonowens Gallery Exhibitions Fonds, Halifax

Language – Emotion + Syntax = Message, 1973
etching (1 of a suite of 6) on copperplate Del paper
73 x 92.1

Peggy's Cove YR BB, 1973
lithograph on Arches paper
64.8 x 63.9
Lithography Workshop, Collection of NSCAD University, Halifax

Glenn Lewis

b. 1935, Chemainus, BC; lives and works in Vancouver, BC

Blue Tape Around a City Block, 1969
16 mm colour film transferred to DVD
9:51

Forest Industry, 1969
16 mm colour film transferred to DVD
94:00
Courtesy of the Artist

Sol LeWitt

b. 1928, Hartford, CT; d. 2007, New York, NY

Using a Black, Hard Crayon Draw Four Contiguous Squares, Forming One Twenty-one Inch Square, Divided into Quarters. Within the First Square (Upper Left) Draw One Line, One Inch Long. Within the Second Square (Upper Right) Draw Ten Lines, Each One Inch Long. Within the Third Square (Lower Left) Draw One Hundred Lines, Each One Inch Long. Within the Fourth Square (Lower Right) Draw One Thousand Lines, Each One Inch Long. All Lines Should Be Drawn at Random, and Straight, 1971
lithograph on German Etching paper
(1 of a suite of 10)
71.1 x 71.1

Within a Twenty-inch Square Area, Using a Black, Hard Crayon, Draw Ten Thousand Free-hand Lines, of Any Length, at Random, 1971
lithograph on German Etching paper
(1 of a suite of 10)
71.1 x 71.1
Lithography Workshop, Collection of NSCAD University, Halifax

Lee Lozano
b. 1930, Newark, NJ; d. 1999, Dallas, TX

The Timecross Casts a Shadow, 1971
ink on paper mounted in Plexiglas frame
21.6 x 28; 31 x 26 framed
Collection of Garry Neill Kennedy

Infofiction, 27 January–13 February 1971
letter to Mezzanine director, exhibition hanging plan, invitation (all facsimiles)
NSCAD University, Gallery Archives, Mezzanine Fonds, Halifax

Ken Lum
b. 1956, Vancouver, BC; lives and works in Vancouver, BC

Entertainment for Surrey, 1978
video documentation of performance
1:45
Surrey Art Gallery; Gift of the Artist

Duane Lunden
b. 1946, Elk Point, Alberta; lives and works in Vancouver

Untitled, c. 1967
suite of 4 identical etchings
43.5 x 56.3 each
Private Collection

Don Mabie (a.k.a. Chuck Stake)
b. 1947, Calgary, AB; lives and works in Nakusp, BC

Assorted Chuck Stake Enterprizes correspondence art projects (29 original drawings and collages), 1972–75
rapidograph pen and ink on paper or cover stock
dimensions variable

Assorted Chuck Stake Enterprizes correspondence art projects (43 offset prints for mailing), 1973–79
offset lithographs on paper
21.6 x 35.6 each

Assorted Chuck Stake Enterprizes correspondence art projects, 1974
offset lithographs on paper, hand coloured with pencil crayon and sewn into vinyl sleeves with plastic toys, buttons, glitter
21.6 x 35.6 each

Assorted Chuck Stake Enterprizes correspondence art projects, c. 1975
5 photocopies of envelopes from slides
21.6 x 28.9 each
Courtesy of the Artist

Allan Harding MacKay
b. 1944, Charlottetown, PEI; lives and works in Toronto, ON

36 Halifax Corner Grocery Stores,1972
paperbound book in library binding
(photography by Lionel Simmons)
26.2 x 18.4
NSCAD University Library, Halifax

Robin MacKenzie
b. 1938, Pickering, ON; d. New Mexico, 2004

Study for Farside/Near, 1975–76
25 azo dye prints mounted on masonite
76.2 x 114.2
Collection of the Robert McLaughlin Gallery, Oshawa; Gift of Allen Weinberg

Arnaud Maggs
b. 1926, Montréal, QC; lives and works in Toronto, ON

Kunstakademie Details 1, 6, 33, and 36, 1980
4 silver gelatin prints, edition of 23
40.5 x 40.5 each
Courtesy of Susan Hobbs Gallery, Toronto

Mainmise, No. 42, December 1974
magazine
Private Collection

John McEwen
b. 1945, Toronto, ON; lives and works in Hillsdale, ON
Blood Tap (or Pressing Out/Pressing Down), 1971
single-channel video transferred to DVD
22:00
Courtesy of the Artist

Bruce McLean
b. 1944, Glasgow, Scotland; lives and works in London, England

King for a Day + 999 Other Pieces/Works/Stuff Etc., October 1970
exhibition invitation, one-page description of booklet
NSCAD University, Gallery Archives, Mezzanine Fonds, Halifax

Médiart, Vol. 1, Nos. 2, 6 and 10, October 1971, October 1972 and October–December 1975
magazine
28 x 22
Issue No. 2 Courtesy of Artexte, Montréal, Gift of Normand Thériault; Nos. 6 and 10, Collection of Jean-Marie Delavalle

Ian Murray
b. 1951, Pictou, NS; lives and works in Toronto, ON

Keeping on Top of the Top Song, 1970
performance (originally performed at Dalhousie University, Halifax, in 1970)
Courtesy of the Artist

The Top Song: An Artist's Design for a Best-selling Record, 1973
side one: *The Top Song* (1970), side two: *Keeping on Top of the Top Song* (from a performance by Tim Cahoon at NSCAD, 1973)
edition of 250, record sleeve and 33 rpm record transferred to CD
31.4 x 31.4
Courtesy of the Artist

Twenty Waves in a Row, 1971
paperbound book
11.3 x 15.5
NSCAD University Library, Halifax

Untitled, 1971
single sheet of paper with text, 10 silver gelatin prints in plastic sleeves
28 x 21.7 (paper); 9 x 13 each (prints)
Collection of Garry Neill Kennedy

Keeping on Top of the Top Song, 25 June–2 July 1973
exhibition invitation
NSCAD University, Gallery Archives, Anna Leonowens Gallery Exhibitions Fonds, Halifax

Image and Appearance, 1974
India ink on book
21.6 x 13.7 x 5

BROADCAST: STATEMENTS WHICH ARE TRUE, OR MOSTLY TRUE, AS APPLIED TO ME/STATEMENTS WHICH ARE FALSE, OR MOSTLY FALSE, AS APPLIED TO ME, 1977
black and white video, UHF, NTSC; continuous local broadcast
Courtesy of the Artist

N.E. Thing Co.

Iain Baxter b. 1936, Middlesbrough, England; lives and works in Windsor, ON
Ingrid Baxter b. Spokane, WA; lives and works in Vancouver, BC

Paint into Earth, S.F.U., Vancouver, B.C., 1966, 1966
silver gelatin print, chromogenic print, lithograph on paper
152 x 101 overall

You Are Now in the Middle of a N.E. Thing Co. Landscape, 1968
offset lithograph on card (postcard)
10.5 x 15
Vancouver Art Gallery, Vancouver

ACT #13—Fallen Logs, 30 Miles East of Hope, BC, Canada (1968), 1968
silver gelatin print, ink, company seal
68.9 x 98.7

ACT #60—Grain Freighter "Sigsilver," Maiden Voyage, Alberta Wheat Pool Bldg., New Brighton Park, Vancouver, British Columbia, Canada and the waters of the world, 1967–69, 1968
silver gelatin print, ink, company seal
70 x 101.4
Vancouver Art Gallery, Vancouver; Purchased with Funds from the Vancouver Art Gallery Acquisition Fund, with Financial Assistance from the Canada Council of the Arts Acquisition Assistance Program

Circular Walk Inside Arctic Circle Around Inuvik, N.W.T., 1969
silver gelatin print, ink, paper, foil seal, offset lithograph on paper
44 x 44

Lucy Lippard Walking Towards True North, 1969
silver gelatin print, ink, paper, foil seal, offset lithograph and paint on paper
37.1 x 45.8

Sixteen Compass Points Within the Arctic Circle, 1969
6 silver gelatin prints, paper, foil seal, ink, labels and offset lithograph on paper
44 x 44 each

Territorial Claim—Urination, 1969
chromogenic prints, ink, labels, offset lithography, paper and foil seal on paper
44 x 44 each
Morris and Helen Belkin Art Gallery, University of British Columbia, Vancouver; Gift of Iain Baxter and Ingrid Baxter

Nothing Project (Nothing is Impossible. Nothing is Something.), 1969
statement on N.E. Thing Co. letterhead
28.1 x 21.7
Collection of Bill Kirby

Telex: Trans VSI Number 14: A Word is Worth 1/1000th of a Picture, 1969
ink on paper (telex)
18.3 x 21.2

Telex: Don't look at this until you are ready for anything, 1970
ink on paper (telex)
32.7 x 21.4

Telex: Trans VSI: Send a Lie, Receive the Truth (Two Dots), 1970
ink on paper (telex)
27.8 x 21.5
Vancouver Art Gallery, Vancouver

P+L+P+L+P= VSI, VSI Formula No. 10, 1970
lithograph on Rives BFK paper with colour slide
61 x 48.3
Lithography Workshop, Collection of NSCAD University, Halifax

Trans VSI Connection NSCAD–NETCO: Sept. 15–Oct. 5, 1969, 1970
paperbound book
27.8 x 21.5
NSCAD University, Gallery Archives, Anna Leonowens Gallery Exhibitions Fonds, Halifax

North American Time Zone Photo—VSI Simultaneity October 18, 1970, 12–30 July 1971
exhibition invitation; one-page project description by Mezzanine director, Charlotte Townsend
NSCAD University, Gallery Archives, Mezzanine Fonds, Halifax

ART is all over (button), 1972
metal pin with text
5.5 (diameter)

N.E. Thing Co. Hockey Team, 1972
chromogenic print
8.9 x 12.6

Eye Scream Restaurant, 1977
Business card, 5.1 x 7.4
Gallery cheque, 21.6 x 10.8
Gallery dishes, commercial-grade china, 22.9 (diameter) x 3 (depth)
Gallery letterhead, 28.1 x 21.7
Gallery opening invitation, 19.4 x 13.6
Gallery receipt, 21.6 x 10.8
Gallery matchbox, 1.7 x 5.5 x 2
Vancouver Art Gallery, Vancouver

N.E. Thing Co.: Sixteen Hundred Miles North of Denver
exhibition catalogue with essay by Charity Mewburn (Vancouver: Morris and Helen Belkin Art Gallery, 1999)
Collection of Bill Kirby

Gunter Nolte

b. 1938, Göttingen, Germany; d. 2000, Fournier, ON

Intervention, 1972
4 black and white photographs of installation at Véhicule Art, Montréal
Collection of Jean-Marie Delavalle

Gestures (tiree de l'album <<Workshop>>, 1975–1976), 1975
screenprint and pencil on paper, edition 5/35
50.8 x 66.5
Musée d'art contemporain de Montréal, Montréal

NSCAD Lithography Workshop

(ephemera), 1970–71

Silver gelatin print of O Canada litho production (Joyce Wieland kissing stone), 1970 (facsimile). Photo: Bob Rogers
Four-page black and white bi-fold brochure for artscanada, April 1970
National Gallery of Canada exhibition catalogue (Joyce Wieland's O Canada print on cover), 1971
Rough proof for O Canada ad in artscanada (August/September 1971). Photo: Bob Rogers
NSCAD University, Gallery Archives, Lithography Workshop Fonds, Halifax

Dennis Oppenheim
b. 1938, Electric City, WA; lives and works in New York, NY

Documentation of *Condensed 220 Yard Dash*, 1969
silver gelatin print
Collection of Bill Kirby
Condensed 220 Yard Dash, 1969
2 plaster-cast footprints from a larger collection
dimensions variable
Art Gallery of Alberta Archives, Edmonton

Material Interchange, 1971
single-channel video transferred to DVD
2:44
Courtesy of the Artist

Reading Position for a Second Degree Burn, 1972
lithograph on Arches Paper
76.2 x 55.9
Lithography Workshop, Collection of NSCAD University, Halifax

Party Fragment 26/2/77, 1977
crushed cigarette package
York University Libraries, Clara Thomas Archives and Special Collections, Toronto

Parachute, Nos. 1–5, October–December 1975 to Winter 1976
magazine edited by Chantal Pontbriand and France Morin
30 x 23
Collection of Chantal Pontbriand

Parti pris, Vol. 2, No. 3, and Vol. 3, No. 6, December 1964 and January 1966
magazine
Private Collection

Andy Patton
b. 1952, Winnipeg, MB; lives and works in Toronto, ON
1st Poster/Description, 1978
instant printed poster on paper
47.2 x 31.8

Untitled (Go-Train station: *1st Poster/Description*), 1978, printed 2010
inkjet print on etching paper
35.6 x 53.3

Untitled (torn: *1st Poster/Description*), 1978, printed 2010
inkjet print on etching paper
35.6 x 53.3

3rd Poster/Description, 1978
instant printed poster on paper
47.2 x 31.8
Untitled (girder: *3rd Poster/Description*), 1978, printed 2010
inkjet print on etching paper
35.6 x 53.3

Untitled (harbour site: *3rd Poster/Description*), 1978, printed 2010
inkjet print on etching paper
35.6 x 53.3

Municipal Election Poster, 1978
instant printed poster on paper (Letraset on paper and 2 colour photographs)
47.2 x 31.8 (poster); 47 x 59.6 each (photographs)

Untitled (hoarding: *Municipal Election Poster*), 1978, printed 2010
inkjet print on etching paper
35.6 x 53.3

Untitled (installation view of *Municipal Election Poster*), 1978, printed 2010
inkjet print on etching paper
35.6 x 53.3
Courtesy of the Artist and Birch Libralato Gallery, Toronto

Périphéries, 1974
catalogue for exhibition at Musée d'art contemporain de Montréal
Collection of Jean-Marie Delavalle

Place & Process and ***AIR ART***
(Edmonton Art Gallery exhibitions), 1969
AIR ART catalogue
Black and white photographs
Exhibition poster
Miscellaneous reviews
"One needs a full stomach to be honest about art," by Virgil Hammock, *Edmonton Journal*, original newspaper article
Collection of Bill Kirby

Edmonton Art Gallery newsletter and archival documents
Willoughby Sharp and Evander Schley, with cinematographer Robert Fiore (New York's Great Balls of Fire Inc.)
Place & Process, 1969
16 mm colour film transferred to DVD
Art Gallery of Alberta Archives, Edmonton

Playback Configuration, November 1974
poster published by Galerie Espace 5, Montréal
Courtesy of InterAccess, Toronto

Zoran Popović
Struggle in New York, 1976
single-channel video transferred to DVD
56:30
Collection of Carole Condé and Karl Beveridge

Québec 75
Québec 75/Arts, 1976
exhibition catalogue (arts section), Musée d'art contemporain de Montréal/Institut d'art contemporain
Collection of Jean-Marie Delavalle

Québec 75, 1978
single-channel video with audio documenting public discussion during the exhibition *Québec 75*
50:00
Vidéographe, Montréal

Québec Underground 1962–1972, published 1973
three-volume book, Editions Médiart, Montréal
Private Collection

Rober Racine
b. 1956, Montréal, QC; lives and works in Montréal, QC

Rober Racine performing Erik Satie's *Vexations* at Véhicule Art, 1978
documentation of performance: single-channel video with audio transferred to DVD
14:00:00
Vexations, annotated score no. 565, 1978
ink on paper
26 x 43
Courtesy of the Artist

Yvonne Rainer
b. 1934, San Francisco, CA; lives and works in Los Angeles, CA

Yvonne Rainer: Work 1961–73, 1974
paperbound book published by The Press, NSCAD
28.5 x 20
NSCAD University, Gallery Archives, The Press Fonds, Halifax

Clive Robertson
b. 1946, Plymouth, England; lives and works in Kingston, ON

A Year Of..f, 1972–73
2 panels with silver gelatin prints and text
76.2 x 21.6 each

Family Music, 1972–73
audio recording transferred to CD
30:00

Identity Transfer, 1972–78
panel with silver gelatin prints and text
76.2 x 21.6

A Conceptographic Reading of Our World Thermometer, 1973
exhibition catalogue published by W.O.R.K.S., Calgary
28 x 22

w.o.r.k.s.c.o.r.e.p.o.r.t., 1975
book published by Beau Geste Press, England
Courtesy of the Artist

Ellison Robertson
b. 1948, Cape Breton Island, NS; lives and works on Cape Breton Island

Tumbling, c. 1970
single-channel video
2:05
NSCAD University Visual Resources Collection, Halifax

Rochdale College
(ephemera), 1968–75

Rochdale Is . . . (poster), 1968,
Sculpture at Rochdale (winter program), 1968
The Eisenhower Years (pamphlet), Thursday, 3 April 1968
Yearbook, 1968
The Catalogue (pamphlet), November 1972
Degree application form, n.d.
Degrees: "B.A.," "Childcare," "Failure," "Non-M.A." and "Nothing", n.d.
Guide Book (yellow), n.d.
Invitation to Rochdale Art Gallery, n.d.
Memo (printed in red), n.d.
Rochdale promotion brochure, n.d.
Thomas Fisher Rare Book Library, University of Toronto, Toronto

Martha Rosler
b. 1943, Brooklyn, NY; lives and works in Brooklyn, NY

Semiotics of the Kitchen, 1975
single-channel video transferred to DVD
6:09
Courtesy of the Artist and Vtape, Toronto

Exhibition invitation (also for Allan Sekula) for *The Bowery in Two Inadequate Descriptive Systems* (1974–75)
21 January–1 February, 1980
NSCAD University, Gallery Archives, Anna Leonowens Gallery Exhibitions Fonds, Halifax

3 Works, 1981
spiral-bound book published by The Press, NSCAD
20.3 x 28
NSCAD University, Gallery Archives, The Press Fonds, Halifax

Tom Sherman
b. 1947, Manistee, MI; lives and works in Syracuse, NY

Trace, 1972
16 mm film transferred to DVD
6:49
Courtesy of the Artist
Distant Interior Sound, from a Photograph by Lynne Cohen, 1977, 1977
silver gelatin print and 2 text panels
170 x 208 overall
Canada Council Art Bank, Ottawa
3 Death Stories, 1977
bookwork, edition of 500
26.6 x 19.7 x 0.5
Collection of Art Metropole, Toronto

Envisioner, 1978
single-channel video transferred to DVD
3:00

TVideo, 1980
single-channel video transferred to DVD
28:00
Courtesy of the Artist and Vtape, Toronto

Rebecca Singleton
b. 1952, Toronto, ON; lives and works in Toronto, ON

How to eat coconut cream pie, 1981 (printed 1998)
selenium-toned silver gelatin print
43.2 x 27.9

How to hold a chihuahua, 1981 (printed 1998)
selenium-toned silver gelatin print
43.2 x 27.9

How to wear a raincoat while wearing a brassiere and slip, 1981 (printed 1998)
selenium-toned silver gelatin print
43.2 x 27.9

How to wear a raincoat while wearing a slip, 1981 (printed 1998)
selenium-toned silver gelatin print
43.2 x 27.9
Courtesy of Christopher Cutts Gallery, Toronto

Robert Smithson
b. 1938, Passaic, NJ; d. 1973, Amarillo, TX

Drawing for Glue Pour, 1969
ink on paper
20.4 x 25.3

Britannia Beach Project: Spill Fluvial Discharge, 1970
ink on paper
27.7 x 21.3

Britannia Beach Project: Spill-White Paint, 1970
ink on paper
27.7 x 21.3

Island of the Dismantled Building—Vancouver, 1970
ink on paper
21.4 x 27.6
Vancouver Art Gallery, Vancouver

Michael Snow
b. 1929, Toronto, ON; lives and works in Toronto, ON

Portrait, 1967
8 sections of hollow, rectangular, grooved aluminum tubing, assembled in 4 pairs as a frame of variable dimensions according to width of passage or

opening, held in position by aluminum slots, nuts and clasps
dimensions variable (approx. 61 x 91)
Private Collection

Authorization, 1969
instant silver gelatin prints and adhesive tape on mirror in metal frame
54.6 x 44.4 x 1.4

Tap, 1969–72
framed silver gelatin print, framed typewritten text on paper, framed documents, CD player, speaker box, wire and sound
silver gelatin print 107.1 x 156.3; text 65.1 x 40; documents 32 x 62.5; speaker box 48.3 x 38.1 x 25.4
National Gallery of Canada, Ottawa

Venetian Blind, 1970
24 chromogenic prints in painted wood frames
126 x 234 overall
Canada Council Art Bank, Ottawa

Works and Films, 17–30 January 1972
exhibition invitation
NSCAD University, Gallery Archives, Mezzanine Fonds, Halifax

Cover to Cover, 1975
paperbound book published by The Press, NSCAD
23 x 17.9
NSCAD University, Gallery Archives, The Press Fonds, Halifax

Jeffrey Spalding

b. 1951, Edinburgh, Scotland; lives and works in Salmon River Bridge, NS

Magenta/Cyan Blue/Yellow, 1973–75
acrylic on canvas
122.5 x 122.5
Diary Painting: One Secret Colour Per Day, 1978
acrylic on canvas
94.3 x 95
Art Gallery of Alberta, Edmonton; Gift of Mr. Leon Liffmann

Lisa Steele

b. 1947, Kansas, MO; lives and works in Toronto, ON

Juggling, 1972
single-channel video transferred to DVD
6:00

Birthday Suit—with scars and defects, 1974
single-channel video with audio, transferred to DVD
13:00

Outlaws, 1974
single-channel video with audio, transferred to DVD
20:00

Internal Pornography, 1975
three-channel video with audio, transferred to DVD
30:00
Courtesy of the Artist and Vtape, Toronto

The Ballad of Dan Peoples, 1977
book, edition of approximately 500
26.6 x 20.3 x .3
Collection of Art Metropole, Toronto

Françoise Sullivan

b. 1925, Montréal, QC; lives and works in Montréal, QC

La promenade entre le Musée d'art contemporain et le Musée des beaux-arts de Montréal, 1970
32 framed silver gelatin prints, facsimile of a roadmap
32.5 x 32.5 each
Montréal Museum of Fine Arts, Montréal; Gift of the Artist

TILT, December 1973
magazine edited by Normand Thériault
Collection of Jean-Marie Delavalle

David Tomas

b. 1950, Montréal, QC; lives and works in Montréal, QC
1000 Seconds: five permutations on the theme of the last 200 seconds before 7:30 am, July 1916, The First Battle of the Somme, 1974
silent Super 8 film transferred to DVD
15:46

Works on the History of Physics, 1975–76
handwritten text on paper in plastic sleeves
22 x 28
Courtesy of the Artist

Serge Tousignant

b. 1942, Montréal, QC; lives and works in Montréal, QC

Ruban gommé sur coin d'atelier—Neuf points de vision, 1973
photostat
63 x 77
Courtesy of the Artist

The Vancouver Tapes, 1970–71

The Vancouver Tapes, No. 1, c. 1970
1. Graham Dube, *Untitled*, 3:33
2. Graham Dube, *Untitled*, 1:34
3. David Askevold, *Fill*, 9:57
4. Jon Young, *Cup*, 3:02
5. Jon Young, *Untitled*, 2:04
6. Vito Acconci, Gerald Ferguson and Bob MacLean, *Trademark*, 8:04
7. Brian MacNevin, *Audio Visual Feedback (completing two cycles)*, 18:52
8. Brian MacNevin, *2-D Images*, 2:58
9. Richards Jarden, *Thigh Waves*, 2:16
10. Barry MacPherson, *Untitled*, 3:00
11. Barry MacPherson, *Eve*, 7:01

compilation 62:21

The Vancouver Tapes No. 2, 1970–71
1. Douglas Waterman, *Calculations*, 5:12
2. Douglas Waterman, *Inhale/Exhale*, 8:55
3. Gerald Ferguson, *Length 4* 21:18
4. Ellison Robertson, *Tumbling*, 2:05
5. Albert McNamara, *Smile*, 18:48

compilation 56:18

The Vancouver Tapes No. 3, c. 1971
1. Harold Pearse, *Gas Stations from Montreal to Vancouver*, 5:19
2. Harold Pearse, *Gas Stations from Montreal to Halifax*, 1:26
3. Harold Pearse, *133 Days in Halifax*, 13:50
4. Wallace Brannen, *Mile Walk*, 12:37
5. Bruce Parsons, *Sound Gap*, 8:00
6. Bruce Parsons, *Aesthetic Machine*, 13:50
7. Allan Harding MacKay, *Repeat the Question*, 3:10
8. Allan Harding MacKay, *Get Out*, 6:17
9. Allan Harding MacKay, *Mike Tap*, 0:51

compilation 65:20

The Vancouver Tapes No. 4 (Pat Kelly), 1971
1. *Catch*, 9:40
2. *Frame Adjustment*, 3:16
3. *Tape Removal*, 4:52
4. *20° of a 360° Rotation*, 3:47
5. *Weight Distribution*, 3:54

6. *Pick Up 10*, 8:00
7. *Animated Video*, 13:54
8. *Front/Back*, 9:00
compilation 56:23
single-channel video transferred to DVD
NSCAD University Visual Resources Collection, Halifax

John Van Saun

b. 1939, Denver, CO; lives and works in New York, NY

Flour Drop, 1969
documentation including diagram on mat board, black and white photograph and drawing of layout for *Place & Process* exhibition
Collection of Bill Kirby

Bill Vazan

b. 1933, Toronto, ON; lives and works in Montréal, QC

Canada in Parentheses, 13 August 1969, printed 1999
5 azo-dye prints, colour photocopy
131.8 x 253.6 overall
National Gallery of Canada, Ottawa; Gift of the Artist

World Line, 1969–71
book (108 pages)
27 x 20.7

Canada Line, 1969–70
map of Canada with 32 silver gelatin prints fixed on map
119.8 x 129.2

Lifeline (with Ian Wallace), 1970–72
postcards (hundreds, but less than 1,000) in binders
Contacts, 1971–73
book (108 pages)
35.7 x 26.8
Courtesy of the Artist

Force Field & Contour Intervals, 15–18 February 1972
exhibition invitation
NSCAD University, Gallery Archives, Mezzanine Fonds, Halifax

Robert Walker

b. 1945, Montréal, QC; lives and works in Montréal, QC

Is Politics Art?, 1975
15 azo-dye prints
51 x 51 each
Musée national des beaux-arts du Québec, Québec

Jeff Wall

b. 1946, Vancouver, BC; lives and works in Vancouver, BC

Landscape Manual, 1969–70
offset lithograph on paper (booklet)
28.6 x 20.8
Vancouver Art Gallery, Vancouver; Gift of Robert Kleyn and Gift of Gerald Ferguson (two copies)

Ian Wallace

b. 1943, Shoreham, England; lives and works in Vancouver, BC

Pan-Am Scan, 1970
5 silver gelatin prints
203 x 122

La Mélancolie de la Rue, 1973
3 hand-coloured silver gelatin prints, oil paint
104.5 x 157.5 each
Vancouver Art Gallery, Vancouver

Theodore Wan

b. 1953, Hong Kong; d. 1987, Vancouver, BC

Untitled (Hornby Island performance), 1975
offset lithograph on paper (booklet) documenting performance
23 x 28

Bridine Scrub (for General Surgery), 1977
10 silver gelatin prints
50.5 x 40.4 each

Theodore Saskatchewan (documentation of name change), 1977
mixed media, newspaper clipping, certificate, silver gelatin print (aerial photograph)
dimensions variable

Artist's Sperm, 1978
silver gelatin print
58.4 x 73

Only the mind is allowed to wander, 1981
offset lithograph on card with text documenting performance
10.1 x 14.5
Vancouver Art Gallery, Vancouver; Gifts of the Estate of the Artist

Douglas Waterman

b. c. 1952, Bridgewater, NS; d. c. 1980, Lunenburg County, NS

Shuffle, 1971
single-channel video
30:00 (5:00 excerpt)
NSCAD University Visual Resources Collection, Halifax

Untitled, 22–26 July 1974
exhibition invitation
NSCAD University, Gallery Archives, Anna Leonowens Gallery Exhibitions Fonds, Halifax

John Wall

b. 1953, Toronto, ON; lives and works in Calgary, AB

I'm a Killer, 1973
single-channel video transferred to DVD
11:00
Courtesy of the Artist and Vtape, Toronto

Lawrence Weiner

b. 1942, New York, NY; lives and works in New York, NY, and Amsterdam, The Netherlands

STATEMENTS, 1968
ink on card
York University Libraries, Clara Thomas Archives and Special Collections, Toronto

Two Common Nails Driven into the Floor One Directly In Line with the Other at Points Determined at the Time of Installation, 1968 (recreation 2010)
text, nails
dimensions variable
Collection Public Freehold; Reinstallation Courtesy of the Artist

5 Works, 7–27 April 1969
exhibition invitation (facsimile)
NSCAD University, Gallery Archives, Mezzanine Fonds, Halifax

Lawrence Weiner: Interview with Harris Sullivan for CJCH TV, Halifax, 1969
single-channel video transferred to DVD
15:30
NSCAD University Visual Resources Collection, Halifax

Flowed, 1971
paperbound book and ring-bound draft mock-up (facsimile)
17 x 11 each

[Turned] Red as Well as Black, March 1972
statement of work
NSCAD University, Gallery Archives, Lithography Workshop Fonds, Halifax

Laid Out Flat, Bent (Now) This Way . . . , 18–22 June 1979
exhibition invitation, recto and verso sides
NSCAD University, Gallery Archives, Anna Leonowens Gallery Exhibitions Fonds, Halifax

Rodney Werden
b. 1946, Toronto ON; lives and works in Toronto, ON

I'm Sorry, 1974–75
single-channel video transferred to DVD
5:00
Courtesy of the Artist and Vtape, Toronto

Irene F. Whittome
b. 1942, Vancouver, BC; lives and works in Montréal, QC

Element. The White Museum. Le musée blanc, 1975
5 printed sheets of paper
27.9 x 21.5 each
Courtesy of the Artist

Joyce Wieland
b. 1931, Toronto, ON; d. 1998, Toronto, ON

Dripping Water (with Michael Snow), 1969
16 mm film transferred to DVD
12:00
Courtesy of the Canadian Filmmakers Distribution Centre, Toronto

O Canada, 1970
lithograph on Arches paper
57.2 x 76.2
Lithography Workshop, Collection of NSCAD University, Halifax

O Canada, 1972
lithograph on silk, edition 7/10
154 x 124
Hart House, University of Toronto; Purchased by the Hart House Art Committee

Pierre Vallières, 1972
16 mm film transferred to DVD
32:00
Cinémathèque Québécoise, Montréal

Martha Wilson
b. 1947, Philadelphia, PA; lives and works in New York, NY

Chauvinistic Pieces, 1971 (exhibition copy 2010)
text on paper
44.5 x 61

Breast Forms Permutated, 1972 (exhibition copy 2010)
9 silver gelatin prints with text
50.8 x 35.6 overall

Posturing Drag, 1972 (exhibition copy 2010)
chromogenic print with text on card
(photograph by Douglas Waterman)
49 x 29 overall
Courtesy of the Artist

Posturing: Drag, 1972
chromogenic print in metal frame with photostat of text card from verso side
(photograph by Douglas Waterman)
20.5 x 25.5 (framed print); 16 x 21.6 (text card)
Collection of Garry Neill Kennedy

Art of Incarnation, 14–21 October 1972
exhibition invitation
28 x 21.7
NSCAD University, Gallery Archives, Mezzanine Fonds, Halifax

Early Work 1972–74
Premiere, 1:33
Routine Performance, 2:10
Art Sucks, 1:25
Appearance as Value, 1:50
Method Art, 6:15
Psychology of Camera Presence, 8:50
Cauterization, 6:45
Deformation, 8:00
black and white video compilation
Courtesy of Vtape, Toronto

Male Impersonator (Butch), 1973 (exhibition copy 2010)
chromogenic print with text on card
(photograph by Richards Jarden)
49 x 29 overall

I Make Up the Image of My Perfection/I Make Up the Image of My Deformity, 1974 (exhibition copy 2008)
2 chromogenic prints with text on card
(photographs by Alan Comfort)
48.3 x 63.5 overall
Courtesy of the Artist

Women's Works, 5–16 August 1974
public service announcement (facsimile)
NSCAD University, Gallery Archives, Anna Leonowens Gallery Exhibitions Fonds, Halifax

Paul Woodrow
b. Leeds, England; lives and works in Calgary, AB

Rearview Mirror, Cover-Up, and Character Generator, 1970–71
single-channel video compilation transferred to DVD

City Signature, 1972
map, silver gelatin print

Bureau of Imaginary Exchange, 1976
poster, silver gelatin prints, plastic sign, rubber stamps, questionnaire forms
dimensions variable

Imaginair Tavel, 1978
silver gelatin print, poster
Courtesy of the Artist

Jon Young
b. 1948, Cape Breton Island, NS; lives and works on Cape Breton Island, NS

Film for Viewing with Eyes Crossed, 16–18 February 1972
exhibition invitation

Tuning to a Tree (performance),
28 January 1974
exhibition invitation
NSCAD University, Gallery Archives,
Anna Leonowens Gallery, Halifax

Tim Zuck
b. 1947, Erie, PA; lives and works in Calgary, AB

Elevator, 1970
single-channel video, text card, 3 silver gelatin prints
20:00 (video); 7.6 x 12.7 each (card and prints); 20.1 x 28.5 overall
Halifax, 1970
single-channel video, text card, 3 silver gelatin prints in plastic sleeves
20:00 (video); 7.6 x 12.7 each (card and prints); 20.1 x 28.5 overall
University of Lethbridge Art Collection; Gift of the Artist

Untitled, 13–21 February 1971
exhibition invitation
NSCAD University, Gallery Archives,
Mezzanine Fonds, Halifax

Author and Contributor Biographies

Grant Arnold is Audain Curator of British Columbia Art at the Vancouver Art Gallery, where over the past twenty years he has organized more than thirty-five exhibitions of historical, modern and contemporary art. He has also contributed a number of essays and articles to exhibition catalogues and journals. Arnold teaches in the Critical and Curatorial Studies Program at the University of British Columbia and has lectured on historical and contemporary art at a variety of conferences and institutions.

Vincent Bonin is an author and independent curator. From 2000 to 2007 he worked as an archivist at the Daniel Langlois Foundation for Art, Science, and Technology (Montréal). As a curator he notably organized *Documentary Protocols (1967–1975)* (two exhibitions and a publication) at the Leonard & Bina Ellen Art Gallery, Concordia University (2007–10). He is co-curator (with Catherine Morris) of *(with occasional political overtones): Lucy Lippard's Six Years Project* produced by the Brooklyn Museum. Bonin is the author of numerous essays about the social meaning of archives and the refashioning of the documentary genre in the field of contemporary art. In 2010 the Canada Council for the Arts awarded him the Joan Yvonne Lowndes Award for excellence in critical and curatorial writing.

Catherine Crowston is Deputy Director/Chief Curator of the Art Gallery of Alberta. She was Director/Curator of the Walter Phillips Gallery at the Banff Centre from 1994 to 1997 and Assistant Curator at the Art Gallery of York University from 1986 to 1994. She was formerly a member of the editorial board of *Fuse Magazine*, and taught curatorial studies and critical issues at the University of Alberta from 2001 to 2005. In 2002 Crowston served as the Canadian Commissioner for the Sydney Biennale of Contemporary Art and was awarded the Royal Canadian Academy of Arts Medal for Outstanding Achievement in the Visual Arts.

Barbara Fischer is the Director/Curator of the Justina M. Barnicke Gallery at the University of Toronto. Fischer was the Director/Curator of the Blackwood Gallery at the University of Toronto in Mississauga from 1999 to 2005 and Curator of Contemporary Art at The Power Plant Contemporary Art Gallery in Toronto from 1988 to 1990. She taught museology and curatorial studies at the University of Western Ontario from 1995 to 1999 and art history and theory at the Ontario College of Art & Design from 1992 to 1998. In 2009, she was Commissioner for the Canada Pavilion of the 53rd International Art Exhibition—La Biennale di Venezia.

Blair French is Executive Director of Artspace in Sydney, Australia. He previously worked in art galleries and museums in New Zealand and the United Kingdom. He is the editor of *Photo Files: An Australian Photography Reader* (Sydney: Power Publications and Australian Centre for Photography, 1999) and the author of *Out of Time: Essays Between Photography and Art* (Adelaide: Contemporary Art Centre of South Australia, 2006) and, with Daniel Palmer, *Twelve Australian Photo Artists* (Sydney: Piper Press, 2009). Recent curatorial projects include an eight-part international performance installation season *Aftermath* (2007) and solo exhibition projects with Shaun Gladwell (2007); Bruce Barber, Rose Nolan and Francis Upritchard (all 2008); Peter Robinson (2009) and Simon Denny (2010), among others.

Jeff Khonsary is a Vancouver-based writer, curator and designer. Recent curatorial projects include *Motto Storefront* (Artspeak, 2010, with Melanie O'Brian and Alexis Zavialoff), *Copy Room* (Langara College Centre for Art in Public Space, 2009) and *Ear to Ear* (Or Gallery/Cornershop Projects, 2008). He is Co-Director of Fillip Editions and Publisher of *Fillip*, a magazine focusing on international art and criticism. With Melanie O'Brian, he commissioned and edited *Judgement and Contemporary Art Criticism* (Fillip Editions, 2010) and convened a symposium of the same name in 2009.

Lucy Lippard is an internationally renowned independent writer, activist and curator. She was among the first writers to address the dematerialization that was central to conceptual art, and was also an early champion of feminist art. She is the author of twenty-one books on contemporary art, including *Six Years: The Dematerialization of the Art Object from 1966 to 1972* (New York: Praeger, 1973), a crucial discussion of the development of conceptual art. She received an honorary doctorate from the Nova Scotia College of Art and Design in 2007. In 2010 she received the Award for Curatorial Excellence from The Center for Curatorial Studies at Bard College, New York.

Chantal Pontbriand is a writer and an independent curator. She was Head of Exhibitions Research and Development at the Tate Modern, London. Pontbriand co-founded, with France Morin, the Montréal-based art journal *Parachute* in 1975 and was editor until publication was suspended in 2007. She has curated a number of exhibitions over the past thirty years, including *HF|RG [Harun Farocki|Rodney Graham]* (2009) for the Jeu de Paume, Paris, and *The Yvonne Rainer Project* for the BFI Gallery, London. She was Commissioner for the Canadian Pavilion at the 1990 Venice Biennale, presenting work by Geneviève Cadieux.

Mari Carmen Ramírez is Wortham Curator of Latin American Art and Director of the International Center for the Arts of the Americas at the Museum of Fine Arts, Houston (MFAH). She has published widely on contemporary and modern art from Latin America. Curatorial projects include *Inverted Utopias: Avant-Garde Art in Latin America* (2004), co-curated with Héctor Olea, and *Hélio Oiticica: The Body of Color* (2007), which was presented at the MFAH and the Tate Modern, London.

Michèle Thériault is Director/Curator of the Leonard & Bina Ellen Art Gallery at Concordia University in Montréal. She has organized numerous exhibitions examining artistic practices in relation to questions of translation, frames of reference, exhibition sites and knowledge of art. She is the author of numerous essays and articles in exhibition catalogues, anthologies and journals. From 1988 to 1996 she was Associate Curator of Contemporary Art at the Art Gallery of Ontario in Toronto. Thériault taught contemporary art and curatorial studies at the University of Ottawa from 1998 to 2003 and is Adjunct Professor with the Department of Art History at Concordia University.

Charlotte Townsend-Gault is a professor in the Department of Art History, Visual Art and Theory at the University of British Columbia. She was Director of the Mezzanine at the Nova Scotia College of Art and Design from 1970 to 1973. Her work with contemporary art is linked to her interest in the social relations activated by First Nations cultural expression. Most recently she curated *Backstory: Nuuchaanulth Ceremonial Curtain and the Work of Ki-ke-in* for the Morris and Helen Belkin Art Gallery at the University of British Columbia. Forthcoming publications include *Masked Relations: Display and Disguise on the Northwest Coast* and a co-edited volume entitled *The Idea of Northwest Coast Native Art: An Anthology*.

Jayne Wark is Professor of Art History in the Division of Historical and Critical Studies at the Nova Scotia College of Art and Design. She is conducting comprehensive research for a book on the history of conceptual art in Canada from the mid-1960s to the present, funded in part by a National Gallery of Canada Research Fellowship and a grant from the Social Sciences and Humanities Research Council of Canada. Dr. Wark has published and lectured extensively on twentieth-century art history and theory. Her book, *Radical Gestures: Feminism and Performance Art in North America*, was published by McGill-Queen's University Press in 2006.

William Wood is an art historian and a critic, having taught at universities in England and Canada. Since 1984 he has published on recent art in journals, anthologies and exhibition catalogues and has held editorial positions with *C Magazine*, *PUBLIC*, *Vanguard* and *Parachute*. He has been interested in Vancouver art post 1960s and is working on a book about contemporary art in Vancouver in the twenty-first century.

Acknowledgements

The publication *Traffic: Conceptual Art in Canada 1965–1980* was organized and coordinated by the Vancouver Art Gallery on behalf of the partner organizations. The exhibition, tour and publication were produced with the generous assistance of the Canada Council for the Arts, the Museums Assistance Program of the Department of Canadian Heritage and the Nova Scotia Department of Communities, Culture and Heritage.

The curators gratefully acknowledge the contributions of the following individuals for essential research and/or work on the myriad details related to production of the exhibition and publication: Heather Anderson, Jo-Anne Balcaen, Geneviève Bédard, Meghan Bissonnette, Joanne Bristol, Matthew Brower, Aimée Brown, Zoë Chan, Pamela Clark, Melanie Colosimo, David Court, Heather Diack, Tonia Di Risio, Peter Dykhuis, Lin Gibson, Rebecca Gimmi, Liz Gomez, Renée Gruszecki, Jessica Hein, Michelle Johnson, Eleanor King, Bill Kirby, Jacob Korczynski, Karen Love, Joni Low, Laura Matwichuk, Valentino Moreno, Erin Peck, Heather Pigat, Bony Poon, Mélanie Rainville, Christopher Régimbal, Sharla Sava, Maureen Smith, Paul Smith, Trevor Stark, Marilou St-Pierre, Jordan Strom, Leah Turner, Ulli Walker, Adam Welch, Jenna Winter and Juliana Zalucky.

Special thanks are extended to Karen Henry for her work in editing and coordinating the production of this publication. Also thanks to Lana Okerlund for her thorough copy editing and proofreading of the English text. The French translation, copy editing and proofreading of this publication were coordinated by Michèle Thériault at the Leonard & Bina Ellen Art Gallery, Concordia University, Montréal. We particularly wish to acknowledge the translation work of Colette Tougas.

Participation of the Art Gallery of Alberta (AGA) was supported by the City of Edmonton and the Alberta Foundation for the Arts. The AGA is a not-for-profit organization that relies on the support of its members, donors, sponsors and government. The AGA is grateful for the generous support of the many public and private donors and sponsors who have made the AGA's New Vision possible, and for the ongoing support of the City of Edmonton, the Alberta Foundation for the Arts, the Canada Council for the Arts and AGA members.

Halifax INK and participating organizations would like to acknowledge financial support for *Traffic* provided by the Canada Council for the Arts and the Nova Scotia Department of Communities, Culture and Heritage. Jayne Wark's research was supported by Halifax INK and the Social Sciences and Humanities Research Council of Canada. Halifax INK is a consortium that represents the publishing interests of university art galleries and artist-run centres in Halifax, Nova Scotia. Anna Leonowens Gallery of NSCAD University, Dalhousie Art Gallery, Mount Saint Vincent University Art Gallery and Saint Mary's University Art Gallery, presenters of the exhibition in Halifax, each receive operational and programming support from their post-secondary institutions and through grant programs offered by the Canada Council for the Arts, the Nova Scotia Department of Communities, Culture and Heritage and the Department of Canadian Heritage. Non-presenting members of Halifax INK are the Centre for Art Tapes and Eye Level Gallery.

The Justina M. Barnicke Gallery gratefully acknowledges the support of its partner galleries at the University of Toronto, including the University of Toronto Art Centre, Doris McCarthy Gallery and Blackwood Gallery. The exhibition in Toronto was financially supported by the Canada Council for the Arts, the Ontario Arts Council, the Toronto Arts Council and the Hal Jackman Foundation. Research was supported by Young Canada Works and the Museums Assistance Program, both of the Department of Canadian Heritage. The conference *Traffic: Conceptualism in Canada* was hosted at the University of Toronto and made possible through financial support from the Social Sciences and Humanities Research Council of Canada and the Canada Council for the Arts. A web-based component of the exhibition hosted by the Centre for Contemporary Canadian Art was funded through the Museums and Technology Fund of the Ontario Ministry of

Tourism, Culture and Sport and a Founders Award from the Toronto Friends of the Visual Arts. Justina M. Barnicke Gallery is part of Hart House at the University of Toronto. Its programs are supported by the Canada Council for the Arts and it receives project support from the Department of Canadian Heritage, the Ontario Arts Council, the Toronto Arts Council, foundations, corporate sponsors and individuals.

The Leonard & Bina Ellen Art Gallery's participation was supported by Concordia University. The gallery is part of the Office of the Vice-President Research and Graduate Studies. Its operations are funded by the university and its programs are supported by the Canada Council for the Arts, the Conseil des arts et des lettres du Québec, the Department of Canadian Heritage, the Iris Westerberg Stern Programming Fund, the Samuel Schecter Exhibition Fund and the Frederick and Mary Kay Lowy Art Education Fund.

The Vancouver Art Gallery acknowledges the support of its members, individual donors, corporate funders, foundations, the City of Vancouver, the Province of British Columbia through the British Columbia Arts Council, and the Canada Council for the Arts. The Gallery is very grateful for generous support for *Traffic* from Concord Pacific and Aymong Family Trust.

The exhibition, tour and publication are generously supported by:

Canada

Patrimoine canadien
Canadian Heritage

Canada Council for the Arts
Conseil des Arts du Canada

NOVA SCOTIA
Communities, Culture and Heritage

Project funding for individual galleries is also provided by:

Alberta Foundation for the Arts

CONCORD PACIFIC
CANADA'S LARGEST COMMUNITY BUILDER

Université Concordia University

The City of Edmonton

Hal Jackman Foundation

HartHouse

Ontario

ONTARIO ARTS COUNCIL
CONSEIL DES ARTS DE L'ONTARIO

Social Sciences and Humanities Research Council of Canada
Conseil de recherches en sciences humaines du Canada

TORONTO ARTS COUNCIL

TFVA
TORONTO FRIENDS OF THE VISUAL ARTS

We are grateful for the assistance of:

Blackwood Gallery
University of Toronto Mississauga

www.ccca.ca

DALHOUSIE ART GALLERY

DMG

UNIVERSITY OF TORONTO

Traffic: Conceptual Art in Canada 1965–1980

Published in conjunction with an exhibition organized by the Art Gallery of Alberta, Justina M. Barnicke Gallery (Hart House, University of Toronto) and the Vancouver Art Gallery, in partnership with the Leonard & Bina Ellen Art Gallery (Concordia University) and Halifax INK, and with the support of the University of Toronto Art Centre, Blackwood Gallery (University of Toronto, Mississauga) and Doris McCarthy Gallery (University of Toronto, Scarborough).

The exhibition is curated by Grant Arnold, Catherine Crowston, Barbara Fischer, Michèle Thériault with Vincent Bonin, and Jayne Wark.

Exhibition schedule

Justina M. Barnicke Gallery (Hart House, University of Toronto), University of Toronto Art Centre, Blackwood Gallery (University of Toronto, Mississauga) and Doris McCarthy Gallery (University of Toronto, Scarborough): 11 September–28 November 2010
Anna Leonowens Gallery (NSCAD University), Dalhousie Art Gallery, Mount Saint Vincent University Art Gallery, Saint Mary's University Art Gallery, Halifax: 18 March–8 May 2011
Art Gallery of Alberta, Edmonton: 25 June–18 September 2011
Leonard & Bina Ellen Art Gallery (Concordia University), Montréal: Part 1, 13 January–25 February 2012; Part 2, 16 March–28 April 2012
Vancouver Art Gallery: 29 September 2012–20 January 2013
Badischer Kunstverein, Karlsruhe: 1 April–30 June 2013

A more extensive chronology of Canadian conceptual art developed during the research for this exhibition can be found at www.ccca.ca/cca.

Editors: Grant Arnold and Karen Henry
Manager, publications: Karen Love
Production coordination: Karen Henry
English to French translation: Natalie de Blois, André Lamarre, Mélanie Rainville, Colette Tougas (principal translator)
French to English translation: Eduardo Ralickas
French revisions: Michèle Thériault
English copy edit and proofreading: Lana Okerlund
French copy edit: Zoë Chan, Micheline Dussault, Michèle Thériault, Colette Tougas
French proofreading: André Lamarre
Chronology (1970–80) research assistance: Laura Matwichuk
Biographical notes: Meghan Bissonnette, Michelle Johnson
Digital image preparation: Trevor Mills, Rachel Topham
Reproduction rights: Danielle Currie
Design: Studio Blackwell; Kelsey Blackwell with Thary Chhom and Bartosz Gawdzik

Printed and bound in Canada by Friesens
Distributed in the US by Publishers Group West 2

Distributed by:
Douglas & McIntyre
An imprint of D&M Publishers Inc.
2323 Quebec Street, Suite 201
Vancouver BC Canada V5T 4S7
www.douglas-mcintyre.com

12 13 14 15 16 5 4 3 2 1

Cover image: Gerald Ferguson, *The Standard Corpus of Present Day English Language Usage arranged by word length and alphabetized within word length*, 1970, detail, reproduced with permission of the estate of Gerald Ferguson

End papers: Brian Dyson, *I will not make any more art (after John Baldessari, 1971)*, 1977, Courtesy of the Artist

Library and Archives Canada Cataloguing in Publication

Traffic : conceptual art in Canada, 1965-1980 / Grant Arnold and Karen Henry, Editors.
Issued also in French under title: Trafic.
ISBN 978-1-895442-88-5
1. Conceptual art—Canada. 2. Art, Canadian— 20th century.
I. Arnold, Grant II. Henry, Karen A III. Vancouver Art Gallery

N6545.5.C66T73 2011 709.71'09046 C2011-906049-3

art gallery of alberta

Art Gallery of Alberta
2 Sir Winston Churchill Square
Edmonton, AB, Canada, T5J 2C1
www.youraga.ca

HALIFAX**INK**

Halifax INK
c/o Saint Mary's University Art Gallery
Saint Mary's University
923 Robie Street
Halifax, NS, Canada, B3H 3C3

JMB.

Justina M. Barnicke Gallery
Hart House, University of Toronto
7 Hart House Circle
Toronto, ON, Canada, M5S 3H3
www.jmbgallery.ca

galerie **leonard & bina ellen** art gallery

Leonard & Bina Ellen Art Gallery
Concordia University
1400 Maisonneuve Blvd. West
Montréal, QC, Canada, H3G 1M8
www.ellengallery.concordia.ca

Vancouver Artgallery

Vancouver Art Gallery
750 Hornby Street
Vancouver, Canada, V6Z 2H7
www.vanartgallery.bc.ca

I will not make

I will not make an

I will not make a

I will not make a

I will not make a

I will not make

I will not make a

I will not make a

I will not make an

I will not make a

I will not make an

I will not make a

I will not make a

I will not make

I will not make